The Wilsonian CENTURY

The Wilsonian CENTURY

U.S. Foreign Policy since 1900

Frank Ninkovich

THE UNIVERSITY OF CHICAGO PRESS

*

Chicago & London

Frank Ninkovich is professor of history at St. John's University, New York. He is the author of several books, including *Modernity and Power: A History of the Domino Theory in the Twentieth Century,* published by the University of Chicago Press.

The University of Chicago Press, Chicago 60637
The University of Chicago Press, Ltd., London
© 1999 by The University of Chicago
All rights reserved. Published 1999

08 07 06 05 04 03 02 01 00 99   5 4 3 2 1

ISBN (cloth): 0-226-58648-0

Library of Congress Cataloging-in-Publication Data

Ninkovich, Frank A., 1944–
    The Wilsonian century : U.S. foreign policy since 1900 / Frank
Ninkovich.
        p.   cm.
    Includes bibliographical references and index.
    ISBN 0-226-58648-0 (alk. paper)
    1. United States—Foreign relations—20th century.   2. Wilson,
Woodrow, 1856–1924.   I. Title.
E744.N545   1999
327.73—dc21
                                                        98-14219
                                                        CIP

To
Paul Barton Johnson
and
Dorothy Greene Johnson

CONTENTS

ACKNOWLEDGMENTS

I would like to thank a number of people for their help in getting this volume into print. My wife, Carol, as usual, has been a source of indispensable support. The copy editor, John McCudden, performed at a level above and beyond the call of duty in bringing order to a very messy manuscript. Professor Lawrence Gelfand of the University of Iowa, one of the outside readers, pointed out numerous errors of fact and interpretation, while an unidentified outside reader made life interesting by questioning some of the nonrealist assumptions that inform my interpretation. Doug Mitchell, a senior editor at the University of Chicago Press, was his usual helpful and encouraging self at all stages of the process, from the time this project was first conceived to the time it was finally accepted for publication. My students in History 1684 and 1685 at Harvard University, to whom much of this material is already familiar, deserve thanks for both putting up with and questioning my way of looking at things.

This book is dedicated to Dorothy Greene Johnson and Paul Johnson. I wouldn't be a historian today if it were not for their encouragement and timely assistance.

Interests versus Interpretation in U.S. Diplomatic History

This work is an outgrowth of my last book, *Modernity and Power: A History of the Domino Theory in the Twentieth Century.* Among my hopes for that monograph was that it would present a clear narrative picture of the distinctly modern features of U.S. foreign relations in the twentieth century. Unfortunately, that ambition was misplaced. For a variety of reasons, *Modernity and Power* turned out to be a work of intellectual history, useful mainly to specialists already familiar with the particulars of the history of U.S. foreign relations. When I proposed writing a broader, factually more inclusive introductory narrative for a nonprofessional audience, my editor at the University of Chicago Press, Doug Mitchell, quickly called it "Son of Book," an apt capsule description of what this volume is about.

Like its predecessor, this book is the product of a long-standing unhappiness with the kinds of explanations offered up by historians of U.S. foreign relations. I was first introduced to American diplomatic history through seminal works like George Kennan's *American Diplomacy 1900–1950* and William Appleman Williams's *The Tragedy of American Diplomacy.* For someone who came of age in the turbulent and rebellious 1960s, each of these books, in its own way, offered a powerful critique of what seemed, at the time, a U.S. foreign policy that was as puzzling as it was unattractive. Kennan explained U.S. misadventures abroad by pointing to America's deviations from the realities of power, while for Williams overseas entanglements were the product of a long-term fixation with economic expansion. Although their dissimilar ideological outlooks made for differences on a host of issues, including the crucial question of whether the U.S. *ought* to base its policies on interests, Kennan and Williams were at least of like mind on one major point: each agreed that foreign policy was best understood by reference to the underlying forces and interests that shape international relations.

The kinds of interest-based explanations employed by Kennan and Williams have enjoyed enormous influence among a broader community of social scientists and diplomatic historians. Of the two, realism, which is based on the idea that external realities or structures of power in international society shape and determine the behavior of states, has been the more influential outlook. According to this view, a nation's interests, past or present, could be defined accurately only by correctly assaying and weighing the distribution of power in international society. Though professionally less powerful overall, partisans of economic explanation have likened economic interests to drives—like sexuality or hunger in individuals—that must find expression in relations with other states.

As one political scientist accurately notes, both of these scholarly frameworks for understanding foreign relations "maintain that there are material causes to which events and actions can be reduced."[1] They treat interests and structures as if they were objective, hard, substantial realities of the kind that are uncovered and explained by natural science. Like natural phenomena whose internal mechanisms may not be immediately obvious, interests can, in principle, be accessed by social scientific methodology and even measured and predicted if enough intellectual elbow grease is applied. Indeed, a contemporary high priest of realism goes so far as to say flatly that "the national interest can be calculated." If true, this would suggest that both policy-makers and historians of foreign relations can penetrate behind the appearances and get in touch with *the* objective causes of international relations.[2]

These sweeping kinds of knowledge-claims deserve to be met with much more skepticism than they typically receive. It is understandable that proponents of objectivity, cashing in on the intellectual prestige deservedy enjoyed by science, should tend to receive the benefit of the doubt. But there is no need to genuflect before such outlooks just because they *claim* to be based on objective certainties, especially if one takes into account their rather sorry record of explanation. Nowhere has the failure to prove objectivist contentions been as evident as in the American habit of ignoring the precepts of power politics and economic self-interest by intervening repeatedly in areas where the nation's strategic and economic stakes were, by most conventional measures, negligible.

If one totes them up, just about all the landmark events of American foreign policy in the twentieth century fail to measure up to strict objectivist standards. The record of failures compiled by realists reads something like this: America's idealism in World War I badly misjudged the world situation, while Woodrow Wilson's plan for a League of Nations was utopianism run amok. Still groggy from the drug of idealism, the U.S. mindlessly attempted to outlaw war in the 1920s. For some realists, the isolationism of the 1930s was emblematic of the American tendency to oscillate between enthusiastic internationalism and sullen withdrawal. The love affair with the Soviets during World War II and the infatuation with the United Nations were, like Shaw's description of second marriages, also triumphs of hope over experience. American interventions in obscure and marginal areas during the cold war, particularly in Vietnam, merely added to an already long list of ideological excesses. On the economic side, the unending obsession with China, where U.S. trade and investment were minor, is the best example of how economic interests could be ignored, but the wars in Korea and Vietnam as well as other episodes could easily be added to the rap sheet.

In trying to account for America's allegedly unrealistic behavior in both world wars and the cold war, Kennan portrayed Americans as naive, idealistic, and prone to fits of misguided popular enthusiasm, a people whose sequestered history had prevented them from adjusting properly to the real world. Self-deception was also a major explanatory tool for Williams, who attributed the otherwise puzzling U.S. preoccupation with China to the powerful spell cast by an expansionist ideology or worldview. The source of these misperceptions lay in America's susceptibility to idealism, myths, and various other fantasies. Unlike earlier historians of American "exceptionalism," Kennan and Williams saw little to celebrate in this phenomenon, the only exceptional quality of America, apparently, being its stupidity. In a pluralistic world, the United States was just another country, more prosperous and powerful than most, but all the more dangerous therefore when driven to act on the basis of illusions. It is as if they agreed with Sigmund Freud's judgment that "America is a mistake, a great mistake."

An occasional distortion here and there is one thing, but to be afflicted with myopia over the course of an entire century, as seems to have been America's diplomatic fate if one is to believe these interpretations, poses a serious problem for interest theories. Granted, one can understand why warped ideas, like sinful flirtations, might at times be attractive for policymakers and historians alike, but it is difficult to see why they should be perpetually seductive, given what ought to be the more compelling claim of science to partnership in a long-term monogamous relationship. Moreover, given what are supposed to be the intractable realities of the world, one would think that the United States would have taken a lesson or two from the school of hard knocks. Yet, somehow, America has not only survived, but thrived on its nutritionally impoverished foreign policy diet.

Sensing that something was amiss, a few prominent political scientists have suggested that the U.S. was motivated by a "coherent system of irrationality."[3] Still, despite deploying some heavy conceptual artillery for dealing with aberrant ideologies, interest theories have not come up with very good explanations for why, as Alfred North Whitehead once put it, "the life of humanity can easily be overwhelmed by its symbolic accessories."[4] Indeed, by having to concentrate on why the ideological tail has been wagging the objectivist dog, interest theories themselves appear to have been overwhelmed by the symbolic accessories of international relations. Time and again, they have been put in the embarrassing situation of trying to explain why the United States has acted in ways that were contrary to its supposedly objective advantage.

Interest-based approaches also conceal serious problems with what ought to be their strong point—an objectivity based on value neutrality. The fact is, they are hardly as neutral and detached as they pretend to be. If, for example, one turns over the hard-shelled views of people like Kennan and Williams, one finds a soft underbelly of subjectivism nourished by what, according to the standards of realism, are the empty calories of values.[5] Kennan's realism could only function by proposing to subvert the democratic process in foreign-policy-making by substituting elite experts like himself as the ultimate judges of the national interest. Williams's critique of economic motivations similarly would replace the nation's free-market culture with a society based on a political economy more in keeping with his radical views. In the end, such interest theories invariably disenchant; instead of providing access to objective truth, they reveal instead the rather ordinary values of people who trumpet their objectivity.

These weaknesses would be of no concern were it not for their practical impact on the way the history of foreign relations is written. But theory matters, however annoying it may be to the many historians who simply want to get on with the apparently straightforward business of research and writing, because it determines the kinds of problems we tend to look at and influences our selection of data and our interpretations of the facts. In diplomatic history, the idolatrous worship of objective reality and a neutral, value-free standpoint of observation creates some serious difficulties for the way in which the narrative of U.S. foreign policy is handled. Surprisingly, objectivism has made it more difficult for historians to fulfil their primary professional responsibility: to provide factual descriptions of the past.

Three problems, in particular, stand out. First, in their capacity as critiques, these objectivist perspectives assume that ideologies are wrong. Typically, historical actors are treated as "judgmental dopes," the term that Harold Garfinkel uses to describe the patronizing way in which sociologists view the people they study.[6] But to adopt this pose of superiority, to write off ordinary consciousness as false consciousness, is to underestimate the extent to which ideologies are useful everyday charts for navigating successfully past foreign policy shoals. Indeed, as I will argue below, ideologies may be the *only* useful instruments of policy knowledge available to statesmen because, in many cases, there are no objectively correct descriptions of foreign policy problems, much less objectively correct answers. If most policy situations are in fact rationally undecidable without the help of values and subjective interpretations, this would mean that the objectivist standard has been falsely applied to foreign affairs.

Second, the objectivist approach provides poor descriptions of what ideologies are actually like. In principle, one ought to be able to give accurate descriptions of viewpoints to which one is hostile, but in historical practice it has worked out otherwise. Because of their need to play ideologies off against the presumably correct objective description, ideologies tend to be portrayed as anemic, narrow, and even silly. In Williams's work, for example, the economic worldview that supposedly drove Americans is presented quite narrowly as purely economic, leaving little room in the picture for issues of politics and values that also take up space in the minds of policy-makers. For his part, Kennan sees a slavish obedience to public opinion as blowing the United States continually off course even though U.S. policy making has in fact been dominated by elites who, more often than not, have had very different ideas about the world than the mass public. Paralleling the narrowness of Williams's economic focus, Kennan and other realists tend to portray policy as simplemindedly "idealistic," to the neglect of other significant nonutopian themes found within the ideology.

Lastly, there is a systematic misreading of the foreign policy impact of these ideologies. Because they are thought to be wrong, the presumption is that they have had harmful consequences. But the United States still exists, its values are intact, and by most contemporary measures of success it appears to be thriving. Might it not be possible, therefore, that these ideologies have been beneficial by providing "real world" guidance to policy-makers of a very practical sort? To the extent that the United States has prospered in world affairs, might not success be because of ideology rather than despite it? For the United States, ideology worked. And, by that rather vulgar pragmatic standard, it was true—all of which helps to

explain why Americans have been uninterested in learning from the alleged mistakes that realists and other critics continue to point out. To be
sure, the U.S. has had its share of misadventures and failures, but what
nations have not? I doubt that anyone can prove that the American record
in foreign relations has been less successful than that of powers presumably driven by greater reverence for realities and hard interests. On the
contrary, one could make a powerful argument for the case that it has
been more successful.

Boiled down, the problem seems to come down to this: By confusing
the way the world is perceived generally, diplomatic historians have confused the way in which policy-makers have perceived the world of foreign
relations. These shortcomings are the product of an inflated, godlike view
of historical knowledge that is inherent in objectivism. Not only is it assumed that the truth is "out there" and discoverable, but that it is already
known by historians, who possess more perfect knowledge than the people
they write about, thanks to their greater command of the facts and deeper
understanding of the reality in question. To hold this kind of view pretty
much mandates that history be written as a story of misperception. Instead
of being told what American policy-makers actually thought, we are
treated to the historical equivalent of Monday-morning quarterbacking
about what are presumed to be their mistaken ideas. Thus, while objectivists would no doubt agree in principle that ideas matter, what they give
us in practice are accounts in which ideas matter most when they are
wrong. What this suggests, to my mind, is that interest-based approaches
have some serious congenital handicaps in understanding what they pur-
port to be explaining.

What are the alternatives? Since the 1960s, the humanities have under-
gone something of a conceptual revolution that sometimes goes under the
name of "postmodernism." Like all "isms," postmodernism is complex,
often contradictory, and impossible to describe accurately with a few
sweeping abstractions. Nevertheless, one major feature of the postmodern
sensibility, as I understand it, is a more modest conception of what knowledge is and what it delivers than the kind of hard, positivist notions of
truth-finding that were formerly in vogue. One can arrive at this less assertive understanding of knowledge by any number of intellectual routes.
Within science itself, as Thomas Kuhn's justly celebrated *The Structure
of Scientific Revolutions* has made clear, research is governed by "para-
digms," which are provisional explanatory frameworks for a knowledge
which is ever incomplete, subject not only to experimental revision but
also to periodic episodes of wholesale reconceptualization. These para-
digms are constitutive of not only of science but "are constitutive of nature

as well." It is these conceptual transformations, the emergence of new ways of looking at the world, rather than objective discoveries, that constitute scientific revolutions. "After a revolution scientists are responding to a different world," says Kuhn.[7] It would appear that the objectivists have reversed the order of things. From this point of view, science, far from being the model of all knowledge, is itself dependent upon preexisting cognitive frameworks for its authority.

In social science, too, ambitious hopes for achieving neutrality and complete objectivity have been blasted. Because scientific observers can never abstract themselves from the experimental situation that they influence, an inevitable degree of subjectivity and distortion is introduced. Then, too, the objects that social scientists study—people rather than structures—are also subjects in their own right, whose behavior is fundamentally different from the phenomena studied by the natural sciences. As one author notes, when studying human beings "the object of our investigations is itself a pre-interpreted domain."[8] Moreover, social science necessarily involves a degree of "reflexivity," a feedback effect in which the knowledge generated and applied by social research becomes part of a new social reality. As far as social science is concerned, then, perfect objectivity, unmediated and therefore undistorted, is not part of the human condition. In spite of all this, objectivists somehow continue to insist that the fundamental structures of objective reality remain constant.

As objects of study, interests are slippery because they have no objective existence apart from the way people constitute and interpret them. Because we shape the world as much as it shapes us, and because meaning is not taken from reality but imparted to it, to understand interests is not simply to mirror nature. There is no objectively given "there" there, just waiting to be discovered, apprehended, and understood as it really is, in all its transcendental purity.[9] As sociologist Herbert Blumer argues: "It is impossible to cite a single instance of a characterization of the 'world' of reality that is not cast in the form of human images. . . . To indicate anything, human beings must see it from their perspective; they must depict it as it appears to them." This assertion, he rightly insists, is "incontestable."[10] We cannot jump out of our skins and discard the conventions, prejudices, creative inspirations, and ideological frameworks that we bring to all of our understandings of the world for the simple reason that these preexisting frameworks are a condition of our knowing.

Over the course of this century, thanks to the insights of a variety of philosophers working in quite different traditions, our sense of how these humanistic "pre-understandings" function has expanded enormously. One important element of such frameworks of understanding is "historicity."

We cannot help but approach the world from a historical frame of mind because it is built-in. We all make sense of the world by situating ourselves historically in narratives that cover our personal lives, our family sagas, and our place in larger national and international dramas. The facts and the narrative frameworks are products of human selectivity and inventiveness, but the need to understand historically is part of our makeup as human beings. Without historical understanding, knowledge would be empty and we would be lost in time and space, devoid of identity. As a form of knowledge, then, history does matter.

Although some historians still aspire to the nineteenth- century ideal of objectivity, it seems clear that history can never divorce itself entirely from literature or from interpretation. History supplies the warehouse of facts, whose storerooms are stocked and managed by historians, but the plot of the narrative is not supplied by the data. If that is true of history as practiced in the universities, it is all the more the case in everyday life, where history is even more plainly a construct, an interpretive story about the world. In the case of national history, our narrative understanding of the country's role in time and space, which has been passed down and reinterpreted from generation to generation, has exercised great influence. The idea that the United States is at the leading edge of history and has a special claim on the future, for example, has been very powerful. But sometimes, as happened with U.S. foreign policy early in the twentieth century, the traditional frameworks lose their scriptural status and the stories have to be revised or new narrative frameworks altogether have to be adopted. That kind of historical understanding, its emergence and its influence, is itself something that can be studied and understood historically, which is what I propose to do in this book.

In principle, it would be marvelous if we were able to base our understanding of the world entirely upon experimentally grounded science, which offers the greatest certainty that human beings can attain. But while hard science and social science are obviously important, the problem in trying to generalize this standard is that we do not live our lives scientifically and cannot hope to do so because reliable scientific knowledge about cause and effect in social and cultural matters is in short supply and is likely to remain so. Thus science was of no help whatsoever to American statesmen in understanding the world of international relations. To be sure, they studied diplomatic reports and intelligence data; they called upon expert opinion; and, increasingly, they tapped social scientists for advice. But in the end, unscientific as it was, only historical interpretation as a form of knowledge was capable of pulling together all that information and making sense of it.

Thus, from a contemporary "postmodern" standpoint, what interest-theorists write off as distortions—"myths" or ideologies or idealism—are actually complex and influential inner worlds of speculative and practical knowledge and understanding that are every bit as worthy of our attention as the objective world beyond appearances that science seeks to penetrate. If I may be pardoned for trying to turn the tables, a study of this subjective dimension of policy-making, by shifting our inquiry into what is the primary sphere of knowledge, promises to make our understanding of diplomatic history *more* objective by taking into account what one social scientist has called "the objectivity of the subjective."[11] Martin Heidegger's assertion that "the humanistic sciences must necessarily be inexact just in order to remain rigorous" suggests the importance of taking into account the nonobjective, nonquantifiable side of things.[12]

In other words, it makes more sense to work from the inside out, by studying the interior world of which we have direct knowledge, than to assume the sanctity of structures whose existence is posited rather than perceived. For historians who make a habit of criticizing historical figures for acting on the basis of unsound ideas, it might be wiser to follow Blumer's advice in this matter. "If the scholar wishes to understand the action of people it is necessary for him to see their objects as they see them," he says. "Failure to see their objects as they seem them, or a substitution of his meanings for other meanings, is the gravest kind of error that the social scientist can commit."[13]

Does this amount to a claim to be more objective than the objectivists, more Catholic than the pope? Not really. Though I would argue strongly that the results of doing history this way are in many ways more satisfying and more accurate, it is important to realize that there is a trade-off involved here. This deeper understanding of the interior world of policy-makers, which can never be absolute, comes at the cost of acknowledging that our supposedly objective knowledge of the social world is not nearly as reliable or all-encompassing as we had once believed. This is not to deny that social science exists, that it can improve our understanding of the world, or that it can play a practical political role, but I would suggest that a social scientific understanding of a problem is, at any given time, only another vocabulary, and not necessarily a superior one, for understanding and resolving social problems. For example, academic knowledge, no matter how seemingly impressive, does not necessarily translate automatically into achievement in the practical world of politics, in which art, cunning, and experience are often more instrumental to success than hard knowledge. "Politics," said Albert Einstein, and with good reason, "is much harder than physics."

As a scholar who also believes in the power of objective "social forces" and acknowledges the integrity of the social sciences as fields of study, I have no difficulty in admitting that international environments have at times taken on a systemic or structural character, e.g., the classical European balance of power or the cold-war order of the 1970s and 80s. These systemic environments, though very much human creations, were indeed objective in the sense that they had taken a life of their own. It is obvious that failure to accommodate oneself to the system, any system, is done at one's peril, be it driving on the wrong side of the road or foolishly attacking a power that belongs to a stronger alliance.

Those are examples of fact-driven forms of understanding. At times, however, understanding, even in the hard sciences, is driven by theory. Just as individuals are forced to navigate in turbulent situations whose complexity they do not fully understand, so too are states. They have to interpret their international environment and to plot courses of behavior without stars, compasses, or accurate nautical charts to guide them. This book argues that in the twentieth century traditional systems collapsed, rendering the old rules of the game and foreign policy traditions out of date. Much of American foreign policy in the twentieth century emerged from the need to develop new rules for navigating through a turbulent and unpredictable modern international environment.

Consequently, new guiding ideas, in the form of Wilsonian interpretations that helped to constitute and transform the world, came to the fore. It took some doing, but these ideas eventually migrated from the realm of speculation into the world of commonsense practice. And, after being subjected to the test of experience, they were significantly revised. If we agree that change in the twentieth century was in fact accelerated, and radical, and global in scope—a crucial point—then drawing conclusions about the implications of this rapid change is pretty much a matter of common sense. "Under stress," according to David Harvey, "reality gets created rather than interpreted under conditions of space-time compression."[14] As a rule, the greater the uncertainty, the greater is the role of ideology—*that* is a fairly straightforward proposition of social science.[15] And this book argues that for the period in question uncertainty, not calculability, was a fundamental fact of life for American policy-makers.

To sum up my argument, objectivist approaches have had serious problems in describing what goes on inside the heads of policy-makers. As a result, they have failed in their attempts to use objective or structural realities to explain why events in the twentieth century turned out the way they did. All this may disturb or even offend those who prefer to believe that statesmanship rests on more solid objective foundations. Realists might still object that, despite somehow having muddled through, Wilsonianism was a misperception of the world as it really was. But to try to determine whether or not Wilsonianism correctly apprehended "external reality," to attempt to figure out whether it was right or wrong, or to wonder if it succeeded despite itself strike me as irrelevant questions that cannot be answered. They suggest that there was a better way of doing things based on an undistorted knowledge of the world. From the perspective of this book, however, such claims are the product less of good science or history than of bad philosophy, for in place of practicality and viability they attempt to substitute a standard that cannot be tested because it essentially lies outside of the experience being studied.

There was nothing arbitrary about the historical interpretations upon which American statesmen relied. Though the frequent mentions in this book of the role played by "historical interpretation" and "historical imagination" might suggest that foreign policy ideas were somehow "made up," and thus capricious and flimsy, they were in fact amazingly solid and durable at the same time that they were pragmatically flexible. As I shall argue, the Wilsonian century was the product of an imaginative interpretation of history that survived not only because it seemed to make sense of a confusing modern world, but also because it successfully passed the test of experience. In the face of numerous crises, Wilsonianism maintained enough plausibility as an explanation of world politics—in fierce competition with realist doctrines, it should be remembered—to convince American statesmen of its rightness. And, to an amazing degree, it succeeded through a pragmatic process of trial and error in structuring the world in accord with its own preconceptions.

One can always suggest that it could or should have been done otherwise. But, for my part, to engage in this sort of thinking is to indulge in a kind of historical fantasizing far more speculative than the outlooks I describe in this book.

THEORY MATTERS, but this book's usefulness as history depends ultimately on its persuasiveness as a story. As a historian, I am less interested in arguing abstractly than in showing concretely. Establishing that ideas and ideology matter is one thing; showing the exact way in which they operate is quite another. This book's purpose is therefore practical rather than theoretical: to show that American policy-makers from Theodore Roosevelt through Bill Clinton have been driven by interpretive frameworks so deeply embedded as to constitute significant foreign policy realities of their own. Indeed, they helped to create the reality they imagined. Because my chief concern is to show how ideology operated and evolved in specific policy contexts, it might be helpful at this point if I stepped down from the pedestal of theory and outlined my argument in advance.

In what follows, I hope to describe the emergence and persistence through the century of *two* quite distinct but related foreign policy ideologies. The first I shall call "normal" internationalism, which was and remains the basic ideology of the country. This ideology was a natural outgrowth of the commercial and cultural internationalism of the nineteenth century, a period when America's political isolation was complemented by a flowering of transnational activity in the private sector. The second ideology, Wilsonianism, was a crisis internationalism that surfaced in bad times, only to give way to normal internationalism once the turbulence had passed. As we shall see, there was nothing natural at all about Wilsonianism. A creative doctrine, it was one possible response among many to the world crisis of 1914–18.

The existence of two conceptual frameworks does not mean that U.S. policy was schizoid. It merely suggests that America's response to modernity, like modernity itself, was double-edged: extraordinarily optimistic and progressive on the one hand, yet afflicted by a sense of extraordinary, perhaps unmanageable crisis on the other, depending on the circumstances. The two were, in any case, closely related, one being an offshoot of the other. The twentieth century has been the best of times and the worst of times, and American foreign policy has been closely attuned to its ups and downs.

In the late nineteenth and early twentieth centuries, American foreign policy turned slowly in the direction of greater international involvement on the basis of an optimistic and unproblematic mental image of global progress. Then, during World War I, Woodrow Wilson painted a disturbing new picture of the world situation and its potentially disastrous impact upon American security. Contrary to the common image of Wilson as a moralist and idealist (which, in part, he was), this book emphasizes the serious and distinctly modern kind of threat that his idealistic solutions were intended to eliminate. This bleak side of his thought needs to be better understood if the meaning of twentieth-century foreign policy is to be grasped. Wilson's views were not immediately accepted; and, when at last they were adopted, they were significantly revised. Nevertheless, from the eve of World War II through the end of the cold war, American foreign policy had a distinctively Wilsonian cast to it.

For half a century, American foreign policy was based on the assumption that world history had stumbled onto new, dangerous, and radically uncertain terrain that obliged American policy-makers to abandon traditional diplomacy. Dealing with this unprecedented situation demanded action more radical than simply abandoning the *American* foreign policy tradition of isolation and time-honored notions of national interest. It required leaving behind a tradition of diplomacy that had been followed in Europe and elsewhere for thousands of years. Modern American foreign policy involved nothing less than a radical break with the past.

The Wilsonian assumptions that later became axiomatic for American statesmen were fairly simple. Straining to make sense of the global scene through the fog of war, Wilson believed that he could discern a number of prominent features in the emerging profile of international relations. First, the advent of "total war" made clear that war itself was no longer a useful or reliable instrument of diplomacy. It had become so destructive and socially disruptive that it was far too costly a means for achieving any ends that might conceivably be gained from military action. Second, it created a new kind of danger that was distinctly different from old threats of physical conquest: the possibility of a poisoning of the world political environment by powers hostile to liberal democracy. Third, it suggested that the European balance of power, formerly the fulcrum of world politics, had been permanently unhinged, beyond possibility of restoration. Fourth, the necessity of American intervention in Europe demonstrated that modern politics and warfare were global in scope. Finally, Wilson assumed that, given the obsolescence of the balance of power and the interconnectedness of the modern world, *any* conflict anywhere, unless nipped in the bud, threatened to escalate into another world war more calamitous than the first.

All of these assumptions, it must be emphasized, were precisely that: assumptions, unscientific inferences rooted in an interpretation of world history. They did not leap immediately to the eye, in bold relief, when one viewed the world situation. And it could not have been otherwise: because modernity cannot be *experienced* locally, it has to be *imagined* as a whole, as a global process. It was Wilson's gift for historical interpretation rather than empirical observation that enabled him to give such a compelling reading of a chaotic world scene. Wilson imposed a narrative form upon a reality that could be (and was) interpreted in many ways, but which, in itself, was mute as to its meaning. Though he was soundly repudiated in his own time by the American people, his reading of history gained in influence as time went on until, eventually, it became deeply ingrained in America's political culture—so deeply, in fact, that its Wilsonian origins went largely unrecognized.

There was nothing utopian about all this. On the contrary, the key to understanding the Wilsonian century is that it was continually haunted by the fear of terrible failure. The interdependence of world society, the globalization of warfare, and the end of power politics and warfare as practical instruments of foreign policy were phenomena that, harnessed to a runaway modernity, could spell disaster for civilization of a kind never before witnessed. In this kind of situation, there was no alternative to basing foreign policy on an ideology relatively free from the grip of interests, old-style guideposts that could provide no more than a partial and inadequate perspective for dealing with problems that were world-historical in scope.

Wilson's modern definition of threat is crucial to understanding American policy in the twentieth century. But Wilson's creative genius—and, despite his serious shortcomings as a statesman, it would be ungenerous to call it anything less than that—extended to solutions as well as to problems, another area where his reputation has been tarred with the brush of do-gooder idealism. Wilson's famous panacea, of course, was the noble but unworkable scheme for a League of Nations. The cement that was supposed to bind together the loose sand of the League's member-states was world opinion, the popular liberal sentiment embedded in all peoples that was being unleashed by the global spread of democracy.

Few concepts in international relations are as vague as world opinion. However, if one accepts Wilson's definition of the modern world's problems, there would seem to be no way out of these difficulties other than to posit something like world opinion as a solution. Admittedly, many foreign policy analysts dismiss it as a fantasy, as more of an empty abstraction than a concrete description, and prefer to start with the supposition that international society is fundamentally anarchic, an assumption that is itself open to question.[16] But, if nothing else, the widespread belief in its existence was itself a significant social fact, if only because it lay at the heart of a good deal of American foreign policy behavior in this century.

To leave it at that, though, would be to view world opinion as a fantasy—significant, perhaps, but a fantasy nonetheless. There is more to world opinion than American naiveté, however. From today's perspective, the existence of world opinion as a fundamental social phenomenon is not so easily laughed off. John F. Kennedy, in summarizing the cold war, once remarked that "the real question is which system travels better."[17] As the twentieth century ends, it is hard to deny that democratic ideas, in the form of a triumphant liberal capitalist ideology, have not only traveled but have taken up residence throughout much of the world. But even that may still be a rather abstract notion. More down-to-earth is the undeniably widespread acceptance of a modern way of life—from wearing certain kinds of clothes, driving cars, living in cities, pursuing careers or working at specialized jobs, consuming mass-produced goods, engaging in nonagricultural employment for the global market, and so on—that presupposes a practical habituation to universal ideas without making an intellectual to-do about it. Yes, the world is still pluralistic, but it is also true, thanks to the acceleration of history that is characteristic of the modern era, that cultures are quicker to change nowadays, with the result that people today are culturally far closer together than ever.

World opinion was flexible enough to be defined and held together in different ways depending upon time and circumstance. At first, it was almost exclusively Western; then Asia began to count; later still the third world. For political purposes, a strongman might serve as a substitute if opinion within a country was either anti-American or suppressed. Most often, world opinion suggested a policy of cooperation. But at times, when global sentiment was running against the United States, American statesmen pretended to know the world's needs better than the passing opinions of the day, which they considered to be distorted, and they chose to go it alone. The upshot is that even though some American policies appeared to stray far from the Wilsonian intellectual reservation, especially during the cold war, the continuing belief in the ultimate historical triumph of world opinion as the American ace-in-the-hole justifies calling those policies neo-Wilsonian.

No single historical approach has the capacity to capture the historical process. Unlike science, which can have only one valid explanation, history offers a menu of narratives from which to choose. Our choice of narrative depends on many things: tradition, current events, ideological dominance, personal preference and politics, and accident, among others. To some extent, however, it depends on a good story that answers in a satisfying way some unresolved questions about the past. I think I have a good, perhaps even convincing, story to tell. I believe that my approach provides a more coherent narrative (consistent with the evidence, I should hasten to add) that helps historians, of whatever description, to better explain some puzzling aspects of the American foreign policy past, particularly a pattern of interventionism where American interests, however defined, were not clearly at risk.

All of this should, I hope, become clear in the text. If I have done my job properly, this work should make clearer the century-long significance of Wilsonianism, whose connection to the cold war, as well as to the internationalism that began and ended this century, has not always been very obvious. While some of the ideas in this book have already been developed in *Modernity and Power,* this book does a better job of contextualizing Wilsonianism, of situating it in relation to world developments and the main currents of American thinking about the world. It makes clear that Wilsonianism was a crisis internationalism and not the country's fundamental foreign policy ideology. The reason it has been so influential—enough so to warrant the title of this book—has to do with long duration of the extraordinary series of crises through which the United States and the world have passed in the course of the past century.

My hope is that this interpretive narrative will promote an understanding of the peculiarly—and I mean peculiarly—ideological character of U.S. foreign relations in the twentieth century. Americans have long tended to think of themselves as unique, but the case for America's singular standing in history is much easier to make when focusing on its distinctive foreign policies than on its allegedly superior domestic institutions. It would have been a remarkable story if the United States had gone from isolationism to world power by following the traditional path of power politics. But the nation took a different and altogether more extraordinary course by radically redefining what it meant to be a world power. American internationalism in the 20th century *was* truly exceptional because it abandoned the idea of interest as traditionally understood over thousands of years, opting instead to identify its national security with global needs.

Other historians have already argued strongly and convincingly on behalf of the independent causal significance of ideology and imaginative frameworks of ideas.[18] Using modernity as its central concept, this book's chief claim to originality lies in its attempt to connect internationalism, Wilsonianism, and the cold war—and thus the entirety of America's foreign policy history during the twentieth century—more directly and convincingly than other works have done. Among other things, I would hope that this work contributes to a reconsideration of events that, all too often, have been interpreted by historians in determinist or reductionist terms. I have tried to suggest how open, problematic, and objectively undecidable foreign policy choices were at the time they had to be made and how creative and imaginative were American interpretations of the world situation. "World society constitutes a world with an open future," says one scholar.[19] That was true when my story begins. It is no less true today.

A few last comments. Inasmuch as this is neither a textbook nor a comprehensive survey, many events have, of necessity, been left out. For reasons peculiar to my perhaps idiosyncratic conception of the historian's duty, it strives to be neither critical nor celebratory. Because the book follows the general line of argument laid out in *Modernity and Power,* I apologize in advance for repeating myself. However, in reformatting my ideas I have clarified some of my views and, in a few instances, some fresh thoughts may even have emerged. Finally, if the account is not as clear and readable as I had hoped, I promise not to try a third time.

CHAPTER ONE

The Emergence of Normal Internationalism, 1900–1913

Modernity, Change, and Globalism

The distinguishing feature of modern times is that they are *radically* different from the past. By the close of the nineteenth century, America had been transformed many times over by the industrial revolution. For diplomatic historians, one common way of measuring the extent of this change is to describe the objective indices of power. By 1900, the United States led the world in extraction of raw materials like coal and iron ore; was the principal producer of agricultural commodities; produced more steel and other manufactured goods than any other country; led in the production and per capita consumption of consumer goods; and was a leading exporter of both goods and capital to the rest of the world.

But this kind of information tells us little or nothing about the kind of American foreign policy that was emerging at this time. "Nothing is so fallacious as facts, except figures," said the British statesman George Canning. Indeed, in history, unlike the quantifiable certainty they provide in science, facts and figures never come close to providing a single definitive explanation of the past. Though easily described in quantitative terms— amount of railroad mileage, the degree of urbanization, the multiplication of invention, the explosion of aggregate wealth, and so on—all the statistics that screamed "more" of this or that failed to capture the qualitative change in the way of life introduced by industrial modernity. So great was the difference that millenniums of history were compressed into a single century. In many ways, an American alive in 1776 would have felt more at home in Periclean Athens or republican Rome than in the industrial America of 1900.

Because the industrial revolution was not fenced in by national borders, the remaking of the United States was only a national episode in a far more elaborate story: the social and cultural transformation of the planet. Just as industrial modernity reshaped the internal functioning of nations by creating new ways of life and politics, many contemporaries believed it would be every bit as revolutionary in its effects on relations between states and societies. In 1900, the world appeared poised on the brink of a great transformation that would carry over to diplomacy and international society the change introduced by the industrial revolution to national societies.

Today, globalism is a cliché, but a century ago it was a fresh and exciting phenomenon, a prominent feature of the most radical burst of change since civilized societies had first emerged thousands of years earlier. At a meeting of the American Academy of Political Science in 1899, one scholar summed up the sense of astonishment that this worldwide process still managed to arouse at the time:

> We have been living in one of the most interesting periods, not only of the last hundred, but of the last three hundred, or even of the last five hundred years. We can take up no newspaper in these days without finding something which reminds us that we are a part of the greater world which has its limits no longer in the civilized life of Europe and the nations which were the outgrowth of that, but which extends to the uttermost confines of the globe and which includes practically to-day, as never before in the history of the world, the whole human race. [Technology has] "brought us together and made us feel the solidarity of the whole human kind in a way quite unparalleled at any previous time."[1]

In 1910, the retired president Theodore Roosevelt, speaking as an accomplished historian, reaffirmed the widespread perception that people were living in an era of historical discontinuity. "The present civilization can be compared to nothing that has gone before," he said. "It is literally a world movement."

The foreign policy consequences of modernity were most spectacularly evident in the tidal wave of imperialism that washed over the world in the 1880s and 90s, when Europe's enormous superiority in military technology enabled her to absorb with ease vast regions of Africa and Asia formerly outside the orbit of modern history. Thanks in part to the military power generated by her new manufacturing muscle, the United States, too, became a full-fledged empire. After defeating Spain in a brief and one-sided war that began as a quarrel over Spain's inept handling of a revolution in Cuba, the U.S. suddenly found herself in possession of far-flung overseas territories, cheek by jowl with other empires.

The reasons for this outburst of imperial expansion remain unclear to this day. Detaching Cuba from Spain was a war aim, but it came as a surprise that Puerto Rico in the Caribbean and Hawaii, Guam, and the Philippine islands in the Pacific Ocean fell into America's imperial embrace. Describing America's acquisition of the Philippine islands from Spain, one writer noted quite accurately that "seldom has an event of the kind been less due to foresight or premeditation."[2] President William McKinley, in issuing instructions to the peace commission concerning the fate of the Philippines, noted that America had proceeded "without any original thought of complete or even partial, acquisition of the islands."[3] If the United States was making a statement by becoming an empire, it was an exclamation more than a declarative sentence.

No single conspicuous cause explains what happened. The traditional simplistic explanation for imperialism over the centuries—gold, God, and glory—was actively embodied in various pressure groups. Some commercial interests were enthusiastic about markets and raw materials made accessible by expansion; missionaries got on the bandwagon; the army and navy, meanwhile, made security arguments. Party politics also had much to do with it, the Republicans being more solidly for empire than the Democrats were against it. Although there was no deafening clamor for empire, seasoned politicians sensed that the public was leaning in favor of acquiring colonies. Contingency or chance also played a part. Theodore Roosevelt's assertive presence as an assistant secretary of the navy ensured that Dewey would steam to Manila Bay for his fateful confrontation with the Spanish fleet. With all these factors at work, the Senate vote in favor of ratifying the peace treaty with Spain was still a close call, thanks to a sizable and vocal anti-imperialist opposition.

This episode could be investigated ad infinitum in ever finer detail in the way that scientists smash atoms with particle accelerators without ever coming up with a final cause. One thing seems clear, however. The Spanish-American War and the acquisition of an overseas empire were not prompted by security concerns. Neither foreign dangers nor the impulse to acquire empire for gold, god, or glory were decisive factors. Given the absence of "hard" causes, it is probably more fruitful to view this episode as part of an identity crisis in which the industrially maturing United States was struggling to define its domestic order and its place in the larger world. Domestically, the populist movement, labor unrest, the new immigration from eastern Europe, continuing racial problems, the rising tide of feminism, and the social and cultural dislocations brought by industrialism made the 1890s a decade of anxiety. Similarly, imperialism was a portent of massive changes afoot in the organization of international society.

Significantly, many members of the younger generation of leaders took their cues from European achievements. As it was nationalizing after the Civil War, the United States was simultaneously internationalizing. Americans in large numbers pursued advanced degrees in Germany's superlative universities. Many a daughter of American industrialists attracted marriage-minded European nobility with their attractive dowries. For the American upper classes, frequent travel on the Continent and a familiarity with European tastes, manners, languages, and customs, were increasingly a mark of social distinction at home. The Old World, once disdained as the alien "other" by earlier generations of Americans, was now part of a common civilization in which the American upper classes, arrivistes and old-money patricians alike, felt increasingly at home. Admittedly, not all Americans reacted in this way. Even for those who did, a sense of American distinctiveness, and often superiority, remained. On balance, though, commonality was beginning to supersede difference.

It seems highly unlikely that American imperialism would have taken place without the prior existence of European imperialism as a model. Rejected a generation earlier because it was not in keeping with American tradition, imperialism was increasingly acceptable to many precisely because it was a contemporary symbol of global success.[4] The idea of participating in a common global drama was not entirely new. In the middle of the nineteenth century, Americans had agreed with the logic of "opening" China, Japan, and other formerly reclusive countries to the incursions of world civilization. Imperialism reflected an even greater willingness to launch the United States into the global stream of time. It was by this new universal standard—the degree to which American foreign policy could secure the nation's place in an emerging global civilization—that American foreign policy would increasingly be measured in the future.

Imperialism was, in any case, a transitional phenomenon and a symptom of change, not a new foundation for foreign policy. The war with Spain and its imperial aftermath were, as one historian has suggested, "but one example of a new American sense of the world."[5] The debate over empire, however furious, was not over the fundamental issue of whether to join the modern world community. As David Healey has pointed out, "both imperialists and antiimperialists foresaw for the United States nothing less than the moral and material leadership of the world."[6] For people like Henry Cabot Lodge and his friend Theodore Roosevelt, "Great power status was the primary goal. Imperialism was attractive, but only insofar as it contributed to that end."[7] Thus when, a few years later, the enthusiasm for colonialism cooled off, the nation resumed its search for a way of operating comfortably within the new global context.

The dramatic events of 1898 and 1899 allowed the nation, hopelessly self-absorbed and isolationist only a few years earlier, to claim membership in the small group of great powers that dominated international relations. Archibald Cary Coolidge, an early scholarly student of foreign affairs, defined the world powers as those nations which were "directly interested in all parts of the world and whose voices must be listened to everywhere."[8] In keeping with the trend toward concentration that was characteristic of the new industrial era, this club of great powers, each of which exercised control over vast geographic expanses, was becoming ever more exclusive.

Besides playing a dominant role in the western hemisphere, the United States was now a major power in the Far East, with interests in the Philippines and China, and it also took a greater interest in European affairs. By Coolidge's standard, it was obvious that the United States deserved to join the small fraternity of industrialized nations with global reach and interests: England, France, Russia, and Germany. Whatever influence the United States hoped to exercise, it would, for better or worse, have to be in the company of these nations. Many assumed the experience would be for the better. "Our civilization is European," said a peace advocate. "It is the great powers of the world that determine the world's peace on a great scale."[9]

How would the U.S. interact with the other members of this small brotherhood? No one knew, exactly. To take but one obvious question: If the United States was becoming more like the European countries in a global society, would this not result in a Europeanization of American foreign policy? Would not political rivalry and conflict be amplified to unprecedented levels? Operating on the pessimistic assumption that the future would recapitulate the past, one forecaster, Theodore Salisbury Woolsey, saw the new situation in this way: "The old theory of the balance of power confined its workings to the European system, to land power, and to political, not commercial growth. There are signs that every one of these limitations is being overridden." He concluded of the new global "balance" that "we cannot be within the sphere of the concert, yet not of it."[10] Woolsey dreaded this change—the Europeanization of the world and the accompanying Europeanization of America—but he saw no way of avoiding it.

Woolsey was an exception. For most Americans who thought about the matter, world power did not mean that their country was being initiated into an irredeemably rowdy and violent gang of cutthroats. Civilization, or modernity, had changed the United States, but, since it was a universal process, it had also changed everything else. The globe was described in terms of shrinkage and contraction, to be sure, which if interpreted as a struggle for space might have triggered fears of overcrowding, but this shrinkage was a consequence of the *expansion* of civilization. Living in an expanding universe was not like jostling against others on an increasingly crowded train. It was more like embarking on a comfortable journey with sociable passengers in a first-class carriage. Despite disagreements about this or that aspect of policy, most would have agreed that "the general tendency of American expansionism is toward human freedom."[11]

As Herbert Croly, the philosopher of progressivism, argued, "The emancipated and nationalized European states of today, so far from being essentially antagonistic to the American democratic nation, are constantly tending towards a condition which invites closer and more fruitful association with the United States."[12] It was not that the United States was becoming like other nations. Instead, Americans believed, in their optimistic way, that a world caught up in revolutionary ferment, whose most advanced expression was American society, was coming to resemble them. As one historian expressed it, in 1902: "The story of America and the story of modern world history are the same story."[13] In any case, even if the degree of convergence was exaggerated, there was little cause to fear for national security. As the reformer Henry Demarest Lloyd put it, "If nobody can lick us, we need not be afraid to play the just and generous big brother among the nations."[14]

The British journalist W. S. Stead's phrase, "the Americanization of the world," captured this widespread feeling that the American present would be the world's future. Many European observers agreed. As early as 1851, the *Economist* predicted that "the superiority of the United States to England is ultimately as certain as the next eclipse."[15] In the 1880s, Lord Bryce wrote in *The American Commonwealth* that "America has in some respects anticipated European nations. She is walking before them along paths which they may probably follow."[16] The U.S. stood, according to one newspaper, "at the pinnacle of the greatest civilization of the world's history . . . a nation that in the opinion of many statesmen is just commencing to play its great part upon the stage of the universe."[17] This was a very powerful and deeply rooted idea. President Dwight D. Eisenhower later recalled of his fin-de-siècle upbringing that "the most confident conviction of my boyhood was that the principles of our free society would be universally accepted around the globe."[18]

World power, then, did not mean retracing the historical footsteps of the *old* Europe, in which competitive political expansion had been the norm. American policy-makers viewed America's new global activism as part of a more encompassing progressive transformation then taking place throughout the world. In their eyes, the future would not bring a global version of power politics; on the contrary, progress would bring peace, growing prosperity, and an integration of the world along liberal demo cratic lines. One writer expected that "the increased respect that nations will have for each other as they come to know each other better, as each one learns to adopt the better features of others and discard its worst features, may lead to the existence of a few great nations which will manage their affairs separately, but which will bear to each other relations like those which exist in a peaceful family."[19] Modernity and civilization, it was widely believed, would produce a harmonious century wholly unlike the conflict-racked millennia that preceded it.

But this optimism coexisted with uncertainty about where precisely history was headed. Ironically, the very engine of historical change that allowed human beings to believe in progress also belched a huge cloud of smoke that reduced visibility into the future. Despite its benefits, modern progress was also unsettling precisely because it was historically discontinuous. It was by definition new, different, and unpredictable, perhaps even uncontrollable. The human creativity embodied in science and technology always produced unanticipated social consequences that left intellectual interpreters playing a permanent game of catch-up. Progressives worried about managing the uneven outcomes of industrialism; others fretted about decadence eroding the character traits that had produced progress; while still others voiced more fundamental doubts about whether society was in fact a perpetual motion machine of progress.

An awareness of the historical breach produced by modern industrial society had already produced a distinctively modern outlook in high culture. The modernist revolutions that swept through art, music, architecture, literature, philosophy, and other intellectual disciplines marked sharp, often shocking breaks with tradition that would in due course merge into a new, antitraditional tradition of modernity. But modernism was not simply about art, or high culture, or about aesthetic enjoyment disconnected from everyday experience. It spoke to the radical change that artists and intellectuals, with their hypersensitive antennae, sensed was going on in the life-world around them. Because modernity was a worldview, it was impossible for it to remain isolated in cloistered artistic and intellectual communities. Inevitably, the sense of discontinuity found in artistic modernity made itself felt in workaday aspects of life, including the understanding of foreign relations.

Even though liberal social transformation was well advanced domestically in most industrial nations, in foreign affairs the revolution had barely begun. Despite changes in the cast of characters, diplomacy in Europe—and hence, in much of the world—was still being conducted pretty much along traditional principles of power balancing that had been in effect since the seventeenth century when the European state system was first established. Philosophically, the system was much older than that. The principles of power had a family tree that could be traced back thousands of years. But if the whole world had changed in fundamental respects, if "the increasing sense of distance from the past"[20] was indeed gaining ground, then *all* traditional definitions of foreign relations would have to face the guillotine of modernity.

Europe was changing its ways, but so too was the United States, where modernity challenged a policy tradition of isolation that appeared to more and more observers a vestige of an earlier and bygone world. Tradition presumed stability, continuity, and timelessness. In Alexander Hamilton's day, nothing had seemed more enduring than the regional truths of geography. The idea of America as a New World had bred a sense of separation from distant conflicts in which foreign relations were truly *foreign*. But, in America's case, isolation did not breed differentiation the way it does in the natural world. On the contrary, commercial and cultural interaction had fostered a growing commonality between the U.S. and Europe. Increasingly, the spread of modern industrial civilization and the emergence of a common global society placed in question the survivability of unique, stationary, and isolated ways of life. With liberal values and a market economy spreading into every crevice of the globe, local distinctions and cultural peculiarities were fated to disappear. As the progressive economist Simon Patten put it, "The earth has but one general environment and can bring to perfection but one type of man."[21]

Increasingly, because the state of the world was so fluid, tradition-based policy gave way to policy based on the historical interpretation of change. Indeed, it could be understood in no other way. To a few statesmen, the demands of the situation were straightforward enough. "When we say that the great historian must be a man of imagination," Theodore Roosevelt maintained, "we use the word as we use it when we say that the great statesman must be a man of imagination."[22] A statement of this kind had extraordinarily radical implications. Taken literally, it meant that interests—commonly thought of as traditional, vested, local, immediate, perceptible by common sense, hard, and selfish—would have to be replaced by imaginative interpretations of volatile and often confusing international situations. It meant that the old commonsense realities of foreign policy would have to be replaced by a wholly new way of seeing the world.

By 1900, that new worldview had yet to be convincingly articulated. Fairly typical of the time was a statement by Cleveland's secretary of state, Richard Olney: "The mission of this country . . . is not merely to pose but to act . . . to forego no fitting opportunity to further the progress of civilization." To be sure, the United States had tangible interests to defend, but in Olney's view "our material interests only point in the same direction as considerations of a higher and less selfish character."[23] This was a very naive and unproblematic way of putting things, to say the least. It assumed that the internationalist journey would be relatively straightforward and painless, and that what was good for the world would automatically be good for the United States. This unclouded optimism failed utterly to anticipate the kind of internationalism that would be needed to deal with the terrifying new dangers that accompanied globalism, the kinds of global threats that in 1900 had yet to be articulated. But even if they had been voiced, dire forecasts would have had little impact at the time.

An appreciation of the power of this sunny, optimistic internationalism is indispensable to understanding the contrasting rhythms of the Wilsonian century. An internationalism of fear, if it were to be taken seriously, required as a prerequisite for its existence a more fundamental and positive internationalism to fear for. The potential dissolution of civilization could be perceived as a threat only to the degree that the United States was thought to be already entangled in it. The construction of that internationalist base, the creation of a sensibility that there existed a normal internationalism worth defending, which was so essential in the decades to come, was achieved by the Roosevelt and Taft administrations.

Roosevelt and Taft: The Transition to Normal Internationalism

Thanks in large measure to the disillusionment fostered by an unexpected and stubborn rebellion against American rule in the Philippines, the infatuation with empire subsided as quickly as it had arisen. As it became apparent that imperialism was not the gateway to globalism, American statesmen resurveyed the international terrain in their search for answers to the riddle of America's place in a fast-modernizing world. In September 1901, on the day before he was assassinated, President William McKinley suggested that close involvement was inevitable. "Isolation is no longer possible or desirable," he insisted. Pointing to the effective shrinkage of space and time brought about by rapid technological improvements in communication and transportation, he asserted that "no nation can any longer be indifferent to any other." McKinley's global vision reflected the prevailing liberal optimism about the basically peaceful thrust of commerce. "Though commercial competitors we are, commercial enemies we must not be," said the doomed president.[24]

Between the Spanish-American War and the outbreak of the Great War in Europe in 1914, the United States made significant strides in the direction of globalizing its foreign policies. McKinley's successors, Theodore Roosevelt (1901–9) and William Howard Taft (1909–13) were the first presidents to self-consciously embark upon the modernization of American foreign relations. Though their internationalist initiatives were quite limited and over-optimistic by comparison with what followed afterwards, they began the task of reshaping American policy to fit the coming global era. Because of their contrasting approaches, they need to be viewed in relation to one another in order to better gauge the radical modernist meaning of America's rise to world power.

Surprisingly, Taft comes out looking far more the pioneering modern than T.R. when the two men are judged on the basis of their contributions to twentieth-century internationalism. Roosevelt was clearly the more charismatic and colorful of the two and the more eager to claim distinctiveness as a trailblazer. Given his legendary exploits in the American West, his heroic cavalry exploits with the "Rough Riders" in the Spanish-American War, his wide-ranging interest in the politics of Europe and Asia, and his endless references to force as the bottom-line factor in international relations, Roosevelt has always seemed to be a founding father of a certain realistic style of American globalism.

But the he-man image of Roosevelt as wielder of the "Big Stick" is a grossly misleading caricature. He was, far more than most, an intellectual politician. With his abiding interest in history, he was more fully attuned than most of his contemporaries to the global revolution then in progress and struggled mightily to reconcile traditional American foreign policy—which was mostly concerned with the goings-on in its hemispheric neighborhood—with global changes. Though often seen as the personification of America's rise to world power, Roosevelt's deep ambivalence about the spread of a universal civilization definitely tilted his foreign policies in the direction of tradition. His foreign policies were an ending, not a beginning, the last chapter in a book, more than a century in the writing, about the consolidation of American power in the Caribbean.

By contrast, Taft authored the first chapter of a new volume in American foreign policy history. Though less active intellectually than Roosevelt in thinking through the global processes at work, he was more fully in sympathy with them and more interested "in keeping the house of the world in order." While undeniably bland and conservative when compared to the Rough Rider, he was, surprisingly, far more innovative in his diplomacy. It is because the basic outlines of his rather thoroughgoing internationalism remain imprinted on American foreign policy to this day that he deserves greater credit for innovation than he has commonly received.

Unfortunately for his historical reputation, Taft's outlook was enshrined in the phrase "Dollar Diplomacy," a phrase that Democrats used for decades as a stick with which to beat the Republicans at election time. But when Taft stated in his message to Congress that "modern diplomacy is commercial," he did not mean to suggest that Dollar Diplomacy was devoted merely to the service of commercial interests. The underlying assumption was that warlike methods—*Roosevelt* methods—were outdated and that peaceful cooperation and commercial expansion were now the order of the day. Though his views were premature, he believed what many political scientists today take for granted—that because of their common framework of values democracies do not make war on each other.

For both presidents, America's future as a world power lay in cooperation with other powers who behaved in a "civilized" manner. In Roosevelt's case, even when exerting a long-awaited American dominance in the Western Hemisphere, he did so, sincerely, in the name of civilization. His policies in Europe and Asia, even though they reflected a hierarchical ordering of foreign policy priorities, also had a civilizational side that amounted to more than window dressing.

But Taft went far beyond TR's tentative steps. During his presidency, Rooseveltian reserve in Asia and Europe was abandoned for a vigorously pursued diplomacy of cooperation. Taft was not simply being idiosyncratic or quixotic (if so, much of American diplomacy for the rest of the century would have to be described in similar terms). Ever since his time, American foreign policy has not been guided by traditional definitions of realism or economic interest. Notwithstanding all the loose, imprecise, and rather ominous talk of "world power," this cooperative global approach would become a recurring theme of American foreign policy throughout the twentieth century, the central feature of normal internationalism.

This cooperative outlook had a transforming impact upon American foreign policy at the start of the century. Within the space of a decade, American opinion about Great Britain, Germany, Russia, China, and Japan underwent a sea change. These images proved to have remarkable staying power, shifting only in response to the ideological upheavals of mid-century. Even then, the standard of judgment would remain pretty much the same as that employed when the century began.

The primary ingredient in changing America's image of these crucial nations was their perceived degree of modernity. Though the specific issues varied from case to case, the common thread tying them all together was the degree to which the other nation adhered to the common global project of civilization. The more modern and civilized the power was perceived to be, the more favorable was the image; the lower the modernity ranking, the more negative the sentiment. Between 1900 and 1913, in the auditions for the much anticipated global drama, events in Latin America, East Asia, and Europe selected the actors and their global roles for a long time to come.

Latin America Policy in Global Context

Throughout the nineteenth century, America's foreign policy horizon was predominantly local. The Monroe Doctrine of 1823 had articulated some long-held assumptions about the ideal conditions of American foreign policy by arguing that colonization in the New World was at an end and that Europe no longer had any right to install monarchical forms of government or to intervene in American politics. Reciprocally, the U.S. stated its willingness to stay out of European quarrels. Though the Monroe Doctrine hardly set Europe's knees to trembling (nor did it much stir Americans until the 1850s, when it finally began to assume its dogmatic status), the Old World's preoccupation with the continental balance of power and a temporary decline in enthusiasm for colonialism meant that the U.S. was not called upon to enforce the doctrine. Fortunately, threats like the independence of Texas and the French occupation of Mexico fizzled out before America's fidelity to the doctrine was put to the test.

In the ten years beginning in 1895, the United States became unquestionably the hegemonic power in the northern half of the Western Hemisphere, fulfilling at long last Alexander Hamilton's injunction in *The Federalist Papers* "to aim at an ascendant in the system of American affairs." This dominance was, in part, a nationalist reaction to the possibility that the rapidly expanding European colonial powers might choose the Western Hemisphere as their next target. But there were internationalist implications to American domination as well, for it would have been impossible for the U.S. to embark on a global course if it had been beset by insecurity in its own back yard. In international affairs as in personal life, cosmopolitanism is dependent on personal security and self-confidence.

Thus Caribbean regionalism of the fin-de-siècle period was as much an expression of globalism as a defensive Monrovian response to global encroachments. However much the fulfillment of a long-standing desire, the Caribbean policy of the United States also owed a great deal to a growing identification with Europe. "The distance between Europe and

America is being diminished," said Herbert Croly, the theoretician of progressivism.[25] This ideological affinity with the Continent produced geopolitical assumptions quite different from those in force in Hamilton's time. Whereas Hamilton assumed the existence of four separate and independent spheres of politics—Europe, Asia, Africa, and the Americas—the sudden burst of American activism in Latin America was based on the growing understanding that those formerly separate spheres were in the process of merging into a single, global political system. The days of depicting the New World as a complete contrast with Europe were over.

The conviction that Europe and America were becoming more alike with every passing year was evident from the way in which each of the major crises in the Caribbean over the span of a decade became entangled, to one degree or another, with global considerations. The Venezuela Crisis of 1895, for example, widely held to be the first drink in America's binge of Caribbean expansion, arose from a boundary dispute between Venezuela and British Guyana. The disagreement had been simmering for decades when the United States decided suddenly, in 1895, to make an issue of it in a bombastic message to Great Britain that presumed to elaborate a new twist on the Monroe doctrine. Secretary of State Richard Olney warned Europeans of the danger they would be courting in bringing imperialism to the Western Hemisphere and threatened to set the boundary unilaterally unless the British consented to arbitration.

There were domestic factors at work in the histrionics of the Cleveland administration, chief among them being a desire to win credit with a mass public that was quickly drifting away from the administration's economic policies. But from a foreign policy standpoint, global factors were quite prominent. The Venezuela crisis was an important step in the emergence at long last of a rapprochement between the colony and its nemesis, the former mother country. In Tyler Dennett's words, the episode was an illustration of "the school of American thought which holds that the most certain way to reach a friendly understanding with John Bull is to begin by giving him a stiff punch in the nose."[26] It was not long before Olney was characterizing his outburst as "liberties of speech which only the fondest and dearest relatives indulge in"—a family quarrel.[27]

A certain segment of the foreign policy elite even hoped to use the Venezuela crisis as a way of bringing the U.S. and Great Britain together! Anglophiles like the American ambassador in London, John Hay, put the point without embarrassment: "All of us who think cannot but see that there is a sanction like that of religion which binds us to a sort of partnership in the beneficent work of the world."[28] By this time, the old animosities were a thing of the past. Even Henry Adams had to confess that "I no longer feel the old acute pleasure in vilifying the British."[29]

The threat of war was like the threat of divorce for a couple linked too closely to part. As one petition in England put it: "All English-speaking peoples united by race, language and religion, should regard war as the one absolutely intolerable mode of settling the differences of the Anglo-American family."[30] But that kind of reconciliation assumed that the two parties could agree upon a favorable global division of labor. If nothing else, the outburst certainly gained London's attention. Once the British recognized American suzerainty in the hemisphere, it was hoped, the two Anglo-Saxon nations would march arm in arm, jointly leading the global march to development.

This co-captaincy of world leadership was usually justified in terms of race, as an expression of the "unity of the Anglo-Saxon race." In the scientifically sanctioned racism of the day, the acid test of racial superiority was a people's level of civilization. Those of Anglo-Saxon descent assumed that their industrial and civic achievements provided the only credentials required for leading the rest of the world the way to modernity. Anglo-American friendship had been building for a long time among the elites of the nations, but it began to acquire political meaning only as the result of a growing conviction in both countries of the common duty to a global civilization.

Once the British gracefully gave way to American demands that the Venezuelan-Guyanan border dispute be arbitrated, relations with the United States began to improve. Further concessions to American sensibilities followed rapidly. Thanks to the British unwillingness to go along, a European attempt to intercede on behalf of Spain during the Cuban crisis in 1898 came to nothing. Shortly thereafter, in the second Hay-Pauncefote treaty of 1901, the British finally acknowledged America's sole right to build and fortify an isthmian canal and, more generally, acquiesced in America's pursuit of regional hegemony in the Caribbean.

The Panama Canal episode would seem, on the face of it, to run contrary to this internationalist trend. In 1903, Roosevelt brazenly fomented a revolution in the Colombian province of Panama after failing to strike a satisfactory bargain with the government in Bogotá. Convinced that the Colombians were intent on extorting money from the U.S., he quickly recognized and granted protection to the breakaway province and then signed a treaty with this new political creation that guaranteed, in perpetuity, American control of a ten-mile-wide canal zone. This was indeed a bravura piece of acquisitiveness. As a de facto extension of the American coastline, the canal made the Caribbean an American security zone in a more compelling way than ever before.

The British, meanwhile, stood by with their arms folded and quietly applauded the American initiative. Shortly thereafter, the royal navy in effect withdrew from the Caribbean basin, leaving it to the United States to enforce security in the region. This move was part of a global retrenchment forced by the need to concentrate limited naval resources on an increasingly worrisome continental situation in which imperial Germany was becoming a formidable naval competitor. But it was made possible in the first place by the British recognition that the United States would preserve British economic interests in the region.

There was also an internationalist logic at work from the American standpoint. The canal was not supposed to be simply an American inter-coastal turnpike but a highway for civilization benefiting the entire world. As one early justification for its construction put the case: "The canal is an international benefit which the United States has no right to take upon itself, except as the representative of civilized commerce. The oceans are the property of mankind."[31] The test of this interpretation of the canal's status came when the U.S. set canal fees for non-American vessels. After some controversy, President Woodrow Wilson in 1914 decided that American ships would pay the same tolls as everyone else.

On a host of other issues, a pervasive spirit of cooperation emerged between the two countries that in the past would have been unimaginable. Shortly after the British had winked at America's rough treatment of Spain, the United States adopted an officially benevolent position of neutrality during Britain's 1900–1902 war with the Boer rebels in South Africa, despite the fact that significant segments of American public opinion sympathized with the Boer insurgents. This willingness to give way in areas where the other English-speaking power had paramount interests was reciprocated when the British deferred to their American cousins in a dispute over the boundary between Canada and the Alaskan panhandle, much to the disappointment of Canadians who had expected more aggressive representation from their guardians in London.

Although incidents in the Caribbean led to a clearing of the air and closer understanding with the British, the exact opposite was true for relations with Germany. Relations between the two nations had begun to sour as early as the 1880s, thanks to quarrels over Samoa, a trade controversy, and some ominous German naval behavior at the battle of Manila Bay in 1898. It was impossible to dissociate these disagreements from the fact that Wilhelmine Germany was a "despotism," to use Roosevelt's term, a nation in which autocracy and Prussian militarism, two distinctly premodern phenomena, were closely allied. The aristocratic symbol of the nation, the Kaiser, struck most observers as something of a wild man, most characteristically when he exhorted his troops to behave like "Huns" when embarking on a punitive expedition to China in 1900 to punish the Boxer rebels. That word was gleefully picked up by the popular press and would long thereafter be used as a metaphor for a militaristic Germany.

In the space of a few years, in American eyes Germany became America's most likely future enemy because of her perceived designs against the Monroe Doctrine, a doctrine that Chancellor Otto von Bismarck a few years earlier had called a "preposterous assumption."[32] The incident that marked a significant turn for the worse in German-American relations was the second Venezuela crisis. This episode took place in 1903, when German, British, and Italian gunboats began bombarding the coastal cities of Venezuela as a way of inducing that country's dictator, Cipriano Castro, to resume payments on his international debts.

Cagily, Castro played to U.S. public opinion by stressing European violations of the Monroe Doctrine. Roosevelt saw no danger in the British intervention. But the public outcry, combined with a fear that the Germans intended to seize a port in Venezuela as they had recently done in China, led Roosevelt to act. Discreetly, but convincingly, he threatened to use naval force if the German navy continued its aggressive debt collection tactics. The quarrel with Venezuela ought to be arbitrated, he suggested, and arbitrated it was.

In contrast to the 1895 spat with Great Britain, the result was not improved understanding with the *Kaiserreich.* Henceforth Germany was plagued with image problems that would shadow it for at least a half century to come. Though the visible flames of conflict were stamped out, the underbrush of distrust between the two nations was left to smolder. Shortly thereafter, the American military drafted a war plan, code-named Black, to deal with a hypothetical German assault against American interests in the Caribbean. Until the eve of the Great War in Europe, according to the then assistant secretary of the navy, Franklin D. Roosevelt, "the power that we were building to guard against was Germany."[33]

But while military planners were thinking in traditional military terms, American statesmen were trying to understand these developments within the modern context of global civilization. Roosevelt realized that the Europeans had a right, according to the international law of the day, to collect on their loans, by force if need be. His concern to establish American dominance in the Caribbean while abiding by international duties was evident in the Dominican crisis, when the failure of the Dominican Republic to pay its debts threatened European intervention. To forestall European military meddling, the U.S. imposed a customs receivership upon the country, the income from which was used to pay off foreign bondholders.

Roosevelt took care to justify his action in traditional terms by announcing the "Roosevelt Corollary" to the Monroe Doctrine, but his 1904 message to Congress spoke a different language. There he was quite frank in talking about an "international police power" exercised on behalf of civilization. Henry Adams had anticipated this development when he said "whatever the American people might think or say about it, they would sooner or later have to police those islands, not against Europe, but for Europe, and America too."[34] As was later pointed out, the Monroe Doctrine had originally been aimed against Europe, not against Latin America. In this case, however, Roosevelt was speaking as if America was the executor of an estate held in common with the Old World.

One might object that these were, after all, variations on the old theme of distancing the United States both ideologically and geopolitically from Europe. But in modern circumstances, a rigid pursuit of separation would have had, ironically, catastrophic consequences. If, as Croly pointed out, the United States insisted on a total exclusion of Europe from the hemisphere, that might lead the Europeans to try to break down a radically isolationist Monroe Doctrine. War for this purpose "would defeat the very purpose which it is supposed to establish. It would embroil the United States and the two American continents in continual broils with Europe." The United States would have to become "a predominantly military power, armed to the teeth, to resist or forestall European attack."[35] Quite unintentionally, America "would become a part of the European political system with a vengeance."

Although Taft refused to follow Roosevelt's lead in other respects, Latin America was one region in which he followed dutifully in T.R.'s footsteps. For the Caribbean nations, the big stick did not smart any the less because Taft claimed to be applying the diplomacy of the dollar. Indeed, in some ways, Taft was *more* nationalistic than Roosevelt. In Nicaragua, he managed to evict European economic interests and replace them by American-funded loans, secured by the kind of customs house receivership pioneered by T.R. in the Dominican Republic. Nevertheless, Taft's policy differed from T.R.'s in its explicit regard for the economic development of Latin America, a topic that stirred T.R.'s martial soul not at all. And economic development was at the heart of Taft's globalism.

East Asia in Global Context

Taft's internationalism was made easier by Roosevelt's successful pursuit
of Caribbean hegemony. Thanks to T.R., America's sense of security in
the hemisphere had never been higher. Hence, in contrast to its rather
narrow-minded application in Latin America, in other areas of the globe
"dollar diplomacy" was free to generate unprecedented proposals for international cooperation. Although the Taft administration sought to promote American investment in Russia, the Ottoman Empire, and in Africa,
among other places, the most notable attempt to use dollar diplomacy as
a way of modernizing international politics took place in East Asia, where
the diplomacy of imperialism in China brought together, in close proxim-
ity, most of the great powers of the coming century. While the image of
Great Britain and Germany was formed largely in relation to Caribbean
issues, America's modern perception of the other powers grew out of their
relationship to China.

After forming an early commercial and missionary interest, the political
connection with China grew out of the Opium War (1839–42), a conflict
that resulted from Great Britain's desire to continue its lucrative opium
trade with China. Unable to resist modern British weaponry, the once
reclusive Chinese agreed to the opening of "treaty ports," commercial
enclaves that were to all extents and purposes outside the control of China.
The Chinese imperial government also lost the power to set its own import
taxes and, by granting the principle of "extraterritoriality" to the British,
relinquished the right to try westerners according to Chinese law. Within
a few years, other powers, including the United States, signed treaties
with China that granted them similar privileges.

For all the expansive rhetoric, America's interests in Asia were actually
quite small. According to a leading historian of U.S.-Chinese relations,
trade with China, though on the increase by the end of the century, "was
never more than an infinitesimal part of American trade."[36] In any case,
the house of commerce could not be built until a modern social foundation
for supporting it had first been laid. Over the long term, America's missionaries played a far more important role in China by addressing the
basics of modernization. Their most significant achievements came after
they shifted their focus from religious to secular conversion. Given the
abysmally small number of Chinese converts, direct evangelization was
replaced by a stress on modern education, in the hope that the appetite
for Christianity would grow as a by-product of an overall elevation of
cultural tastes. In this way, evangelization and westernization were closely
tied together.

The absence of significant "hard" interests has led some historians to argue that China's importance had to do with visions of the future, e.g., the enormous profits to be made from selling to a market with many hundreds of millions of potential customers. For some, China undoubtedly did possess such allure. But this kind of salesman's fantasy alone was not enough to supply the energy to propel American diplomacy. More important as a motive force was the idea of China as a field of collaboration, the main theater in which the cooperationist drama of modern civilization would be played out. For here was where America, the Orient, and the Occident came together in a new global diplomacy. Again, in his thinking about Asia, Herbert Croly took an accurate reading of the progressive pulse. "While the American nation should never seek a positive place in an exclusively European system," he said, "Europe, the United States, Japan, and China must all eventually take their places in a world system."[37]

For many Americans, China policy was the symbol of the new internationalism. China would demonstrate how the old rust-bucket diplomacy could be abandoned in favor of a more modern design. Over the course of the nineteenth century, numberless statements pointed to the Far East as the locus of the nation's foreign policy destiny. Albert Bushnell Hart, a leading historian, believed along with many others that America's global future lay across the Pacific: "Who can doubt that the purpose of the American people is not only to make this nation felt as a world power, but also to spread western civilization eastward?" he asked. In China, interests were defined in terms of the future; not according to what the United States had, but what it might create; not in terms of China alone, but in global perspective.

The turn of the century hardly seemed a propitious time for such cooperation. In the late 1890s, spheres of interest in China seemed ripe to become outright possessions. In response, the United States declared the "Open Door" Policy, which sought to maintain the status quo of the imperialist treaty port system in effect since the 1840s. The British, having the greatest commercial stake in China and being hard pressed elsewhere, were content with this arrangement; indeed, some British diplomats suggested a joint open door announcement with the United States. Other powers in China were less pleased with the Open Door idea, but they went along with it because a breakdown of the treaty port system might lead to runaway competition. Whatever their aspirations in China, they were not yet worth war with another major power.

At first, the principal challenger to the Open Door approach appeared to be Russia. The degradation of the peasantry, the utter absence of democracy, a general backwardness and primitivism, combined with an exalted sense of Russia's mission—all these were extremely off-putting to Americans who visited the gargantuan Czarist state. American travelers were typically appalled at the crudeness of Russian society. According to newspaperman Julian Ralph, Russia was not "the last and most primitive corner of Europe," but "the first and most advancing country of Asia."[38] "Scratch a Russian and you find a Tartar," said Carl Schurz. According to Andrew D. White, "Russia has been coming slowly out of the Middle Ages—indeed, out of perhaps the most cruel phases of medieval life."[39] Even that interpretation of the Russian past was too optimistic for some. Arguing that the country was beyond the civilized pale, Henry Adams insisted that "Russia had nothing in common with any ancient or modern world that history knew."[40]

For many observers, Russia's semi-barbarous level of development, combined with the country's enormous resources and population, seemed to spell trouble for the future. "Russia's objective," said Frederick Wells Williams, "is international monopoly. There is no place in her scheme for countries that her garrisons do not occupy."[41] Henry Cabot Lodge described the Russians as "a people whose fundamental ideas, whose theory of life, and whose controlling motives of action are utterly alien to [our] own. There is no common ground, no common starting-place, no common premise of thought and action." Lodge wondered "how soon they will reach the point of dangerous and destructive rivalry."[42]

These kinds of suspicions were amply justified by firsthand diplomatic experience of Russia's tactics in China. In 1900, the antiforeign Boxer rebellion prompted the treaty powers to send expeditionary forces to China to rescue the western legations besieged in Peking by the rebels. The United States took part by dispatching a contingent of its troops from the Philippines. Suspecting that other powers might use the intervention as a pretext to keep their troops in China as a prelude to assuming full colonial control, Secretary of State John Hay in July 1900 issued a second Open Door note, which urged the other powers to maintain China's "territorial and administrative entity," i.e., to avoid partitioning China.

Instead of promptly withdrawing their troops, the Russians lingered on and expanded their sphere of influence in Manchuria and Korea. Seeking to augment their privileges without specifically overturning the status quo, they extorted further concessions from the moribund Qing dynasty in Peking. In response to repeated expressions of concern from American officials about the protection of U.S. commercial interests, the Russians replied evasively and showed no intention of pulling in their horns. Their self-aggrandizing behavior alarmed Americans on the scene, who had no doubt that the Russians felt nothing but contempt for the Open Door. Repeated protests came to nothing.

This overbearing Russian behavior certainly exasperated President Roosevelt, not least because it frustrated his sense of how an imperialist division of labor ought to work in East Asia. Thinking about optimal regional arrangements in the new global order, T.R. "thought it for the interest of the world that each part of the world should be prosperous and well policed."[43] At first, he believed that Russia was the power best suited to dominate China, that it could do for the Far East what the United States was doing on behalf of civilization in the Caribbean region. He changed his mind soon enough, however. Writing to his ambassador in St. Petersburg, Roosevelt recalled that "for years Russia has pursued a policy of consistent opposition to us in the East, and of literally fathomless mendacity. She has felt a profound contempt for England and Japan and the United States, all three, separately or together. It has been impossible to trust any promise she has made."[44]

Another point of controversy with Russia centered on her treatment of Jews. Long noted for its anti-Semitic policies, the Czarist government typically required its Jewish population to live within a narrow band near Russia's borders known as the Pale of Settlement. Occasionally, official policy tolerated and encouraged anti-Semitic riots and massacres known as pogroms. In 1903, John Hay delivered a petition to St. Petersburg put together by American Jewish leaders to protest the notorious Kishinev pogrom, in which forty-five Jews were killed. More important to the prestige of the United States was the ill-treatment accorded Jews who had become American citizens. By 1911, the situation became so critical that the Taft administration decided unilaterally to annul the commercial treaty with Russia first signed in 1832.

The treaty relationship was abandoned largely for reasons of domestic politics, not from any serious expectation by Taft that the Russian government would change its behavior. Prior to this point optimism had governed trade and investment with Russia. "Russia is the country of the future," said one such optimist. "Investments are inherently safe."[45] This move puts the allegedly compelling allure of the China market into some perspective, for within three years trade with Russia dropped from 85 to 31.3 million dollars. The China trade, by comparison, was much smaller.

The fast-worsening image of Russia was evident from the Roosevelt administration's attitude toward the Russo-Japanese war of 1904–5. While Americans could only fume and, in any case, U.S. interests in the region hardly merited more than verbal protests, other nations were in a position to take action. The Japanese, who harbored designs of their own for expanding northward into Manchuria from Korea, took a far more alarmist view of Russian behavior. Fortified by the signature of the Anglo-Japanese Alliance in 1902, the dynamically expanding Japanese empire was in a position to protest with bared teeth. With tension running high over the future of the northern portion of Korea, the Japanese launched a surprise attack on Russian naval forces at Port Arthur. Initially, Roosevelt silently cheered on the Japanese from the sidelines. He excused the sneak attack, applauded early Japanese victories, and argued that the Japanese were in effect defending American interests in the Far East.

However, the pro-Japanese tilt of American policy soon disappeared because images of Japan and China were also beginning to shift at this time. Only a few years earlier, it had been fashionable to see Japan as "the Great Britain of Asia," a nation that "with every day is making some new stride toward the Western spirit of enterprise and civilization."[46] But the positive American view of Japan at the start of the Russo-Japanese War faded quickly in the face of growing concern about the purposes to which Japanese power was being put. Jingoist expressions of Japanese national pride led Roosevelt to express doubts about the degree to which Japan actually subscribed to Western values. By that time, the bloom was off the rose for the Rough Rider, who settled finally on promoting a "balanced antagonism" in East Asia, a realistic power balance between the two foes.

The Treaty of Portsmouth, mediated by an impartial T.R., reflected the military balance of the day. Despite having won most of the battles, the financially exhausted Japanese were unable to bring the stalemated war to a conclusion. Meanwhile the Russians, though hardly victorious, were far from defeated. Ideally, T.R. would have preferred one or the other nation to provide civilized leadership in the region of the kind provided by the U.S. in the Caribbean, but both of the leading candidates for the role turned out to have serious shortcomings. Therefore a regional balance of power, besides reflecting geopolitical realities, also seemed best from the civilizational standpoint of regional development.

The Portsmouth mediation, far from signaling a new willingness to get mixed up in East Asian complexities, was the beginning of an American retreat in the region. With the rise of Japanese power in East Asia, Roosevelt saw the handwriting on the wall. Formerly a leading pro-imperialist, he was now convinced that the Philippine islands were a strategic liability for the U.S., a "heel of Achilles," so distant that they could not be defended adequately against a major Asian power. Concerned with the vulnerability of the islands, in 1905, Taft, then secretary of war, visited Tokyo and signed an agreement with Prime Minister Katsura Taro which recognized the preeminent interests of each nation in Korea and the Philippines. In 1907, Roosevelt shut down the U.S. consulate in Korea and the Japanese annexed the peninsula outright in 1910. In 1908, Secretary of State Elihu Root signed still another accord, the Root-Takahira agreement, which reaffirmed the status quo in the Pacific and the Open Door in China.

Following the announcement of the Portsmouth peace terms, Roosevelt's doubts were confirmed by the overwrought Japanese popular reaction to his successful mediation effort. The anti-American riots that broke out in Japan were the result of the Japanese government's willingness to make Roosevelt the scapegoat for its failure to achieve ambitious war aims. No sooner was the war crisis surmounted than the Japanese-American relationship was again inflamed by the discriminatory treatment of Japanese immigrants to the U.S. The number of immigrants was small enough, but the decision of the San Francisco school board in 1907 to segregate Japanese students was construed by Tokyo as an insult to national and racial pride. To be sure, the Japanese government also discriminated against foreigners, but the point was that it did so uniformly.

At issue was not the American government's authority to control immigration or define citizenship, which were fundamental rights of sovereignty, but its discriminatory treatment of Asians. Roosevelt realized that the racial dispute was loaded with political dynamite. Privately, he called the Californians "damned fools" for their blind stubbornness. Nevertheless, the absence of any federal role in local education meant that Roosevelt had no option but to thump away on his bully pulpit in the hope of getting his backsliding flock to see the light. Eventually, a solution was worked out. The Japanese agreed to limit exit visas for individuals bound for California—no Japanese, no discrimination—while the school board rescinded its discriminatory measures.

From this point on, U.S.-Japanese relations were never the same. Increasingly, commentators claimed to discern war clouds on the horizon. In the belief that the Japanese needed to better appreciate the power of the United States, Roosevelt sent the fleet on a round-the-world-voyage, without advance congressional appropriations. The "great white fleet" was greeted effusively by the Japanese after it docked in Japan. But it did little to quell growing talk of a "yellow peril" or predictions of a looming showdown between East and West that presumably would decide the destiny of the world. As one sensationalist account put it, the world would thus be forcefully delivered "from the yoke of an oriental civilization."[47] Though President Taft pooh-poohed any possibility of war with Japan, the adoption in 1911 of War Plan Orange, a contingency plan for war against Japan, was a sign that the times were changing. However, it was indicative of the mixed feelings toward Japan that a basic treaty of commerce between the two countries was signed that same year.

As Japan's civilized status declined in American eyes, China's rose. To this point, Japan had been the East Asian success story, while China was often compared to a narcotized giant, a society in deep slumber incapable of westernizing reforms. Roosevelt was openly contemptuous of the Chinese and skeptical of their capacity to modernize. However, this overwhelmingly negative attitude was turned upside down by the time the first decade of the twentieth century had passed. By 1911, China was seen as the best candidate for introducing American-style modernity in the Far East.

By this time, the American missionary effort had been reoriented from its original emphasis on conversion to the goal of modernization. A host of American educational institutions had sprung up in China. The remission of the Boxer indemnity, the penalty imposed upon China for tolerating the Boxer rebels, was channeled into education. The Rockefeller Foundation began investigating plans to create a modern university in China, deciding finally that its goals could be met with less resistance by creating a world-class medical school in Peking. The idea, as foundation president Raymond Fosdick later put it, was "to make over a medieval society in terms of modern knowledge."[48] Thanks to these numerous private initiatives, the American cultural presence in China overshadowed that of all other China powers.

This optimistic view of China's capacity for development was also visible in the way the Taft administration reframed the Open Door policy. As originally defined in 1899 and 1900, the Open Door was very much a defensive doctrine, but the Taft administration made two significant changes. First, going beyond the protection of what little commerce there was, it emphasized the investment of capital over the sale of goods. An agrarian China could purchase few American-made products, but a China industrialized with the help of American capital investment had the potential to become a valuable trading partner.

Second, in contrast to Roosevelt's acceptance of a balance of power and the regional diplomacy of imperialism centering on China, Taft sought to set in place a more cooperative structure of relations. In its eagerness to open up investment opportunities in China, his administration took a particular interest in the financing of railroads. Taft was quite proud of gaining admission into the all-European investment syndicate or consortium then charged with lending money to the Chinese imperial government in the building of a north-south line between Peking and Canton. This was the so-called Four Power Consortium.

More was involved here than investment for investment's sake. Painfully aware that the Open Door generated little enthusiasm from the other powers, Taft viewed the consortium as an instrument ideally suited to ending the competitive diplomacy of imperialism in China. Quite simply, by acting on the principle of consensus, the consortium could prevent roguish behavior by a single power. "Where nations invest their capital" wrote Secretary of State Philander Knox, "there they are intent upon preserving peace and promoting the development of the natural resources and the prosperity of the people."[49] Once all the powers were aboard the moving train of peaceful cooperation, it would be difficult to transfer back to the diplomacy of imperialism.

This brainstorm was put to the test in Manchuria, where Knox envisioned a neutralization scheme for the railways of that province. The idea was deceptively simple: a consortium would lend China the money to purchase the Japanese and Russian railroads in Manchuria and would run the system until China paid off the loan. The benefits would be manifold. Inasmuch as these railroads had furnished the pretext for imperialist expansion in Manchuria by Japan and Russia, the neutralization scheme would preserve China's territorial integrity, foil imperialist competition, and make piles of money, while the railroads would provide an indispensable platform for China's modernization.

The plan ran into opposition from all quarters. The Chinese were unenthusiastic. They would have preferred to use the Boxer funds to buy the railways outright instead of earmarking the moneys for education, as the Americans insisted. The British, afraid of alienating their Japanese allies, equivocated. The Japanese and Russians, meanwhile, were adamantly against Knox's idea. Indeed, a common resentment of American interference led the former enemies to put aside their hard feelings and sign a treaty in 1910 that defined with some precision their respective spheres of influence in Manchuria. Not least, Taft suffered the indignity of being scolded by his former mentor, Theodore Roosevelt, who urged him to "never draw unless you mean to shoot," to which Taft responded that this was hardly a wild-west gunfight. Still, the neutralization scheme had boomeranged, its only tangible result being to reinforce the diplomacy of imperialism.

This might have seemed a fiasco had not the situation been salvaged by events. Just then, the 1911 revolution toppled the decrepit Qing dynasty and inaugurated the republican era of Chinese history. With China at last on the brink of western-style reform, hopes for China's modernization soared among Americans. With this development, the Japanese and the Russians realized that control of the Manchurian periphery was no substitute for a comprehensive China policy. China proper was where the action would be. With the new republican government of China urgently requesting stabilization loans, Tokyo and St. Petersburg demanded admission to the bankers' fraternity, which in 1912 became a six-power consortium. This club of six anticipated in structure and intent the kinds of great-power partnerships that would later be established to prevent nationalist breakaways, the most famous being the League of Nations Council. Not only would any power that insisted on going its own way forgo the advantages of unity, it would also have to deal with the possibility of facing a united front arrayed against its lone-wolf policies.

The six-power consortium, which snatched victory from the jaws of defeat, proved to be remarkably long-lived. Upon becoming president in 1913, Woodrow Wilson withdrew the United States from the club of 6, arguing from his progressive reform perspective that it was biased toward big American banks, which was indeed the case. However, he soon saw the error of his ways, especially after Japan in 1915, in the so-called 21 Demands episode, sought to expand dramatically its sphere of influence in China. In May 1920, the consortium idea was resurrected, according to one historian, "as a way of checking Japanese expansion and assisting in the modernization of China."[50] Because it did precious little business with China, the consortium was a failure as a modernizing instrument. But it remained quite useful as a device for preventing independent, and potentially disruptive, expansionist behavior by the China powers.

With some ups and downs, then, Far Eastern diplomacy prior to 1914, by emphasizing the need for cooperation among the China powers, was successful in holding competitive imperialism in check. While the other powers chose cooperation as a matter of self-interest, for the United States cooperation in the Far East was representative of a larger global process working itself out.

Europe in a Global Context

China was the symbol of the new American globalism, but Europe, the political and cultural center of civilization, remained the region of utmost practical importance. Writing in 1908, Archibald Cary Coolidge noted that the United States had "shown a greater disposition than of old to

take part in European questions."[51] Though most actively engaged with
European nations in Latin America and Asia, the U.S. was also beginning
to show a concern for what formerly were thought to be purely continental
affairs. In 1906, the United States attended the Algeçiras conference and
helped to mediate the first Morocco crisis between Germany and France.
The very fact that the U.S. was trusted by both sides to mediate suggested
that she had no political role in Europe; but, by the same token, this trust
implied a recognition of America's new status as a power.

Here, too, as in the Caribbean, Germany seemed to be the major problem. Only a few American observers, like Brooks Adams, had stopped
to consider the consequences of an end to the relative period of stability
following the Congress of Vienna. Remarking on the "gangrene" causing the weakness of France, Adams could see in the making a German-
dominated system which promised "at no distant day to consolidate northern Europe and Asia in a mass hostile to the interests of all external races."
Such a situation would be most immediately threatening to England. But
Adams also believed that England was "essential to the United States, in
the face of the enemies who fear and hate us, and who, but for her, would
already have fleets upon our shores."[52] His brother Henry believed that
modernity was capable of producing further consolidation through either
peaceful or warlike means. "Either Germany must destroy England and
France to create the next inevitable unification as a system of continent
against continent—or she must pool interests," he wrote in his *Education.*[53] Trusts and combinations, all the rage in the world of business,
seemed also to be the future of diplomacy.

Looking into the future, historian Albert Bushnell Hart also saw trouble
brewing across the seas. "If there is to be in the coming century a great
battle of Armageddon—once more Europe against the Huns—we can no
more help taking our part with the hosts of freedom than we can help
educating our children, building our churches, or maintaining the rights
of the individual."[54] Speaking of American public opinion, one journal
concluded that the American people would "realize the moment they are
called upon to reflect seriously on the matter, that Britain and France stand
for liberal ideas, and that the Germans as at present organized stand for
the reverse. We have not the slightest fear as to which side their sympathies will incline to."[55]

These pessimistic thoughts belonged to the minority. Far more popular
was the idea that civilization had progressed to the point where war was
no longer likely. Even Theodore Roosevelt agreed (with less than wholehearted enthusiasm, it is true) that as countries became more civilized,

they were less likely to go to war with one another. Because Europe was the acknowledged historical core of modern global civilization, the idea of civilization would scarcely be workable without cooperation among its leading nations. The two Hague peace conferences held in 1899 and 1907, while not accomplishing very much, nevertheless were widely viewed as "a germ out of which better and better things will be developed in the future."[56] Not surprisingly, Americans believed that progress toward peace and cooperation was most advanced in Europe.

Sharing the overall sense of optimism that permeated the time, Taft's dollar diplomacy was closely connected to a burgeoning peace movement that had been around since the 1820s as a reformist outgrowth of Protestant revivalism. By the early 1900s, it had been taken over by the more secular-minded upper classes. Andrew Carnegie's decision to fund the Carnegie Endowment for International Peace, a foundation backed with ten million dollars, was perhaps the most flamboyant indicator of the optimism that characterized the peace movement of these years. So confident was Carnegie that he gave the trustees of his endowment the discretion to use the funds for other worthy causes once enduring peace had been secured.

Nicholas Murray Butler, the president of Columbia University and a leader of the endowment, was a crucial figure in the peace movement. His view of how peace would take root was instructive. Butler believed in "the international mind," a cosmopolitan elite that would be the modern global successor to the old European aristocracy. Rather than being steeped in power politics and reaction, however, this new mentality would be based upon the universality of modern liberal principles, and spread by the new mass media which were creating "the psychological unity of the world."[57] Far from disappearing, the idea of an "international mind," more commonly referred to as world opinion, would in somewhat more democratic form become a central factor in American foreign policy in the coming decades, from Woodrow Wilson's League of Nations to cold war foreign policy.

The most significant European initiative of the Taft administration was the decision to negotiate arbitration treaties with England and France. The idea of arbitration had been around for a long time and had been resorted to from time to time by the United States. Even Roosevelt had signed a number of such treaties, only to see them foiled by a U.S. Senate jealous of maintaining its hold on the treaty power granted it by the Constitution. Taft's treaties differed in two significant respects from prior efforts. First, they covered even questions of "national honor," i.e., vital interests essential to sovereignty that traditionalists believed could never be arbitrated. Second, instead of relying on the practical expediency and power calculations of arbitration through compromise, they sought to institutionalize the notion of "justiciable disputes" by making international law the basis for settling disagreements. As one might expect, the treaties as drafted contained safeguards against defining an issue as "justiciable" unless the U.S. agreed beforehand that it was.

Agreements with England and France were concluded without great difficulty. A notable aspect of the treaty with England, and a signal of the growing closeness between the two countries, was the stipulation, included at the insistence of a Canada still fearful of its southern neighbor, that the Anglo-Japanese alliance could not be applied against the United States. Taft hoped that these two arbitration pacts would create such a favorable impression in world opinion that Germany, Russia, and Japan would have little choice but to sign up as well.

As was the often the case at this time, the Senate undid the president's work. A treaty going to the Senate, John Hay once remarked, "is like a bull going into the arena"—the bloody and fatal outcome was foreordained.[58] The Senate insisted, contrary to the spirit of the treaties, that only it could determine, in each and every instance, whether or not an issue was justiciable. With that, there seemed no point in having any general arbitration treaties at all. After a feeble attempt to rouse public opinion, Taft threw in his hand, but without abandoning his optimism about the future of cooperation. In coming years, his commitment to world peace would find an outlet in his leadership of the League to Enforce the Peace, a private organization established during World War I to lobby for the creation of an international peacekeeping organization.

DURING THE Roosevelt and Taft years, 1900–1913, American foreign policy was refitted to equip the United States to sail the global high seas. But in its maiden voyage, the ship of state remained in shallow waters close to shore. For all the anticipation of radical change, America's so-called "rise to world power" was a period of change without crisis—a remarkably smooth and uneventful period in which the nation, instead of having to worry about its security, had the luxury of reshaping its identity. With the exception of the Western Hemisphere, the nation's policy departures generated little in the way of new commitments. And, to judge by the scanty references to the United States in the memoirs of foreign statesmen, America's new status had little or no effect upon the intrigues of the other powers. With the exception of some grinding of gears in the process of

becoming an empire, the upshift from the commercial and cultural internationalism of the nineteenth century to the cooperative great-power internationalism of the twentieth was smooth and seamless.

If the outward thrust of this global reorientation was not very far-
reaching, its domestic sweep was equally modest. It was very much an
elite phenomenon that, with the temporary exception of imperialism, enjoyed little in the way of enthusiastic or spontaneous public support. The
nearly total absence of foreign policy debate in the three-sided election
of 1912 between Taft, a reinvigorated Theodore Roosevelt leading the
progressive Bull Moose Party, and the Democratic candidate, Woodrow
Wilson, suggested that America's world-power status had not noticeably
overturned foreign policy tradition. Congress, especially the Senate, continued to wreak havoc upon the novelties embedded in treaties. Not least,
tariff policy continued to be poured in the protectionist mold in existence
since the Civil War, hardly the best pattern for casting an internationalist
economic policy. There were, to be sure, increasing calls during these
years for downward tariff revision, reciprocity, flexible tariffs, and the
much-discussed idea of a "scientific" tariff commission. But in the
end, economic nationalism, greased by the logrolling of special-interest
groups, remained the key to understanding how the tariff was set.[59]

This internationalism was also extraordinarily optimistic in its assumptions of great-power cooperation. For good reasons having to do with
the often violent and anarchic character of international relations, foreign
policy has usually been based on fear. But the policies of Roosevelt and
Taft, each in their own way, placed far more emphasis on the benefits
than on the dangers of international involvement. They overestimated the
degree to which global cooperation could be made a reality with "civilized" powers, many of whom, for their part, viewed the United States
as a half-breed, itself only partly civilized. Neither Roosevelt nor Taft
understood that the negative images of Germany, Russia, and Japan that
emerged in the course of their presidencies created a roster of potential
enemies that America would have to contend with for much of the century.
But these disturbing omens had little impact so long as America's ideal
world of international relations differed so little from the real world in
which it found itself.

Normal internationalism, then, was in this setting quite abnormal. As
an outlook it existed mainly in the ideas of a small group of internationally
minded Americans and some like-minded liberals abroad. It was relatively
new and untested, an ideological product of the nineteenth century that
was very different from the more cynical view of international politics

that had been held by the founding fathers of the country and continued to be the European norm by which foreign affairs were conducted.

The optimism of the day makes perfect sense if one understands that America's so-called rise to world power was viewed by many as the culmination of a long historical journey of progress whose happy ending for mankind—or western man, at least—lay just over the horizon. From our standpoint at the end of the twentieth century, however, it looks more like a self-deluded beginning. But as the world sailed into a period of turbulence that threatened to unhinge civilization itself, the sunny internationalism of the Roosevelt and Taft years quickly gave way to dark and dreadful images of the modern world.

The Great War: Wilsonianism
as Crisis Internationalism

The most prominent feature of twentieth-century American internation-alism, the obsession with global dangers, first surfaced in the administra-tion of Woodrow Wilson. Wilson's internationalism has often been la-beled "idealist" because of his crusade against the evil of war. But Wilsonianism in its mature formulation was not a utopian doctrine rooted in a naive progressive urge to do good. Though Wilson was indeed a reformer, we tend to forget that the progressive state of mind emerged out of the widespread sense of crisis that hung over a rapidly industrializing America at the turn of the century. Progressive reform was a response to an industrial system run riot.

Just as the progressives sought to shore up the shaky domestic founda-tions of capitalism, Wilson attempted to repair the potentially fatal interna-tional defects of modern industrial civilization. His campaign on behalf of international organization was, in retrospect, a response to the crisis of a civilization that, if left to the old methods of regulating foreign policy behavior, appeared destined for self-destruction. To be sure, Wilsonianism did have a starry-eyed side, but in comparison to the cheerful and blithely confident views of prewar internationalism, its image of the world was utterly terrifying.

With only a few unconvincing conjectures about the "yellow peril" or the long-range danger from a despotic Russia or a militarist Germany making the rounds, no compelling sense of threat had emerged prior to Wilson's time. It occurred to only a few that the rosy future of progress might be imperiled by a dreadful collapse of modern institutions. This bright picture of internationalism clouded over significantly as the appall-ing enormity of the European war that broke out in August 1914 became clear. With that, the turbulent side of modernity began to surface in a convulsion that contemporaries called, significantly, the Great War for Civilization. As the fierce winds of the European storm howled, with occasional gusts carrying across the Atlantic, the novelty of the war's all-consuming character led Wilson to revise radically the American vision of modern history and to recast the nation's role as a world power.

This reinterpretation would make Woodrow Wilson one of the country's greatest presidents, the creator of a worldview that shaped American foreign policy for the remainder of the century. Wilson was a crusader, but his long-term influence would have been minimal had he not also been the first statesman to understand the self-destructive side of modern international relations and to formulate a comprehensive new approach that promised to salvage international society's progressive machinery. According to his grim diagnosis, only a radical experimental treatment promised any hope at all for a cure. With salvation linked closely to survival, the life-and-death atmosphere of the crisis gave to Wilsonianism a sense of urgency and historical necessity.

Wilson believed that he was fated by temperament, talent, and training to achieve political greatness. As one of the country's first home-grown Ph.D.'s from Johns Hopkins University, Wilson became a founding father of political science and a leading student of public administration who later achieved national renown as a modernizing reform president of Princeton University. But he was also an accomplished historian at a time when the various social sciences had only begun their drift away from their mother discipline of history into increasingly narrow and specialized channels. Wilson's ability to give meaning to highly confusing present-day events by placing them in historical perspective was a key to his response to the Great War.

When still a young academic, Wilson had expressed "an unquenchable desire to excel in two distinct and almost opposite kinds of writing: political and *imaginative*."[1] The Great War granted him the opportunity to do both. After puzzling out the ways in which this war differed from previous conflicts, Wilson managed to impart his view of the war's meaning to a large number of people who sensed its revolutionary character but who, unlike Wilson, had been unable to break loose from the grip of traditional conceptions. Wilson's novel approach to international relations makes little sense unless one understands that it was rooted in an imaginative understanding of the utter historical novelty of the war. That understanding, which relied on a creative interpretation of danger that went beyond traditional conceptions of interest, was itself thoroughly modern in both form and content and made Wilsonianism a tremendously original intellectual achievement.

WILSON WON the presidency as a domestic reformer. With foreign affairs only a minor concern when he first entered the White House, Wilson chose William Jennings Bryan as secretary of state. Had Wilson been able to anticipate the magnitude of the foreign policy crises soon to come, there is little chance that he would have chosen the thrice-defeated Democratic standard bearer in recognition of his status as the elder statesman and titular head of the party. Though an intelligent man, Bryan was much too stuffy a provincial for the job, a teetotaler whose "grape-juice diplomacy" upset the diplomatic corps when he banned alcoholic beverages from diplomatic receptions. Indeed, the State Department as a whole was an incredibly sleepy place by modern standards. But then, it hardly needed to be the guard dog of the republic when the tariff was still the burning foreign policy issue of the day in Washington.

Nevertheless, the absence of debate over foreign policy in the campaign of 1912, apart from a few flurries over dollar diplomacy, had been misleading. In the course of Wilson's academic career, he had often commented on international issues. In the 1890s he welcomed imperialism as a token of new national vitality, never doubting that the United States would, sooner or later, play a leading role in world affairs. "Now civilization is closing in upon us," he stated in 1905.[2] A few years later, he remarked that "we have come out upon a stage of international responsibility from which we cannot retire."[3] Unfortunately, like most everyone else of his generation, he found it difficult to go beyond the bromides about peace, progress, and commerce that passed for the political wisdom of the day. Still, as a progressive who was well-versed in foreign affairs, Wilson had no intention of ignoring the country's foreign relations.

Early in his presidency, Wilson's liberal internationalism was confined to rather humdrum matters of commerce and culture. Consistent with his Democratic free trade leanings, he pushed for a downward revision of the tariff. The Underwood tariff of 1913, which lowered duties from 38 to 30 percent and placed a number of items on the free list, was a modest achievement. His thinking about cultural exchanges emphasized the desirability of free trade in ideas. "Comprehension must be the soil in which shall grow all the fruits of friendship," he said in a 1913 speech in Mobile, Alabama. His target audience in that address was Latin America, but the theme was no less valid for the rest of the world. It had been a leitmotif of his pre-presidential rhetoric that a common understanding of one another and the world situation would illuminate the path to peaceful resolution of international problems.

In the same speech, Wilson delivered a typically "idealist" pronouncement. "It is a very perilous thing to determine the foreign policy of a nation in the terms of material interest," he said. He was here reacting to dollar diplomacy, a policy that, in his somewhat jaundiced partisan view, toadied to special economic interests at the expense of more important considerations. It was far more preferable, he suggested, "to think of the progress of mankind rather than of the progress of this or that investment."[4] But these kinds of assertions, typically cited as evidence of Wilson's idealism, could equally well be used to support the argument that he saw the world from a wider—indeed, global—frame of reference. As we shall see, Wilson's idealism had more to do with the non-empirical way in which he understood the world than with moral judgment.

Though primarily concerned with domestic reforms, Wilson also harbored reformist ambitions for foreign affairs that went beyond the Taft administration's emphasis on great-power cooperation. "I think that the whole temper of the opinion of the world now is so in favor of doing the reasonable thing for the promotion of peace that we needn't despair of accomplishing a great deal," he said early in his administration.[5] As a token of his interest, he backed Bryan's quest to negotiate "cooling off" treaties that required nations to pause and reflect in times of crisis in the expectation that sober second thoughts would suppress the intoxicating impulse to make war. In the spring of 1914, he allowed his confidant, Colonel Edward House, to sound out the major European powers about the feasibility of embarking upon a general program of disarmament.

When forced to respond to events, Wilson started rather shakily, especially in his Latin American policy. Despite an early critique of imperialism and an apparent rejection of the "Big Stick" and "Dollar Diplomacy" of his two Republican predecessors, he himself intervened in Mexico in April 1914 in an attempt to depose the new dictator, Victoriano Huerta, who had seized power by deposing and assassinating the popularly elected liberal president, Francisco Madero. Upset by Huerta's rise to power and Europe's flirtation with his regime, Wilson refused to grant diplomatic recognition to Huerta's government, thus departing from a pragmatic tradition that went back to the first Washington administration.

Following a petty incident in which the Mexicans refused to fire a fourteen-gun salute to placate an insulted American admiral, American troops occupied the Gulf ports of Veracruz and Tampico. But it was not long before Wilson began to appreciate the pitfalls of promoting democracy through force. Unexpectedly, the intervention stirred up a hornet's nest of anti-American nationalism in Mexico, achieving the unlikely feat of uniting Huerta and his enemies against the Americans. A mediation effort by the ABC powers (Argentina, Brazil, Chile) begun in the summer soon settled on a plan for a face-saving withdrawal of American troops, though Huerta's chief opponent, Venustiano Carranza, refused to agree to it. Fortunately for Wilson, Huerta's resignation in July made possible the withdrawal of U.S. troops, and Wilson recognized Carranza's government the following year. Overall, the president saw no reason to regret his actions. "We got Huerta," he said. "That was the main thing I had in mind."[6]

Later in the year, he tried to set things right by proposing a Pan-American initiative which, he hoped, would also establish a standard for the rest of the world. The pact guaranteed each nation's territorial integrity under republican forms of government. Besides trying to make amends for his Mexican policy, Wilson hoped to create a model which might be used to mediate an end to the war that only recently had broken out in Europe. He wanted to set "an example to the world in freedom of institutions, freedom of trade, and intelligence of mutual service."[7] However, long nurtured territorial disagreements in South America undermined this pet project.

In some other respects, Wilson's policies in the Caribbean brought little change. However much he tried to distance himself from the foreign policies of Roosevelt and Taft, some problems in Latin America were beyond his ability to resolve by idealistic means. In 1915 and 1916, he authorized military interventions and occupations in Haiti and the Dominican Republic in response to revolutionary disturbances. Though reluctant to intervene in Haiti, the revolutionary violence there was so gruesome that Wilson finally concluded that "there is nothing for it but to take the bull by the horns and restore order." In the Dominican Republic, already an American protectorate thanks to Theodore Roosevelt's customs receivership, Wilson intervened to preserve a duly elected American-backed government from being overthrown by revolutionaries.

It may have seemed a distinction without a difference to Latin Americans, but Wilson's justification for American domination of the Caribbean was different from that of his predecessors. The anxiety about European intervention and the economic rhetoric that were characteristic of Roosevelt's and Taft's Caribbean policies were now replaced by Wilson's desire to spread law, order, and constitutional democracy as the chief justification for intervention. "I am going to teach the South American republics to elect good men," he said in 1914.

Faithful to his chief's desires, Admiral William Caperton, initially responsible for the Dominican occupation, insisted that "the country must be disarmed, revolutions must be wiped off the calendar, and the people made to deal honestly." Though the U.S. was determined to instil the values of constitutional government, the people of the occupied countries, in the words of one historian, "refused to cooperate in their own salvation."[8] Once installed, American troops were not withdrawn until 1924 in the Dominican Republic and 1934 in Haiti. While the results of these interventions were not encouraging, they showed that Wilson was not shy about using force to promote his democratic ideals.

World War I: Neutral Rights versus Misguided Mediation

After the crisis in the Balkans had escalated from the assassination of the Austro-Hungarian crown prince to a general war in the space of little more than a month, Wilson took immediate refuge in tradition. In proclaiming neutrality he declared that "The United States must be neutral in fact as well as in name during these days that are to try men's souls. We must be impartial in thought as well as in action, must put a curb upon our sentiments as well as upon every transaction that might be construed as a preference of one party to the struggle before another."[9] The point on curbing sentiments was well taken. For one thing, Wilson was painfully aware that within the United States lived a large number of first-generation "hyphenated" immigrants with strong feelings for their mother countries. Moreover, the president might well have been referring to people like himself, he being an out-and-out admirer of England and its institutions who believed strongly in the "unity of the English-speaking peoples."

But neutrality was not simply a matter of avoiding emotional identification with one side or another; legally, it was an assertion that U.S. *interests* were fundamentally different from those of the belligerents. As a foreign policy doctrine, neutrality meant that the U.S. expected to exercise all the rights of neutrality under international law. Specifically, neutral rights meant the right to trade with the belligerents or with anyone else. American cargoes could be seized only under strict rules governing "contraband," or illegal cargo, which had been codified in international law in the nineteenth century. No matter how fierce the struggle between belligerents, its effects were not supposed to spill over and damage neutral commerce. Why, the thinking went, should peaceful bystanders be made to suffer from the quarrels of other powers?

In the past, the insistence on neutral rights had often spelled trouble, since warring nations who were determined to apply maximum economic pressure against deadly foes showed little solicitude for the plight of neutrals. For the first twenty-five years of its existence, the U.S. had struggled to avoid becoming a helpless pawn of the embargoes and counterembargoes applied by the belligerents in the wars that ravaged Europe in the wake of the French Revolution. During the Civil War, the shoe was on the other foot: the North was the blockading power and the Europeans were the offended parties, their commerce with the South thoroughly obstructed by the Union blockade.

In the Treaty of Paris of 1857, following the international congress that ended the Crimean War, neutral rights were systematically acknowledged and codified by treaty for the first time. A later attempt to enumerate specifically what kinds of cargoes were legal or illegal was made in the 1909 Declaration of London. The general adoption of this document was cut short by the outbreak of World War I when, understandably, the British and other powers lost interest in ratifying a measure that might hamper their effective prosecution of the war.

Nevertheless, America's stake in the war could not be boiled down to the profit motive. No matter how technically correct his public position, privately Wilson rooted for England and the Entente for reasons that went beyond his emotional attachment to Great Britain. Given the serious global consequences, a German triumph would be quite worrisome. As his confidant Colonel E. M. House noted, "if Germany won it would change the course of our civilization and make the United States a military nation."[10] An Entente victory therefore seemed preferable. "I cannot see now that it would hurt greatly the interests of the United States if either France or Russia or Great Britain should finally dictate the settlement," said Wilson.[11] Implicit in these kinds of comments was the idea that, strategically, the modern world had become a very dangerous place. A public exposition of this viewpoint would not come, however, until the United States itself had entered the war.

This larger perspective also affected Wilson's thinking about neutrality which, although it was legally correct, ran at cross-purposes with his notion of civilization. Often he talked in the same breath about defending "neutral and human rights," as if they were one and the same thing.[12] But he realized from the start that traditional neutrality was rooted in a narrow conception of national interest which was, after all, the cause of the conflict in Europe. Having once described "mere national patriotism" as "a narrow and provincial feeling," Wilson believed that there were broader and more meaningful perspectives from which to approach the world.[13] Thus, while the United States was not a party to the war, its insistence on protecting its commerce mimicked, in its own way, the egoism of the belligerents, a trait that Wilson saw as being contrary to the nation's global mission.

Troubled, Wilson worried about how to reconcile this selfish doctrine with the nation's role in promoting civilization. Just before the war erupted, he said: "One of the most serious questions for sober-minded men to address themselves to in the United States is this: What are we going to do with the influence and power of this great nation? Are we going to play the old role of using that power for our aggrandizement and material benefit only?"[14] In other words, neutrality ought to possess a nobility, a universal validity, that transcended the narrow profit motive. When challenged in 1915 to stand up and fight for the country's neutral rights, he responded that "I am interested in neutrality because there is something so much greater to do than fight."[15]

Specifically, Wilson saw neutrality as a platform from which he could mediate an end to the conflict. He preferred to see neutrality in terms of "our duty to prevent it, if it were possible, the indefinite extension of the fires of hate and desolation kindled by that terrible conflict."[16] For Wilson, this modern notion of neutrality was far more compelling than the traditional concept. While neutral rights became the *casus belli,* this altruistic sense of neutrality grounded in civilizational concerns became the conceptual bridge to Wilsonian war aims.

The wartime issue that more than any other brought out this high-minded American approach to neutrality was the provisioning and feeding of Belgium, a small nation sympathetically depicted by the press as "a martyr to civilization."[17] Although Belgium had been guaranteed neutrality by long-standing treaty, the Germans felt they had no choice but to invade France via Belgian territory if they were to make a success of the Schlieffen plan. Once in control, the Germans refused to feed the Belgians, arguing that their privations were caused by the British blockade. Why, after all, should Germany take food out of the mouths of its soldiers? The British, for their part, were convinced, should supplies and foodstuffs be allowed to enter Belgium, that they would be diverted to the German army, thereby undermining the blockade.

Enter Herbert Hoover and the Americans. Hoover was a successful expatriate businessman headquartered in London who agreed to organize the provisioning of relief to Belgium on a private basis. Contrary to this image of private charity, much of the money for Belgian relief came from the French and British governments, both of whom were eager to avoid the propaganda disaster that would result if the Belgian people succumbed to mass starvation. Propaganda was by this time already a potent foreign policy force. The so-called "Rape of Belgium," a British-compiled propaganda catalog of abuses, real and imagined, inflicted by the occupying Germans, helped to stir anti-German sentiment within the United States and elsewhere. But, contrary to British hopes, Belgian relief did not put Americans on the side of the Entente. Belgium mattered to Americans primarily because it embodied the kind of elevated and disinterested neutrality that they hoped to bring to bear upon the war in Europe.

In May 1916, Wilson outlined the kind of mediated peace for which a neutral America would serve as midwife. In an address to the League to Enforce Peace, an organization created the previous year to lobby for the creation of an international peace-keeping organization, he suggested that it would be "our privilege to suggest or initiate a movement for peace among the nations now at war." That peace, he insisted, "must henceforth depend upon a new and more wholesome diplomacy." Arguing that "the interests of all nations are our own also," he revealed his support for U.S. membership in a "universal association of the nations" whose purpose would be to prevent war.

But the kind of mediation Wilson had in mind had no chance of success. He assumed that the belligerents could put aside their differences in the interest of creating a permanent structure of peace. Indeed, he wrongheadedly believed that there was a basic identity of war aims among the warring nations, oblivious to the fact that each side saw the war as a life-and-death struggle. Nor did he understand that the belligerents failed to see the United States in the same high-minded and disinterested light in which Wilson perceived his country. The British believed they were fighting *America's* war, while the Germans saw U.S. policy as being de facto pro-British. Moreover, Wilson's *status quo ante bellum* approach expected the warring powers to behave as if nothing had happened, to trade in the substantial gains and losses on the battlefields and the potential rewards of victory for a pie-in-the-sky scheme for international peace.

For the first three years of the war, Wilson was caught between conflicting impulses: affirmation of neutral rights, which tended to drag the United States into the war, and civilized mediation, which suggested that the United States ought to remain above the battle. Neither proved very satisfactory as a springboard for launching his lofty conception of mediating an end to the war on the basis of a peace that put an end to international politics as usual. In the end, only American entry into the war offered Wilson the opportunity to make a reality of his peace program.

Legal issues of neutrality quickly caused problems with both sides. One of the first questions requiring attention was the matter of loans to the Entente. Secretary of State Bryan argued vigorously, but to no avail, that money was the worst contraband of all. Quickly, Washington ruled that nongovernmental loans were beyond the state's authority to regulate. Wall Street investment banks soon began floating bond issues on behalf of the Entente nations, the proceeds of which were used to purchase war material from the U.S. Because Great Britain controlled the high seas, the Central Powers were effectively excluded from American financial markets. This laissez-faire loan policy stimulated a flood of American exports overseas and made virtually inevitable a collision between the United States and the economic warfare of the belligerents.

Incidents on the high seas were not long in coming. After a number of minor episodes, 128 Americans went down with the torpedoed passenger liner, the *Lusitania,* off the coast of Ireland in May 1915. Although the *Lusitania* was a British ship that was carrying munitions in its hold, international law of the day entitled citizens of neutral powers to travel aboard belligerent passenger liners in the full expectation of safety. The outpouring of anti-German emotion was nothing short of breathtaking. In suggesting that the problem with German behavior was its resort to a "barbaric" weapon that did not fit well within the existing codes of war, the *Lusitania* episode suggested that "civilization" could be a powerful ideological theme sanctioning American participation. "No nation has the right to change the rules of war," said Wilson, although he acknowledged that "the conditions of war have changed radically."[18]

Bryan resigned because of Wilson's hard-nosed approach, but the president did not want war at this time. The provocation was not great enough, while the benefits of American neutrality, financial and civilizational, beckoned. After threatening to hold the German government to "strict accountability," Wilson was satisfied with the response from Berlin. However, the German willingness to accommodate the president was due primarily to the lack of a sufficient number of submarines for conducting an efficient campaign and to a concern with the military impact on Germany of American belligerency. Another serious incident took place on March 24 of the following year, when the Germans torpedoed a French passenger ship, the *Sussex,* in the English channel, injuring a number of Americans. Following yet another ultimatum from Wilson in which he threatened to break off relations and, presumably, go to war, the Imperial Government agreed to halt the sinking of passenger ships and merchantmen, but only if the British in turn ended their illegal blockade practices.

From that point on, Wilson was at the mercy of the changing tides of strategic opinion within Berlin. For the time being, the civilian leadership was able to hold the military hotheads at bay. But if the military situation had been more desperate, or if Germany's crash program of submarine construction had come to the point of making a submarine blockade fully effective, the outcome would undoubtedly have been different. Wilson was painted by his party as a peace candidate in his victorious election campaign of 1916 on the slogan "He kept us out of war." But he realized full well that the decision for peace or war lay with the Germans.

With the issue of neutral rights for the moment played out to its limits, Wilson focused increasingly on the universalist side of neutrality. As 1916 progressed, he became increasingly determined to offer a mediated peace. For a time he placed his hopes in the House-Grey memorandum, signed early in 1916, in which the United States sought to promote the holding of a peace conference by promising to enter the war on the side of the allies if the Central Powers should refuse to attend such a gathering. This memorandum proved to be nothing more than a useful device for the British to tie the United States to the Entente, making it less likely that the U.S. would resort to drastic measures in retaliation against British blockade violations on the high seas. The truth was, neither London nor Paris was remotely interested in a *status quo ante bellum* settlement of the kind envisioned by Wilson as the prerequisite to permanent peace. Too many lives had been lost, too much treasure had been expended to warrant settling for an impasse. Episodes like this leave little doubt that Wilson's understanding of the war during this period was naive and superficial and his diplomacy of mediation misguided.

The chances for mediation, never very good in the first place, vanished entirely early in 1917. Wilson's neutrality had become somewhat more impartial in 1916 as he protested British violations such as the blacklisting of American firms, illegal seizures of cargo on the high seas, and searches of American mails. When he delayed a mediation appeal until after the presidential election, the Germans decided to beat him to the punch. This was both a propaganda move and an attempt to forestall further Wilsonian meddling in the war. Nevertheless, upon hearing of the German démarche, Wilson jumped on the bandwagon and asked both sides to spell out their war aims, hoping that this might bring about the long-awaited parleys.

For a moment, everything seemed to be within reach. Perhaps the finest example of Wilson's rhetoric was his "Peace without Victory" speech of January 22, 1917, in which he outlined his conception of a lasting peace. "Is the present war a struggle for a just and secure peace, or only for a new balance of power? If it be only a struggle for a new balance of power, who will guarantee, who can guarantee, the stable equilibrium of the new arrangement?" he asked. Because a new balance of power was sure to break down and lead to another war, he insisted that "there must be, not a balance of power, but a community of power." In what would this community be rooted? In the common ground of democracy, as he made clear: "No peace can last, or ought to last, which does not recognize and accept the principle that governments derive all their just powers from the consent of the governed." One detects here a more sober note that contrasts with the image of Wilsonianism as a crusading doctrine. "I speak of this." he said, "because I wish frankly to uncover realities. Any peace which does not recognize and accept this principle will inevitably be upset. It will not rest upon the convictions or affections of mankind."[19]

Unfortunately, the Entente and the Central Powers were worlds apart in their war aims. Secret treaties signed among the Entente powers in 1915 promised Constantinople to Russia, much of the Tyrol and the Adriatic to Italy, and Alsace-Lorraine to France, while partitioning the Middle East for good measure. The Germans, anticipating a sweeping military victory, also harbored extraordinary territorial ambitions. These incompatible goals of the combatants alone would have been enough to frustrate Wilson's plan, but he was also thwarted from within by the scheming of anti-German officials like Secretary of State Robert Lansing, who went behind Wilson's back to urge Entente representatives to produce equivocal replies to Wilson's request for public statements of war aims. Indeed, all too often Wilson found himself working at cross-purposes with his pro-British advisers and representatives.

Shortly after Wilson's speech, the German High Command chose to gamble everything on an all-or-nothing submarine campaign. By this time, the naval blockade was having a disastrous impact on Germany's food supplies. The military brushed aside as irrelevant the arguments of their diplomats about the dangers of American intervention. The U-boats were ready. If all went well, the war in Europe would be over by the time the Americans had assembled a military force. The announcement of unrestricted submarine warfare came as a terribly unwelcome surprise in Washington, where only a few days earlier Wilson had looked forward to mediating a revolutionary peace. Now, instead, he was faced with the need to make good his threats, repeated over the years, of stern measures against Germany should she resume unrestricted submarine warfare.

Understandably, Wilson was not at all enthusiastic about taking this route. A few months earlier, he said "it would be a crime against civilization for us to go in."[20] War, he believed, might Prussianize the country by subordinating everything, including his ambitious domestic reform program, to military necessity. It might also stoke the fires of hatred and passion to a point where a sound progressive peace based on cool reason would become impossible. Hoping against hope to avoid intervention, for a time he played with the notion of armed neutrality, even going so far as to authorize the arming of merchantmen on dubious statutory authority when Congress refused to grant permission to do so.

In the end, his attempt at staying out was futile. The British government managed a stunning propaganda coup when it intercepted a telegram, sent by the German Foreign Office to the ambassador to Mexico, instructing him to propose a German-Mexican alliance, using as bait the prospect of recovering the territories in the American southwest lost in 1848. The release of the Zimmermann Telegram provided an emotional spark that inflamed American public opinion. German sinkings of American merchantmen also began to mount. These pressures, combined with the absence of any possibility of mediation, left little choice but to go in. In his second inaugural address, delivered on March 5, 1917, Wilson suggested that neutrality, of whatever variety, was no longer possible. He complained that external forces, over which the U.S. had no control, "have drawn us more and more irresistibly into their current and influence. It has been impossible to avoid them."[21]

Wilson delivered his war message on April 2, 1917 and Congress voted the declaration of war on April 6. Though neutral rights had taken the United States into the war, Wilson did not forget the larger postwar aims that he had hoped to achieve through mediation. "Neutrality is no longer feasible or desirable where the peace of the world is involved and the freedom of its peoples," he said. That larger sense of the democratic potential of a global civilization, formerly the key to his hopes for neutral mediation, would henceforth be the positive pole of Wilson's wartime rhetoric. In a memorable phrase, Wilson summed up the ideological justification for the war by telling Congress and the American people: "The world must be made safe for democracy." Or, as he put it after the war, the U.S. was fighting for "a world fit to live in."[22]

The Great War and the Internationalism of Fear

To this point, there is little doubt that Wilson had been naive about the war. His efforts at mediation were shot through with grand illusions about the attitudes of the belligerents. Contributing to his ineffectiveness was the figure of Colonel House, who, in his zeal to secure American intervention on behalf of Great Britain, slyly subverted Wilson's ideas while continuing to enjoy the full confidence of the president. Ironically, the failure of mediation and America's entry into the war made it possible for Wilson to attain a deeper understanding of the central political issues of the modern world and to provide a more logical basis for his reformist ideas. The wartime Wilson would no longer be a naive idealist.

With the U.S. now a belligerent, the president began to address the problems of modern world civilization from a more balanced historical perspective that took full account of the threatening features of change. In time, he explained why this war was so unlike past wars; why it was a *world* war (though the Second World War was the first truly global conflict, for people like Wilson World War I encompassed all of the world that mattered); why it was so much more violent and revolutionary than past conflicts; and why it had the makings of an enormous tragedy. In brief, Wilson understood and drove home the point that this war was a watershed event, a point after which international history would flow in a different direction.

Besides defining the ideals for which the United States and the Entente powers were fighting, he explained why his war aims were not only desirable but absolutely necessary; and he explained why they could not be achieved by any means other than war. In his wartime rhetoric, his optimistic forecast of a coming era of peace was anchored in an understanding of the dismal implications of power in the modern era. The creation of a league of nations, formerly something merely desirable in the abstract, now became a historical necessity, as his idealism went from "ought" to "must."

Wilson's wartime views on the meaning of this conflict provided his outlook with an intellectual coherence that had formerly been lacking. To this point, there had been a poor fit between the provocation and Wilson's grandiose war aims. As the war's dangers became clear, Wilson closed this gap between self-interest and selflessness by tying his supranationalism closely to the imperative of survival. By defining the threat in apocalyptic world-historical terms, he overcame the incongruity between neutral rights as a mundane *casus belli* and his aspiration for a celestial peace program. Now the global problem and the universal solution fit hand in glove.

These larger historical issues came to the fore when Wilson and his advisers were forced to decide upon the form of American participation in the war. Would the U.S. merely provide arms and money, fight a naval war, or send troops to Europe? There were many sensible arguments on behalf of limited participation. Tradition suggested a naval war as a logical way of fitting the punishment to the crime. On the Continent, France and Britain initially assumed, as French Ambassador Jules Jusserand reported, "that a war of logistical aid was the most urgent and useful thing that the United States could give us."[23] If soldiers were to be sent, the Europeans preferred to integrate small units of American troops into their armies. Should this happen, General Tasker Bliss foresaw that "we might have a million men there and yet no American army and no American commander."[24] In any case, army planners had failed to anticipate a historically unprecedented strategic situation that called for sending a massive force to Europe.

Wilson and others wondered how complying with French and British wishes might affect the peace settlement. Even at this early stage of American belligerency, Wilson was convinced that "the problems of the settlement were urgent." He knew full well that the secret treaties and special arrangements among the Entente threatened to create a world order every bit as corrupt, backward, and dangerous as the old one. Without full American participation, the peace was likely to be vindictive and self-defeating. Carthaginian peace terms would be "a great disaster."[25] Hoping to maximize American influence, General Bliss argued that "the time has come for the France and England to stand fast and wait until our reinforcements can reach them in such a way as to give the final, shattering blow."

The decision to send an expeditionary force, then, was taken partly to influence the peace settlement. America's initiation into the club of victors would have to take the form of a blood ritual. A weighty American military contribution was all the more necessary as the war aims of the United States and the allied governments were likely to be quite different. Carefully distancing himself from the old-style politics of his de facto partners, following the declaration of war Wilson showed no interest in forging an alliance with the Entente powers, preferring instead that the U.S. be described as an "associated" power.

But sending a massive army to France made little sense if it was aimed solely at satisfying an idealistic urge for a just and lasting peace. As it happened, a weightier and strategically novel rationale emerged out of the worsening military situation in Europe. After being stalemated for three years, an increasingly precarious position on the western front and a succession of Russian military reverses in the east suddenly made a German victory, once treated as merely a hypothetical possibility, appear quite achievable. As time went on, it became clear that American forces were needed not only to guarantee a liberal peace; they were essential to staving off a disastrous defeat.[26]

The grave military situation added another dimension to Wilson's interpretation of the war's meaning. Well before the United States had become a belligerent, Wilson had begun to question the continuing utility of war as an institution. For all its violence, war had always had its uses. It had paid in the past. It had made sense in systemic terms: as an acceptable

means for achieving calculable ends; as the balancing ı
balance of power; and as the chief instrument whereby i.
ety maintained and reconstituted itself. But now, war as
ized activity had become far too destructive, demanding :
and treasure that threatened to devour the very societies
to serve. Impartially considered, the enormous social an
of war overshadowed any conceivable profits to be gained by victory, as
the crowned monarchs of Europe would soon discover.

Wilson's theme of peace without victory had spoken to the widespread
sense that modern war under permanently stalemated battlefield conditions was futile. However, once America entered the war, he began to
realize that it was more complicated than that. Victory was still possible,
and if the Germans should win war would still pay, though for all the
wrong reasons. The peaceful and prosperous global civilization glimpsed
before the war might collapse and disappear entirely. In adopting this line
of reasoning, Wilson's thinking about the war developed an inner tension,
complexity, and gravity that were formerly absent. He remained convinced of the obsolescence of war as an institution, but he also realized
that the global implications of this war required a total military commitment from the United States.

In a series of speeches and private communications in the summer of
1917, Wilson painted a new picture of what was at stake. Speaking of
the expansionist ambitions of the German warlords, he predicted: "If they
succeed, America will fall within the menace. We and all the rest of the
world must remain armed, as they will remain, and must make ready for
the next step in their aggression."[27] In a speech in Buffalo to the American
Federation of Labor, he insisted that victorious German power "can disturb the world as long as she keeps it."[28] Speaking to the officers of the
Atlantic fleet about militarism and its consequences, he vowed that "we
do not intend to let that method of action and of thinking be imposed
upon the rest of the world."[29]

At this point, Wilson's view of the German peril paralleled that of anti-
German advisers like House, Lansing, and ambassadors Walter Hines
Page in London and James Gerard in Berlin. For example, in his *War
Memoirs,* Lansing wrote: "The German government, cherishing the ambition of world power which now possesses it, must not be permitted to
win this war or to break even, though to prevent it this country is forced
to take an active part."[30] "If victory is theirs," wrote House, "the war lords
will reign supreme and democratic governments will be imperilled
throughout the world."[31]

Wilson was among the first to articulate a danger that would become

...aple of American foreign policy for much of the century: world conquest. He was not referring to direct military conquest; the Germans did not possess the capacity to conquer the United States. He was talking about fighting a prussianized system within Germany, and its external manifestation, the scheme for continental domination known as *Mitteleuropa*, which would enable the Germans to impose their rules of conduct upon the rest of the world. As some informal advisers put it, *Mitteleuropa* was "a system by which adventurous and imperialistic groups in Berlin and Vienna . . . could use the resources of this area in the interest of a fiercely selfish policy directed against their neighbors and the rest of the world."[32]

Pointing to the horror of modern war was one way, according to Ambassador Page, to "shake the world into liberalism."[33] But this global dimension of the war's dangers was something else again. A few farsighted analysts like the diplomat Lewis Einstein and the journalist Walter Lippmann had predicted that the disruption of the European balance of power, especially if it ended in Britain's defeat, would have serious consequences for the U.S.; a few theoretical writers in the exotic and intellectually dubious new discipline of "geopolitics" had suggested that control of Europe would make possible control of the world; and some sensationalist works had pointed to a pan-German program that aimed at "nothing less than the domination of Europe and the world"—but no policy-maker had anticipated anything at all like this.[34] For Wilson, a world once favorable to American isolation and internationalism was on the verge of being destroyed. "Everything will go by the board if we don't win," he said.[35]

In effect, Wilson the wartime leader was admitting that the prewar Wilson had taken the United States into the war for reasons that were, by comparison, trivial. Neutral rights had offered a legal basis for belligerency, while the promise of permanent peace had provided an idealistic goal. But the new perception of threat made American intervention absolutely necessary if a world environment hospitable to liberalism was to survive. "We were a long time . . . seeing that we belonged in the war," he said in 1919, "but *just so soon as the real issues of it became apparent* we knew that we belonged there."[36] In this context, making the world safe for democracy took on an entirely different and altogether more urgent survivalist meaning. Departing from the sanguine internationalism of the past, Wilsonianism had become an internationalism of fear.

Of course, fear was also the precondition of power politics and balance-of-power diplomacy, but Wilson's wartime analysis of the danger facing the United States was not intended to reaffirm the truths of traditional realism. The threat, as he saw it, emanated from the death throes of the balance of power, formerly the mainstay of the international system. The breakdown of the balance that had caused the war was not simply the latest in a succession of periodic failures, but the final convulsion of a European institution that had functioned for more than two and a half centuries. The threat was not so much any inherent evil on this institution's part as the consequences of its overstaying its time. However useful it may have once been, it was no longer applicable to international relations in the modern era.

In his fourteen-points address of January 8, 1818, Wilson made clear that this war marked a rupture with the past:

> The day of conquest and aggrandizement is gone by; so is also the day of secret covenants entered into in the interest of particular governments and likely at some unlooked-for moment to upset the peace of the world. It is this happy fact, now clear to the view of every public man whose thoughts do not still linger in an age that is dead and gone, which makes it possible for every nation whose purposes are consistent with justice and the peace of the world to avow now or at any other time the objects it has in view.[38]

The balance of power was not an invisible hand, working magically to produce equilibrium. Indeed, the proliferation of an obscure Balkan episode into a general European war and then into a global conflict from which the United States could not remain aloof indicated that new cascade dynamics had taken hold. In modern circumstances, small conflicts, insignificant in themselves, could spiral quickly out of control until the entire world was engulfed. Nor could the trend to limitless violence and universal participation be reversed once the modern globalizing dynamic of war had taken root. Therefore, some new system, based on different principles, was necessary to ensure that a great conflict of the kind now being experienced could never again occur. Necessity, not nicety, was driving the world toward internationalism.

But the balance of power was itself only a product of an old social system that was itself perishing. According to one newspaper editorial that interpreted Wilson's insights into the war: "He sees that it is the first great test of an industrialized world community, and that so far in this test all of the old traditions and systems have broken down."[38] Thus Wilson defined the war in terms of an epochal struggle between forces representing the past and those bearing the standard of the future. It was "the last decisive issue between the old principle of power and the new principle of freedom."[39]

In his modern classic, *The Consequences of Modernity,* the sociologist

Anthony Giddens has argued that under contemporary conditions of "time-space distantiation," i.e., the emergence of the world as a single unit of time and space, societies can operate only on the basis of trust. In contrast to the kinds of intimate, face-to-face familiarity typical of traditional, locally rooted societies, the operation of institutions over long distances requires a trust in the professional efficiency of strangers, be they Japanese automotive engineers, producers of Korean electronics, or Greek shipping magnates who assure the delivery of a continuing supply of oil. This kind of impersonal trust in the automatic working of things is an inherent part of normal internationalism.

Wilson was suggesting that there was another side to internationalism, however. Just as trust was different under modern circumstances, so too was fear when things began to go seriously wrong. Modern fear was also impersonal and faceless thanks to high-consequence events taking place far away. Like trust, under modern conditions of interdependence a fear of the effects of global disruptions would have to become the product of an abstract sensibility rather than something that was automatically felt in the pit of one's stomach. It required the ability to diagnose the malfunctioning of complex systems and to suggest intricate solutions in which strong feelings like patriotism and the desire for revenge were suppressed.

At one level, Wilson could point the finger of blame at flesh-and-blood villains. The war was the product of antiquated social systems, undemocratic societies in which privileged castes made war for their own purposes. The German people were "themselves in the grip of the same sinister power that has now at last stretched its ugly talons out and drawn blood from us."[40] But the roots of the crisis ran deeper still. Wilson saw the war as a symptom of structural problems that were embedded in the heart of the modern world-system, problems that Germany, the Kaiser, and the *Junker* aristocracy only embodied. It was not bad people, or bad governments, as such, that made the world such a dangerous place; it was a design flaw built into modernity. The enormous amount of power concentrated by the global industrial system could lead to disaster if released in an uncontrolled way.

The very forces that made progress possible—technology, trade, a global division of labor, and interdependence—also made possible the system's destruction if pushed in the wrong direction and not checked. The greater the degree of integration, the more explosive would be the disintegration produced by a runaway modernity. Thus Wilson recognized one of modernity's most prominent and paradoxical features: as the world became more industrialized and integrated, it became more orderly and predictable; at the same time, breakdowns of the system, though perhaps less frequent, were more calamitous. As one historian has remarked, "it is one of the great ironies of the period that a world war became possible only after the world had become so highly united."[41]

Wilson's natural inclination as a Progressive was to formulate a solution in which top-down control was sanctioned by mass democracy. In the past, the balance of power was often likened to the law of supply and demand, an example of market forces working themselves out until equilibrium was attained. Wilson believed that the world could no longer afford to allow its affairs to be determined by the irrational functioning of power. To replace an uncontrolled balance of power that threatened to run amok, therefore, he proposed an organized and rationally directed community of power. He had already hinted at something of the sort in his second inaugural address: "We realize that the greatest things that remain to be done must be done with the whole world for stage and in cooperation with the wide and universal forces of mankind."[42]

That community of power would operate on the basis of what came to be known in the 1930s as the principle of collective security. If aggression took place, all the members of the League of Nations would unite to embargo the aggressor and, if necessary, to make war upon him. The world would function as a community, as opposed to a collection of self-absorbed and competing nation states. And what exactly was supposed to enforce cohesion upon this habitually squabbling family of nations? There seemed only one answer: world opinion, which was the antithesis of power nationally organized. "If my convictions have any validity, opinion ultimately governs the world," Wilson had said in 1915.[43] A year later, he confessed that "I am willing, no matter what my personal fortunes may be, to play for the verdict of mankind."[44] Organized democratic world opinion, institutionalized in a League of Nations, would have to take the place of the Invisible Hand.

Well aware that a world of immense diversity had a long way to go before it attained the required degree of consensuality, Wilson was at first skeptical about relying on world opinion. But, with a world structure so vulnerable to runaway catastrophe, world opinion seemed the only force capable of checking such outbreaks before they began. In any case, the idea was not so far-fetched, Wilson believed, because there were trends at work in the modern era that would make world opinion a force to be reckoned with. First, there was the democratization that would come about as a result of the war. Autocratic governments would not be able to sustain their legitimacy after committing the folly of making disastrous war for reasons obscure to their populations. Wilson assumed that the democratic governments emerging in autocracy's place would be governed by the will of the people, who would never permit a calamity of this kind to happen again.

Just as important, if not more so, Wilson believed that this war had lessons which were universally applicable. He was convinced that his interpretation of the war's meaning accurately expressed the deepest wishes of what he called the great silent masses of mankind. His insistence upon dealing with a German republic when it came time to negotiate an armistice in November 1918 suggested his conviction that even the German people were with him. He was their spokesman, their chosen instrument. He intuited the language of their hearts that could not be given voice:

> the thoughts of the mass of men, whom statesmen are supposed to instruct and lead, has grown more and more unclouded. . . . National purposes have fallen more and more into the background and the common purpose of enlightened mankind has taken their place. . . . Statesmen must follow the clarified common thought or be broken.[45]

The victory of democracy, in combination with popular understanding of the meaningless horror of modern war—demonstrated by experience and interpreted by Wilson—would provide the foundation for the new diplomacy.

Many of Wilson's ideas were not original, as he would have cheerfully admitted. Some years earlier, he confessed that "Any individual mind, no matter how rich in its contents or in its power, would be impoverished if it were isolated. It takes the vital processes of its life, like the plant itself, from the atmosphere, from the intellectual and moral atmosphere in which it lives."[46] The new era of interdependence, the dangers of Prussianism and Bolshevism, his liberal economic ideas, the structure of an ideal peace, the conflict as a "great war for civilization" or a "war to end war"—these and many other ideas were, as Wilson readily acknowledged, plucked from the air. Indeed, the fact that ideas like world opinion and great power cooperation were put into play both before and after Wilson's presidency suggests that Wilsonianism was an outgrowth of normal internationalism. It was normal internationalism mobilized.

To take but one example, a *New Republic* editorial in 1914 had floated the idea of collective security. "A modern nation which wants the world to live in peace," it suggested, "must be willing and ready, whenever a clear case can be made out against a disturber of the peace, to join with other nations in taking up arms against the malefactor."[47] A potent lobby, the League to Enforce the Peace, had been created to pursue such a program. Kindred ideas had been floating around in England and on the Continent. However, no one surpassed Wilson in his ability to synthesize all the issues or in his capacity to argue them with such persuasive elegance. And no one managed to balance the positive and negative features of modernity in so masterful a fashion. Combined with his ability to put American power into the scales, it was small wonder that Wilson's rhetoric made him a messianic figure to so many people.

He fully intended to have such an effect. "The historian is also a sort of prophet," Wilson once said.[48] True to his word, he had the genius to furnish what was, for many perplexed onlookers, a convincing historical explanation of the war's larger meaning. While some saw the war as a repetition of humankind's propensity to violence, only on a larger scale, Wilson viewed it as an unprecedented event, too exceptional to be understood in traditional ways. With humankind committed to a voyage of progress and change in which it would no longer be hugging the coastline of tradition, historical interpretation was the only instrument available to chart its new location. With change so swift and far-reaching, there was no other way of getting one's bearings.

Because its conclusions cannot be grounded in the objective certainty afforded by scientific method, historical thinking, by its very nature, is idealistic. Though it was not particularly utopian, Wilsonianism as an ideology was indeed idealistic *in a philosophical sense* because it was, at bottom, an attempt to impose form upon what was otherwise chaotic historical content. But that does not mean, necessarily, that it was erroneous, or that superior modes of explanation were readily available. Like most new ideologies, it was designed to make sense of some extraordinary events that prevailing belief systems were at a loss to explain. Wilson understood that the war was so novel that *only* historical interpretation could make sense of what was going on around him. That is why he was so convincing to so many: because of the urgent element of historical necessity—not the "moral necessity" he spoke of in 1916—that lay at the heart of his thinking about the war.[49]

Wilson's wartime ideas were important because, at a minimum, they rejuvenated the Entente by turning the war into an ideological conflict whose stirring message the nationalistic Germans could not hope to match. "At the bottom, I believe that the peoples of the Allies are with me," he said.[50] Although Wilsonianism gave an ideological boost to the Allied war effort, it was not enough to keep Russia in the war. Wilson had welcomed the March 1917 revolution that brought down the Czarist regime as a sign of the potency of democracy. Unfortunately, the provisional government, bent on keeping its treaty commitments to the Entente, collapsed entirely in November when confronted with a Bolshevik coup. This calamitous event only confirmed Wilson's analysis of the war, for

Bolshevik communism was an example of the price paid by modern societies for imposing the intolerable burdens of modern war upon their civilian populations.

For the moment, Bolshevik ideology, however repulsive, was less a matter of concern than the new regime's impact on the course of the war. Shortly after coming to power, Lenin, bent on assuring the survival of his shaky government, threatened to take Russia out of the war entirely. With the eastern front no longer in existence, Germany could redeploy her troops and perhaps deliver a knockout blow in France. Because the Bolsheviks were seen as pro-German and as hostile to liberal capitalism, Wilson finally caved in to the repeated demands of his allies for intervention. Beginning in the summer of 1918, American contingents were sent to Vladivostok on the Pacific and Archangel in the Arctic north and were left to languish haplessly until finally withdrawn in 1920, nearly two years after the war had ended.

The Russian intervention was long used by the Communists as proof positive of the unremitting hostility of the capitalist world. However, that estimate of the West's intentions probably overstates the perceived seriousness of the Bolshevik danger, which, Wilson believed, was like a fever that would eventually break. "My policy regarding Russia," he said, "is very similar to my Mexican policy. I believe in letting them work out their own salvation, even though they wallow in anarchy for a while." Because the Bolshevik threat was ideological rather than military, he favored leaving Russia "to settle her own affairs in her own way as long as she does not become a menace to others."[51] Intensely disliked and distrusted as the new regime was, it would be another quarter century before Bolshevism replaced Germany, within the Wilsonian framework, as the foremost strategic menace to civilization.

The war's ominous character only deepened as time went on. Far more worrisome than Bolshevism as an ideology was the effect Russia's withdrawal would have upon the already uncertain military outcome of the war. To prevent the worst-case disaster of Wilson's new strategic vision from coming to pass, the United States first had to assure victory. Then and only then could it take the lead at the peace conference to ensure that the settlement would not be based on the power principles of the old order. Both tasks proved enormously difficult.

The war effort of the Entente powers was already sputtering by the time the U.S. entered the fray. The energetic leadership of David Lloyd George and Georges Clemenceau in prosecuting the war could not reverse the discouraging developments on the front lines. The armies were dispirited. Mutinies erupted throughout the trenches of the French army in the spring of 1917 following the immense slaughter of the ill-conceived Nivelle offensive. In the east, the Bolsheviks were obviously looking to take Russia out of the war to preserve their revolutionary power. The fourteen points, enunciated in January 1918, were in part intended to restore fighting spirit among the Allies and to keep Russia in the war.

The fourteen points are the best-known statement of Wilsonian war aims. Among Wilson's chief aspirations were: disarmament; free trade; freedom of the seas (the *casus belli*); an end to secret diplomacy ("open covenants openly arrived at"); an end to imperialist competition by "an impartial adjustment of colonial claims"; and, of course, a general association of nations to replace the balance of power. But the fourteen points were only the specific expression of more general principles, such as those announced in September 1918, in which Wilson repudiated revenge as a motive, declared that special interests would not be the basis for the treaty at the expense of "a common interest of mankind," and insisted that no special economic arrangements would be made. This league would not be a closed club of the victors.

The signature of the Treaty of Brest-Litovsk in March 1918 between Germany and Bolshevik Russia added greater urgency to American mobilization. With Russia out of the war, the Germans had regained the manpower advantage on the western front that enabled them to attempt a knockout blow. The remainder of the war was a desperate race against time for each side as the Germans sought to deliver the coup de grâce while the Allies hung on until the fresh American armies arrived. Following a series of violent German offensives that came very close to success, the Yanks disembarked in force in the summer of 1918. From that point on, with more than one million fresh American soldiers available, the revitalized Allies launched counter-offensives that set the German army reeling backwards to defeat.

Suffering on the battlefield and on the home front, where Bolshevik revolution threatened, the Germans requested an armistice, with the understanding that the peace treaty would be based on the fourteen points. Wilson and his French and British allies each held out for more. Wilson wanted to see the abdication of the Kaiser and a democracy installed in Germany, while the Allies were more concerned to ensure that the Germans agreed to the principle of paying reparations for war damages. Prompted by the High Command's understanding that the war was lost, Germany was in no position to reject these conditions. Thus the Kaiser abdicated and the *Kaiserreich* was succeeded by a republic declared in

Berlin on November 9. Convinced that further fighting was futile, the German High Command agreed to sign an armistice on November 11, 1918.

The Peace Treaties and the League of Nations

Achieving the physically difficult but conceptually simple objective of winning the war was easier than nailing down a complicated peace. In an extraordinary decision that kept him out of the country for nearly six months, Wilson decided that he would be the chief negotiator for the United States. No president had taken a trip abroad before while in office, much less acted as a chief peace commissioner. Yet, so intent was Wilson on securing *his* kind of peace, the only viable kind, in his mind, that he insisted on going. Naturally, the other four peace commissioners wound up playing bit parts to the president's starring role.

Wilson had a difficult time in Paris, where he had to deal with formidable leaders who had strong ideas of their own. Because the treaty was originally slated to be a negotiating draft, the various committees tended to insert maximum demands in the expectation that they would be softened in later negotiations with the defeated enemy. Things worked out altogether differently, however, as the "preliminary peace conference at Paris" became, to all intents and purposes, the final peace conference. With opinion against Germany hardening, the Entente statesmen felt compelled to return home with something to show their electorates. Consequently, the Germans were called in only to sign a take-it-or-leave-it peace, a *Diktat,* whose spirit bore little resemblance to the nonpunitive fourteen points.

In a world whose domestic politics were increasingly democratic but whose foreign affairs continued to be based on power politics, Wilson believed that the logical solution was the extension of liberalism in foreign affairs. "Liberalism must be more liberal than ever before, it must even be radical, if civilization is to escape the typhoon," he said in January 1919. Contrary to Wilson's predictions, the peace treaty as it was finally presented to the Germans in June 1919 was far from liberal in many respects. It took territory away from Germany in the east, committed Germany to signing a blank check for reparations to repair massive war damages, demanded an admission of war guilt from the Germans, drew contested borders for the Austro-Hungarian successor states of central and eastern europe, and failed to address the problem of Bolshevism in Russia. But at least—and this was its saving grace in Wilson's eyes—it did provide for a League of Nations.

The Treaty of Versailles was viewed by many at the time and later as a bad treaty, vindictive and shortsighted. While the Germans understandably hated it, liberal opinion in the United States was also shocked by its severity. That Wilson had been forced into many compromises to get a treaty at all did little to mitigate the widespread belief that he had abandoned his principles. Karl Marx once said that he was not a Marxist, in a narrow, dogmatic sense; no doubt Wilson felt the same about the need for flexibility in the face of messy realities.

In its Far Eastern provisions, the treaty was even more un-Wilsonian. Despite tumultuous Chinese protests that erupted in May 1919, Wilson gave in to the Japanese demand to assume German rights in China's Shantung province, that being the price Tokyo had set in advance for entering the war on the side of the Entente. Had Wilson not buckled, he felt that Japan might not have joined the League, thereby crippling that body from the start. Though Wilson had hoped to "find some outlet to permit the Japanese to save their face and let the League of Nations decide the matter later,"[52] he had to rest content with an oral promise from Japan to retain Germany's economic privileges only, leaving nominal sovereignty to China.

To liberals who viewed Japan as a potential troublemaker, this was nothing less than a sell-out to old-style power politics. Relations with Japan had been tense enough during the war as Tokyo took advantage of the distractions of the European war to acquire additional special privileges in China. The crisis caused by the 21 Demands episode of 1915–16 was papered over only by the ambiguous Lansing-Ishii accord of 1917, in which Japan acknowledged the Open Door principle in return for U.S. recognition of Japan's "special interests" in China. The bad feelings left over from this disagreement were magnified when Wilson discovered that the Japanese, as part of the Russian intervention, had landed far more troops in Siberia than seemed warranted by the situation.

Making matters worse was Wilson's leading role in defeating a declaration of racial equality, which was backed by China and Japan. If adopted, it would have removed what little ideological justification remained for keeping intact the European empires. Naturally enough, the British would not hear of it. Wilson himself, a Virginian whose racial prejudices were typical of his time and place, was not enthusiastic about the Japanese proposal. Consequently, his Far Eastern decisions alienated both the Chinese and the Japanese. They also underscored the rather narrow Euro-American boundaries of Wilson's conception of world opinion.

With traditionalists feeling that he had gone too far and liberals complaining that he had not gone far enough, Wilson knew that he would have trouble in getting the Senate to agree to the treaty. Just before returning to Europe on March 5, following a brief visit to the United States, Wilson was confronted by a "round robin," a document that opposed the League of Nations covenant as Wilson had crafted it. Although it was signed by thirty-seven senators, more than enough to send the entire treaty down to defeat, Wilson thought it was a bluff. "You cannot dissect the Covenant from the treaty without destroying the whole vital structure," he said. As always, he believed that the people were with him.

Organizing the opposition to the treaty was the formidable Henry Cabot Lodge of Massachusetts, chairman of the Senate Committee on Foreign Relations. Though there was more than a touch of personal animosity between the two men, Lodge was driven primarily by principle. No light-weight in his understanding of foreign affairs, he had long been an inti-mate of Theodore Roosevelt and was one of the guiding spirits of the 1890s on behalf of a "Large Policy." Lodge's conception of foreign rela-tions differed considerably from Wilson's. His willingness to approve the French security treaty, although without entering the League, was itself a radical departure from tradition. Wilson had entered into this treaty of guarantee, at Clemenceau's insistence, in the expectation that it would become a redundant insurance policy overridden by the primary coverage offered by the League.

Lodge's skillful obstructionism went a long way toward defeating Wilson's dream. Over the course of the summer, he invited treaty oppo-nents of every shade to ventilate their views before his committee. A fron-tal assault against the idea of a League, Lodge knew, would be suicidal, but a string of amendments might eliminate the most offensive features of American membership. Wilson's fourteen points were thus shadowed by fourteen reservations, many of them unobjectionable. The main stick-ing point was the attempt to water down the American commitment to Article X of the League Covenant, which obligated all members to "pre-serve as against external aggression the territorial integrity and existing political independence" of all League members.

Wilson feared that without an unreserved commitment to Article X, which he called "the kingpin of the whole structure,"[53] the League mem-bers were bound to waver and fudge in moments of crisis when, as collec-tive security advocates believed, "the will to war is everything."[54] Without Article X, the League would be limited to dispensing aspirins to an inter-national community in need of chemotherapy. In trying to persuade those senators who were inclining towards compromise that the essentials could never be bargained away, Wilson argued that the Lodge resolution "does not provide for ratification but, rather, for the nullification of the treaty."[55]

Faced with this challenge to the League's credibility, he dug in his heels. Following a meeting with the senators, he agreed to a number of changes but vowed afterward to make no further concessions. Given his unwillingness to placate the large number of reservationists in the Senate, defeat was a certainty. But Wilson believed that he could play his trump card by taking the issue to the people. On September 4, he set out by train on a demanding cross-country speaking tour. If public opinion was to be the savior of the world, and if America was to be at the core of this global consensus, Wilson the democrat and the statesman had no other choice but to arouse the force on which everything depended.

His speeches were characteristically eloquent. He mentioned the crusading sacrifices of the war. And he drove home again and again the point that without American participation in the League and without full commitment to Article 10 the League would be stillborn. Most eerie, in retrospect, were Wilson's uncanny prophecies about what would befall the world if America failed to enter the League of Nations. "I do not hesitate to say that the war we have just been through, though it was shot through with terror of every kind, is not to be compared with the war we would have to face the next time," he said.[56]

Misfortune struck Wilson in the form of illness, most likely a stroke, on the return leg of his trip. In late September, the train returned to Washington with the crippled president. For a long time to come, the severity of his condition was hidden from the country by his protective wife and by complaisant physicians. Bedridden throughout the treaty fight, the president became more stubborn and unyielding. Indeed, some historians have suggested that the stroke clouded his political judgment. How else, they reasoned, could a masterly politician like Wilson have failed to agree to the compromises without which the Senate was bound to reject the treaty? Reject them he did, however. In a series of votes in the fall of 1919 and the winter of 1920, the Senate rebuffed both the Lodge reservations and Wilson's treaty.[57]

The League of Nations was a major issue in the election of 1920. The Democratic candidate, James M. Cox, and the vice presidential nominee, the young Franklin Delano Roosevelt, stated the Wilsonian case with vigor. But Republican candidate Warren G. Harding's promise of "normalcy" struck a deeper chord with the American public. Despite strong suggestions by some Republican internationalists that the United States would indeed enter the League with reservations, Harding refused to give a solid commitment. Following his overwhelming electoral victory, all mention of joining the League was dropped.

No doubt the United States could have joined the League had the president been willing to bend, as his critics have been fond of pointing out. They assumed that American membership, even on modified terms, would have made the League a going concern and prevented the disastrous cycle of events of the 1930s. However, for Wilson, American membership without American *leadership* was of little value. "America is the only altruistic country," he had said at the peace conference.[58] By this he meant that other nations were bound to look at crises from their own narrow perspectives instead of from the global point of view that was needed to make the League work. This was, in retrospect, a pretty accurate forecast. If the U.S. abandoned its commitment to global leadership right from the start by reserving the right to remain aloof in future crises, other nations could hardly be expected to make a success of collective security. To agree to reservations was akin to condoning conditional vows of marriage. To compromise on this issue would have required Wilson to abandon Wilsonianism.

And yet, given his predictions of a more devastating war, his stubbornness guaranteed, by his own logic, that such a war would indeed take place. Compromise, however illogical, would at least have given the new organization a better chance of muddling through, though Wilson no doubt felt it had no chance whatever of succeeding. In fairness, he had a point. Indeed, it seems likely that even Wilson's purist League would not have worked. One of the lessons of the twentieth century is that no international organization can prevent a great power from making war if it is determined to do so. For all the passionate controversy generated by this episode, in the end Woodrow Wilson's shortcomings as a leader probably had little to do with the international failure of collective security.

Domestically, the League project collapsed because Wilson's historical interpretation of the war was, at bottom, not *believable* to enough people who had their own interpretations of what it was about. If it was a war against autocracy, well, then, had not autocracy been defeated and sent packing? With that problem out of the way, the world could continue on the unproblematic path it had been treading prior to the war's eruption. It was much easier to see the Prussian monarchy as the source of danger than to pin the blame on some less visible and arguable structural conditions embedded within modernity. From this point of view, the war was only a temporary blockage of a road to international cooperation that had been fully reopened.

There were still other impediments to the full-fledged adoption of Wilson's views. Many Americans had gone to war to defend neutral rights, to teach the Germans a lesson. Beyond that, nothing further needed to be done. And for many liberals, the war was indeed a crusade, not the life-and-death conflict articulated by the wartime Wilson. When Wilson returned from Paris after having compromised on reparations, boundaries, and imperialism, he suffered defections from liberals who had taken him at his questing word.

Whatever the novelties of the war—its immense scale, its geographic breadth, its all-consuming character—Wilsonianism seemed more novel still. It was at the same time too idealistic and too alarmist, a strained combination of extremes that failed to produce the necessary base of support in public opinion. Visions of heaven and hell are indispensable religious motivators, but the secularized Wilsonian equivalents—the League, the collapse of civilization—failed to evoke the same kind of concerned response from people for whom the sense of the matter continued to lie somewhere in between. Wilsonianism was altogether too radical a departure for the American people to support given the traditional justifications for entering the war. Wilson's historical interpretation ran too far ahead of the store of collective experience upon which the acceptance of his views ultimately depended. Most people prefer to lead their lives on the basis of experience rather than imagination. Nations are no different.

Woodrow Wilson's moment was brief, the product of a unique moment in time. Following the Senate's rejection of the peace treaty, the political waters that had briefly parted came together again, making impassable the road to membership in the League. And the waters would never part again. During the 1920s and 1930s, a League of Nations Association and other die-hard enthusiasts tended the Wilsonian flame in the expectation of the second coming of collective security. Despite their efforts, time worked against realizing the concept of collective security in an American-led international organization.

Wilsonianism would survive and eventually flourish, but only by altering its form over time. It took an isolationist turn in the 1930s. During World War II, it became the ideological legitimator for a United Nations project that was very different in conception from the League. And, after World War II, cleansed of utopian expectations, it came fully into its own, not in an international organization, but as the dominating conception of American foreign policy in the cold war.

For the time being, the lessons of experience pointed in the direction of adopting a less disturbing and demanding vision of internationalism. Such a vision was in fact already waiting in the wings. Having already passed a prewar audition under William Howard Taft, this more optimistic outlook was ready to take over the role of leading foreign policy ideology in the coming decade. Wilsonianism would be replaced, not by isolationism, but by normal internationalism.

CHAPTER THREE

The 1920s: Normal
Internationalism as Utopia

"All great human catastrophes are more or less alike," complained Ray Stannard Baker, one of Woodrow Wilson's disciples. "No sooner had the war ended than the high emotional and moral enthusiasm which marked its concluding year began to fade away."[1] From the perspective of the 1920s, the Great War for Civilization was a rare occurrence, more like a three-hundred-year flood than the first in a succession of disasters. For the United States, the war's impact was even less traumatic than for the other major participants. Having borne only a small fraction of the combined casualties, some 150,000 soldiers killed in action during a comparatively brief period of belligerency (more than half of those deaths being non-battle-related), the shock of the war was not powerful enough to deflect the nation from its prewar course.

The tendency following catastrophes is to rebuild and to return to business as usual, a process made easier in this case by America's still vibrant sense of historical optimism. Warren G. Harding's evocation of "normalcy" promised a reversion to the pre-Wilsonian internationalism of the Taft years, not to nineteenth-century isolation. With the war seen as a singular interruption, the world once again took on the nonthreatening aspect of the prewar years. While Wilsonianism lay in ruins, the national consensus in favor of admission to the League, with reservations, suggests that pre-Wilsonian internationalist ideas—less demanding and less apocalyptic—were alive and well.

This fundamental internationalist sentiment was reflected in American foreign relations throughout the 1920s, which traveled farther down the pre–World War I road of optimistic global cooperation opened up by Taft's dollar diplomacy. Taft had argued that modern diplomacy was economic, and American statesmen of the 1920s fully agreed. "The dominating fact of this last century," said Herbert Hoover, then secretary of commerce, "has been economic development. And it continues today as the force which dominates the whole spiritual, social and political life of our country and the world."[2] Following the Wilsonian interruption, the emphasis was once again on the basics of commerce, culture, and international cooperation.[3]

There were, however, some major differences between the 1920s and the prewar years. Perhaps the most striking conceptual departure was the globalization of the Open Door policy over the course of the decade. Originally, the Open Door was an American policy that had China as its focus. Because the U.S. had shown no willingness to fight to uphold the Open Door principle, the idea clearly ranked far below the more forceful Monroe Doctrine in strategic importance. But that changed in the course of the decade as the Open Door was promoted from its relatively humble station to a policy of the first rank and, at the same time, was expanded to global dimensions. Correspondingly, the Monroe Doctrine was declawed and aligned more closely with Open Door principles. The upshot was that the idea of the Open Door was universalized. Originally identified with China, it was now the guiding idea behind America's promotion of an open world.

The success of the Open Door outlook depended, as before, on world opinion, whose benign and unitary functioning presupposed that the world was heading in the liberal direction first charted by America. With autocracy having been convincingly trounced and shoved aside, the cohesive world opinion created by the universal civilizing process appeared finally to have crossed the threshold of maturity and become a force capable of creating and maintaining international harmony. Without making an uncalled for Wilsonian fuss about things, now that autocracy had been defeated there appeared to be few obstacles to consensual behavior among the great powers. The modern dream of great-power cooperation could at last be put into practice.

Another notable change was that the United States was no longer a peripheral actor. Long typecast as a supporting player, the U.S. had never before enjoyed marquee status in international politics. That changed in the 1920s. Although the Wilsonian sense of danger disappeared, a belief in the rightness of American world leadership persisted. But leadership requires followers, which were in plentiful supply during the decade. For other nations, America's absence from the League of Nations did not diminish their reliance on the United States as the world's foremost economic and political power. That being said, U.S. leadership was of a peculiar variety. Throughout the decade, America remained aloof and po-

litically disengaged, as the absence of conflict and the apparent commitment to a cooperative framework of relations among the great powers
appeared to make political commitment unnecessary.

There was also a much greater emphasis on coordination and planning
in the 1920s than during the Taft years. Despite the fading of the twenty-
year burst of Progressive reform, business and global market forces were
not given a completely free hand. As an impressive amount of historical
research has shown, leading Republican ideologues of the decade like
Herbert Hoover were not out-and-out laissez-faire types. They believed
in coordination and planning, so long as it was not imposed by the government. This "voluntarist" philosophy was equally evident in America's approach to foreign relations throughout the decade. As economic issues
took pride of place, reliance was often placed on the leadership of industrial statesmen, the economic experts of their time. As Michael Hogan
has put it, the Republican administrations were interested in "putting private power in the service of public policy."

Technocracy—the reliance on neutral expertise—can work only if political and ideological issues have been banished to the sidelines. The
fondness for using business leaders to solve international economic problems was but one illustration of liberalism's ongoing temptation to define
society solely in economic terms. It was part of a technocratic mind-set
of the 1920s in which, ideally, politics was being displaced by administration, with an emphasis on efficiency and rationalization. "Political boundaries and political opinions don't really make much difference," said one
of the decade's high priests, Henry Ford.[4] At the very minimum, the vogue
for technocratic solutions to international problems required a frame of
reference that transcended purely national considerations of self-interest.

By relying on technical fixes, the intention was not so much to avoid
power politics as to replace it altogether with the modernization process.
Matters once settled irrationally by power could now be resolved by rational agreement based on the intricacies of economic science, which had
developed an international language of its own. The popularity of "Ford-
ism" in countries as different as Germany and the Soviet Union suggested
that such a transnational language was indeed emerging. It was, in any
case, the only common tongue available. However much they admired
America's technical achievements, Europeans continued to look down
their noses at American culture, while European politics seethed with anti-
democratic countercurrents.

So closely linked were international commerce and diplomacy in the
minds of the nation's leaders that the creation in the Commerce Department of a career foreign service, a group of foreign policy professionals

made possible by the Rogers Act of 1924, was justified largely on commercial grounds, leading one critic to imagine the American diplomat's briefcase being replaced by a "salesman's satchel with dollar marks all over it."[5] In 1928, a retiring consul took the common notion of the depoliticization of international relations to an uncommon, but logical, extreme. "As diplomatic functions today are mainly economic," he reasoned, "this places the Department of Commerce in control of the substance of diplomacy, and leaves the State Department with social relationships."[6] Indeed, under Herbert Hoover's energetic direction, the Commerce Department's Foreign Service, complete with attachés posted abroad, vied with State for control of America's international commercial relations.

The result was a foreign policy of involvement that was neither Wilsonian nor assertive in a macho "lone ranger" style of unilateralism. By exercising leadership without responsibility, American statesmen of the decade attempted to construct a world without politics. If one compares the outlook of the decade with Wilson's pessimistic appraisal of the serious structural defects embedded within modern global society, it is the Republican-dominated foreign policy of the 1920s that comes across as positively utopian. Wilson's League would have done away with politics as usual; the Republicans tried to do away with politics altogether. It is this politically uncommitted internationalism that a later generation would define as isolationism.

The Globalization of Latin American Policy

In the 1920s, the change in U.S. policy was more pronounced in Latin America than in any other region. The greater degree of movement took place because regional policy, suffering from arrested development, had to catch up to the now-prevailing global sensibility in Washington. Whereas the Caribbean regionalism of the 1890s had been at the forefront of America's new globalism, the Roosevelt corollary had long since begun to lag behind more recent trends. The reason for this retrogressive character of Latin American policy seems fairly clear. Despite his flirtation with globalism, Theodore Roosevelt, throughout his various Caribbean escapades, had remained faithful to the traditional Hamiltonian dictum of four separate political spheres. While Taft and Wilson opted for shinier new models of internationalist policy for the rest of the world, for travel closer to home they retained the tried-and-true vehicle of hemispheric policy, content for the most part to replace a few parts here and there as necessary to keep it running.

But a thoroughgoing internationalism suggested the desirability of a de facto mellowing of the Monroe Doctrine, or perhaps even its outright abolition. After the war, the United States finally began to bring its policies toward Latin American in line with its global outlook as not only the Roosevelt corollary but the Monroe Doctrine itself began to fade as coherent patterns of geopolitical belief. This is not to suggest that the Monroe Doctrine was dethroned as a cultural icon. It was not. But by the end of the decade, the United States was well on the way to displacing it with the Good Neighbor Policy, an internationalist approach that only masqueraded as regionalism. Afterwards, the Western Hemisphere would remain special, but only as a local habitat within a single, all-encompassing global environment.

One major test of America's new emphasis on business universalism took place in Mexico. The United States had twice sent troops into Mexico during Wilson's presidency, in 1914 and 1916 (in an unsuccessful effort to chase down Pancho Villa's raiders), and then had refused to recognize the new revolutionary government that came to power in the wake of the adoption of the Constitution of 1917. For American business interests, the most objectionable feature of the new constitution was article 27, which retroactively defined subsoil mineral rights as the property of the Mexican nation. Americans who had invested in Mexico with the specific expectation of exploiting underground riches viewed this clause as nothing less than confiscation, a brutal nullification of contractual property rights.

Significantly, the U.S. did not choose to employ the Big Stick. Realizing that a hard-line insistence on property rights would poison the relationship between the U.S. and Mexico and probably damage trade and investment in the long run, the Coolidge administration, thanks to the skillful negotiating efforts of the international banker Thomas Lamont, quickly worked out a live-and-let-live arrangement. The document known as the Bucareli Agreement of 1923 was vague, so full of reservations on both sides concerning property rights that it led a future ambassador to wonder: "was an agreement or even an understanding reached?"[7] Within both countries, there was strong opposition to the agreement as a sellout. Nevertheless, it gave the U.S. an excuse to recognize the government of Alvaro Obregón.

In 1925, under Obregón's successor, Plutarco Calles, the Mexicans resumed their campaign for national control over resources by passing legislation to implement article 27. Though a minority of hard-liners in the State Department called for an embargo on Mexican oil shipments or even war, Washington responded with moderation. Thereafter, the strained relationship improved greatly with the appointment of Dwight Morrow, a partner in the Wall Street banking firm of J. P. Morgan, as ambassador to Mexico in 1927. Despite some fears that his appointment presaged war in defense of American financial interests, exactly the reverse was true. Speaking for the American investment community, financier Lamont declared that "the theory of collecting debts by gunboat is unrighteous, unworkable and obsolete."[8] Dollar diplomacy was finally living up to its name.

Almost magically, a tense situation was transformed. The Mexican government, hurt by declining oil revenues and beset by other internal difficulties, backtracked from its extreme position on property rights by passing compromise legislation in 1928. Unlike many out-and-out racists within the State Department who looked down on Mexicans as an inferior people, Morrow soothed their prickly revolutionary nationalism by displaying a genuine interest in Mexican culture. This was not simply a matter of cynical calculation; the decade of the 1920s was a time when many Americans were fascinated with things Mexican. Interest ranged from art, literature, and other cultural achievements to an appreciation by American radicals of the political achievements of the revolutionary regime.

In addition to a noticeable warming between the United States and Latin America, the 1920s also brought closer relations between the U.S. and Great Britain in the region. There was some concern as the war was drawing to a close that the allies were bent on creating closed spheres in what would amount to an economic partition of the world, but these fears proved to be unfounded. Agreements were reached with British oil, cable, and radio interests in the region that reflected a broader global commitment to the Open Door principle.

Doctrinally, the United States began to climb down from the interventionist perch upon which Roosevelt had placed it. In 1928, the State Department released a long memorandum by Undersecretary J. Reuben Clark, which declared that the Monroe Doctrine had asserted no U.S. right to intervene in Latin America. According to Clark, the original Doctrine "states a case of United States vs. Europe, and not of the United States vs. Latin America." This did not mean that the right of intervention was being given up entirely. At the sixth Pan American Conference in Havana in 1928, American delegate Charles Evans Hughes defended American "interposition" in certain circumstances. "When governments break down and American citizens are in danger of their lives. . . . Are we to stand by and see them butchered in the jungle?" he asked, rhetorically. But this defense of the right to intervene rested on the generally accepted principles of international law instead of on the legally dubious Roosevelt corollary.

The advantages as well as the shortcomings of this new approach were illustrated by American policy in Nicaragua. After landing troops to intervene in a civil war in 1926, Coolidge sent Henry Stimson, formerly secretary of war in the Taft administration, to mediate a settlement. While working out a temporary cease-fire, Stimson organized American-supervised elections in 1928 and arranged for the creation of what was supposed to be an impartial National Guard as the sole military force in the country. Unfortunately, this attempt to take the army out of politics quickly backfired, as the new National Guard, under the control of General Anastasio Somoza, commandeered the political system. In this way, the United States unwittingly created the instrument that would be the basis of the Somoza family's dictatorial grip over Nicaragua for the next five decades. Nevertheless, the solution served its main purpose of limiting American involvement, and by 1933 American marines were out.

The trend away from interventionism occurred not because of any return to the first principles of Monroe, but because the business internationalism of the 1920s was allergic to old-style geopolitics. It was only a short step to the repudiation of intervention altogether. President-elect Herbert Hoover suggested the possibility of further improvement in relations during a good-will tour of Latin America in January 1929. Though the historical title to the Good Neighbor Policy would be appropriated later by the Roosevelt administration, it is clear that the original claim was filed by Hoover.

Thus dollar diplomacy, once a code word for American imperialism, finally began to take on a developmentalist meaning for U.S.–Latin American relations as growth began to take precedence over gunboat diplomacy. More American money than ever before, much of it speculative, began to flow south of the border in the expectation that profits, economic expansion, and democratization would follow. Some historians have argued that this was only a shift from naked political imperialism to a more subtle form of economic control in which invisible cords of commercial power replaced the old military manacles. To be sure, American economic influence was often overwhelming and development remained a will-'o-the-wisp throughout much of the region, but the fault was hardly America's alone. The social structures of these countries imposed barriers to modernization that, short of intervention for this purpose, the United States was unable to remove. And, as Mexico showed, revolution provided no magical answers. In any case, the renunciation of intervention, however lacking in utopian outcomes, was something that the Latin Americans themselves had long been avidly seeking.

This internationalization of the Monroe Doctrine requires a moment's reflection. That it should have become so bland and denatured was the result of a change in the fundamental conditions of the world that had called it into being in the first place. The 1920s differed radically from the 1820s. No longer was there a danger that Europe would seek to reestablish colonialism in the Americas, restore monarchical government, or export the balance of power to Caribbean shores. In practical terms, then, the apparent realization of a cooperative world civilization made the Monroe Doctrine unnecessary. Whereas formerly the doctrine had existed in a state of conceptual tension with the Open Door, the one emphasizing the part, the other the whole, the two basic foreign policy tenets were now harmonized.

Typically, the U.S. Senate, weighed down by parochial political ballast, saw things differently. In considering various treaty commitments throughout the decade, it took compulsive care to protect the Monroe Doctrine "from any conceivable curtailment."[9] But the Senate was prostrating itself before idols in which policy-makers and businessmen no longer believed. By the end of the 1920s, far from restoring the Doctrine by scraping off the barnacles of the Roosevelt corollary, Republican administrations had gone a long way toward placing it in drydock as a regional policy. This process of internationalizing the doctrine would be taken farther still in the 1930s with the Good Neighbor Policy of the Roosevelt administration.

The Internationalization of the Open Door

Nowhere was the triumph of cooperative internationalism more evident than in the international acceptance of the Open Door Policy by the China powers. The policy, formerly little more than an annoying pebble that Americans had bounced off the windows of the great imperial powers in the hope of gaining their attention, now became the foundation stone of a region-wide settlement that ended the diplomacy of imperialism. Building on the legacy of Taft's dollar diplomacy in East Asia, China policy became the showpiece of the Harding administration's devotion to great-power cooperation.

The European settlement at Versailles was flawed, but the peace conference had done an even worse job of applying liberal principles to Asia. That may have been due in part to Wilson, who, while writing off the European balance of power as beyond resurrection, seemed willing to acknowledge old habits of force in the Far East. Indeed, in the immediate postwar years, the "new diplomacy" seemed wholly out of place in this region: colonialism remained entrenched, racial equality was denied, and the old diplomacy of imperialism, based on expansion into China and the Anglo-Japanese alliance, was still in effect. Moreover, tensions continued to run high. In 1919, the United States and Japan became embroiled in a nasty dispute over the tiny island of Yap, worthless but for its lying astride a cable route. China was in turmoil, in the midst of a bout of civil war called the "Warlord Period," and the future of the Open Door was once again in question.

From the American perspective, something needed urgently to be done. The United States, the great power with the least to fear from immediate threats, was leading the world in armaments expenditures. Thanks in large measure to the unsettled situation in the Far East, there was the danger that a burgeoning naval arms race in the Pacific would spin out of control. In 1919, the Royal Navy had 42 capital ships—battleships and heavy cruisers—to America's 16 and Japan's 14, but in another five years the accelerated building programs of all the powers would have raised those numbers to 43, 35, and 22. For antimilitarists and Republican conservatives alike, this kind of wasteful expenditure needed to be reined in.

Domestic politics played a role, too, in the push to fashion a cooperative settlement in the Far East. Senator William Borah, best known as one of the die-hard "Irreconcilables" opposed to American membership in the League of Nations in any form, competed with President Harding to demonstrate that Wilsonianism was not the only path to peace. Referring to the "driving power of public opinion," Borah insisted that "Governments are inherently against disarmament" while "the people are unalterably for it."[10] Expressing the optimistic mood of the decade, he contended that "No nation can long defy the public opinion of the world."[11] Similar domestic pressures and initiatives made themselves felt in Great Britain and Japan.

In July 1921 the U.S. issued invitations for a conference on naval limitation to be held in Washington later in the year. Contrary to Borah's desires, the conference agenda was expanded to include all Far Eastern questions. The State Department had already signalled the future direction of American diplomacy in 1920, when it revived the moribund six-power consortium in China, a body from which Wilson had withdrawn in 1913 in the belief that it had been a creature of Wall Street monopoly interests. However, as the years went by, it began to look better and better as a tool for managing a potentially volatile Chinese situation in which an expanding Japanese sphere of influence threatened to ride roughshod over the Open Door idea. At the very least, the consortium would "neutralize China for development."[12]

The key figure at the Washington conference was Charles Evans Hughes, Harding's secretary of state. As the Republican candidate for the presidency against Wilson in 1916, Hughes was a man of some stature. A believer in rationality and the harmony of interests, Hughes called peace "a state of mind" which could "find expression in agreements and institutions, in the willingness to assume obligations of mutual self-restraint." In particular, if economic diplomacy were to succeed, wasteful arms races would have to stop. "If peoples have really become convinced that war and preparation for war are poor business, we may hope for peace, provided a sense of security can be created and maintained and disputes find processes of peaceful adjustment," he said.[13]

The conferees at Washington (even Henry Cabot Lodge was a delegate) arrived at a number of important agreements that, taken together, replaced the old "diplomacy of imperialism" in Asia. Most spectacular were the naval arms limitation accords, which resulted in actual reductions of forces in being. The moving force here was Hughes, who in his opening address proposed radical and specific reductions. After some negotiations, the parties arrived at the famous $5:5:3$ parity ratio of capital ships for the U.S., Britain, and Japan. Since the U.S. and Britain had global responsibilities, they needed larger navies. The smaller Japanese ratio, combined with a nonfortification agreement (Pearl Harbor and Singapore being the sole exceptions), was thought to be more than adequate to defend imperial interests in Asia. Indeed, the ratio was subsequently criticized by military realists as overly generous to Japan.

The naval reductions were only the concrete expressions of larger assumptions about international cooperation that guided the powers assembled in Washington. The Four Power treaty, for example, was designed to replace the Anglo-Japanese alliance, which since 1902 had been the linchpin of an East Asian balance of power. Getting rid of the alliance had long been an American objective, since it was conceivable that under its terms the United States and Great Britain might some day be pitted against each other. Though the British were hardly enthusiastic about terminating an arrangement that had, on the whole, worked quite well in defending their Asian interests, pressure from Canada and the realization that American ill will would more than cancel out any gains from continuing the alliance sufficed to gain their agreement. The Japanese, too, most notably Foreign Minister Shidehara Kijuro, realized that a broadly based consultative pact would be the only kind of agreement acceptable to the newly ascendant world power, the United States.

Whereas the Five Power treaty created a rough naval balance in East Asia, the Four Power consultative pact did away with the balance of power as a political principle. According to its terms, the signatories were obligated only to consult in the event that there was a threat to the peace or the interests of any of the parties were endangered. As with the consortium, the Four Power pact was supposed to operate by unanimity, on the assumption that no fundamental conflicts of interest would arise among the signatories. Indeed, Borah went so far as to claim that "article 2 of this treaty and article 10 of the League of Nations Covenant contain the same moral obligations exactly."[14] It all seemed too easy to those cynically inclined, but if Hughes were to be believed, "The great things are the simple ones." He claimed that "when this agreement takes effect we shall have gone further in the direction of securing an enduring peace than by anything that has yet been done."[15] If nothing else, the agreement codified the optimistic internationalist beliefs of the day.

Finally, the Washington conference gave the United States an opportunity to write the Open Door policy for China into international law. To this point, the Open Door was nothing more than a statement of American preference. Although nations had been careful not to contradict it openly, it had no legal force as a precept for the conduct of great-power diplomacy in China. That situation now changed as the conferees in Washington wrote the Open Door principle into a multilateral agreement. The " 'open door' in China has at last been made a fact" said Hughes. With the Nine Power treaty recognizing the Open Door as the basic framework for dealing with China, the beginning of the end of the imperialist treaty port system was at last in sight.

Despite this statement of good intentions, the unequal treaties would remain in force for the foreseeable future, much to the dissatisfaction of the increasingly nationalistic Chinese who demanded an end, here and now, to all foreign special privileges. Various particularistic advantages acquired in the old days also lingered on, with some modifications. For example, though the Japanese promised to get troops out of Shantung as soon as possible, they still considered that province to be a Japanese "sphere." Regardless, it was widely assumed that tariff autonomy would be restored and extraterritoriality abolished at some point in the future. Meanwhile, collaborative development, the offshoot of great- power cooperation, would become a guiding principle to replace the nationalistic exploitation of China.

The agreements would later come in for their fair share of criticism: they were too idealistic; they conceded regional hegemony to Japan; no provisions for enforcement existed in the event of a breakdown of regional order; the special privileges had not been revoked outright. In retrospect, all these objections were valid. But, at the time, the agreements appeared to embody a cooperative spirit in world opinion whose potency could not be denied. In any case, the agreements were utterly consistent with

American diplomacy in the region. With the exception of the Philippines, whose acquisition had rapidly become a matter of regret, American interests in the Far East had never been substantive to the point that they required forceful defense against another power. True, force had been used against the Chinese, but that was easily explained away as action in the name of civilization. And, to the degree that increasingly rabid anti-imperialist resentments within China contributed to the breakdown of the new order, it could well be argued that the agreements were not idealistic enough.

The agreements marked the high point of what the diplomatic historian Tyler Dennett had called "the cooperative policy" in East Asia. According to J. V. A. MacMurray, the chief of the Far Eastern Division in the State Department, America's Far Eastern policies had been "formulated with a new precision" at the Washington conference. But the Washington treaties were also a triumph for American diplomacy and an expression of the nation's new global stature. The United States had managed the amazing feat of reconciling the policies of nations whose interests in the Far East had in the past diverged significantly from its own. Indeed, things had changed to the point that the idiosyncratic outsider was now setting the rules for the entire fraternity.

The internationalization of the Open Door was evident also in American policy in the Near East, where American oil companies, with State Department support, sought access to the petroleum resources of the region. With the amazing spread of machinery based on the internal combustion engine, oil was quickly becoming the natural resource most vital to the functioning of modern industrial economies. The same was true for modern military organizations, as navies and armies relied increasingly on petroleum for their mobility. In a move reminiscent of Taft's railway diplomacy in China, a consortium of American oil companies, with the State Department's blessing, was granted entree by the British into Persia. Similarly, Jersey Standard was given access to Indonesian oil fields following negotiations with the Dutch government. This application of the Open Door principle favored the large corporations over smaller companies. But perhaps that was only to be expected in an industry where gigantism was the normal prerequisite for cartel-like cooperation and in a decade in which corporatism was the prevailing ideology.

The Globalization of European Politics

Ever since the eighteenth century, isolationism had meant isolation from Europe. As the Great War receded into memory and came increasingly to be viewed as an historical aberration or mistake, America's traditional aloofness from the Continent's affairs appeared, at least on the surface, to become even more deeply embedded. "A change of ministers in France," according to the *Los Angeles Times,* "is of less importance to the residents of Los Angeles than a change of grade on an important thoroughfare."[16] So fearful was the new administration of guilt by association with the League of Nations that the State Department, for a time, refused even to answer mail from Geneva. As the decade wore on, the public got used to the idea of American participation in various League conferences, but membership was out of the question. Because the League was considered very much a European organization, its disappearance as an issue in domestic politics meant that America's concern with Europe's politics had faded away, as well.

If political cooperation was ruled out, economic entanglement certainly was not, nor did absence from the League indicate a lack of concern with the Continent's problems. Economic experts like Thomas Lamont and Herbert Hoover recognized from an early date that European prosperity was indispensable to America's economic well-being. As George Wickersham put it: "Our interests are indissolubly united with the interests of Europe, and until we have reorganized a sound, a normal condition of affairs in Europe . . . we shall not have healthy times at home."[17] The failure of Europe to recover, besides producing economic and political chaos on the Continent, would depress significant segments of the American economy that depended on Europe as an export market. Such was the simple but compelling logic of economic interdependence.

Ominously, the postwar international economy was misfiring. Civilization might have been saved in the Great War, but the titanic conflict had also created a host of problems for the postwar order. All sorts of issues cried out for resolution: restoring the currency convertibility once provided automatically by the gold standard; freeing up trade; and opening up the channels for productive capital investment. The restoration of a flourishing commercial and financial environment also appeared to require progress on disarmament, lest huge sums of capital be wasted in military spending.

We now know that American policy-makers recognized, with an extraordinary degree of sophistication, the connection between all these issues and were aware of the need to act on them. They also knew that the U.S. had the power to compel solutions. Wilson had accurately predicted that, following the war, the United Stated could "force [the Europeans] to our way of thinking, because by that time they will, among other things, be financially in our hands." America, long a debtor nation, was now the leading creditor nation, the world's banker. Thanks to the historic wartime turnaround in its balance of payments, New York had replaced London as the world's chief exporter of capital. "Our influence in central bank circles," said Benjamin Strong of the Federal Reserve Bank of New York, "is almost predominant."[18]

Economically, at least, the challenge of internationalism lay in *undoing* much of the peace settlement rather than in getting America to abide by it. The most intricate and difficult financial problems inherited from the war revolved around the related issues of reparations and war debts. A restoration of prosperity in Europe was not likely to be achieved while the 1920s generation was saddled with the huge load of debts run up by its political forebears. So long as these massive obligations existed, it was impossible to expect normal conditions of trade and payment, just as one cannot envision normal blood circulation in an artery containing a huge embolism. Only the United States was in a position to do something about removing the blockage.

A critical problem was the 12 billion or so dollars owed to the United States from loans made during the war. Until the French and British agreed to a reparations settlement and negotiated debt repayment agreements with the United States, Harding gave notice that future loans, however badly needed for recovery, would not be forthcoming. Foreseeing that an ongoing snarl of debt would make for a sluggish world economy, some leaders like Herbert Hoover agreed privately that the logical thing to do was to wipe the slate clean by canceling debts and reparations. But because the loans had been subscribed by the American public, cancellation would in all likelihood have required a politically unthinkable tax increase. Thus President Calvin Coolidge's position—"they hired the money, didn't they?"—became the standard political refrain.

Most experts realized that the ability of the Allies to meet their debt obligations to the U.S. was conditional upon their receipt of reparations payments from Germany. France and England had so insisted from the very beginning. Unfortunately, the demand for massive reparations payments from Germany was the most controversial and problematic economic aspect of the peace treaty. At the time of the treaty's signing, a total sum had not yet been fixed; only the respective percentage shares to be allocated among the victors had been decided. Not until 1921 did an allied reparations commission announce that Germany would be obliged to pay the then-astounding sum of 33 billion dollars in gold, a demand far in excess of what might reasonably have been expected a few years earlier.

Early critics of the settlement like British economist John Maynard

Keynes called the attempt to squeeze enormous reparations sums from Germany "one of the most serious acts of political unwisdom for which our statesmen have ever been responsible."[19] In all likelihood, the amount could never be repaid and reparations would continue to act as a drag on international finances. There was no way in which Germany could earn such huge sums in gold from her own foreign sales nor transfer such amounts to the victors without seriously damaging her own financial stability. Even if it were granted, for the sake of argument, that Germany could pay up if she made a supreme effort, how could she be forced into that frame of mind? Defeat can impose economic slavery, but it cannot force the slave to work with the vigor of the person who labors for personal gain. When the shoe was on the other foot in the matter of repaying of war debts, England and France were quick to point out the hardships that came with making one-sided financial transfers of this unprecedented magnitude.

Interested American observers were not far behind Keynes in their criticism of the Versailles settlement's economic provisions. Herbert Hoover, for example, believed that the reparations settlement was "entirely unworkable" and stated privately in 1923 that "continental stability cannot be secured unless there is a settlement of interlocked debts, reparations and disarmament."[20] It was not simply an abstract question. If Europe failed to recover, the forecast for the American economy was likely to be quite bleak, too. The United States was, to be sure, remarkably self-sufficient, but its marginal dependence upon exports could still make an enormous difference. In some areas—agriculture, for example, which remained an economic soft spot throughout the 1920s—continued exports to Europe were essential if the plight of American farmers was not to worsen still further.

This internationalist perspective was by no means a universally accepted economic creed in the 1920s, a decade when economics as a social science had not yet attained the prestige that it would enjoy after World War II. Nor was it political dogma for statesmen, many of whom had been weaned on the nationalist economic outlooks of the late nineteenth century, or for members of Congress whose economic vision extended no farther than the parochial interests of their constituents. But for those bankers, industrialists, and government officials with foreign exposure, the commanding global economic position of the United States and its significant stake in foreign economic outcomes could not be denied.

In 1923, all the presentiments of catastrophe seemed on the brink of coming true. Following a German default on reparations, French and Belgian forces invaded and occupied the heavily industrialized Ruhr Valley with the aim of extracting reparations by force. The German government urged workers in the Ruhr to respond with passive resistance by refusing to work on behalf of the invaders. However, the decision to support the Ruhr work force through governmental payments caused monetary chaos. With the printing presses running overtime, the situation soon spun wildly out of control. In the famous hyperinflation of 1923, paper money depreciated in value so quickly as to become worthless. The collapse of the German currency system meant that the fallout in Europe from this economic volcano could not be far behind.

In stepped the Americans, with an ingenious private-sector solution that was an outgrowth of the voluntarist and nonpolitical standards of the decade. For some time, Secretary of State Hughes had been urging that the reparations issue be turned over to financial experts. In 1924, the Chicago banker Charles M. Dawes joined a new subcommittee of the Reparation Commission that soon drafted a plan bearing his name. This exercise in voluntarism was deceptive, for Dawes's appointment came as the result of considerable backstage maneuvering by the government. In any event, Dawes's scheme had Germany resuming reparations payments at a reduced rate of interest. In return, private bond issues were floated by some of America's most prominent investment banks, thereby raising the necessary capital for Germany's economic reconstruction and financial stabilization. An American was appointed agent general for reparations, to assure that the German economy functioned in accord with the details of the program.

The Dawes plan worked spectacularly well. The $200 million loan to Germany, 110 million of which was raised in the United States, was quickly oversubscribed by enthusiastic American investors. But the Dawes loan was only the first dose of a monetary stimulant for the German and world economies. Over the course of the decade, the United States injected billions more into Germany for reconstruction. Among other uses, American money allowed the Germans to produce the budget surpluses needed to make reparations payments. So close did the two nations become as a result of American efforts to modify the reparations settlement that, according to one German diplomat, the United States was "not only the best friend but actually the only friend which the *Reich* has in international society."[21]

By making the Allies responsible for converting reparations payments into gold, it was hoped that the Dawes plan would "commercialize" the reparations problem, i.e., take it out of politics altogether. This commercialization of reparations continued in the Young plan of 1929, so named after the American industrialist Owen D. Young. This plan further reduced the sum owed by the Germans to $9 billion plus interest, and came up with a less onerous system of annual payments. Without openly saying so, this renegotiation of reparations settled on sums which approximated quite closely the sum due the U.S. in payment of World War I loans.

In practice, then, if not in principle, the U.S. acknowledged the connection between reparations and war debts, something it had long recognized in private. The World War Foreign Debt Commission, created by Congress in 1922 to act as the nation's collection agency, was originally supposed to take a very tough line. But with reduced reparations resulting in a lessened capacity to pay war debts, the U.S. position softened. An agreement reached with Great Britain in 1923 paved the way for a general European stabilization scheme. Over the course of the decade, the commission turned into "a very lenient creditor"[22] by negotiating repayment agreements with its biggest debtors and by scaling back payments on the basis of ability to pay. All this amounted, in effect, to a policy of partial cancellation.

The Dawes plan also produced some spectacular political benefits. By promoting Germany's prosperous integration into the world economy, the inflow of dollars had the effect of curbing any revival of German nationalism. With the French and the Germans now convinced of the folly of continued economic confrontation, a series of treaties was signed the following year at Locarno, Switzerland, institutionalizing for Europe the same spirit of cooperative internationalism that the Washington treaties had set in place for the Pacific. The borders between France, Belgium, and Germany were recognized as sacred. Various arbitration treaties were agreed to. It was also decided to end Germany's outcast status by allowing her to join the League of Nations. The "spirit of Locarno" that made possible these accords expressed the optimistic internationalism that infused European diplomacy after 1925.

The economic settlement could not salve some festering political problems, however. Little thought was given to the problem of the European balance of power or to remedying the territorial excesses of the peace treaty. Confirming the boundaries in the west had been fairly easy. Alsatians, for example, long accustomed to thinking of themselves as French, had no difficulty in being reassimilated to France. But there was no "eastern Locarno" to resolve the territorial problems arising from large areas with mixed ethnic populations. With respect to eastern Europe, all German governments of the 1920s were "revisionist." That is, they were committed to eventually undoing the territorial settlement in which large German-speaking areas had been taken away from the *Reich*.

Had Americans thought seriously of restoring a balance of power, they would have been more sympathetic to France. Instead, by continuing a pattern of disagreement that had emerged during the peace conference, France played the role of European villain throughout much of the decade. Extravagant French demands seemed to lie at the core of the reparations tangle. As a result, Secretary of State Hughes "often became impatient with them, deploring their irrationality and obstinacy."[23] The French were also the most stubborn in resisting America's insistence on repayment of war debts. What seemed like generosity to Americans appeared to the French as a tight-fisted unwillingness to recognize the disproportionate sacrifices that France, with some 1,400,000 war dead, had made in a common cause. "Was that not 'money in the bank' to us, the energy of these young men lost?"[24] complained the retired Clemenceau. Not least, French diplomacy seemed obsessed with maintaining military superiority over Germany and with relying on outmoded prewar power-balancing techniques. A newspaper cartoon that depicted France trying on a German spiked helmet depicted as well as anything America's exasperation with her former ally.

Germany, by contrast, appeared the more virtuous of the two nations. Temporarily humbled by defeat, newly democratic of necessity, and desperate for friendship, the Germans reached out for a helping hand to the two powers that remained beyond the European orbit: the Soviet Union and the United States. In 1922, in a move that shocked the other European powers, the two outcasts signed the Rapallo Treaty in which they agreed to economic and (secretly) military cooperation. Realizing that economic prosperity and defense against unreasonable French demands depended upon America, the Germans also made sure to cultivate close relations with the United States. This turnaround in opinion showed how easily strategic relationships could be upset by the new global economic logic.

The Kellogg-Briand Pact

Legal internationalism was yet another non-Wilsonian way, more traditional and far less controversial, of pursuing international cooperation. The treaties negotiated by Roosevelt and Taft had been attempts to extend an American tradition that went back to the early nineteenth century of using arbitration treaties to settle international differences. In 1926, after lengthy Senate debate, the Coolidge administration sought American membership in the World Court. The American terms were hedged about with qualifications, the most serious being the Senate's insistence on the right to veto advisory opinions that involved the United States. However much the Europeans desired an American presence, American admission on that basis was turned down. Nevertheless, a number of distinguished Americans, Elihu Root among them, did serve as judges on the international tribunal at The Hague.

Yet there was more than one arrow in the quiver of legal internationalism. In 1928, the United States adhered to the Pact of Paris, better known as the Kellogg-Briand Pact, which outlawed war as an instrument of national policy. The "outlawry of war" was an American inspiration, bred in the imagination of a Chicago lawyer named Salmon O. Levenson who claimed that wars occurred because they were wholly legal activities for states to engage in. Take away the legal justification for wars, he reasoned, and nations would think twice about starting them.

The diplomacy of outlawing war evolved out of a French proposal. Ever since the United States had rejected the security treaty of 1919 along with the League of Nations, French diplomats had been seeking an American commitment to guarantee their nation's security. In 1928, Aristide Briand, somewhat nervous about the testy state of relations between the two countries, proposed a rather innocuous-sounding treaty in which the U.S. and France pledged not to go to war against each other. This was far from what the French really wanted, but it was at least a first step in weaning away the U.S. from its isolationist position.

Smelling a rat, the American secretary of state, Frank Kellogg (with backstage prompting from Senator Borah), suggested that the treaty be made accessible to all interested nations. Briand had no choice but to comply, and the Pact of Paris soon became a multilateral treaty, signed by fifteen countries to start with. Interestingly, most of the signatures were conditional. With everyone claiming the right to self-defense, war was not renounced absolutely. Other exceptions, as in the case of Great Britain and her empire, were also made. The U.S. Senate, as one might expect, hastened to add its reservation. Nevertheless, at the time the pact was viewed as a great accomplishment. Indeed, even Kellogg, who was at first quite wary of this snake oil remedy, now testified to its amazing medicinal properties. For foreign governments, particularly Great Britain and France, the value of the treaty lay not in any expectation that the United States would intervene against a lawbreaker—clearly it would not—but rather in the hope that it would abandon its traditional insistence upon pursuing an even-handed policy of neutral rights.

For some American internationalists and Wilsonians, the treaty was a tentative first step on the road to a community of power. Perhaps, they reasoned, Wilson and his followers had attempted to soar farther than a fledgling internationalism could comfortably fly. In contrast to the League, which was supposed to function immediately as a robust adult, they hoped that this treaty would naturally and in due course grow into the larger wings of collective security. Even Senator William Borah on one occasion suggested that it was "quite inconceivable that this country would stand idly by in case of a grave breach of a multilateral treaty to which it was a party."[25]

Of course, if nations did choose to go to war illegally, aggressors could not be punished by some international tribunal because the pact contained no definition of aggression and made no provisions for sanctions. The hope was that world public opinion would keep aggressors in check in the first place. The treaty's "sole sanction lies in the power of public opinion of the countries, constituting substantially the entire civilized world," explained Secretary of State Henry Stimson in 1929. According to the internationalist scholar James Shotwell, "the will to peace is paramount in the civilized world; and it is in this fact that the Pact of Paris resides."[26] "Public opinion will suffice to check violence," said President Hoover.

In the scathing dismissal of historian Robert Ferrell, the Pact of Paris demonstrated the foolishness of relying upon anything so insubstantial as world public opinion. "Nations were to discover," he wrote, "that public opinion was in part an invention of the merchants of toothpaste and to-bacco, that its larger manifestations were difficult to predict or measure, that it was subject to national prejudices, that, in short, it could not act as an international force for peace and indeed might do the opposite."[27] Whatever the truth of that judgment, the Kellogg-Briand Pact was, at the time, another step down the road of internationalism and yet another manifestation of the belief in the ability of modern world opinion to maintain peace.

The Failure of Economic Management

Ultimately, the sustained effort of three Republican administrations to forge a cooperative global structure without political commitments failed miserably. A significant part of the problem in the late 1920s could be traced to the inconsistencies of American economic policy. First and foremost was the continuation of the traditional high tariff policy of the Republican Party. If the United States was to be the world's banker and a leading exporter of goods, there was only one way for importing nations to repay their loans and their purchases: by having the United States open its markets to foreign products, thereby allowing nations to earn the dollars needed to repay their obligations to America. Woodrow Wilson, a free trader, once expressed the common sense of the matter: "If we want to sell we must be prepared to buy," he said.[28]

However, the United States showed little interest at this time in opening its markets. While economically internationalist Republicans were in charge in the executive branch, in Congress protectionism still ruled the roost. The Fordney-McCumber Tariff of 1922 reversed the Wilson administration's downward revision of tariffs, but the Hawley-Smoot Tariff of 1930 went even farther in the direction of protectionism, raising rates to near all-time highs.[29] Complaints from American economists were dismissed by Senator Smoot as coming from "the cloistered halls of theoretical universities." At the time, many experts viewed these high rates as a comparatively minor and correctable problem. They were more concerned with the question of how the tariff could be used to promote a general downward revision of rates. The inclusion of the unconditional most-favored-nation clause rather than reciprocity, which favored bilateral mutual tariff-cutting concessions, was believed to be a victory for the idea of stimulating the creation of an open world market.

But with downward revisions of duties few and far between, the result, contrary to internationalist economic logic, was a persistent trade surplus. Compounding the problem, a steady weakening of American exports throughout the 1920s would have made it impossible to justify running a trade deficit for the sake of a creating a healthy global economy. Agricultural sales to Europe performed well until the Continent's farm industry righted itself by mid-decade, and thereafter it was industrial exports that took over. Europe was the primary customer, but increasingly Japan was a major market. China, though as ever symbolically important, was still racked by poverty and turmoil in the 1920s and incapable of purchasing from the United States in significant amounts.

Herbert Hoover believed that America's balance of payments surplus would be offset by tourism, loans, and remittances sent back to their home countries by American immigrants. Another important way of compensating for the imbalance was to lend money abroad, which could then be used to pay for American imports. Realizing that speculative loans were an invitation to disaster, Hoover suggested governmental supervision of foreign loans to ensure that they be granted only for productive investments that were likely to contribute to the expansion of the borrowing nation's wealth. The State Department had its own motives for agreeing to such a policy, since it could be used as an instrument of coercion for bringing economically recalcitrant governments to heel.

Predictably, bankers were not pleased by this assertion of governmental authority. But while they had little choice but to submit their proposals to Washington for review, international banking practices were, with only a few exceptions, not controlled by an iron hand. The voluntarist ideology of the decade was too powerful to allow heavy-handed interference by the state in one of the most sacred processes of the free economy—the market in money. The result was that overseas loans were ruled by market considerations. As time went on, loans were increasingly diverted from Europe to more risky debtors in Latin America and Asia. By the end of the decade, money available for lending to Europe was beginning to dry up, as investors flocked to chancier, but higher-paying capital markets elsewhere. Most of these loans would be defaulted in the 1930s.

The situation began to unravel in 1929, in the wake of the stock market crash and the onset of the Great Depression in the United States. Although economic historians still disagree on the causes of the depression, it was clearly a global economic downturn whose epicenter lay in the United States. As the economic slump took hold in America, the reservoir of capital dried up and the spigot of loans to Germany and Europe began to sputter. Foreign loan issues declined from $1.25 billion in 1929, to $229 million in 1931, and to zero in 1932, thereby eliminating a major stimulus to economic expansion abroad. With the flow of loans cut off, Germany could no longer make reparations payments, the British and French could no longer pay back their war debts, and foreign imports of American goods declined.

When the expanding depression reached Germany, Hoover made a desperate attempt at freeing up the world economy by cutting away the tangled roots of debt that were clogging the pipe of world investment and trade. In June 1931, he proposed a one-year moratorium on all intergovernmental debts. It was, however, too little, too late. To no avail, the English invoked internationalist arguments on behalf of outright cancellation, arguing that "it will not profit a creditor country to collect a few million pounds or dollars if it thereby perpetuates a world disorder." Further European efforts to wipe out Germany's reparation obligations in return for American cancellation of war debts were met by Hoover's rather lame contention that there was no connection between the two issues. Meanwhile, the depression continued its epidemic-like spread through industrial societies.

Could anything have been done? American policy on debts and tariff, strongly tinged by nationalism, worked contrary to the requirements of the international system. According to historian Joan Hoff: "Only strong loans control in conjunction with lower tariffs, increased imports on the part of the United States, and cancellation of the outstanding intergovernmental debts would have changed the world financial situation before

1929."[30] But all this would have required a huge reversal of American assumptions about how to link together the domestic and international economies. And, in the absence of hard knowledge of the causes of the depression, it is impossible to say with certainty whether even this would have been enough.

What is clear is that America's economic internationalism was not internationalist enough, its halfhearted application being the major cause of undermining great-power cooperation. To others, U.S. policies looked very much like selfishness. With economic internationalism apparently incapable of assuring prosperity, many nations chose go-it-alone courses of national self-sufficiency. High tariffs, abandonment of the gold standard, competitive currency devaluation, and exchange controls became standard instruments of economic warfare. State-managed economies became the vogue for governments of the left and the right. In the absence of assured access to raw materials and markets, and in the face of international economic competition that threatened to devastate domestic industries and jobs, economic nationalism became the default position.

In other respects, too, the 1920s produced powerful anti-internationalist undercurrents. Racism was on the upswing, as were nativism, aggressive nationalism, and doctrines of cultural relativism, all of which rejected the idea of the unity of mankind. More ominous still, some nations began to look to military expansion as a way of creating self-sustaining economies. In the 1920s, disarmament was thought to be a necessary feature of the new world order, the assumption being that less military spending would contribute to economic prosperity and increase mutual confidence among the powers. But the collapse of League-sponsored disarmament negotiations in Geneva in 1932 was a signal that military competition would once again become a key feature of international politics.

After the heartening success of the Washington conference in 1922, disarmament began to encounter increasingly heavy weather. Following a failed conference in Geneva in 1927, a naval agreement on smaller warships was reached at London in 1930, only to run into vehement opposition from Japanese militarists who argued that the ratios of 10:10:6.97 on destroyers, which limited Japan to seven destroyers for every ten allowed the British or the American navy, were an insult to their nation. Negotiations on land armaments in Geneva failed even to reach the stage of drawing up a draft agreement, thanks to a Franco-German impasse. Scheme after scheme failed to break the deadlock caused by the French demand for security and the German demand for equality. As far as the French were concerned, only a militarily inferior Germany would guarantee the security of the French nation. A dramatic call by Hoover for the elimination of all offensive weapons and reduction of remaining weapons by one-third encountered resistance from the French, Germans, and British. A few months later, Adolf Hitler was chancellor of Germany and disarmament was dead.

The Manchurian Crisis and the Collapse of Apolitical World Order

Despite the ominous storm warnings coming from Europe, the internationalism of the 1920s began to unravel most noticeably at the edges of the world system. Early in the decade, the Washington treaties had sought optimistically to replace the diplomacy of imperialism with a new cooperative order. Unfortunately, orderly cooperation among the signatories proved elusive when dealing with an unruly China that was increasingly loathe to accept any imperialist supervision, even if ostensibly for its own good. Other regional powers also had difficulty in accepting the new order. The Soviet Union, still an outcast nation, viewed the Washington system as but a new variation on the old theme of imperialism. Through flamboyant propaganda and the signing of a treaty in 1924 which returned some treaty rights previously extorted from China by the czars, the Soviets added revolutionary expectations to the region's increasingly unstable mixture of ideologies.

The radical message played well in a newly nationalistic China. The years 1917–27 are known as the Warlord Period because of the absence of centralized rule following the collapse of Yüan Shi-kai's government in 1917. The country lapsed into disunity, its major regions controlled by autonomous generals who commanded armies as their instruments of authority. Despite the disintegration, in part because of it, ever since the demonstrations of May 4, 1919, the day when the peace conference failed to authorize the return of Shantung to China, the spirit of nationalism was running high.

Determined to restore Chinese unity and independence, the Kuomintang or National People's Party, based in Canton in the south, made its bid for power. Under the leadership first of Sun Yat-sen and later his military disciple, Chiang Kai-shek, the Kuomintang reorganized itself so as to more efficiently pursue its nationalist goals. The most convenient organizational model was the Leninist party—small, secretive, highly disciplined, and flexibly efficient. Hoping to take advantage of Communist organizational know-how, in 1924 the Kuomintang formed a common front with the fledgling Chinese Communist Party and accepted Russian advisers. Even if this was only a marriage of convenience, it suggested that western suitors had been firmly rejected.

As a result of this new militancy, relations with the treaty powers grew increasingly tense. In 1925, sentiment against the "unequal treaties" led to student demonstrations in Shanghai and Canton, which were met by gunfire from British forces. The Chinese responded with a boycott of British goods. In 1926, the situation grew still more explosive as Chiang Kai-shek launched his famous Northern Expedition, a military campaign of unification. The following year, after the capture of Nanking, the Communists stirred up trouble by attacking foreigners within the city, killing six.

As the decade wore on, the powers went their own way in dealing with a Chinese nationalism that was increasingly impatient with the gradualist approach to sovereignty. The U.S. responded to the antiforeign outrages by holding Chiang responsible, but the other China powers responded as they saw fit. The British gave up concessions in order to dim the luster of the Russians. Japan sent troops in 1927 to protect its nationals and businesses in the north as Chiang's armies approached Peking. The Japanese withdrew their forces in 1929, but not before a Chinese boycott had been launched against their products. In all, Chinese nationalism was finally doing what imperialist competition had been unable to achieve: breaking up the common front of the China powers. Even so, the treaty powers might have weathered the squall of Chinese nationalism had not the Great Depression extinguished the flickering flame of internationalism.

On September 18, 1931, the Japanese army fanned out from its garrison areas in Manchuria and proceeded rapidly to conquer the entire Chinese province. The pretext for this action was an explosion on the Japanese-owned South Manchurian railway. The Japanese blamed the explosion on Chinese "bandits" when in fact it was master-minded by extremist officers in the Kwantung army. Though the plot was undertaken without the foreknowledge of the government in Tokyo, the Manchurian conspirators had the backing of their army superiors in Japan, who prevented the civilian leadership of the country from interfering with the consummation of this military adventure. Within a few months, Japan was urging the rest of the world to recognize its puppet regime in Manchuria, now called Manchukuo.

With its export-based economy badly damaged by the global depression, Japan had already set out on a neomercantilist course that abandoned the economic internationalism of the 1920s. That decision was far-reaching in its own right, but the military conquest of Manchuria raised problems that the international structure of the 1920s had not been designed to handle. That system had been constructed on the assumption that problems could be handled without any need for hard-nosed political guarantees. As for the Kellogg-Briand Pact, that treaty did not seem to apply, since the Japanese were careful not to declare war.

In the United States, the Manchurian crisis fractured the internationalist consensus of the decade as policy-makers in the Hoover administration anxiously debated a course of action. The crisis stimulated a debate between those who, like Secretary of State Stimson, favored a revived Wilsonianism in which the world community would be backed by force and those who, like Hoover, were content with a normal internationalism that stopped with the imposition of the moral sanctions of world opinion. Stimson was convinced that, in the modern world, war was a contagion, no matter where it began. "In the interconnected and industrialized world of today war has become immeasurably more destructive and likely to spread than in former ages," he later wrote. "Unless it is controlled, our civilization will be in real peril."[31] For Stimson, the seizure of Manchuria was a violation of both the Nine Power treaty and the Kellogg Pact. Because the Manchurian episode had taken place in East Asia, a region that Stimson called "our part of the world," he believed it was America's responsibility to take the lead in dealing with the challenge.

But Hoover disagreed vigorously. He had sat at Wilson's right hand as a valued economic adviser in Paris, but his slant on the need for peace was always more economic than military. Throughout the 1920s, he was a leading advocate of technocratic solutions to global problems. Hoover's thinking had always been colored by an awareness, derived from his far-ranging business travels, of the world's enormous cultural and racial differences. Should world opinion fail, then the situation was beyond salvaging in any case, and American separateness from the rest of the world was always a viable alternative. He had little patience with Wilsonian strategic prophecies of doom. If anything, his experience with the Great War taught him that American intervention was likely to be more catastrophic than American forbearance. Moreover, he had been in China during the Boxer Rebellion, and his understanding of Chinese history, which was more than superficial, suggested that China could once again absorb its invaders.

After waiting fruitlessly for liberals in Tokyo to regain control, Hoover and Stimson compromised on a policy of nonrecognition. Although Stimson wanted something tougher, perhaps the threat of an economic embargo, he agreed that world opinion, as expressed through nonrecognition, might well succeed. "As has been shown by history in the past," he wrote to Senator Borah, the force of world opinion would "eventually lead to the restoration to China of rights and titles of which she may have been deprived."[32] For his part, Hoover felt that this legalistic approach was quite consistent with tradition and with America's limited interests in China. Nonrecognition became a convenient way out for other nations who also wished to avoid taking hard action against Japan. Meanwhile, the League of Nations, after investigating the Manchurian situation and accepting the report of an investigative commission report that was surprisingly easy on Japan, received notice from Tokyo of Japan's withdrawal from the League.

The Manchurian crisis was a historical watershed. Apart from serving as a reminder that Wilsonianism had not been half-baked fantasizing, after all, it discredited the optimistic internationalism of the 1920s. The breakdown of world order in the 1930s demonstrated that dollar diplomacy was a fair-weather craft only, unsuited to navigation in politically turbulent waters. In the belief that great-power cooperation was the norm, the internationalism of the 1920s failed to take seriously the possibility of a reversion to previous strong-arm methods. "The world of credit is essentially a world of peace," said one optimist in 1929, parroting the line that capitalism equals peace.[33] But that kind of world was fast disappearing.

THE 1920s WERE a period of international relations without politics, a decade in which the U.S. displayed an unprecedented degree of leadership, but without commensurate political commitment. This kind of limited involvement only makes sense when one considers the abiding faith in a modern, progressive global civilization. That faith, which has maintained its grip throughout the century, assumed that economic growth, the force that produced a modern global civilization in the first place, was the key to its continued improvement. In the 1920s, a global harmony of interests seemed less a utopian possibility than a commonsense truth. Commitment seemed beside the point as long as there were no fundamental threats to the nation's existence or sense of identity.

American statesmen failed to recognize that, in an interdependent world where mutual vulnerability was the flip side of progress, political and economic crises required one nation to take responsibility to prevent the system from crashing. They also neglected to take into account the possibility that international economics had every bit as much potential for disruption as power politics. The goal of technocratic management of the international economy was inherently flawed, partly because the state of economic knowledge was still quite primitive, in part because even the experts tended to interpret international needs from their particular national perspectives, but most of all because it refused to recognize the political aspects of economics.

In brief, there was little concern with the possibility of catastrophic economic or political "systems effects" or of limiting them if they occurred. Once economic collapse led to a revival of nationalist thinking and policies, including a new enthusiasm for war, there was nothing in place institutionally—neither an effective League of Nations nor a restored European balance of power—capable of stopping the slide into chaos. Wilson had at least taken into account the need for political action through collective security; but the system of the 1920s had no such safeguard.

After Manchuria, foreign policy debate in the U.S. took a new turn. On one side, neo-Wilsonians increasingly saw a need to go beyond apolitical internationalism; on the other side were those who advocated a retreat not only from the internationalist assumptions of the 1920s but also from the more limited internationalism of traditional neutrality. In short, the Far Eastern crisis set the stage for a debate in the 1930s on the question of whether *any* kind of internationalism at all was desirable. Perhaps, many of the new isolationists wondered, it had been a ghastly mistake to welcome the worldwide process of integration set off by industrialism. The single world created by modernity was not working well. Was it worth keeping? Was it worth fighting for?

Answers to those questions were slow in coming. Wilsonianism would make a phoenix-like recovery, but not before the optimistic images that dominated the historical imaginations of policy-makers, images of a world civilization tending naturally and almost automatically to peace, prosperity, and cooperation, were brutally shattered in the 1930s. Yet though the world tumbled into the abyss, it would take the better part of a decade to revive the Wilsonian sense of danger. Even then, it was by no means universally accepted. Ironically, its eventual triumph owed more to historical accident than to the overpowering sense of historical necessity that roused Wilson to action.

CHAPTER FOUR

The 1930s and World War II:
The Crossroads of Modern Internationalism

The Great War for Civilization was widely perceived as the crisis of the old order. Wilson had tried to suggest that it was more than simply a crusade against autocracy, but most Americans were unprepared to accept the disturbing possibility that the conflict was a crisis of the modern world. This basic confusion was absent from debates about the historical meaning of the 1930s and World War II. If nothing else, these years were clearly a crisis of the triumphant liberal world order that had replaced the power politics of the past. This time, modern internationalism was itself on trial. Thus, far from being a repeat performance, for Americans the Second World War was unambiguously about global issues. As far as public consciousness was concerned, World War II was the first truly global conflict, the great war *of* civilization.

For a time, the worldwide upheaval triggered by the Great Depression brought to a halt and even reversed what only a few years earlier seemed an inevitable trend toward the creation of a liberal global civilization. As the optimism of the 1920s evaporated and the frail-born League of Nations struggled feebly to find its legs, more vigorous ideologies, basing their appeal on narrower grounds of race and nationality, made a bid for ideological supremacy. Suddenly liberal internationalism, once synonymous with modern high fashion, was hopelessly behind the times.

In contrast to the faceless, behind-the-scenes technocratic style of the 1920s, the 1930s featured a series of electrifying diplomatic and military performances by powers thoroughly hostile to the post-Versailles status quo. By the time Herbert Hoover left office, the Japanese conquest of Manchuria was complete. The Washington treaties and the Kellogg-Briand Pact had done nothing to stop Japan's military advance except to erect a flimsy barricade of words and paper. In Europe, where the traditional balance of power was no longer effectively in operation, the League of Nations made a weak stab at preventing another war. With the ascent to power of Adolf Hitler and his Nazi movement in 1933, Germany moved swiftly to undo the peace settlement of 1919 and the accords of the 1920s. Following their departure from the Geneva disarmament conference in 1933, the Germans announced rearmament in 1934, and in 1936 unilaterally remilitarized the Rhineland, all in violation of treaty obligations.

As events tumbled forward swiftly and ominously, the 1930s were years of extraordinary uncertainty about foreign policy. With the old diplomacy banished and the new diplomacy of collective security ineffective as its stand-in, it was not clear to liberals how they should proceed. The confusion was perhaps most pronounced in the United States, where Americans rejected the Republican version of internationalism that held sway throughout the 1920s, but without being able to settle on an alternative. While they continued to spurn Wilsonianism, by mid-decade they also rejected what used to be the default position, the traditional policy of isolation based on neutral rights.

As the country drifted ideologically, President Franklin D. Roosevelt managed eventually to set internationalism on a new course by emphasizing the catastrophic implications of modernity's downside. Although the economic collapse of the 1930s put American institutions under great immediate stress, FDR believed the international crisis to be potentially far more threatening to the American way of life. As a result of FDR's successful articulation of this apocalyptic global strategic threat, the Wilsonian sense of danger that was missing from the internationalism of the 1920s finally took center stage in American diplomacy, a position it would not yield until the end of the century.

FDR's penchant for tacking with the prevailing political winds has baffled contemporary observers and historians alike, but there is no doubt whatsoever that he was an internationalist who was convinced of the absolute necessity of preserving a liberal global civilization. After cutting his teeth on the abrasive foreign policy rhetoric of his cousin Theodore, a mature FDR gravitated to Wilsonianism. He served in the Great War as assistant secretary of the navy, and in the election of 1920, as the running mate to Democratic presidential candidate James Cox, he campaigned strongly on behalf of American membership in the League. During the 1920s, he outlined a program of international cooperation that went beyond the limited internationalism of dollar diplomacy, whose myopic focus on American economic interests was too selfish to suit his taste. In suggesting a more altruistic and cooperative approach, he hinted at an internationalism that placed greater emphasis on the good of the whole.

More importantly, FDR never lost touch with the new Wilsonian view of security. During the interregnum between the election and his inauguration in March 1933, in a series of interviews with Henry Stimson, he glimpsed flashes of lightning in the distance that signaled the approaching storm of war. Taking a gloomier view than Hoover of the deterioration of relations with Japan, he privately "admitted the possibility of war and said flatly that it might be better to have it now than later."[1] FDR, it was clear, did not view World War I as a historical aberration. It was, instead, the harbinger of new dangers to which the United States had become permanently exposed.

Like most Wilsonians, however, FDR believed that cooperation was the normal condition of modern internationalism. This fundamental outlook was most tellingly revealed in an address delivered in 1933 at the Woodrow Wilson Foundation's annual dinner. Speaking to an audience that was eager to keep lit the Wilsonian flame, FDR asserted that the world's problems were caused by a relatively small minority. Though he harbored some doubts about the Germans, he believed that "in every country the people themselves are more peaceably and liberally inclined than their governments."[2] He suggested that:

> The blame for the danger to world peace lies not in the world population but in the leaders of that population. . . . Back of the threat to world peace lies the fear and perhaps even the possibility that the other 10% of the people of the world may go along with a leadership which seeks territorial expansion at the expense of neighbors. . . . If that 10% of the world population can be persuaded by the other 90% to do their own thinking and not be so finely led, we will have practical peace, permanent peace, real peace throughout the world.[3]

Inasmuch as FDR still tends to be viewed as a realistic statesman, it is worth pointing out how directly contrary this statement of personal belief was to the kinds of assumptions that underlay the traditional realist approach. In his famous recipe book for statesmen, *The Prince,* Niccolò Machiavelli had maintained that "a man striving in every way to be good will meet his ruin among the great number who are not good."[4] In contrast, FDR's contention in his 1936 annual message to Congress that "peace is jeopardized by the few and not by the many" reversed the proportions of Machiavelli's ingredients by emphasizing that the world was fundamentally a moral and peacefully inclined place.

FDR was long accused, along with his secretary of state, Cordell Hull, of resorting to a preachy style in foreign relations, and preachment was an essential element of his early foreign policy views. "It is only through constant education and the stressing of the ideals of peace that those who still seek imperialism can be brought in line with the majority," he said.[5] FDR was not engaged solely in the missionary task of converting a small group of infidels. Precisely because there existed a great body of believers, FDR assumed, like any good pastor, that the function of preaching was to remind his congregation, which might be occasionally susceptible to heretical views, of the generally accepted precepts of internationalism, while hoping at the same time to win back the few genuine apostates.

Shrewd politician that he was, FDR realized that the Wilsonian creed could not be read literally. Practically speaking, he knew that American membership in the League of Nations was a dead issue. At best, the United States might become affiliated with League organs like the World Court and its functional agencies. But, with opponents calling the court "nothing but a court of babble, ballyhoo, and bunk—a court of intrigue," the Senate decisively rejected American membership in January 1935, thereby severely limiting the president's options for linking the nation to collective security.[6]

Direct political association with the League was out of the question. Should the League decide to embargo an aggressor under article 16, the United States might conceivably help out by cooperating with League economic sanctions. But that kind of limited and indirect collaboration, even though motivated by Wilsonian sympathies, was a far cry from the American leadership that Wilson had believed indispensable to the success of the world organization. Much as he may have disliked it, FDR always understood that domestic political realities prevented Wilsonianism from ever being resurrected. Whatever future it had would be the result of reincarnation, not a rebirth.

Roosevelt's Wilsonian sense of international crisis was at first obscured by his desperate desire to find a way out of the depression, even if that meant having to abandon, for the time being, international economic cooperation. Like many other governments of the day, FDR's New Deal was drawn to the new ideological fashions in which the idea of national planning seemed a plausible and attractive alternative to the marketplace ideal. The rising challengers to liberalism, fascism and communism, championed collectivist and statist ideas of social and economic organization that had as their immediate focus the salvation of the nation. But the Stalinist program of building socialism in one country and the nationalist economics of fascism were not alone in their faith in managed economies. In the United States, where the depression was more severe than anywhere else, Americans for a time also turned away from international cooperation in order to explore domestic paths to economic recovery. With nationalist solutions in the ascendant, economic—and political—internationalism would have to be placed on hold.

Thus one of the first major foreign policy decisions of Roosevelt's presidency was his refusal to follow the internationalist script written by Hoover for the London Economic Conference of 1933. Hoover tried, without success, to get FDR to commit himself to a program of international currency stabilization in the hope that fixed currency ratios, free of unsettling devaluations, would restore predictability and confidence to international markets. FDR thought otherwise, however, and lectured the other powers at London about slavishly following the "old fetishes of so-called international bankers." Domestic recovery measures, especially nationalist attempts at currency reflation aimed at reversing the plummeting wage-price spiral, seemed more promising at the time than international fixes that might restrict domestic policy flexibility.

Given the sorry state of the world and the abysmal condition of the American economy, a policy of international engagement would have been very difficult to justify in any case. The 1932 presidential campaign was fought almost exclusively on domestic issues, as the American people refused even to recognize fast-growing international problems, never mind the remedies that Woodrow Wilson had prescribed to deal with them. That reluctance to deal with the rest of the world extended even to the traditional policy of neutral rights, which had governed American foreign policy for a century and a half during the heyday of isolationism. In the intellectual climate of the 1930s, American participation in World War I was viewed as a *mistake,* not the historically necessary enterprise described by Woodrow Wilson nor even the righteous defense of America's national interest as conceived by irreconcilables like Senator Borah.

This conceptual confusion also extended to American views of communism and fascism. While neither of these ideologies stood much chance of striking deep roots in the United States, there was during Roosevelt's first term a surprising willingness among large numbers of Americans to give them the benefit of the doubt. Mussolini made the trains run on time, it was said, allowing Italian-Americans to feel an enhanced pride as Americans in the new status of their ancestral homeland. Germany seemed a paragon of economic efficiency and prosperity. And the Soviet Union, a beehive of activity with its new Stalinist command system, seemed positively dynamic in comparison to the crippled American economy.

Many Americans detested these ideological newcomers, to be sure, but not from any likelihood that they would make war on the United States. It was their internal appeal, not their ominous external behavior, that gave people pause. Not until the late 1930s, when fascism appeared to be making a grasp for global control, did Americans begin to grapple seriously with the national security implications of totalitarian foreign policies.

The Good Neighbor Policy as Global Model

Ever since the creation of the republic, the nation's policy of Caribbean regionalism, to be properly understood, has needed to be placed in global context. From the 1890s onward, American behavior in Latin America offered solid clues to understanding the changing direction of American policy outside the Western Hemisphere. In the 1930s, Latin American policy, which only a decade earlier had been behind the times, once again stepped to the forefront. The Roosevelt administration continued the trend of the 1920s in which the strict regionalism of the Monroe Doctrine was being shunted onto the tracks of the new internationalism. Beyond that, however, the Good Neighbor Policy, while narrowly regional in one sense, became for a time the lead locomotive in FDR's global train of thought.

The Good Neighbor Policy had been planted in the Hoover administration, but FDR has understandably received most of the credit. As with any grand tree, people are more inclined to pay attention to the magnificent branches and foliage than to the root system. Nevertheless, under Roosevelt's horticultural care, it grew into a very different kind of plant. In its evolution over the course of the decade, the Good Neighbor approach was extraordinarily flexible and could be sold to quite different audiences. It was a regional program—"Peace, like charity, begins at home," FDR explained[7]—but the policy was also meant to operate in "a world of neighbors," not simply a hemispheric community.

The Good Neighbor approach was intended to be a standing counterexample to the bad neighbor policies being pursued in other regions. In Rio de Janeiro in 1936, FDR explained that "The fine record of our relations is the best answer to those pessimists who scoff at the idea of true friendship between nations."[8] He hoped the model would be emulated. "Democracy is still the hope of the world," he said in Buenos Aires. "If we in our generation can continue its successful application in the Americas, it will spread and supersede other methods by which men are governed."[9]

Chameleon-like in its shifting coloration, the Good Neighbor could be either isolationist or internationalist, depending on the political background. For domestic critics of internationalism, it could be defended as a logical outgrowth of hemispheric isolationism. Lining himself up for the time being with the antiwar movement and those who sought to limit

American export profits in the event of another war, FDR promised to do everything possible to ensure that the nation was not once again sucked in." However, he also warned that "We can and will defend ourselves and our neighborhood."[10] Later in the decade, when sounding the global alarm bells, the Good Neighbor Policy would become the basis for community mobilization to ward off a global fascist threat. Capable of being customized into several possible models, the Good Neighbor Policy could be marketed to people with very different foreign policy preferences.

The Good Neighbor got off to a shaky start in 1933 in Cuba, which for thirty-five years had been a protectorate of the United States. A revolution on the island had brought to power Ramon Grau San Martìn, a president too left-wing for the State Department and for America's man in Havana, FDR's good friend and Dutchess County neighbor, Ambassador Sumner Welles. At first, Welles favored military action to force out Grau, but wiser heads prevailed and action was restricted to a more discreet display of warships. Grau's exit was speeded by America's manipulation of the sugar quota, which was vital to Cuba's monoculture economy as the chief source for earning foreign exchange. Only after the administration was assured that control of the island's political system lay in trustworthy hands did it announce the end of the Platt Amendment, which since 1901 had justified intervention in Cuba's internal affairs.

The administration soon put behind it these opening-night jitters and began to speak its lines with greater assurance. At the Montevideo Pan-American Conference of 1933, the U.S. finally renounced the right of intervention it had so arrogantly proclaimed some thirty years earlier under Theodore Roosevelt. Unfortunately, with American envoys no longer acting as proconsuls, the new hands-off attitude meant that the resulting power vacuum was often filled by the military and other authoritarian elites. Distasteful as these developments were, the Roosevelt administration stood by its course. It took Pan-Americanism still farther at the 1936 conference in Buenos Aires, where a number of pathbreaking cultural agreements were signed. The Buenos Aires meeting, said FDR, "should be an inspiration to all peoples of the Americas and an example to the rest of the world."

Indicative of the administration's determination not to stir up trouble south of the border was the agreement reached with Mexico over that nation's 1938 nationalization of foreign-owned oil properties. Though obviously unhappy with the high-handed manner of the Mexican action, the administration swallowed its pride and settled for compensation that amounted to only a few cents on the dollar.

Another important component of the Good Neighbor approach was the administration's opening up of commercial policy. Secretary of State Cordell Hull believed passionately that free trade was a miracle drug suitable for treatment of many different ailments. Besides its economic benefits, its potential usefulness extended also to a liberalization of world politics, since Hull, like many other liberals, was convinced that "the political line-up followed the economic line-up." By promoting an interdependent world economy, free trade made less likely the need or the desire to create self-sufficient empires based on military conquest.

The Reciprocal Trade Agreements Act of 1934 came nowhere near to creating the free trade utopia envisioned by Hull. With FDR still scrambling to find domestic exits from the Great Depression, the moment was hardly ripe for economic internationalism. The accords that were concluded under this act, mostly with Latin American nations, settled for bilateral reciprocity instead of creating a new global system. But, as in other elements of his Latin American policy, FDR was more interested in setting an example to a global congregation of believers. In retrospect, the reciprocal trade agreements bill was the beginning of an historic turnaround from protectionism to free trade. From this point, America's commitment to the freeing up of world trade would gather momentum as the century progressed.

Later in the decade, as the U.S. leaned toward interventionism in Europe and Asia, the Good Neighbor Policy took on a military coloration. In conferences at Lima in 1938 and Havana in 1940, the European danger was stressed. The Lima Declaration announced a determination by American nations to resist "all foreign intervention or activities that may threaten them." To the last, however, the Good Neighbor Policy could be interpreted in radically different ways. Hemispheric solidarity was obviously useful as a strategic platform from which to fight a war in Europe or in Asia. On the other hand, it also made sense if the United States should choose to sit out the war in a regional Fortress America.

The New Neutrality

By 1936, the United States had retreated to a position of neutrality that was entirely new. Isolationism 1930s-style was no mere escape to the past. In contrast to the previous long-standing adherence to neutral rights, which had frequently sucked the United States into foreign complications, the object of the new neutrality was to avoid war, even if that meant abandoning the allegiance to neutral rights. Indeed, the new conception of neutrality in the 1930s was so pervasive that it permeated every foreign policy position. The foreign policy debates of the 1930s envisioned three basic options, all of them different kinds of neutrality: the traditional insistence on neutral rights, a neutral form of collective security, and a new isolationism which was bent on avoiding war at all costs. In each case, the idea of American world leadership, a common theme of the preceding three decades, was absent.

According to psychologists, when individuals experience a confusing disorientation called "cognitive dissonance" they often take comfort in bedrock truths. With trouble brewing abroad in the 1930s, one might have expected Americans to revert to a familiar policy based on neutral rights. But that did not happen. In trying to provide explanations for why the U.S. had intervened in the Great War, isolationists of the 1930s rejected both Wilson's internationalist rationale and the neutral rights argument for involvement. Neither internationalism nor national interest as traditionally understood seemed appealing. With the discrediting of the sunny internationalism of the 1920s and the emergence of the new neutrality, the United States was operating, for the first time since the War of 1812, without an effective foreign policy tradition.

By the mid-1930s, America's involvement in World War I was widely viewed as an enormous blunder in which the nation had been maneuvered into belligerency by special interests. Many lurid accounts suggested that money was the cause, whether lust on the part of munitions makers for the obscene profits of war or the desire of Wall Street investment bankers to profit by lending money to the Entente powers. The Nye Committee, created by the Senate in 1934 to investigate the issue, gave its blessing to this simpleminded account of America's entry into the war. Because the money power was unpopular for its role in provoking the depression, it was not surprising that the prevailing suspicion of big business should have rubbed off on foreign policy. Roosevelt himself bore some responsibility for creating a climate of domestic politics that was hostile to internationalism, for by diverting resentment of the robber barons into domestic reform channels, he was implicitly discouraging a policy of international engagement.

Inasmuch as the quest for commercial profit was at the root of neutral rights, a return to traditional isolation seemed out of the question. The isolationist Bennett Champ Clark of Missouri, in the course of Senate arguments on the first neutrality act, realized that there was no going back. "The United States of America cannot," he insisted, "turn back to a policy of so-called neutrality that finally pulls us into a conflict with one or all of the belligerents."[11] In a backhanded way, this argument recognized the strength of Wilsonian arguments that modern war was too terrible to contemplate fighting. "Let us not claim as a right what is an impossibility," he said. "The only way we can maintain our neutral rights is to fight the whole world." Clark concluded that "the detour around another devastating war is to be found only in new conceptions of neutrality."[12] For the new isolationists, then, the evils of modern war overshadowed the benefits of fighting for trade.

Clark's view, shared by many other isolationists, recognized that a basic prop of the old isolationism was no longer in force: the existence of an occasionally bothersome but fundamentally friendly and manageable international environment. In its recognition that this comfortable global milieu had disappeared, the isolationist fear of war was an expression of one of the deepest concerns about the irresistible pull of global modernity. However, unlike Wilson, who had concluded that modern conditions of war made it impossible to stay out, those who rejected traditional neutrality believed that there was a way. The Great War, they contended, had been a *European* war and not the kind of global conflict into which the United States could not help but be drawn.

The floodwaters of isolationist legislation started to rise with the Johnson Debt Default Act of 1934, which forbade any new private loans to governments who had defaulted on their World War I debt. With the exception of Finland, just about all of America's debtors had defaulted by June 1934, which many Americans thought every bit as reprehensible as the treaty violations committed by Germany, Italy, and Japan. Still more expressive of the temper of the times was the Ludlow Resolution, first introduced in 1935, which called for a constitutional amendment that would have required a public referendum on war. Although as many as 73 percent of those polled in 1937 favored its passage, Roosevelt rallied his troops in the House, arguing that such an amendment would "cripple any President in his conduct of our foreign relations." Proposals like the Ludlow amendment, he maintained, "appeal to people who, frankly, have no conception of what modern war, with or without a declaration of war, involves."[13]

Unfortunately for FDR, internationalist arguments fared no better than traditional views in this fear-ridden new climate of opinion. By the time he became president, Roosevelt had already discarded any ambitions for having the United States join the League of Nations, though he continued to believe in collective security. In the absence of American membership, for a time he thought that it might be possible to engineer a solution in which the United States could cooperate to good effect with the League without becoming a member.

The scheme was launched by Norman Davis, America's representative to the Geneva disarmament conference in 1933. Seeking to breathe new life into the flagging negotiations, Davis suggested, with FDR's approval, an approach in which the United States would pledge not to interfere with any economic sanctions placed by the League against aggressor nations. This voluntary cooperation with the League, by renouncing any desire to trade with aggressors, was an abandonment of neutral rights policy. "These former rights of neutrality which are becoming somewhat obsolete today are now merely rights to get into trouble as the world has evolved today," said Davis.[14] In 1933, legislation was introduced before Congress which would have given the president the discretion to declare an embargo—a cutoff of trade—with aggressor nations.

However, this legislation was soon reworked by congressional isolationists in a way that subverted the president's intentions. Instead of giving Roosevelt the right to penalize an aggressor, the bill was rewritten to apply mandatorily to *all* belligerents. In the event of war, the United States would help the League by not trading with the aggressor, but an impartial embargo might at the same time hurt the victims of aggression. As for cooperation with collective security, this isolationist enactment was supposed to take effect whether or not the League acted.

By 1935, after fermenting in committee for the better part of two years, the first of the neutrality acts embodying the new isolationism was distilled by Congress. It provided for a mandatory arms embargo against *all* belligerents. The Neutrality Act of 1936 took matters a step farther by banning loans to belligerent powers. Still another bill in 1937 banned travel on belligerent vessels and authorized Roosevelt to provide that certain raw materials other than munitions be purchased on a "cash and carry" basis. "Today marks the downfall . . . of the internationalist," crowed Senator Hiram Johnson of California.

The first application of the neutrality legislation, in response to Italy's invasion and conquest of Ethiopia in October 1935, showed how uncertain its effects abroad could be. Italy complained about the U.S. arms embargo even though the U.S. continued to export other industrial materials of war. Meanwhile, the League dithered as Ethiopia was swallowed up. The "malevolent neutrality" toward the Spanish Civil War which started in 1937 was equally disadvantageous to the victim of aggression.[15] Technically, the embargo provision did not apply to civil wars, but FDR invoked the neutrality act anyway to keep the isolationists happy. The U.S. embargo paralleled an arms cutoff imposed by Great Britain and France against the Republican government in Madrid. Unfortunately, with the Germans and the Italians freely providing covert military aid to Francisco Franco's forces, U.S. policy worked to the advantage of the fascists.

In passing legislation designed to make war less likely, Congress was acting on the basis of "lessons of the past." To be sure, there was some fear that history would repeat itself. But the deeper fear was of history itself, of the implications of the global modernization process which was fast entangling the nation in global webs that no one could fully comprehend or control. The influential historian Charles Beard was one of the few who understood that the debate over America's course, far from being about interests, was at bottom an argument about how the nation chose to understand and respond to world history. "Horrible as the thought may be for simple minds," he wrote of the conspiracy-tinged isolationist mind in *The Devil Theory of War,* "it is a fact that such a policy, indeed every large public policy, is *an interpretation of history*—past, in the making, and to be made."[16]

Himself an isolationist, Beard believed that the United States was ready to abandon the global interpretation of history that had guided the nation into the twentieth century. Convinced that the old traditions had been played out, he had enough self-assurance to believe that he could, with his pen and his imagination, create yet another compelling historical vision, "an ideal conception of the American nation in its world relations." *The Open Door at Home* was his attempt to portray an alternative future in which the United States was politically and economically disconnected from the world, blessed with a self-contained economy which, with only a necessary modicum of planning, would be capable of providing full employment and social justice.

According to Beard, to give up isolation "for a mess of pottage in the form of profits on cotton goods, tobacco, petroleum, and automobiles, is to make grand policy subservient to special interests [and] to betray the security of the American nation."[17] Nationality, not interests, ought to govern American foreign policy. For Beard, internationalism was merely an illusion, a pretty ideological mask concealing the ugly realities of special interests operating beneath. "If we go to war," he argued, "let us go to war for some grand national and human advantage openly discussed and deliberately arrived at, and not to bail out farmers, bankers and capitalists or to save politicians from the pain of dealing with a domestic crisis."[18]

Beard's radically nationalist message fell on deaf ears. With few exceptions, isolationists of the 1930s were not ready to accept the thorough-going program of economic nationalism that would have been required to make a reality of Beard's continentalism. But even if more intellectuals had jumped on Beard's rather lonely bandwagon, isolationism as a political movement was incapable of creating a compelling new worldview. Much of isolationism's broad appeal was attributable to the fact that it

was a coalition composed of widely varying types: belligerent nationalists, pacifistic internationalists, leftist radicals, conservatives, and foreign-
oriented supporters of either fascism or, at certain times, communism. But
a combination of this breadth, while well suited to the political task of
rejecting internationalism and traditional policy, could only be united by
negatives. And, in any case, the isolationists were hardly capable of creating an alternative worldview virtually overnight. Given these formidable
limitations, the eventual victory of internationalism in the 1930s may have
been due less to its merits than to the shortcomings of isolationism.

But at least the issues were being clarified. FDR's decision to accept
rigid neutrality legislation in 1935 was based, quite apart from the need
to bow before the politically inevitable, on his agreement with the isolationists that neutral rights, rooted in narrow notions of economic interest,
was indeed an old-fashioned justification for war.[19] The choice between
isolationism and internationalism as it emerged in the late 1930s was not
a choice between tradition and Wilsonian utopianism. It was, rather, a
choice between a *new* kind of isolationism that was far more radical and
consequential than the old and a *new,* or neo-Wilsonian, internationalism.[20]

In this match-up, Wilsonianism possessed a number of advantages: it
had a well-defined sense of what constituted a modern global crisis and
it benefited, despite its novelties, from being more deeply grounded in
tradition. Whereas the isolationism of the 1930s was, by comparison, a
historically rootless doctrine, internationalism reached back well into the
nineteenth century. Wilsonianism's idealistic side remained attractive to
a few believers, but far more important than utopianism to its revival was
its latent ability to evoke the sense of global peril that Wilson had tried
unsuccessfully to convey in 1917 and after. Although the distressing trend
of global events in the late 1930s would go a long way toward making
possible the revival of Wilsonianism, it could not provide indisputable
objective grounds for its victory. To the very last moment, it remained
possible to make a credible isolationist case against involvement. No matter how alarmist its outlook, Wilsonianism remained a form of idealism
because even its definition of threat was rooted in historical imagination.

The Two Wars, 1937–1941

The existence of heavy public resistance to interventionism right down
to the morning of the Japanese attack on Pearl Harbor, not to mention the
confusing manner in which the United States became involved, suggests a
historical problem of enormous dimensions that is even more debatable

than the knotty issue of intervention in World War I. Yet American involvement in World War II has generated very little in the way of historical controversy, far less than would have been predicted at the time. A neo-isolationist critique was indeed launched after the war, by Beard and a few others, but it swam in vain against the current of opinion. This relative immunity from historical criticism was the result of the belated triumph of a now-dominant Wilsonian worldview. Much of that triumph was due to the reawakening, by events between 1937 and 1941, of Wilsonianism's dormant sense of fear.

In 1937, the smoldering underbrush of Chinese and Japanese hostility was ignited into the blaze of the Sino-Japanese War. In Europe, after a period of respite following the Rhineland episode, Hitler began to move very rapidly. In March 1938, the Führer's forces marched into Austria and united that country with Germany, contrary to the Treaty of Versailles, in the famous *Anschluss.* That summer, Hitler raised tensions over the fate of the Sudeten Germans in the neighboring country of Czechoslovakia by threatening war if they were not reunited with the Reich. This crisis ended with the famous Munich accords in October, in which the French and the British agreed to "appease" Hitler. In return for the transfer of the Sudetenland and its three and one-half million Germans, Hitler pledged not to make any more territorial demands.

However, the appeasement episode was only a prelude. In March 1939, the Wehrmacht goose-stepped into Prague, effectively eliminating the Czechoslovak state. Shortly thereafter, Hitler provoked a crisis with Poland over the "Polish Corridor," a narrow strip of real estate created at Versailles that gave Poland access to the sea at the cost of separating the main body of Germany from East Prussia. This time, Britain and France made clear, there would be no further appeasement: a German war with Poland would mean a general war in Europe. Hitler then amazed the world by signing a nonaggression pact with the Soviet Union, his chief ideological enemy, in August 1939. Besides guaranteeing a single-front war for the German army, a secret annex to the treaty partitioned Poland between the two formerly hostile totalitarian powers. This deal allowed the USSR to retrieve the territory it had lost to Poland in 1921.

The situation continued to evolve with breathtaking swiftness. The Nazi invasion of Poland on September 1 was successfully completed in six weeks. During a period of "phony war" in the west, the Germans invaded Denmark and Norway. In May 1940, German mechanized forces poured into France via Belgium and the Ardennes Forest and routed a confused and demoralized French army. By the end of June, France had surrendered and the collaborationist regime of Marshall Pétain had taken control of the unoccupied portion of France from the new capital city of Vichy. Meanwhile, the evacuation of the British expeditionary force on the beaches of Dunkirk in Belgium narrowly averted another major victory for Germany.

Next, Hitler prepared for an invasion of the British Isles. While readying an invasion fleet in the channel ports, the Luftwaffe attempted to soften up the British population by a campaign of terror bombing. Fortunately for the British, the "Battle of Britain" remained largely an air war. The Royal Air Force, assisted enormously by its possession of secret radar technology, regularly intercepted the German air fleets and inflicted unacceptable casualties. The invasion barges being assembled for a cross-channel assault were mercilessly strafed and bombed to pieces by the RAF.

Failing to bring Britain to heel, Hitler next turned against the Soviet Union. On June 22, 1941, German armies launched "Operation Barbarossa" against their erstwhile ally, fully expecting to deliver a quick knockout punch. Although the German armies, ill-equipped for winter warfare, bogged down outside of Moscow and Leningrad as the harsh Russian winter set in, most experts anticipated an assault of redoubled fury in the next campaigning season. If the USSR collapsed, Hitler would be master of the continent.

In Asia, the tempo of events also picked up. While continuing their war of expansion in China, the Japanese set their sights on the southwestern Pacific, a region attractive to Tokyo for its mineral resources and oil. Recognizing the connection between events in their respective spheres of action, the Japanese and the Germans signed the Tripartite Pact in September 1940, a treaty that sought to keep the United States out of the war. Should one party be attacked by a nation currently neutral in the world conflict, i.e., the U.S., the others were supposed to come to the aid of their cosignatories. Another fateful diplomatic bargain was concluded shortly thereafter. On the mistaken assumption that Hitler and Stalin would remain allies, Japan concluded a non aggression pact with the Soviet Union in April 1941, thereby confirming the policy of "Southern Advance." Then in July, as a prelude to further advances in the region, Japanese forces occupied southern Indochina, the northern portion having been occupied the previous year, with no resistance from a helpless Vichy French colonial regime.

Dismaying and ominous as they were, none of these developments made American intervention inevitable. What mattered was how Americans interpreted these events, for there existed no hard or objective criteria of national interest that compelled the United States to get involved.[21] Nor did there exist a compelling international "structure" that might have made U.S. intervention mandatory in Europe or Asia, or in both regions. FDR once confessed that "in spite of every possible forethought, international relations involve of necessity a vast uncharted area."[22] Given the ambiguity, indeterminacy, and confusion built into the world situation, America's slow tilt toward intervention was the result of the president and his advisers acting from a Wilsonian interpretation of the situation. But it need not have been this way. Another president, one who shared Herbert Hoover's outlook, for example, might have reacted in an altogether different manner and generated very different outcomes.

Interpretation and creation are very closely related human activities. Besides providing a key for decoding current events, FDR's global Wilsonian perspective was to some extent self-fulfilling, for it was only as a result of American participation that the two separate wars in Europe and Asia were united into a Second World War. World War II was, in a literal sense, the product of America's historical imagination.

FDR and the Wilsonian Definition
of the Global Threat

It was against this rapidly changing background of events that the United States drifted into the war. By the end of 1941, FDR had managed to steer the ship of state to an internationalist heading by committing massive quantities of aid to Great Britain, while in the Pacific the U.S. took the lead in stiffening the backs of an anti-Japanese coalition. But this bare-bones résumé gives American policy the appearance of being more clear and purposeful than it seemed at the time. The Roosevelt administration did have a clear sense of the totalitarian problem; its internationalist solution, however, was based on little more than a leap of faith in the correctness of the internationalist vision of history.

For a time, FDR himself was laid low by the isolationist bug. Indeed, he would have been a poor excuse for a politician had he not been so smitten. In 1936, he explained that he had long since decided that "the United States could best serve the cause of peaceful humanity by setting an example."[23] Reading another verse from the isolationist bible, FDR declared that "We are not isolationists except in so far as we seek to isolate ourselves completely from war."[24] "I hate war," he insisted, and promised that he would do everything possible to prevent America from becoming involved in yet another world conflict.

This was, however, a qualified isolationism that failed to deal with the sources of the problem as defined by principled isolationists like Beard or, later, by Herbert Hoover. For Beard, trade was the taproot of overseas involvement; for FDR, international commerce always remained part of the solution. "Without a more liberal international trade, war is a natural sequence" he told the same audience in 1936.[25] So, unless the world reverted to liberal ways, war was unavoidable, after all.

As HIS CONTINUED emphasis on disarmament and free trade suggested, FDR was never content to accept the unruly world of the 1930s as the normal state of affairs. Along with Secretary of State Hull, who spoke endlessly of the need to abide by fundamental principles, Roosevelt continued to champion liberal change in the international order. Until 1937, American policy was dominated largely by preachment in an attempt to win over the remaining 10 percent of world opinion. In his 1935 State of the Union address, noting the rise of undemocratic regimes, FDR said: "I hope that calm counsel and constructive leadership will provide the steadying influence and the time necessary for the coming of new and more practical forms of representative government throughout the world wherein privilege and power will occupy a lesser place and world welfare a greater."[26]

Deep down, Roosevelt must have had his doubts about relying on world opinion alone without the sanction of force to back it up. Wilson, after all, had been convinced that world opinion without power was futile. As the failed policies of the 1920s had shown, an internationalism without force, a politics without commitment, was unlikely to succeed. It must have been with some measure of relief, then, that Roosevelt in 1937 went back to his earlier emphasis on cooperation with the international community. By that time, the Italian invasion of Ethiopia had succeeded, the fascist challenge to the leftist government in Madrid had erupted into the Spanish Civil War, and the Japanese invasion of China proper was well under way. Ultimately, FDR's bent for political cooperation, gradually extended year by year, would bring the United States into the war.

FDR's quarantine address, delivered in October 1937, announced that "a reign of terror and international lawlessness" had "now reached a stage where the very foundations of civilization are seriously threatened." Comparing the situation to an outbreak of epidemic disease—a telling metaphor, since plagues often spared isolated human communities—FDR suggested that in such circumstances "the community approves and joins in a quarantine of the patients in order to protect the health of the community against the spread of the disease." Using Wilsonian language, FDR declared that "war is a contagion" that could "engulf states and peoples remote from the scene of original hostilities"—including, obviously, even the United States. The decent 90 percent of the world population "can and must find some way to make their will prevail," he said.

The critical uproar provoked by this speech made clear that the public was not ready for the kind of international cooperation suggested by FDR. A ready-to-hand occasion for displaying a united sense of purpose, a meeting in Brussels of signatories to the 9-power treaty of 1922, failed to agree on any sanctions that might put some bite into their condemnation of Japanese behavior in China. And, as if to confirm the lack of consensus in the United States, the panic at the possibility of war that followed the Japanese bombing of the gunboat *Panay* on the Yangtze River in China demonstrated the absence of even the minimal resolve that FDR had in mind. A greater sense of alarm at events abroad, a perception that war was the lesser danger, as well as a better articulation of the stakes—all these would be necessary if Roosevelt hoped to rally the American public.

Roosevelt himself was not yet prepared to cast policy into a neo-Wilsonian mold. Indeed, as late as 1938, it was apparent that he had not wholly abandoned his reliance upon a non-mobilized world public opinion. This was evident from his acceptance of the results of the "appeasement" policy at Munich, which assumed that Germany, once she was glutted with territory, would reenter the community of nations. One of the biggest revelations of the Munich accords, FDR revealed to a number of his correspondents, was the existence of a widespread "will to peace," which translated into an isolationist desire to avoid war. His optimism was evident, too, from his desire to convene a world economic conference, originally proposed by Under Secretary Sumner Welles, that would guarantee access to markets and raw materials for the "have not" powers. The willingness to engage in economic appeasement suggested that the administration believed an agreement on reestablishing a liberal world order, a world of normal internationalism, was still within reach.

In the aftermath of Munich, and especially the officially sanctioned anti-Jewish riots of *Kristallnacht* that took place throughout Germany in November 1938, FDR abandoned his reliance upon words. His new policy had two points of reference. First, instead of looking to world opinion, he now sought to educate the American public. Second, he no longer focused on the evils of war. As the situation in Europe and Asia deteriorated, he began to emphasize instead a more pressing danger: the intolerable situation that would face the United States if the Axis powers won. Wilson had also raised the possibility of global domination, but his rhetoric had clearly targeted war as the biggest problem facing the world. For FDR, the issue of war became secondary to the global threat.

The danger envisioned by FDR can, without putting too fine a point on it, be summed up in two words: world conquest. Though the Nazis had no immediate plans to take on the United States and the Japanese were content to carve out an empire in Asia and the Pacific, Roosevelt believed that these two expanding systems would, in combination, pose a mortal threat to the United States. Economically, German and Japanese control of large portions of the world would foreclose any possibility of free trade. Commerce would have to be politically managed. To get along on the basis of reciprocity, the United States would undoubtedly have to impose export and import controls. Looking for precedents, FDR pointed to the economic depression caused by Thomas Jefferson's embargo policy. "The whole fabric of working life as we know it—business and manufacturing, mining and agriculture—all would be mangled and crippled" under a Nazi-dominated world system, he insisted.[27]

The economic danger was but one dimension of the problem, since Germany and Japan expanded by military means. Nazi ideology glorified war and violence as basic elements of life, while Japanese society was increasingly dominated by military values. New military technology, FDR believed, would soon enable the enemy to reach the U.S. in a matter of hours. Merely holding these nations at arm's length would call for a huge military establishment in a high state of permanent readiness and would require an ongoing willingness to engage in arms races in which the other side might well possess superior resources. It would, moreover, require a diplomacy steeped in the cynical pragmatics of power, allying with one party or the other as warranted by circumstances. In one of his broadcast fireside chats, FDR argued that "to survive in such a world, we would have to convert ourselves permanently into a militaristic power on the basis of war economy."[28] In the phrase of the day, the U.S. would have to become a "garrison state" that in many ways mimicked its ideological opposite numbers.

Most worrisome of all, perhaps, were the ideological implications of allowing Germany and Japan to have their way. To some extent, international ideologies are fruits that grow from the tree of power. If the fascist nations had been allowed to carve up the world for themselves, then it seemed quite possible that the tree of democracy might disappear from the global orchard. The Spanish Civil War was quite disturbing in this respect. "The war in Spain is certainly not a civil war. It is an international conflict for the testing of the world's spirit by the fascist international,"[29] said FDR's ambassador to Spain, Claude Bowers. The conflict suggested that the future would fall to either fascism or to communism, while the democratic powers stood irrelevantly to the side, rubbing their hands raw with worry.

Could democracy continue to exist in one country as a purely national creed? Or, stripped of its universalist pretensions, would the doctrine that "all men are created equal" lose its legitimacy? FDR doubted whether liberal democracy, an ecumenical creed, could survive as an ideological atoll in a rising sea of totalitarian doctrines. Even isolationism had presumed the capacity to influence all mankind for the better through the power of example. Perhaps America could hold out in a totalitarian world, but only if America redefined itself. If expansionist totalitarianism triumphed abroad, the American way of life would have to be radically transformed. America's self-conception as a nation, its political and economic culture, the American creed, all these would have to change.

Conceived of in this way, the threat was very modern. The problem was not a direct menace to the nation's existence. Rather, the threat to America's identity and the American way of life emanated from the deterioration of the international environment. The choice confronting the nation was the kind faced by people in a crime-ridden community in which traditional police methods had failed. In the face of rampant thuggery, one could put bars on the windows, install alarms, and remain perpetually alert to repel intruders. FDR's worst fears envisioned the U.S. as "a lone island in a world dominated by fear . . . a people lodged in prison, handcuffed, hungry and fed through the bars from day to day by the contemptuous, unpitying masters of other continents."[30] This kind of world would have been, in FDR's words, "a shabby and dangerous place to live in." It would also have been quite different from the friendlier international environment of the past.

In the final analysis, it was irrelevant whether or not the United States was immediately or directly threatened by Japan or Germany. The central issue for internationalists was not whether the United States could survive in a world dominated by totalitarian states (it could); far more important was the question of *how* it would have to survive. Democracy in one country was even less viable than the idea of socialism in one country. "The sphere of our international relationships would shrivel," predicted Cordell Hull, "until we would stand practically alone among the nations, a self-constituted hermit state."[31] If the price of survival was the loss of the American way of life, FDR believed that the price, exacted by not going to war, was too high to pay.

Still, the emergence of this kind of world was, by Roosevelt's own admission, quite conjectural. Given its hypothetical nature, it is not surprising that this internationalist sense of danger was criticized by the isolationists. Even some of FDR's closest advisers from time to time questioned the reality of the perils being conjured up by the president. William

Bullitt, for example, once warned FDR that "there is no basis of policy more unreal or disastrous than the apprehension of remote future dangers."[32] Had the United States chosen to do nothing at all, this nightmarish world might not have come into being. Britain might well have survived, a balance-of-power peace might have established itself in Europe, a negotiated solution might have been arrived at, and the Japanese might have discovered, as Herbert Hoover predicted, that in invading China they had bitten off more than they could chew. Age-old principles of power balancing might well have reasserted themselves. And the effects of the new military technologies could be interpreted in more positive ways. For example, the isolationist Senator Robert Taft (son of the president) maintained that "air power has made it more difficult to transport an army across an ocean and that conquest must still be by a land army."[33]

Why take steps toward involvement, then, if danger was not staring one directly in the face? Why take seriously a threat that, according to University of Chicago president Robert Maynard Hutchins, rested "on a pyramid of assumptions, hypotheses, and guesses"?[34] Why make policy on the basis of worst-case assumptions about the future? Because, Roosevelt believed, in the modern world one couldn't afford not to do so. Allowing the totalitarian nightmare to become a reality was "a possibility no farsighted statesman could afford to permit."[35] The point was also made in a State Department draft of a radio address for FDR. "There has been a tendency," it said, "on the part of all of us to concentrate too much on the immediate present as it concerns us rather than to think of the ultimate consequences to this nation of a continuance of this collapse of law and order."[36] After awakening to such a reality, there would be no second chance to set things right.

Diplomacy and strategy in the modern world were different. The old rules of power and diplomacy and warfare no longer applied. Modern technology had annihilated distance, FDR was fond of pointing out, having shrunk the globe to the point that geographic isolation offered no guarantee of security. The economic integration of the world meant that time, space, and history were the same for all. Moreover, the speed with which events moved in the modern world made things all the more frightening. The rapidity of totalitarian conquests meant that one could not afford to sit by and wait until the fog of peace had lifted. By that time it might be too late. Because time, space, and velocity had changed—the basic forms with which one constituted the world—one had to gauge the trajectory of events beforehand, lest history pass one by.

Events in 1939 and 1940 appeared to confirm FDR's bleak view. The signing of the Tripartite Pact in September 1940 solidified the image among American internationalists of a global conspiracy of gangster nations. Structurally, the danger FDR was describing was clearly Wilsonian in provenance. The end of the European balance of power, the danger of world conquest, the corresponding danger of world war, the newly discovered importance of out-of-the-way places to American security, the danger of revolution—all these themes had been present in Woodrow Wilson's attempt to define the Great War's radical historical meaning. Now, as war loomed on the horizon, FDR was able to embroider each of these points in grim detail. In so doing, FDR did not have to worry about neutral rights as a complicating factor.

By contrast, it would appear at first glance that the isolationists, who insisted upon responding to immediate and obvious threats, operated from an outlook more deserving of the name "realist." Their unwillingness to become involved in another war unless America was directly threatened in its own back yard suggests that a sense of imminent, objective danger was the touchstone of their policy. If, however, the dynamics of the modern world are radically novel, one cannot say with any certainty that the isolationists had a superior grasp of the issues. Indeed, the isolationist fear of involvement was itself rooted in the intuition that modern war was different and that the international environment had changed radically. Fear of war was fear of the Wilsonian world. And isolationists had no conclusive proof that FDR was not right. Roosevelt was at least working from a well-established sense of international history of which his version of Wilsonianism was but an elaboration. The isolationists, meanwhile, in rejecting even the limited internationalism of the past, were operating in a historical void.

Not surprisingly, then, given the different assumptions and the absence of any objective standard of proof, the two sides talked past one another in the great debate of 1940–41. The White Committee, an internationalist group that sought to awaken public opinion to the threat, argued that the survival of Great Britain was essential to American security. America First, the isolationist lobby, insisted that aid to Britain would bring war, thereby endangering the U.S. Ostensibly an argument over what the United States ought to do, at a deeper level the great debate was a hopelessly irreconcilable quarrel about how threats ought to be defined in the first place. The peril, depending on one's point of view, was isolation or involvement.

How could so many people differ on a subject on which, one would think, agreement could be readily reached? One of the cherished assumptions of internationalism holds that knowledge of the world is destructive of the isolationist mentality. But the great debate was a quite remarkable demonstration of the difficulty of defining national security in a modern environment in which danger was not objectively manifest and in which there existed no objective grounds of knowledge. There was no way of viewing the situation realistically. Because the old cultural definitions no longer held authority, the society possessed no equivalent of animal instinct, which automatically triggers a defensive response. Each side's argument was quite rational, based on its assumptions. There was no correct answer to be arrived at by referring to strategic realities because the argument was about history, or interpretations of history, and not about strategy based on hard economic or political interests visible to everyone, like an army massing at the border. Reality was itself very much in flux and its definition up for grabs.

The Conflict between Strategy and Worldview

More often than not, FDR's approach has been characterized as a global realpolitik. It is true that he believed that "the hostilities in Europe, in Africa, and in Asia are all part of a single world conflict" and that "our strategy of defense must be a global strategy which takes account of every front." Nevertheless, there are a number of reasons to doubt FDR's realism. The first has to do with the distinctive neo-Wilsonian way in which he defined the Axis threat to the United States. Instead of acting to protect well-established economic and strategic interests, FDR chose instead an idealist definition of threat in which the liberal course of world history was endangered. The second has to do with the strange manner in which the United States got into the war. All the steps that FDR took with a view to aiding Britain, Russia, and China while keeping the U.S. out, instead sucked the country into the war with an inevitability that seems clear only in hindsight. In this way, FDR pioneered a strategy that took Wilsonianism beyond the collective security framework and provided a preview of the kind of dilemmas that would plague policy-makers in the cold war.

The third reason has to do with outcomes. It has often been suggested that the United States was pursuing a realistic diplomacy after all in its concern to prevent Europe from being dominated by a hostile power and thwart Japan's desire to become the hegemonic power in Asia and the Pacific. The problem with this argument is that the U.S., by intervening, effectively *destroyed* the balance of power in these two regions of the world. That outcome cannot be explained in terms of traditional realism. Thus perception, action, and outcome were closely related. The way in which the threat was defined ruled out any "realistic" way of dealing with it, which in turn led to an outcome that violated realist standards.

FDR's administration was caught in 1940 and 1941 between the conflicting demands of a novel sense of global danger and a traditional understanding of strategy that made it necessary to rank specific geographic regions in order of importance. Roosevelt was never able to reconcile the two. This tension between the differentiations of traditional strategy and the holistic Wilsonian worldview created a huge conceptual gap between the war plans of the administration and the way it actually got into the war. Ultimately, internationalism, despite all its uncertainties, took precedence, yielding spectacularly successful results.

The administration unambiguously preferred a Europe-first strategy which defined Germany as the primary threat. The RAINBOW plans (which implied that the next war would be "multicolored," i.e., the U.S. would have more than one major opponent on its hands) appeared late in 1939. The next year, RAINBOW-5 was selected and refined in the navy's Plan D. Early in 1941, talks with the British and Canadian military staffs led to approval of a document called ABC-1. According to these plans for a two-front conflict, the U.S. would fight a defensive war against Japan until Germany was defeated. By implication, diplomacy would play a vital role in implementing this strategy. Ideally, a skillful diplomacy might be able to avoid war with Japan altogether by stringing out negotiations until Germany had been defeated.

Things never worked out that way. While the military, still operating on a traditional realistic wavelength, generally pushed for the diplomats to step on the brakes in the Pacific, the State Department, which was attuned to a modern Wilsonian assessment of the crisis, stepped on the gas. The end result was a crisis that led the country into war on two fronts at the same time, a war that it prosecuted, moreover, with equal vigor despite the selective strategy called for by Rainbow-5. Thus America, on the basis of a unified understanding of events that were not necessarily connected to each other, transformed two quite separate wars in Europe and in Asia into World War II.

The suddenness with which the war arrived stood in contrast to the agonized and uncertain diplomacy that led to it. Between 1939 and 1941, American policy retreated from the isolationism of the mid-1930s to a posture of openly pro-British neutrality, but only through a series of incremental steps. This tentativeness was attributable to a variety of factors. Internal divisions between hard-line "hawks" and softer "doves" often produced inconclusive debate and nuanced decisions, as in the case of the embargo of aviation fuel to Japan. Public opinion was in a confused state, with most people expecting war and backing FDR's various steps, while refusing at the same time to support outright interventionism. But probably the biggest cause of uncertainty was the novelty of the policy being implemented. It was not clear, exactly, how to meet the baffling and conflicting demands of the situation. FDR's famous deviousness may, to some extent, have been the product of an indecisiveness produced by the inherent indeterminacy and complexity of the situation.

As soon as the war in Europe broke out, Roosevelt sought a revision of the Neutrality Acts. In November 1939, the arms embargo was repealed, on condition that the belligerents pick up their weapons and munitions at American ports on a cash-and-carry basis. This worked well in the Atlantic, which was dominated by the Royal Navy, but was of little help in the Pacific, where the Japanese had blockaded the China coast. By November 1941, the act was further modified to allow American merchant vessels to deliver cargoes to belligerent ports. No doubt these legislative changes would have led to a maritime crisis not unlike that of 1917, had other events not supervened beforehand. Sensing a major crisis in the offing, in September 1940 Congress mandated peacetime conscription for the first time in American history with a view to training some two million troops.

While Congress was moving back to traditional neutrality, FDR was pushing the nation into uncharted waters, often through liberal use of executive agreements as a way of muting the constitutional voice of the Senate in treaty-making. In response to a request from Prime Minister Winston Churchill for help for the overstretched Royal Navy, in September 1940 FDR promised to hand over fifty World War I destroyers in return for the right to garrison some British bases in the Western Hemisphere. Importantly, too, the agreement stipulated that the Royal Navy would flee to American waters in the event of a British surrender rather than be scuttled or turned over to the Germans. The destroyers-for-bases deal was vintage Roosevelt, capable of being viewed admiringly, like the Picasso portraits that combined both frontal and profile views, in either an interventionist or isolationist light.

In December 1940, FDR plunged further ahead, with a proposal that was designed to make the United States "the arsenal of democracy." The British had by this time exhausted the dollar assets with which they were purchasing American supplies. The straightforward course would have been to provide financial credit to Great Britain, but this avenue was closed off by bad memories of the World War I experience. So, instead of advancing money, FDR proposed to supply the goods directly, using the ingenious analogy of lending a fire hose to a neighbor whose house was on fire. Since no money was actually changing hands, and the loaned supplies were to be returned at war's end, the administration was able through this clever tactic to circumvent the intent of the Johnson Act.

Following a fierce last-gasp debate between isolationists and international-ists, Lend-Lease, which had been given the patriotic docket number H.R. 1776, passed with comfortable majorities in March 1941.

Given the persistence of powerful isolationist sentiment and the less articulate but widespread public fear of war, the destroyers-for-bases deal and Lend-Lease could not be justified in straightforward Wilsonian terms. But other arguments were readily available. Aid to Great Britain, for ex-ample, made sense as a way of preserving a traditional European balance. If Britain's survival was a precondition of hemispheric security, the aid could be justified as a measure that sought to restore the relatively benign and familiar world order of old. Moreover, Lend-Lease was hardly a full-blooded interventionist measure. It was an example—an extreme exam-ple, to be sure—of the kind of limited internationalism that FDR had been trying unsuccessfully to sell since the early 1930s. Whatever the mea-sure's actual strategic logic, its publicly stated rationale portrayed it as a way of keeping the United States out of war.

Presciently, FDR saw to it that the Soviet Union would be eligible for Lend-Lease. He had welcomed the Soviet Union back into the family of nations in 1933, when the policy of nonrecognition put into place fol-lowing the Bolshevik revolution was finally lifted. The promise of job-creating trade was one reason for the changeabout, but so too was FDR's premonition that the Soviets might one day become a useful strategic part-ner. At the same time, FDR believed he had resolved some outstanding issues that had clouded the relationship between the two countries. An accord on the Czarist debt was reached and the right of worship within the USSR was acknowledged by the Soviet regime. Moscow also agreed that hostile propaganda against the U.S. would cease.

Although the relationship cooled after the recognition deal and the se-ductive image of trade proved to be a mirage, Roosevelt made sure to maintain a working relationship with the Soviets. For a sizeable stretch of the 1930s, the State Department and significant portions of public opinion viewed Soviet communism as a greater threat than Nazi Germany, a sign perhaps that fear of left-wing radicalism at home was weightier than fears of aggression from abroad. The Ribbentrop-Molotov Pact and the bullying Russo-Finnish war that broke out a few months later further tarnished Stalin's image in American opinion. But FDR's refusal to treat Hitler and Stalin as coevils put him in a position to make the Soviets quickly eligible for Lend-Lease aid after Hitler's invasion on June 22, 1941. This pro-Soviet tilt to FDR's foreign policy, his ability to look beyond ideology to common strategic needs, is the strongest argument in support of those who see him as a realist. But one swallow does not a summer make.

By this time, the administration was taking more assertive steps in the Atlantic. In April, the U.S. signed an agreement with the Danish governnment to prevent the invasion of Greenland and extended the area of its naval patrols to west longitude 26°. In July, Iceland was occupied by U.S. troops, ostensibly to forestall the possibility of its becoming a German base. Shortly thereafter, the navy began convoying merchantmen halfway across the Atlantic. By September, after some controversial incidents between American destroyers and German U-boats, FDR ordered the U.S. navy to "shoot on sight" at any German submarines found within U.S. defensive waters. Still, however nakedly interventionist these steps appeared to the president's isolationist critics, they were fairly consistent with the premises of the Lend-Lease Act. The unsatisfactory consequences of the embargoes of the mid-1930s and the cash-and-carry revision of the neutrality acts had made clear that a failure to assure the safe arrival of the goods in England, far from promoting even-handed neutrality, would simply have made for unneutrality of a different kind.

That American foreign policy in Europe was still unable to step outside a rather limited vision of international cooperation became clear in August 1941, when FDR and Churchill conferred for the first time off the coast of Newfoundland. The meeting produced a document known as the Atlantic Charter that sought to define a common Anglo-American vision of the postwar world. It promised an end to territorial aggression, with future boundary changes requiring the consent of the peoples involved, and it looked forward to an era of democratic government, free trade and the Open Door, economic cooperation, freedom from want and fear, and freedom of the seas.

Although this joint statement of war aims was a bold step in the direction of involvement, the document was also quite cautious in some crucial respects. When Churchill attempted to secure an explicit American pledge to defend Britain, FDR refused to commit himself. And while the charter was certainly internationalist in its promotion of anti-imperialism and free trade, it was missing the supranational dimension of Wilsonianism. The prime minister had tried to get FDR to agree to a new league of nations, but was forced to settle instead for disarmament of the aggressors *pending* the establishment of some general system of security. Thus the meeting in Placentia Bay, too, could easily be interpreted as committing the nation to the kind of armed, internationalist neutrality that had been proposed earlier in the decade.

The absence of any explicit plans for collective security was quite important, for it meant that this war would not be another universalist crusade. This time there would be not even the hint of a peace without victory, which had envisioned all the belligerents participating as equals in a collective security organization. Instead, peace would be imposed and maintained by the victors. While the war would be fought to ward off very real Wilsonian dangers, it would not be fought for the chimerical prize of a Wilsonian peace. The Atlantic Charter suggested, then, that as far as Europe was concerned the administration was quite gun shy about Wilsonian interventionism and a Wilsonian-style peace.

If the Europe-first strategy in practice was more tentative than it appeared, FDR's policy toward Japan was far tougher than called for by realist strategy. Indeed, FDR's anti-interventionist critics would have done better to focus their attention on his policies in the Pacific, where his administration stumbled into a new kind of global strategy that made his policy toward Germany look cautious by comparison. Not only would this strategy take the country into World War II, it foreshadowed much of America's policy in the cold war, when Asia would become the primary military battleground against outbreaks of global political contagions.

Indeed, FDR's policy in Asia had been significantly tougher and strategically more globalist, from a much earlier date, than his policy toward Germany. In the Pacific, the fleet was anchored at its forward base in Pearl Harbor, Hawaii, rather than on the Pacific coast. In 1939, hoping to send a strong economic message to Tokyo, the State Department canceled the 1911 commercial treaty, which meant that trade would henceforth be regulated on an ad hoc basis. A series of embargoes on high-octane aviation fuel and scrap metals followed shortly thereafter.

Japan's determination to gain possession of the oil-rich Netherlands East Indies was redoubled after negotiations in the winter of 1940–41 with Anglo-American oil companies failed to secure sure supplies of crude. In July 1941, Japanese forces occupied all of Indochina as a prelude to further expansion southward. In response, the U.S. froze all Japanese dollar assets held by American banks. This translated effectively into an oil embargo against Japan, since dollar funds were no longer available to pay for their petroleum purchases. The embargo turned out to be a de facto decision for war, since Japan relied on the United States for roughly 80 percent of its oil. As the embargo took hold, the declining stockpiles of the imperial army and navy meant that a decision for war would have to be made sooner rather than later, lest the lifeblood of the military machine dry up.

All this ran counter to ABC-1, which suggested the desirability of pursuing a softer line toward Japan while getting tough with Germany. Roosevelt had not at first intended an action with such far-reaching consequences, but after discovering that hard-liners in the bureaucracy had been denying Japan the necessary permits and clearances to purchase oil he felt obliged to continue the embargo for fear of looking weak. Despite some opportunities to compromise or arrange a modus vivendi, Washington chose to dig in its heels against Japan, despite the fact that Japanese behavior in East Asia had not changed in any fundamental respects over the preceding four years. If anything, it was American perceptions of the situation that had changed. In particular, the September 1940 signing of the Tripartite Pact had convinced the administration of the world-wide character of the threat. From a global perspective, whatever its effects on military strategy, going easy on one of the gangster nations could only make the situation worse by being interpreted as appeasement or isolationism. Taking a hard line at least left open the possibility that Japan would ultimately back down.

But the Japanese did not see things that way. Since caving in to American demands was unthinkable, they decided to launch a preemptive strike on the American Pacific fleet moored at Pearl Harbor in Hawaii and to seize control of Southeast Asia and the Southwest Pacific by attacking Malaya and Singapore, the Philippines, and the Netherlands East Indies. Japanese action was simultaneously a decision to fight, a way of securing the resources necessary to wage war upon the United States, and a giant step toward creating the self-sufficient empire toward which Japanese policy had been tending since 1931. Overlooking the complexities, FDR predicted that December 7, 1941, would be "a date that will live in infamy" and easily obtained a declaration of war from a suddenly galvanized Congress.

In retrospect, the decision to play hardball with Japan looks very much like a diplomatic intrigue on behalf of taking a "back door to war." This "back door" metaphor suggests that the U.S. somehow "sneaked into" the war rather than manfully walking in through the main entrance in the Atlantic, and that the Far East was a strategic sideshow to the European main event, as suggested by Rainbow-5. It is true that there was a widespread sense in Washington of an Anglo-American division of labor. Making a stand against Japan was viewed as an important contribution to preserving the British position in Europe. Without the empire and its line of communication, Britain's survival was problematic. There was also considerable sympathy for the notion that East Asia was, as Stimson had described it, "our part of the world," a region where the United States was traditionally a major player. Moreover, the tough line against Japan was popular with the American people, in contrast to the less provocative but more controversial measures being initiated around the same time against Germany.[37]

But the back-door approach was not necessarily intended to lead to war, nor did it inevitably lead to war with Germany. Some policy-makers, believing that the Japanese were not foolish enough to delude themselves about their chances of winning a war against the United States, had been convinced that economic pressure alone could bring Japan to heel. In any case, if worse came to worst, there was no *assurance* that involvement in the Pacific would automatically precipitate war with Germany. Indeed, following the Japanese preemptive strike on the Pacific fleet at Pearl Harbor Hitler did the United States a huge favor by declaring war even though he was not obligated to do so under a strict interpretation of the terms of the Tripartite Pact. Given Roosevelt's growing naval activism in the Atlantic, Hitler probably believed that war with the United States was inevitable, no matter how tightly he held the reins on his U-boat commanders. Thus, what for the conspiratorially minded was the biggest success of the "back door" approach was shot through with contingencies.

The back-door metaphor was therefore not quite accurate. The situation was actually more like a plunge through a trap door that put the U.S. into a vertiginous free fall toward the ground of global conflict. Though it left military-diplomatic coordination in tatters, the outbreak of the Pacific war and the German declaration of hostilities a few days later was a vindication of the global definition of threat that was so central to Wilsonianism. For FDR, pointing out the gap between strategy and diplomacy would hardly have been considered a devastating criticism of his administration's ineptitude; it was simply a confirmation of the distinctiveness of *modern* political realities, of a gap that was built into the situation. Indeed, it would become a standard feature of cold war policy in years to come.

The Far Eastern origins of the war were significant in yet another respect: the symbolic role that Asia and the Pacific would continue to play. It is difficult to agree with those historians who argue that the U.S. took a hard line against Japan because of American economic interests in China. Because those interests were minuscule in dollars-and-cents terms, it is clear that China played a role in American policy that transcended its economic importance. But the imaginary friendship with China and the myth of the Open Door Policy also had little to do with the inflation of China's worth. Instead, issues which in the past had not been worth a war now assumed extraordinary importance because of their symbolic value to global policy. In the past, China policy had been an excellent barometer of the state of global civilization. It was no different now when the barometric pressure was dropping.

With Japan, the symbolic became the substantial, unlike in World War I, when Asia had been largely a sideshow. This is important to understanding America's participation in the war, for if Japan had not been a revisionist power in the 1930s, then history would have been much different. Without Japan in the picture, there would have been less reason, in Wilsonian terms, for the United States to go to war against Nazi Germany alone. That would have been a *European* war, always a tough sell to Americans. But Japan justified a *global* interpretation of the threat to America just as the attack on Pearl Harbor finally justified American participation in the war. Die-hard isolationists preferred to believe that the administration had crawled through a secret back door to war in the Far East, but for most the Japanese attack appeared to confirm the Wilsonian belief in the global character of modern warfare between major powers. Thus, what for isolationists was the back door to European war was for internationalists the front door to global conflict.

In that sense, Pearl Harbor was a godsend to the United States, so much so that many suspected the administration had secretly connived at allowing the attack to occur, especially after it was revealed that military intelligence had cracked Japanese codes. All this was important because Pearl Harbor put a stop in an instant to all the bickering and uncertainty that had roiled American public opinion. The conspiracy theory has never been proven because, it appears, the administration had at the same time too much inconsequential information from its "Magic" intercepts but not enough hard data to piece together Japanese intentions. But what seemed like conspiracy can more easily be explained as the strategic outcome of a Wilsonian ideological framework. Even so, it is hard to argue with the contention that Pearl Harbor was a stroke of good fortune for Roosevelt.

It used to be the common wisdom that, with Pearl Harbor, the American people became internationalists, but today that is by no means clear. Certainly the Pearl Harbor attack made it *seem* as if the death of isolationism was sudden and decisive. It is, however, easy to imagine all kinds of scenarios in which the United States might well have stayed out of war if different leaders had been at the helm or if other accidents of history had occurred. In any case, the destruction of the kind of deep-seated fears of internationalism that undergirded isolationism could not be accomplished in the course of a day by a single event. After the war, internationalists would have good reason to nurse their continuing suspicion that the American public had been converted more for reasons of convenience than from genuine faith. Like many Romans and barbarians who agreed to be baptized once Christianity became the official religion of the empire, the conversion was only skin-deep.

But, for the time being at least, the foreign policy debate was at an end. Pearl Harbor and World War II eliminated the ambiguities and uncertainties of the decade by enshrining the Wilsonian strategic outlook as the "realistic" one. So powerful was this new mind-set that, in future, interest-based critiques of American policy were easily shrugged off as outdated and irrelevant. It only remained for the foreign policy community to mute the idealistic side of Wilson's thinking, which focused on international organization, rather than great-power cooperation, as the key to maintaining the peace. This process of ideological revision would be undertaken in the course of planning for the postwar world.

Beyond Wilsonianism: Planning the Postwar Era

Once in the war, the United States was faced with two main problems, winning the war and formulating a specific postwar program. The declaration of the United Nations on New Year's Day, 1942, signed in Washington by twenty-six nations, sought to address both issues. First, it formed the "Grand Alliance" between the U.S., Great Britain, the Soviet Union, and China, and committed the signatories to stick together until the successful conclusion of the war. Ideologically, the declaration committed the coalition to the principles of the Atlantic Charter, thereby presumably disposing of any potential conflicts over postwar goals. But it quickly became clear that more practical plans would have to be drawn up to see the Grand Alliance through to an era of postwar peace.

The diplomacy of the Grand Alliance had its share of rocky moments. A beleaguered Stalin had good reasons for counting on the Americans to fulfil their promise to open a second front sometime in 1942 to relieve German pressure against the Red Army. However, British opposition to a premature assault on the Continent quashed that possibility. Even the second-best form of support to the Soviets, the delivery of Lend-Lease supplies, was suspended for a time because of horrible convoy losses at the hands of German U-boats. There was also some diplomatic tension early in the war over the question of whether the Soviets would be permitted to hang onto the ill-gotten gains of their treaty with Hitler. However, by late 1943, Stalin was apprised of the British and American commitment to a 1944 cross-channel invasion. With the D-Day invasion of Normandy on June 6, 1944, these wartime disagreements receded into the buried archives of memory.

Winning the war remained FDR's priority throughout. As the conflict ground ineluctably to a close, FDR's advice to Chiang Kai-shek in April 1944, in response to Chiang's complaint about a border incident with the Soviets, was typical of his first-things-first mentality. "Leave it on ice," said FDR. "Any attitude which would be harmful to our united effort in winning the war would be unwarranted and I am confident that misunderstandings which may arise among members of the United Nations can be dispelled by the exercise of restraint and goodwill." Roosevelt's habit of putting off potentially divisive postwar issues, though much criticized afterwards, was based on the need to win the war first and on his belief that the postwar order would, in consequence, be a cooperative one.

The war in Europe ended with the Allies behaving amicably enough, as their forces retreated to predetermined zones of occupation in Germany following V-E Day, May 8, 1945. In Asia, the war ended far more ambiguously. Following the explosion of an atomic bomb over Hiroshima and another over Nagasaki on August 6 and 9, the Japanese agreed to surrender terms on the fifteenth. Unlike in Europe, Japan's surrender was not wholly unconditional. Eager to end the fighting, the U.S. agreed to allow the Japanese to retain the emperor institution. This meant that the military occupation would be indirect, with the existing Japanese bureaucracy and government institutions acting as an intermediary, whereas in Europe the German government would disappear altogether. Meanwhile, on August 8 Soviet armies invaded Japanese forces in Manchuria, providing an additional incentive for Japan to capitulate.

Some historians have suggested that the U.S. was engaging in "atomic diplomacy" in the hope of forestalling Soviet participation in the Pacific war and perhaps intimidating the USSR in order to gain diplomatic leverage in postwar diplomacy. However, the rather slow evolution of the cold war between the U.S. and USSR, coupled with the desire to end the war, suggests that political motives could not have been so well developed at this time. FDR, not unlike Wilson, believed in his own way that the war would generate solutions to postwar problems, with wartime collaboration generating the habits of trust necessary for successful postwar cooperation. His vice president and successor, Harry S. Truman, who ordered the nuclear bombings, fully agreed.

Cooperation, however vapid it appears to contemporary eyes, seemed the only possible policy at the time. Essentially, it presupposed the desirability of taking another stab at creating the kind of world that statesmen had aspired to, but botched, in the 1920s. Apart from being repugnant as a matter of principle, a return to more traditional balance-of-power policies was pretty much ruled out as a practical matter by the understanding that Germany and Japan, each the most logical balancer in its region, had forfeited their great power roles. The few people who anticipated a serious falling out with the USSR were in no position to deflect policy from its collaborative course.

Even so, some kind of blueprint for a constructive peace had to be drafted by allies who had joined the war at different times and for different reasons. A series of conferences beginning with a summit in Tehran in November 1943 began to sketch the outlines of a postwar order. Besides confirming the decision for an Anglo-American invasion of the Continent in the spring of 1944, the first meeting between FDR, Churchill, and Stalin also discussed some basic postwar issues. Roosevelt secured Stalin's agreement to enter the war against the Japan shortly after victory was nailed down against Germany. There seemed also to be a consensus on harsh treatment of Germany, though the details were left to be worked out later.

The February 1945 summit at Yalta, a former Czarist resort in the Crimea, seemed to set the seal on postwar cooperation. Germany was divided into four zones of military occupation pending the reestablishment of civil government (France was included as an occupying power largely at Churchill's insistence). Reparations would once again be exacted from Germany, though within limits. Meanwhile, the British and the Americans had cooled on the idea of partitioning Germany. That would have created long-term nationalist resentments and might have been an invitation for the powers to try their hand at spheres-of-influence politics. Allied discussions on partition were to be continued, but sentiment was clearly leading in the direction of running Germany cooperatively.

Other important decisions were made at Yalta. Polish borders were set roughly 150 miles farther to the west, thus allowing Stalin to keep the fruits of the Nazi-Soviet Pact, and the country would be governed largely by pro-Soviet Poles until free elections could be organized. In a move that reassured the Americans, Stalin joined in signing a Declaration on Liberated Europe in which the victors promised to reestablish democracy in eastern Europe. At the same time, FDR admitted privately that since "the Russians had the power in eastern Europe," that "the only practical course was to use what influence we had to ameliorate the situation."[38] Stalin also confirmed his promise to join in the war against Japan, provided that the Soviets regained some territories and concessions in the Far East lost forty years earlier in the Russo-Japanese war.

Wartime developments in economic policy turned out to be far more important in the long term than the short-lived political agreements. To assure that disastrous global economic crises like those of the 1930s would not be repeated, an economic agreement was hammered out at a meeting of Allied finance ministers in the New Hampshire resort of Bretton Woods in the summer of 1944. Those present were well aware of the failure of economic management in the 1920s and 30s. With a view to restoring an open world economy, this American-inspired accord established a World

Bank to finance basic development and an International Monetary Fund to help maintain stable currency ratios.

A modified gold standard, with the U.S. dollar serving as the benchmark currency—effectively as good as gold—would provide both liquidity and an acceptable international standard of value. All of this presumed the existence of an open trading system, which would be promoted by a post-war General Agreement on Trade and Tariffs (GATT). The commitment to creating a truly open world economy this time around would go a long way toward explaining America's staying power over the next fifty years. Just as international security was no longer assumed to be self-regulating, the global economic environment would also require close attention.

These economic plans were only one example of a revival of normal internationalism. Less obviously, the same outlook was present in the negotiations to create a successor to the failed League of Nations. For many Americans, the most significant achievement of Yalta was securing Stalin's final approval for membership in the postwar United Nations Organization. The creation of this new body had received its first big impetus in October 1943, when Secretary Hull met with his Soviet and British counterparts in Moscow and obtained a commitment to create a new postwar organization.

Back home, the announcement was greeted with great enthusiasm by Wilsonians, who dreamed of entering, after years of wandering in the wilderness, their leader's promised land. Quite in contrast to Wilson's political ordeal (of which everyone was conscious), the domestic politics of gaining consent for membership in an international organization were almost painless. In 1944, the House and Senate passed the Fulbright and Connally resolutions, assuring that after this war there would be no repeat of the obstructionism of 1919. Later in the year, a conference held at Dumbarton Oaks outside Washington, D.C., hammered out the text of a charter for the new United Nations Organization.

The United Nations was an American project. As the interplay between Asia and Europe demonstrated, only the United States had a wholly global approach, one that recognized both the positive and the negative facts of life of international society in the modern era. In contrast, other nations had become involved and continued to fight with regional and particularist stakes uppermost among their concerns. Churchill was concerned primarily with Europe and the British empire, while Stalin seemed bent on realizing the old Czarist dream of a pan-Slavic empire in eastern Europe and restoration of the pre-1905 Russian position in the Far East.

But this successor to the League was not what it appeared to be. The U.N. was widely viewed as a "second chance" for Wilsonianism, but the public failed to realize, and FDR failed to tell them, that collective security already had three strikes against it. It was a telling fact that FDR, who after all had brought the U.S. into the war by employing a Wilsonian strategic logic, was reluctant to rekindle the passions of Wilsonian idealism. Like many others, FDR agreed that the League had been ineffective, but he parted company with those who believed that some organizational tinkering here and there, coupled with American membership, would assure that things were done right this time.

Over the years, Roosevelt had come to believe that *no* international organization could prevent the kind of great-power conflict that had caused two world wars. Indeed, in this respect he more closely resembled his cousin Theodore than his mentor Wilson. There were certain kinds of issues that could be resolved in no other way than through war. While Wilson placed war on a par with world conquest as evils, FDR clearly relished the exhilarating challenges of this global conflict; in his more pessimistic moments he even downplayed any grand hopes of ensuring that this would be the last conflict of its kind.

It followed from this perception of the organization's limited potential that the U.N. was not given the power to stop great-power disagreement by threatening force. Despite some glaring flaws in its architectural design, the League as a structure was supposed to be able to withstand the stresses of continuing great-power antagonism. By comparison, the U.N. could not be the vehicle of Wilsonian collective security because it could not act against the veto of one of the great powers with a permanent seat on the Security Council. "Veto" is the negative postwar term for what was referred to at the time as the "principle of unanimity," the basic rule for Allied cooperation throughout World War II.

Those who jumped to opposing and more cynical conclusions about the organization's purpose were also off the mark. Although the U.N. was supposed to be the peacetime continuation of the wartime alliance, it was not a revival of the Concert of Europe, the great-power club of the post-Napoleonic period that sought to maintain stability in Europe. To be sure, some State Department analysts saw the U.N. as bearing "every earmark of a great power alliance," but FDR did not interpret the new body's charter as a license for an ongoing American presence in European affairs. Significantly, he told Stalin at Yalta that the United States would have its troops home from Europe within two years. Without a continuing military presence on the Continent, America's political role there would necessarily be limited.

In his conception of the U.N., FDR did not envision American global political involvement, much less global leadership. Instead, he imagined a regional division of labor in which each of the Security Council members—originally the "four policemen"—would act as the local cop in its own neighborhood. True to its traditions, America would be more active in the Caribbean and the Pacific than in Europe. In Europe, meanwhile, the U.S. would serve as a mediator between the British and the Soviets. This limited internationalism bore more than a passing resemblance to the kind of "civilized" cooperation envisaged by Theodore Roosevelt and Taft just prior to World War I. From this perspective, the U.N. was designed to be a *pre*-Wilsonian body.

But it is also possible to view the U.N. as a *post*-Wilsonian organization. Whatever the built-in shortcomings of Wilsonianism, now that the global threat was on the verge of being eliminated, there was no need for collective security as a substitute for war. The U.N. was created on the assumption that the kinds of great power conflicts that had led Wilson so passionately to champion a league had been resolved by history. Despite their ideological differences, the Allies had learned to cooperate during the war and were presumably united, as well, on the absolute necessity of avoiding another cataclysm.

Whether the U.N. is termed pre-Wilsonian or post-Wilsonian is of little consequence; it is a matter of perspective whether one sees it as a reversion to the past or an original program for the future. The central point is that it was neither a collective security organization in the Wilsonian tradition nor a great-power alliance. Instead, it was founded on the view, in currency before World War I and dominant in the 1920s, that a stable world could be based only on an unforced, natural great-power harmony—"civilized" cooperation. Banal as it may seem, the idea of normal internationalism, which was incorporated into the structure of the U.N., once again demonstrated its enormous staying power.

What, then, *was* the new world body supposed to do? Essentially, it was an organization of the great powers designed to prevent the lesser powers from becoming too rowdy, a League of Nations "lite," as it were. As the Mexican delegate at the June 1945 San Francisco conference said, under the U.N. Charter "the mice would be disciplined, but the lions would be free."[38] With power politics having been replaced by cooperation among the great powers, the peace of the strong would be imposed upon the weak. Here too, the United Nations bore more than a passing resemblance to the kind of international organization much talked about before World War I. Theodore Roosevelt, for example, had this kind of international cooperation in mind when arguing that "warlike intervention by the civilized powers would contribute directly to the peace of the world."

Given its built-in incapacity to check the kinds of global dangers that had so disturbed Wilson and FDR, the United Nations was fated to spend the postwar years on the margins of world politics once great-power contentiousness resurfaced. But the organization's limitations ran deeper than that. If the life-and-death issues of world politics were beyond the ability of international organization to resolve, the same would prove true of many of the minor issues. Thus, the U.N. during the cold war was often ineffectual in the little things as well as the big things. In retrospect, of course, one might argue that the U.N. was created a half century too early. But, as the 1990s have demonstrated, it is not clear that a post-Wilsonian U.N. true to the original intentions of the founders could succeed even in that more modest role.

By 1945, it appeared as if Wilsonian internationalism was history in the sense that Americans commonly understand the term—past, dead and buried, irrelevant to the present. Following FDR's articulation of a Wilsonian global threat, his wartime diplomacy had dispensed with Wilsonian solutions in the belief that they had not worked and, in any case, were no longer necessary, thanks to great-power cooperation. The world appeared ready at long last to resume its twice-interrupted journey down the road of civilized cooperation. It seemed as if history had nowhere else to go.

But that kind of confidence failed to reckon with the unresolved ideological conflicts still lurking within modernity. Indeed, it is a humbling commentary on the limited insight into the future enjoyed by human beings that World War II's statesmen failed utterly to predict the ideological conflict of the postwar years. World War II was, among other things, a war between nationalist and internationalist points of view. The defeat of Germany and Japan marked a historical point of no return in which local perspectives could no longer hope to dominate world politics. Ethnically rooted nationalism had been selected out by history and prevented from becoming the dominant species of international politics. The problem henceforth would not be great-power nationalism. The determination to control Germany and Japan would see to that.

American statesmen presumed that the Soviet Union would join the main road of New Deal internationalism; or, if it chose for the time being not to enlist in the Bretton Woods scheme, that it would continue, like some harmless communal experiment in utopian socialism, to pursue socialism in one country. In either event, the assumption appeared to be that the postwar years would bring a reprise of the kind of great-power cooperation envisioned by President Taft and by the Republican administrations of the 1920s. It did not happen that way. Instead, the postwar

period turned into a tumultuous struggle to decide which road to internationalism, the socialist or the market-based capitalist approach, would be
the pathway to humankind's future.

For the duration of this struggle, Wilsonianism, rejected in the 1920s
and controversial in the 1930s, would finally find an institutional home
in the most unlikely of places—the U.S. government. A marginal creed
to this point, Wilsonianism would only become central to U.S. foreign
policy in the postwar years, following the failure of cooperation under
the aegis of the United Nations and the reemergence, this time in the form
of the Soviet threat, of the cluster of modern global problems first
glimpsed by Wilson and later described in detail by FDR. As Wilsonian
problems returned, neo-Wilsonian solutions based on world opinion were
also dusted off and pressed into service.

The strange thing about the triumph of Wilsonianism was that it was
not acknowledged as such. Indeed, so deeply did the Wilsonian worldview
burrow into the American diplomatic mind that it became second nature
to American policy-makers. What once had been widely considered to be
a historical fantasy was transformed into a modern realism that few both-
ered to question. Within five years, most everyone in Washington was
speaking Wilsonian prose without knowing it. Wilson never got to see
the promised land in which his ideas flourished, but his people never knew
they entered it.

CHAPTER FIVE

Cold War Wilsonianism: The Normalization of Crisis Internationalism

Defining the Cold War

Realism, because it stresses the limitations of power, is a foreign policy doctrine that is essentially regional in outlook. Ideologies, by contrast, tend toward universality. Doctrinally speaking, then, this suggests that the cold war, which was nothing if not global, was an ideological conflict rather than a stretch-limousine version of a classical power struggle. In World War II, an America acting from a global perspective fought against countries who defined themselves in localist frameworks of nation and region, but whose combined actions were perceived to have planetary consequences. During the cold war, the strategic stakes differed little, but ideologically the situation was far more sharply defined. Now the United States was faced, for the first time, with a Soviet adversary whose outlook was every bit as global as its own. The two ideologies were, in a literal sense, *world*views.[1]

During World War II, Roosevelt had assumed that the USSR would continue its attempt to develop "Socialism in One Country." This approach, articulated in the late 1920s, had marked a retreat from "scientific socialism" to a position that Marx had criticized as "utopian socialism," the belief that the new world could be created exclusively through the power of attraction of a socialist version of the Puritan "city on a hill." But the warm feelings born of wartime cooperation grew chilly over time. After five years of steady increase in postwar tensions, policy-makers in Washington concluded that Communist expansionism was motivating the Soviet Union and that the Soviets possessed both the will and the capacity to challenge the American conception of world order. By 1950, the ideological lines were tightly drawn and the battle was joined.

As the conviction dawned on policy-makers in Washington that the Soviets had taken their global ideological ambitions out of storage and returned to wearing their revolutionary garb, dormant Wilsonian fears were resurrected. But in this revival of Wilsonianism, the crusading utopianism that for many was its central feature was almost entirely absent. This want of perfectionism was the result of a transformation of Wilsonian thought that Wilson himself might have found strange. Most obviously, despite a continuing emphasis on international cooperation, it became very much a national program. Wilsonianism was also routinized in some unexpected ways. As an offshoot of normal internationalism, it had been intended to deal with dangers that, however menacing, were supposed to cause only occasional disruptions to a liberal global civilization. In the cold war, however, Wilsonianism was normalized as a way of dealing with a threat of indefinite duration. It became a way of conducting business as usual. Stranger still, Wilsonianism was internalized to the degree that its modernist character as historical interpretation was forgotten. In a reversal of traditional geopolitical logic, Wilsonianism became the cold war's realism.

IN THE IMMEDIATE postwar years, American policy-makers sought to make a go of Roosevelt's policy of "cooperation." And for a time, readjustment to peacetime conditions, the absence of compelling international crises, and the realization that cooperation was bound to have its ups and downs provided compelling reasons to continue along the course set by FDR. With the war's end, the politics of demobilizing a military establishment some 16 million strong and reconverting the war machine into a peacetime manufacturing economy took precedence over foreign policy. Overseas, with the dust of war not yet settled, it was difficult to get a clear view of the international landscape. The situation was further confused by FDR's death in April 1945. All in all, this was not unlike floating placidly down a stream just prior to reaching an unanticipated waterfall ahead. Unprepared for what was to come, President Harry S. Truman, who was "awfully vague" on FDR's wartime policies, would soon be struggling to keep his head above water in the suddenly treacherous torrent of international politics.[2]

Although the Truman administration's relationship with the USSR was bumpy at first, the paved road of cooperation nevertheless lay stretched out in full view. Shortly after assuming the presidency, Truman had a shouting match with Stalin's foreign minister, Vyacheslav Molotov, over the alleged failure of the Soviets to live up to the Yalta agreements on Poland. In part because of displeasure with Stalin's actions, a badly needed ten billion dollar reconstruction loan to the Soviet Union failed to materialize. Truman quickly realized, however, that he was on shaky ground. He sent Harry Hopkins, FDR's closest adviser, to meet with Stalin in Moscow, where Hopkins patched together a compromise on Poland and apologized for the haste with which Lend-Lease had been canceled following the end of the war in Europe. Truman's subsequent summit meeting at Potsdam in July 1945 was amiable enough to warrant favorable comparisons between Stalin and "Boss" Tom Pendergast of Kansas City, Truman's political mentor. "I can deal with Stalin," Truman concluded.

Not until early 1946 did a growing inventory of problems began to cause serious concern in Washington. Within the Soviet Union, there were worrisome signs of a return to ideology, which were taken to mean that the idea of cooperation was being scrapped. During the war, Stalin (ostensibly) abolished that much-hated instrument of anticapitalist subversion, the Comintern or Communist International, and showed little bashfulness about appealing to Great Russian patriotism as a way of motivating his people. In the postwar years, however, the regime veered ideologically to the left. In February, Stalin delivered a speech that reaffirmed the Marxist-Leninist prediction of capitalism's violent self-destruction and asserted that the Soviet design was "a far better form of social organization than any non-Soviet social system." As time went on, Moscow cranked up the ideological volume in an attempt to drown out all non-Soviet influences. Foreign cultural importations, including Mickey Mouse, were attacked as "bourgeois cosmopolitan" deviations from the truth; cultural exchanges, modest to begin with, were all but cut off.

In Germany, optimistic hopes for a successful joint administration of this all-important country faded quickly. The Potsdam agreements of August 1945, which envisaged a whole German economy and rudimentary centralized agencies, failed to go anywhere, leaving each occupying power free to do as it pleased in its area of occupation. The steady socialization of the Soviet zone of occupation under the puppet regime of Walter Ulbricht, which included a forced merger between the communists and the Social Democratic Party, bred suspicions that Stalin was seeking to use the eastern zone as a springboard for control of all Germany. Similarly, in Korea, a former Japanese colony, no progress was made toward reuniting the Soviet-occupied north and the American-occupied south. Forward movement in drawing up peace treaties with the Axis puppet states—Italy, Hungary, and Romania—was agonizingly slow. Meanwhile, the Soviets showed no interest in joining the new multilateral economic institutions like the World Bank and the International Monetary Fund.

These developments produced heightened concern and suspicion in

Washington, though as yet American policy-makers felt more bewildered than beleaguered.[3] There were, as yet, no systematic intelligence appraisals of the USSR. Into the intellectual vacuum stepped a Soviet expert in the American Foreign Service, a career diplomat named George F. Kennan. Dispelling the confusion that clouded American thinking about communism and the Soviet state, Kennan offered the first persuasive explanation of Soviet motives in the early postwar years. He also suggested a policy of "containment" to deal with the communist colossus. Though Kennan portrayed a far more hostile Soviet Union than the amiable partner that most Americans had expected to deal with, in the end his screenplay for containment was not fundamentally different from Roosevelt's rough sketch of how postwar cooperation might function.

As second in command in the American embassy in Moscow during the war, Kennan had looked on with ill-concealed gloom at Washington's naive determination to establish an enduring friendship with the Soviet Union. No intimate collaboration was possible, he believed, with a nation so xenophobic, insular, and backward as the USSR; a country that was run, moreover, by a group of ideological conspirators habituated to viewing the rest of the world with intense distrust. When asked early in 1946 to provide an analysis of what seemed, to less knowledgeable observers, inscrutably truculent behavior on Moscow's part, Kennan gave the State Department an analysis, "the long telegram," that became a canonical text of American postwar policy.

According to Kennan, the Soviets took "capitalistic encirclement" as an article of faith. Soviet policy, therefore, sought to deepen divisions between the imperialist powers and to take advantage of the revolutionary opportunities that presented themselves in the chaotic aftermath of capitalist wars. Wherever possible, he predicted, "efforts will be made to advance official limits of Soviet power." This "neurotic view of world affairs" had "little to do with conditions outside Russia," according to Kennan. Instead, it arose from "basic inner-Russian necessities" that originated deep in the Czarist past. In a subsequent essay published under the pseudonym "X" in the influential journal of the foreign policy establishment, *Foreign Affairs,* Kennan suggested that "containment" of the Soviet union was the only appropriate course of action to follow, a "patient, long-term, and vigilant use of counter-force" whenever and wherever the tentacles of Soviet power were extended.

The long telegram and X article gave American policy-makers a vivid sense of the Kremlin's basically hostile psychology and outlined, in very broad terms, an *anti-Soviet* course of action that appeared to make sense.

Although Kennan waffled on the issue of how closely the Kremlin hewed to Marxist doctrines, he was a self-professed realist who believed that the objective facts of power could be understood by all, including even the self-deluded intriguers in Moscow. Though Stalin hailed from Georgia, the Soviet leaders were, after all, Russians first and foremost, and it stood to reason that communist ideology would have to be filtered through their Russian sensibilities. Imperial Russia had been expansionist and anti-Western in its own right, but it had also been a functional member of the family of nations. Whatever their commitment to promoting worldwide communism, the Soviet leaders understood power and would respond prudently in the face of overwhelming Western strength and determination. In this respect, they were no different from the Czars who preceded them. One source of confirmation for this view was that Soviet domestic repression bore a comforting resemblance to the harsh practices of the Czarist era.

The thrust of Kennan's analysis was reassuring. If Kennan had wanted to stir up trouble, he could easily enough have done that by playing to the widespread belief that a breakdown of wartime cooperation would lead inevitably to World War III and by portraying Stalin and his cohorts as dedicated communist fanatics who were willing to stop at nothing in pursuit of their ambitions. Instead, Kennan insisted that the West *could* deal with the Kremlin, not in the impossibly chummy way attempted during the war, but by resorting to the traditional techniques of diplomacy. Kennan believed that the Soviet regime was "impervious to reason" but "highly sensitive to [the] logic of force," which suggested that if situations were "properly handled there need be no prestige-engaging showdowns." A recent study of Soviet foreign policy grounded in Russian language sources, which views the Kremlin's behavior as "the result of the symbiosis of imperial expansionism and ideological proselytism," indicates that Kennan's diagnosis was not wide of the mark.[4]

Communist ideology, Czarist history, and Russian culture dovetailed closely, but there was yet another way in which ideology mattered. It was, according to this meaning of the term, a mask, a way of justifying cruel and repressive Soviet rule for a ruling elite that otherwise would have stood exposed as just a motley group of political adventurers. Marxism was "the fig leaf of their moral and intellectual respectability," said Kennan, in a now-famous description. "Without it, they would stand before history, at best, as only the last of that long succession of cruel and wasteful Russian rulers who have forced their country on to ever new heights of military power in order to guarantee external security for their internally weak regimes." This desire to hang on to their positions further suggested that the Soviet leaders were not interested in fanatical martyrdom.

Perhaps the most distinctive feature of Kennan's containment policy was his assertion that, if war could be avoided, history would render a favorable verdict. At some point in the future, the hollowness of communism would become evident to all. The task of the West, therefore, was to hold on until that day when an unnatural form of government, established in power by a freakish accident of history in World War I, would either "mellow" or be replaced by a more moderate regime. Seen in this light, the cold-war policy of containment was a profound act of faith in the benign course of history. This confidence in the future existed despite the fact that there was no objective assurance that things would turn out as Kennan predicted. Indeed, it is ironic that Kennan, whose historical outlook was in many ways profoundly pessimistic and antiliberal, should have reinforced the optimistic American belief in the ultimate triumph of normal internationalism, especially as realism, with its gloomy view of progress and human nature, suggested no reason to expect any improvement in the situation.

Had Washington had been more pessimistic, if policy-makers had believed that time was on Moscow's side, or if communist ideology had been perceived as being even more zealous, then the cold war would have been a far more serious, and perhaps deadly, affair. It might have made sense, in that case, to argue on behalf of a preemptive war, to take advantage of the West's nuclear monopoly before the Soviets had fully developed an atomic arsenal of their own. A few hyper-zealous officials and the renowned philosopher Bertrand Russell advocated precisely this move. Or it might have been better to adopt as guiding principles the cynical precepts of power politics, in which force, and only force, was the bottom line. Instead, Americans opted, without much discussion, for a policy that expressed the abiding belief in the continued vitality of a progressive world society, the same belief with which the U.S. had entered the twentieth-century world.

History mattered enormously, then, as the prize for which the cold war would be fought and as the means for defining the conflict. The cold war was a historical struggle over which ideology or way of life would be able to form the basis of a global civilization. It was intended to be a peaceful struggle, but it would be a war to the finish: Whichever side emerged triumphant, it would be impossible for the other to survive with its ideology intact. It was hardly surprising that Americans would cling to a faith in the progressive outcome of history. But it was a massive irony that the United States, long thought to be a nation "outside history," a country moreover whose people tended to view the past with indifference, should choose to enter such a fateful confrontation from a standpoint that made sense only within the interpretive framework of global history.

The long telegram, which was restricted to governmental circulation, was soon followed by a speech in which Winston Churchill coined another term that would become a staple image of the cold war. Delivering a commencement address at a small college in Fulton, Missouri, Churchill pointed to the "iron curtain" descending over eastern Europe in all the countries occupied by the Red Army. The imposition of communist-dominated governments made a mockery of the Declaration on Liberated Europe signed by the Big Three at Yalta. American policy-makers had been quite willing to acknowledge that governments in this region should have foreign policies friendly to the Soviet Union, but they had assumed that these governments would be freely elected. Instead, Europe was being divided into "spheres of influence" that betokened a return to the failed power politics of the past. Ominously, Moscow described Churchill's words as the ravings of a "warmonger."

The effect of Kennan's long telegram was, as he later put it, "nothing less than sensational," making him, for a time, a celebrity in Washington. He was recalled from Moscow to take charge of the newly formed Policy Planning Staff in the Department of State. From that position, he was given entree to policy deliberations at the highest level and had a shaping hand in many of the early cold war's most important policy departures. It was not long, however, before Kennan came to the rueful conclusion that he had done his job of warning the United States all too well, while failing to sell Americans on the more moderate implications of his analysis.

Over the next few years, he struggled to put across a "realistic" view of containment that emphasized the use of mainly political means to achieve limited foreign policy objectives in Europe and Asia. Containment, he claimed, had been intended as a measured *political* approach, not as a prescription for global military confrontation. As time went on, Kennan was increasingly frustrated at seeing his views rejected in favor of a militarized global outlook that, he believed, exaggerated the Soviet threat and worked against a withdrawal of Soviet power from the heart of Europe. Ironically, his calls for negotiated agreements with the Soviets resembled more and more the unflappable cooperative approach advocated by FDR during the war, a strategy that Kennan, at the time, had ridiculed for its starry-eyed romanticism.

Kennan's rapid estrangement from American cold war policy suggested that his ideas were only a point of departure, a starting point for American cold war internationalism. He had succeeded in defining the Soviet Union as a hostile power (a view long held by conservative circles in the United States) and deserved credit for suggesting a grand strategy of containment for avoiding World War III. Nevertheless, he failed to articulate a convincing historical context in which the Soviet threat or the history of the twentieth century could be understood. Kennan's historical vision was not liberal. His views, which derived from the European balance-of-power tradition, saw containment as a temporary policy for preventing the communization of western Europe pending the restoration of a purely European balance of power. In that sense, his view of the future differed markedly from the normal internationalism that most Americans expected would be the fruit of containment. It is not surprising, then, that his diagnoses and prescriptions were soon overtaken by the only surviving brand of American internationalism: Wilsonianism. The revival of the Wilsonian sense of threat and the institutionalization of neo-Wilsonian solutions over the next fifty years would fill out the remainder of the Wilsonian century.

First Attempts at Defining Cold War Policy

Containment as a policy was not born fully formed. Years of education in the hard school of experience remained before it reached mature adulthood. In the four years following the long telegram's appearance, American perceptions of the Soviet threat and the type of containment needed to control it became more pessimistic and expansive. This was, assuredly, a period of revolutionary change in American foreign policy, but the Truman administration seemed forever to be playing catch-up as all its measures, however novel by comparison with past efforts, seemed insufficient to manage a problem that became more serious with every passing year. In the beginning, a more rigid attitude and harsher words seemed enough. It was not long, however, before Washington was forced to back its words with money, then with military commitments, and finally with force.

In 1946 came the first of many crises. In Iran, the Soviets failed to withdraw Red Army troops from the northern section of the country, contrary to promises made following a joint Anglo-Soviet occupation in August 1941. Ignoring the complaints of the Iranian government, they attempted to create a separatist puppet regime in the oil-rich northern province of Azerbaijan. Embarrassing publicity in the United Nations Security Council finally induced the Soviets to end their intrigues and withdraw, albeit grumbling all the while about the hostility of their alleged allies.

Although it seemed as if exposure to the light of discussion in the U.N. made Iran a textbook example of how Wilsonianism was to operate, the resolution of the crisis was misleading. It may have been more the visit of the U.S.S. *Missouri* to Istanbul and the call for renewed conscription by Truman that turned the trick, methods that pointed in an entirely different direction for dealing with the Soviets. In any case, it would not be long before American policy-makers concluded that the U.N. was helpless to resolve great-power conflicts—as indeed it was designed to be.

The Turkish straits crisis in the summer of 1946 was more indicative of what the future would bring. For some time the Soviets had been pressuring the government in Ankara for joint administration of the narrow straits between the Black Sea and the Mediterranean. By international law, these waters were under the control of the Turkish government, which would close them to warships in time of war. With diplomatic pressure and troop movements on the frontiers menacing the beleaguered Turks, Soviet behavior appeared to be bent on creating a confrontation. "We might as well find out whether the Russians were bent on world conquest now as in five or ten years," said Truman, in deciding to stand up to Moscow.[5] Washington dealt with this crisis by dispatching a naval carrier force to the eastern Mediterranean as an unambiguous hint to the Soviets that they ought to retract their claws. With that, the pressure on Turkey eased.

Yet another fateful development in 1946 was the collapse of negotiations for an accord on the internationalization of atomic energy. Fearing that a monumental and perhaps disastrous armaments race would break out unless some international controls were put in place, early in 1946 the United States proposed a plan for the formation of an International Atomic Development Authority under U.N. auspices. Essentially, the plan called for world government in all areas pertaining to nuclear matters: mining and refining of uranium, research and development for peaceful and military purposes, stockpiling, and a system of strict controls and inspections to ensure that nations could not secretly acquire and hide nuclear arsenals. As the system came closer to becoming foolproof, the United States promised to destroy its atomic stockpiles by phased stages. Bernard Baruch, the American negotiator, added a significant wrinkle by insisting that the veto would not apply in decisions to punish violators of atomic safeguards.

The Baruch Plan, as it was called, got absolutely nowhere, in part because his proposal for eliminating the veto violated the basic principle on which the U.N. was founded. The crux of the problem surrounding the veto was this: without it, the U.N. would not have been created; but with it, nothing of compelling political importance could be accomplished. By proposing "condign [i.e. suitable] punishment" that could not be vetoed, Baruch was in effect proposing "an atomic League of Nations." He was trying to turn back the clock to a Wilsonian conception of international organization and world opinion that FDR and the Soviets had long since abandoned.[6]

Not surprisingly, the plan was summarily rejected by the Soviets, who proposed instead that existing stockpiles be destroyed first, after which an international accord would be hammered out. Their plan was rebuffed by the U.S. because it would have amounted to unilateral nuclear disarmament without any assurance that satisfactory controls could in fact be imposed in the future. Though some criticized the United States for hanging on to its nuclear monopoly as long as possible, this was probably the only way in which congressional approval could have been gained. In the event, the tender shoots of hope for international control were trampled underfoot. For the time being, Americans could rest secure in the knowledge that their nuclear monopoly was likely to endure for another ten or fifteen years, as officials assured them it would.

While these problems bobbed up, many others churned beneath the surface. In Germany, negotiations stalled on creating a self-supporting economy that would also enable Germany to pay sizeable reparations. In the absence of a coherent economic plan, the four separate zonal economies brought the country to the verge of economic destitution. Western Europe was not much better off, as the anticipated postwar recovery failed to kick in for a host of reasons. In Washington, the suspicion was gaining ground that this impoverished situation suited Moscow very well because the swamp of economic chaos provided an ideal breeding ground for communist movements. The economic malaise, coupled with the intimidating presence of the nearby Red Army, seemed sufficient to push the Continent into the arms of the communists without an overt threat of attack.

As the economy in western Europe continued to worsen, the Truman administration turned a major corner in March 1947 in its response to a crisis in Greece. In the wake of the German army's withdrawal from Greece, a civil war had erupted between monarchist and communist forces. Using Yugoslavia and Bulgaria as safe havens and areas of resupply, the Greek communists appeared to be on the verge of winning the civil war. To this point, the British, as the occupying power in Greece, had used military force to prevent this from occurring. But, early in 1947, the financially exhausted British tossed the Greek hot potato into America's lap in the expectation that the U.S. was now prepared to take its turn as world leader.

After some hasty huddling in Washington, Truman decided to commit

American financial resources to the struggling Greek government. He went before Congress in March and requested 400 million dollars in aid, a portion of which would go to the hard-pressed Turks. But the administration's analysis of the problem did not stop with Greece and Turkey. In arguing his case, Truman emphasized the worldwide struggle between contrasting ways of life. In future, Truman declared, "it must be the policy of the United States to support free peoples who are resisting attempted subjugation by armed minorities or by outside pressures."

The Truman Doctrine, as it was soon called, was a landmark of American foreign policy. Although critics viewed it as a declaration of ideological warfare, the address made no specific mention of containment, nor did it use the word "communism." That omission was not the result of a desire to prod the Russian bear as little as possible. Instead, the crisis was cast in broader historical terms than the cold war. Noting the expenditure of 341 billion dollars during World War II, Truman argued that it was "only common sense that we should safeguard this investment and make sure that it was not in vain." In other words, the U.S. was facing yet another version of the kind of strategic danger it had recently vanquished.

Notable, too, was the unilateral character of the pronouncement. It was ironic that Truman, who was far more devoted to the idea of international organization than FDR, sounded the death knell for collective security as it had traditionally been perceived. In this fateful step, the president was announcing the Americanization of internationalism and the intention to provide a national home for collective security. "The free peoples of the world look to us for support in maintaining their freedoms," he said. The United Nations, by contrast, was "not in a position to extend help of the kind that is required." In a decisive manner that contrasted with the fuzzy obligation to the U.N., the president signaled a willingness to commit American resources to distant and unfamiliar places, if need be. The United States would no longer be a spectator on the sidelines; henceforth it would be at the forefront of the struggle to control the ideological direction taken by the world.[7]

Although the request for aid to Greece and Turkey passed through Congress handily enough, the Truman Doctrine was greeted with a flurry of criticisms. Among the loudest complainants were those liberals who refused to believe that their investments of hope in the United Nations were, like Confederate money, now worthless. But those kinds of criticisms were from diehards who failed to recognize a lost cause when they saw one. More significant for the future were critiques that sided with the administration on the necessity of unilateral action while disagreeing with the specifics of the new global picture.

Realists like Kennan thought the address was too overstated to make good policy. Though the doctrine did not promise American involvement anytime, anywhere, much less argue for military action, Kennan's acute nose correctly detected the odor of universalism in the address. One could not write a blank check to cover all contingencies in the future, he argued. Realism demanded that priorities be set; that ends and means be in balance. But when the administration insisted shortly afterward that all future requests for assistance would not automatically receive approval, advocates of aid to faltering regimes like Chiang Kai-shek's nationalist China suggested that the administration was employing a double standard in which, contrary to its soaring universalist rhetoric, it was actually pursuing a Europe-first policy. From the left came accusations that Truman was trumping up yet another "red scare" to mobilize an American public that otherwise might have yawned at the prospect of providing aid to a Greek government barely worthy of the name.

These criticisms were wide of the mark. Kennan's objection, though it rightly sensed the doctrine's global pitch, failed to take into account the impossibility of any American president formulating a foreign policy from the standpoint of "realism" because that had never been part of American foreign policy tradition—unless, that is, one counted isolationism as realism. Critics on the left believed that the Truman Doctrine was an ideological ruse in which the government used the exaggerated threat of communism to sell foreign policy in the same way that sex appeal is used to sell cars or shampoo. But these complaints failed to credit the belief of American officials that the nation and the world had come to an historic turning point at which a declaration of America's commitment was absolutely necessary.

Apart from its allusions to a global threat, Truman's statement announced the triumphant reemergence of some other important, but long buried, elements of Wilsonianism. One had to do with the indispensability of America's leadership role. The Truman Doctrine, much more so than the willingness of the U.S. to enter the United Nations, marked the point of no return from prewar isolationism. Yet another element had to do with world opinion. Policy-makers believed that a failure in Greece would have devastating consequences for morale throughout the world. "Any partial action," said one official, "would raise a very grave doubt in the minds of the Greeks and the Turkish people and the other people in the world who are watching this matter and would throw doubt in the minds of people where we want to restore hope and some optimism."[8] Indeed, it would have been all too easy for Europeans to become demoralized, given the preceding history of the twentieth century.

Why, after all, should a marginal country like Greece have mattered so much? It was not so much Greece as the fate of western Europe in the event of a rout in Greece that worried policy-makers. Truman did note that "confusion and disorder might well spread throughout the entire Middle East," but that was the least of it. As Undersecretary of State Dean Acheson informed the president, "it is not alarmist to say that we are faced with the first crisis of a series which might extend Soviet domination to Europe, the Middle East and Asia."[9] A meeting of the secretaries of state, war, and navy on February 26, 1947, "recognized that the Greek and Turkish problems were only part of a critical world situation confronting us today in many democratic countries and that attention must be given to the problem as a whole."[10]

If America failed to act in the Mediterranean, western Europeans might lose faith in America; and with that, the Continent might swing voluntarily to the left, accommodating itself to Moscow's desires. Ultimately, as Acheson told a group of startled legislators in the White House, the situation came down to "a question of whether two-thirds of the area of the world and three-fourths of the world's territory is to be controlled by the Communists."[11]

However momentous the Truman Doctrine may have seemed—and it was a huge step forward in defining a world role for the United States— it took only a few weeks before the administration concluded that the United States could not afford to rest on its policy oars. By the spring of 1947, Europe seemed on the brink of economic collapse. The long-anticipated economic recovery was being stifled by poor weather and meager harvests, coal shortages, economic dislocations due in significant measure to the fact that Germany had become a poorhouse, and a shortage of dollars known as "the dollar gap" that made it impossible for Europeans to purchase necessary imports and capital goods from the United States. Without a normally functioning economy, it was impossible for them to earn foreign exchange to pay for their needs by exporting abroad. As for Germany, despite a merger of the British and American zones early in 1946, the country was nowhere near to becoming self-supporting. The situation was actually worsening as the U.S. pumped in large dollar amounts of aid to keep afloat an economy in which currency had become nearly worthless.

By early 1947, the economic problem could no longer be ignored. Taking their marching orders from Moscow, sizeable communist parties in Italy and France seemed poised to assume power by peaceful means, their appeal heightened by the radicalizing effect of the dismal economic situation. Should that happen, the Continent would come under the control of a single hostile power and much of the wartime achievement in Europe would have been negated. Something had to be done, and quickly, but what? From a variety of sources within the American government, including Kennan's hastily mobilized Policy Planning Staff, came suggestions for a massive program of economic aid. Unlike World War I, in which the U.S. government provided loans, this aid, to the tune of 12 billion dollars, would take the form of outright grants. In a June commencement address at Harvard University, Secretary of State George Marshall broached what came to be known as the Marshall Plan.

Like much American foreign policy during the cold war, the Marshall Plan was not conceived in narrow terms of national self-interest. But neither was it an act of pure benevolence. It proceeded from the assumption that American safety and affluence could flourish only in a broader setting of peace and prosperity. To be sure, the U.S. economy accounted at the time for about half of the total industrial output of the world and was enjoying huge export surpluses. But how long could that prosperity endure if the rest of the world remained impoverished?

Economist Robert Heilbroner compared international trade to a poker game in which, when "one player gets all the chips, the game breaks up." But in this game, playing was the thing. "It would be a gloomy prospect," Heilbroner concluded, "to feel that an export-import balance would never even out; that we must forever go on facing an incipient export collapse and bailing it out with further loans." No, the other players would have to earn their own chips.[12] Economic policy, therefore, would have to look beyond the deceptive affluence of the moment to assure the long-term well-being of the world economy. In February 1948, a communist coup in Czechoslovakia, the sole remaining democracy in eastern Europe, inspired a wavering Congress to make up its mind in favor of Marshall aid. Congress swallowed hard, but after a long period of debate that featured a relentless public-relations program by the Truman administration, at length it approved a first installment of 6 billion dollars for Europe, with 6 billion more to come over the next four years.

Marshall money was not distributed in no-strings-attached grants. Instead, European governments were expected to come together and hammer out an integrated plan that prescribed recovery for the entire continent. This meant that each nation had to subordinate its specific economic desires to the good of the whole. On a rather less enlightened note, despite the comparatively miserable performance of the U.S. economy throughout the 1930s, American administrators rather arrogantly expected Europeans to defer to superior American economic know-how in planning their reconstruction.

Although it would have made good sense to advocate something of the sort even if relations with the USSR had been harmonious, the Marshall Plan nevertheless had enormous consequences for the cold war. As American policy-makers anticipated, the Soviets refused to have anything to do with it. They did show up at the conference in Paris convened by British Foreign Minister Ernest Bevin in the vain hope that American money would be handed out with no questions asked, as had been their experience with Lend-Lease aid during World War II. But once it became clear that the Soviet and east European economies would have to be plugged into a larger European market economy, Molotov walked out and took the satellite nations with him. The communists had no intention of giving up control of their economic destiny, which was based on a system of centralized planning directed from Moscow; nor would they permit eastern Europe to gravitate economically toward the western orbit.

As Europe finally entered a period of spectacular economic expansion, the Marshall Plan became perhaps the greatest success story of American postwar policy. So stunning was its reputation for achievement that every so often there were calls for Marshall Plans for different regions. More recently, some historians have argued that the recovery of Europe was on the verge of taking off even without Marshall aid. That is probably true, but the Marshall Plan's objectives went beyond pure economics. A key target of the program was morale, specifically the reversal of a defeatist psychology in Europe that inhibited the willingness to save and invest which was so necessary to capitalist enterprise. What was the point, after all, of working hard and saving if communism appeared to be the wave of the future? If, on the other hand, the United States could prove to the Europeans that America was standing behind them, that the United States had faith in Europe's destiny, then the confidence and morale indispensable to recovery might resurface.

As a confidence-building measure, the Marshall Plan introduced the camel's nose into the tent. It began the institutionalization of a process in which requests for sizeable foreign aid and military assistance programs became a regular feature of the annual budget process during the cold war. Though foreign aid was highly unpopular with Congress, the legislators typically loosened the purse strings in the face of what seemed to be compelling national security arguments. Here, too, foreign aid programs and military assistance were less geared to promoting development or assuring security in measurable terms than in boosting the morale of nations who otherwise might lean to the Soviet side.

The Marshall Plan seemed to promise a relatively painless and nonprovocative way out of western Europe's problems. But, like all solutions, it created problems of its own. In particular, it forced a decision on an issue of the highest importance that had remained unsettled since the war's end: the future of Germany. Restoring Europe's economic health entailed a willingness to bring the German economy back to life. American policy makers deemed it unlikely that the rest of Europe would be able rebuild if Germany, the continent's dynamo, remained out of commission. Compelling though German economic revival was in liberal economic terms, it was bound to upset the Soviets, who had much harsher ideas about how Germany ought to be treated.

The Parting of the Ways on German Policy

For a time toward the end of World War II it seemed likely that the U.S. and the Soviets would be of one mind on how to manage the German problem. Both allies had an interest in controlling Germany, lest nationalism rear its head and result in another bid for domination. The Morgenthau Plan, broached by FDR's anti-German secretary of the treasury, suggested a deliberate policy of deindustrialization—destroying the country's factories, flooding its mines, and turning the land into a bucolic nation of shepherds and peasants. For those who hoped to secure U.S.-Soviet harmony, this policy of harshness promised to pay some extra dividends. German industrial plants could be dismantled and shipped eastward as in-kind reparations that would help the USSR repair the devastation inflicted by the German Wehrmacht. A harsh peace, by this calculation, would be beneficial to everyone but the Germans. The British, for example, presumably would stand to profit by stepping in to take over Germany's former export trade.

Though seriously considered at the highest levels, the Morgenthau Plan was finally scrapped because it ran afoul of liberal sentiment. World War I had imposed a punitive peace, but its provisions had been self-defeating, succeeding only in sowing dragons' teeth for the future. Its political harshness had contributed to the rise of fanatical Nazism while its shortsighted economic provisions were in no small measure responsible for the global depression of the 1930s. To classical liberals within the administration like Secretary of War Henry Stimson, who were "horrified by the Carthaginian attitude of the Treasury," deindustrializing Germany, a policy of "turning such a gift of nature into a dust heap,"[13] would be a crime against civilization. It would "surely lay the seeds for another war."[14] If only Soviet views did not have to be taken into account, democratization and integration into the world economy would have been a far better and more obvious solution to the German problem.

The Morgenthau Plan was killed off, but it had a long bureaucratic afterlife. As set out in the army's occupation directive, JCS 1067, the U.S. would provide economic aid only to prevent "disease and unrest." Otherwise, if Germany experienced economic chaos, so be it. The Germans would have to accept the consequences of their actions. The ghost of Morgenthauism also haunted international agreements. At the Potsdam Conference, held on the outskirts of a gutted Berlin in July and August 1945, the victorious allies agreed to hold the Germans to a very low standard of living. The German economy would be self-supporting, but only just barely. Exactly what it would take to reach this low level, was to be determined in subsequent negotiations.

Into the spring of 1946, the parleys over Germany's future "level of industry" chugged along reasonably well until they hit a snag over the Export-Import Plan, the amount of export industry that would be allowable to pay for needed imports. The Russians wanted reparations removals to begin flowing immediately; the western allies preferred to wait and see if the German economy was indeed self-sustaining before allowing reparations to be siphoned off. This chicken-and-egg disagreement was not beyond reasonable resolution, but by this time cold war suspicions had come to Germany as the Allies began trading propaganda accusations about their ultimate goals. The Russians suggested that the western powers were holding up the creation of a unified Germany; the westerners charged in turn that the Soviets were committed to a program of impoverishing and enslaving the German people.

As the propaganda battle heated up, the economy in the western zones continued to worsen. For the second time in the century, German currency was worthless. Shortages of fuel, food, and housing afflicted the miserable population. With economic activity pretty much at a standstill, it was not long before a critical mass of policy-makers began to realize that Europe's economic problems were connected to Germany's. If the Marshall Plan hoped to succeed in jump-starting Europe's economy, it would have to promote a modicum of German recovery as well. However, accepting this line of reasoning meant that the unspoken Soviet-American agreement on a Carthaginian peace, and with it the hopes of cooperation, would have to be abandoned.

Slowly, the United States and Britain began the turnaround, dragging a very reluctant French government behind them. A merger of the Anglo-American zones went into effect at the end of 1946. By mid-1947, a more generous occupation directive, JCS 1779, replaced the punitive JCS 1076. Early in 1948, the London Program spelled out Germany's eligibility for Marshall funds and agreed to the formation of a government for the western zones. Soon after, the Americans and British realized that economic recovery would require monetary reform. A new currency would have to replace the utterly useless Mark then in circulation in all four zones. Consequently, in the spring of 1948, the Deutsche Mark was introduced in the western zones and in the western sectors of Berlin.

Because of these moves, the Soviets no longer had any voice in economic policy in the West. Hoping to restore their influence over Germany as a whole, they resorted to their one clear source of leverage in the country by blockading the western sectors of Berlin. The former German capital, located some 110 miles within the Soviet zone of occupation, had been placed under four-power occupation as a symbol of Allied determination to maintain unity in the postwar control of Germany. "You Germans will not be able to divide us," said the joint occupation. However, once the garment of four-power occupation began to split at the seams, Berlin's location made it a convenient pressure point for use against the capitalist powers. Unfortunately, too, for the West, from a narrowly legalistic standpoint, the Soviets were within their rights in closing off the city to land, rail, and river traffic. There was nothing in the agreements on Berlin that spelled out Western transit rights to the city.

Faced with the choice of seeing the population of West Berlin starve or capitulating to Soviet demands that might obstruct European recovery, the Truman administration took a gamble: it proposed to resupply the city by air, sensing that the Soviets would not risk a war by shooting down Allied transport planes. The wager paid off. Transport capacity was strained nearly to the breaking point, weather conditions over Berlin were frequently miserable, and Western pilots were frequently harassed by Soviet fighter planes, but the airlift persisted for nearly a year before the Soviets called off the blockade.

In this first major crisis between the U.S. and the Soviets in the postwar period, the Berlin airlift, for all its tensions, posed only a minor risk of war, though at first apprehensions in Washington were running high. It should be made clear "that we are prepared to stand and fight on this," urged Averell Harriman.[15] But the mere fact that Stalin was unwilling to make the blockade of the city airtight was a signal that he wanted to avoid war; indeed, the city continued to receive considerable quantities of supplies from the Soviet zone because the blockade had only closed off *western* supply routes. For its part, the airlift, which was portrayed as a symbol of American determination, had also been undertaken with a view to avoiding shooting. Moreover, the confrontation did not signify an end to discussions of the problem. As the airplanes roared in and out of the city, the diplomats continued to drone on in negotiations behind the scenes. What did Stalin want? He wanted to be dealt back in on all-Germany issues, the American ambassador in Moscow reported.

As time went on, it became evident to the Soviets that the blockade was not only a propaganda disaster, but that it had also added momentum to America's plans to proceed with a separate plan of action in the western zones. Once Stalin agreed to call off the blockade in return for a meeting of foreign ministers on German issues in 1949, he discovered that the clock could not be turned back to 1946. No peace treaty for Germany had been put on the diplomatic agenda, the assumption at the time being that it would be better for the Allies to "feel" their way into a prudent solution than to make a treaty on the basis of passions still ablaze from the war. Now the prospect of a treaty was more distant than ever. Indeed, even the provisional agreements hammered out at Potsdam could no longer keep together the wartime allies. The result was a further tightening of Soviet and American spheres of influence on each side of the iron curtain.

The Hardening of Lines in Europe, 1949

The Berlin crisis was not just about Germany. Western Europe's low body-temperature had been raised, but the rising confidence of postwar western Europe was still susceptible to the chill of the cold war. Because Germany was crucial to European recovery, the airlift brought home to Europeans and Americans how easily the Continent could be demoralized by military threats. With the prompting of influential Europeans, Washington soon came to the conclusion that, in addition to the Marshall Plan, a military comforter was in order.

In 1948, the western European countries took a number of steps to assure their own security. The signature of the Brussels Pact by Great Britain, France, and the Benelux countries early in the year was a token of Europe's willingness to defend itself. But many believed that western Europe alone was relatively helpless. Largely at the urging of British Foreign Minister Ernest Bevin, talks began in Washington in 1948 looking toward the formation of a broader collective security organization that would include the United States. By the spring of 1949, the North Atlantic Treaty, with its key provision that an attack against one would be considered an attack against all, even an attack by a member state, was ready for signing.

There were a number of noteworthy features about this alliance. Most obviously, it ended the hallowed tradition, laid down in George Washington's Farewell Address some hundred and fifty years earlier, of avoiding "entangling alliances" in peacetime. NATO also furnished the guarantee of European security that continental nations, particularly France, had been seeking since 1919. Though clearly inconsistent with the U.N.'s conceptual framework of great-power harmony, NATO found legalistic sanction in articles 50 and 51 of the U.N. Charter, which provided for regional self-defense. The United States had already taken the opportunity under this section to sign the Rio Pact in 1948 and to create the Organization of American States.

Despite the regional language, the old cocoon of regionalism had by this time been left far behind, having been transformed into the butterfly of collective security. NATO in particular was justified as a collective security organization, a catchphrase that still had considerable resonance among old-line Wilsonians. For Bevin, NATO incarnated in regional form way what the U.N. "should have been had the Soviets cooperated."[16] While many balance-of-power realists scoffed at this description and preferred to view NATO as a traditional alliance, we shall see in the next chapter that NATO indeed possessed a structure and logic that fully justified its being described in such Wilsonian terms.

But for the time being, the North Atlantic Treaty was merely a piece of paper that recorded the respective commitments of its signatory members. It was a statement of intentions, not an organization. It commanded no armies, nor did it yet have anything resembling a viable military strategy. For now, the organization's reason for being was more to reassure the West than to deter the Soviets. Indeed, military deterrence was not a priority item for Americans at this time, as Truman was still pushing very hard to cap the U.S. military budget at 14 billion dollars. The emergence of NATO as an effective institutional presence, the North Atlantic Treaty *Organization,* would come somewhat later as the cold war was militarized.

Belated attempts to divert the surging waters of the cold war into different channels failed miserably. For example, Kennan, who by this time had become a critic of containment, believed that the Marshall Plan was sufficient to persuade the Soviets into withdrawing their forces from central and eastern Europe. That was a dubious assertion, but he was on more solid ground in predicting that NATO would harden the cold war by practically assuring the continued partition of Germany and the Continent. In a last-ditch effort to head off this eventuality, Kennan proposed that a mutual withdrawal of forces from central Europe be negotiated with the Soviets, after which a neutral European federation could be set in place. Before he could make any headway with his plan, its appearance in the newspapers raised a big ruckus in western Europe, particularly in France, where Kennan's ideas aroused fears of an independent Germany. Clearly, America's allies had their hearts set on NATO. Indeed, it had been pretty much their idea in the first place, "an intelligent way of achieving steady American protection for the future," as one historian put it.[17]

Kennan was also very much in the minority in Washington. Following Truman's near miraculous come-from-behind victory in the 1948 presidential election, the president appointed a new secretary of state for his second term. Dean Acheson had served in various high-level posts off and on for more than fifteen years, most notably as undersecretary of state in 1945 and 1946. Less convinced than Kennan that the Soviets were willing to negotiate with the West, Acheson was more interested in building up "situations of strength." But at first he was quite willing to give a hearing to Kennan's views, especially to his arguments about the German problem. If Germany remained divided, Kennan suggested, a malignant German nationalism was every bit as likely to fester as it had after the First World War.

Acheson listened, but in the end concluded that Kennan's proposals, if adopted, would lead to the undoing of more than two years of policy. Those policies had been painfully arrived at after protracted and often difficult negotiations with America's allies and with Congress. To adopt Kennan's proposals would not only throw the West into an uproar, it would be to buy a pig in a poke, because there was no certainty that Kennan's policies would succeed. And if Europe was not attracted to the U.S., it would be drawn inevitably toward the Soviet magnetic pole. As one policy paper argued, "the idea that Germany or Japan or other important areas can exist as islands of neutrality in a divided world is unreal."[18] Better to go with a known quantity, then, than to leap dangerously into the void of uncertainty.

With the U.S. decision to hitch its wagon to NATO's star, the implications for Germany were clear. Taking precedence over unification, at least for the time being, was the need to normalize the political situation in the three western zones and to integrate them into Europe. Beginning in 1948, a Parliamentary Council began meeting with a view to writing a constitution for the western zones. Finally, in the autumn of 1949, the new document went into effect, creating a new political entity: The Federal Republic of Germany. As the new government assumed its functions in the small Rhenish city of Bonn, the occupation was simultaneously civilianized. Henceforth, ultimate authority in the Federal Republic was exercised by an Allied High Commission that oversaw issues of high politics pending full restoration of sovereignty or the signature of a peace treaty. For their part, the Soviets upgraded the eastern zone into the German Democratic

Republic, whose formal existence the West refused to acknowledge. With these developments, Germany and Europe were divided ideologically and politically along the military frontiers established at the end of the war.

From one point of view, the partition of Germany and Europe was a solution in the tradition of realism and spheres of influence. From the inside, though, things looked rather different. If Germany alone had been at issue between the U.S. and the Soviets, a mutually satisfactory agreement could probably have been reached. But the future of Germany was never considered in isolation. Partition was an unintended outcome of conflict over larger issues having to do with Germany's relationship to Europe and the world.

The partition solution raised numerous collateral problems. Even if the new Federal Republic had been granted full sovereignty, the West Germans would not have been disposed to close the book on the results of World War II. Germany, they believed, would be restored to itself only when reunification took place. At a minimum, that would require some way of reintegrating the Soviet zone. Indicative of the West German state of mind was the name of the Federal Republic's founding legal document, which was called the Basic Law rather than the Constitution. A constitution would become the governing blueprint only after reunification. Because the United States felt compelled for cold-war reasons to back West German nationalist ambitions, these unsettled issues of sovereignty and reunification would become major *global* issues in the decades to come.

By the end of 1949, the first phase of the cold war in Europe had played itself out. In the hope of preventing the communization of the Continent, the Truman administration had articulated the Truman Doctrine, passed the Marshall Plan, joined NATO, and accepted a de facto partition of Germany. In other circumstances, policy-makers might well have rested on their laurels and retired to write their memoirs. However, the many further crises and policy initiatives that lay in store showed that this series of events was only a preliminary phase of the cold war in Europe. Subsequent changes were in large measure the consequence of developments in the Far East, the Soviet possession of the atomic bomb, and a reevaluation of Soviet intentions that took place in Washington in 1949 and 1950. The problems of Germany and western Europe, while crucial, were part of a larger global conflict between two worldviews whose differences could not be negotiated.

The Postwar Far East as Global Catalyst

Just as an understanding of how the crisis of the 1930s unfolded into a world war requires an appreciation of America's global interpretation of

Japanese conduct in the Far East, the cold war cannot be understood without taking into account the global impact that Asia had upon American foreign policy. Despite an obvious Europe-first orientation that stretched throughout the century, one of the long-standing puzzles of American diplomacy is why, since the 1930s, most of the hot wars have started in Asia—Pearl Harbor, the Korean War, and Vietnam being the most notable events. From the standpoint of political realism or economic interests, it is odd that the U.S. should have fought for areas that were of little intrinsic strategic or economic importance, but the puzzlement evaporates once one comes to appreciate the role played by the Far East in the rather different Wilsonian framework.

China had long been a secondary factor in American policy. This was as true of the China theater during World War II, which remained a strategic backwater, as it was of the 1930s, when the Sino-Japanese War took a back seat to the threat from Hitler's Germany. But its symbolic status was far more important than its substantive value, thanks to the long-standing connection between the Open Door Policy and global issues. The Open Door was revered because it expressed in a nutshell the American image of a modern world: an absence of great-power antagonism, coupled with cooperation in the great project of promoting modernization and development free of imperialism.

That was the "normal" image of the Open Door, a view that neatly complemented normal American internationalism, but the remarkable sequence of events that culminated in the Pearl Harbor attack demonstrated that the image of an open world could also be interpreted in Wilsonian crisis terms. The same was true for the cold war in the Far East. Until the remarkable expansion of economic growth in the 1960s and 70s, Asia had a symbolic importance out of all proportion to its actual economic and strategic value. The faint signals emitted from crises in Asia, which formerly would have been confined to the region, were amplified and transmitted globally by Wilsonian ideology.

The U.S. became more heavily involved than ever in China's internal politics during the war, when General Joseph Stilwell, as Chiang Kai-shek's chief of staff, placed heavy pressure on the Generalissimo to reform his corrupt and inefficient regime in order to better fight the Japanese. Frightened by the vigor of a new Japanese offensive, the U.S. even went so far as to send an informal observer mission to the communist base area in Yenan in remote north China to explore the possibility of enlisting the rebel Mao Zedong's forces in a new common front against the Japanese. This so-called "Dixie Mission" (because it was in rebel territory) was undertaken by the Office of Strategic Services, a wartime precursor of the Central Intelligence Agency. Although many State Department "China hands" favored making common cause with the militarily more effective communists, Roosevelt decided by late 1944 that it was better to leave the China situation, snarled as it was, unchanged. As the Japanese offensive waned, the Chinese theater lost its military importance. Chiang's nationalist armies, however ineffectual, continued to hold down large numbers of Japanese troops who otherwise might have been used to lethal effect against American forces in their island-hopping advance across the Pacific Ocean.

With the war's end, the on-again, off-again civil war in China went into its final innings. Ostensibly neutral, the United States nevertheless provided considerable support to Chiang by ferrying his troops to Manchuria and the northern cities, thus enabling them to jump the line ahead of Mao's communist forces in accepting the surrender of the Japanese army. American troops also provided training and guarded Chiang's lines of communications. Hoping to mediate an end to the civil war, early in 1946 Truman dispatched General George Marshall in a futile year-long effort to bring the two sides together peaceably in a coalition government. With Marshall having to contend with a tradition in which there could be only one legitimate ruler under the "mandate of heaven," the prospect of creating a coalition of equals was never good. At the same time, neither party was willing to be the junior partner. By the end of the year, Marshall threw in the towel and returned home to become Truman's new secretary of state. China's fate would have to be settled on the battlefield.

As early as 1947, the handwriting was on the wall and Washington knew it: Chiang Kai-shek and the hapless nationalist forces were doomed. With the emergence of the cold war and the withdrawal of Soviet support for Chiang, Mao was now free to pursue a policy of military victory in the civil war. Much as the Truman administration might have wished otherwise, there was little it could do to turn the tide. Financial and military aid seemed fruitless, as Chiang's corrupt regime was sure to divert most of the money to personal uses. "Thieves, every last one of them," complained Truman. The administration's reluctance to provide aid touched off a squabble in Congress, where so-called Asia Firsters, prodded by an effective China lobby on Capitol Hill, insisted that the Truman Doctrine ought to apply to China as well as to Greece and Turkey. For reasons of domestic politics and a reluctance to admit defeat to the communists, in 1948 the administration capitulated to congressional passage of the China Aid Act, which provided 125 million in funds.

The money did little to stave off a nationalist collapse. The inevitable occurred in October 1949, when a victorious Mao announced the People's Republic of China in Beijing. Chiang's routed forces, meanwhile, had fled across the Formosa Strait and installed themselves on the island of Taiwan, hoping to lick their wounds and prepare a return to the mainland. But the prospect of a turnaround in Chiang's fortunes struck policy-makers in Washington as a fantasy. Most expected the People's Liberation Army, after a brief period of preparation, to successfully invade Taiwan and finally put an end to the long-running civil war.

For the Truman administration, this outcome was a setback, to be sure, but hardly a disaster. Following a period of "waiting for the dust to settle," the U.S. hoped to recognize the new regime. Though communist, the PRC was thought to be, first and foremost, intensely nationalist in outlook. The feasibility of national communisms existing beyond Moscow's control had already been demonstrated by the noisy dispute between Stalin and Marshall Tito's Yugoslavia in 1948. Tito had come to power on the strength of his leadership of the anti-Nazi Partisan guerrilla movement during World War II. Unlike the satraps in the eastern bloc, his existence did not depend on the presence of the Red Army. U.S. policy-makers hoped that a communist China, whose creation owed little to Stalin's support, might likewise be separated from the Soviet flock and, with some skill and luck, played off against Moscow to America's advantage.

However, events abroad and at home failed to unfold according to expectations. In 1949, Mao announced that the PRC would side firmly with the socialist camp. A number of incidents in which American diplomats were held in virtual captivity underlined the deep animosity of the new regime towards the United States and the West. The Sino-Soviet Treaty of February 1950 provided further evidence that communist foreign policies, despite a long history of Sino-Russian enmity, were being defined in terms of ideological antagonism with the West, and not, as originally anticipated, by national interests.

At home, things were no better. The collapse of the nationalist regime on the mainland led to heated accusations that the Truman administration had "lost China." Despite Acheson's attempts to pin the blame on Chiang's ineptness, Republican right-wing critics assigned far greater importance to the wartime flirtation with Mao as an explanation for the debacle. This dalliance was attributed to the existence of a large body of treasonous communist sympathizers within the Department of State, a group that was alleged to be conspiratorially responsible for the fall of China to communism.

The Truman administration responded that China was not America's to lose, which was quite true, but it was drowned out by a pack of critics that howled even louder at the scent of blood. The fall of China, it turned out, had an extraordinarily demoralizing effect upon many Americans who had long assumed that America's China policy lay at the heart of the nation's effort to reorder the modern world away from traditional politics. If China policy was a failure, so too, by implication, was global policy.

The administration also badly miscalculated the possibility of letting bygones be bygones with the PRC. However shrill and even hysterical the criticisms of China policy, Mao's decision to align with the USSR gave the critics a powerful debating point that the administration found impossible to rebut. Ideological solidarity *did* appear to be more powerful than nationalism, as indeed it was, if only for the time being. Like the dog who walked on its hind legs, the surprise was not that it was done well but that it was possible at all. With some warrant, then, the Truman administration soon arrived at the conclusion that the U.S. was faced not by a coalition of nation states but by a monolithic international movement centered in Moscow. Thus, instead of becoming the norm, Tito's Yugoslavia turned out to be the exception that proved the rule.

The emergence of a communist China contributed enormously to this sense of monolithic threat, as roughly one-third of the world's population was now living under communist rule. "The manpower and the resources of the world will be mobilized against us," warned William Bullitt. Viewed in traditional national and regional terms, there was little to hold the PRC and the USSR together. But, just as the loose coalition of Axis powers in the late 1930s came to be perceived in undifferentiated global terms, the combination of European and Asian dangers in 1947 sensitized American policy-makers to the looming world communist threat, with a shared global ideology providing even greater justification for holding such a view. Thus, while the force of nationalism was granted in principle, in practice communism was viewed as monolithic. Today, our understanding is more nuanced. Nationalism did not disappear in the communist bloc, but we also know that internationalist ideology exerted a powerful force of mutual attraction among Marxist countries. Indeed, the same was true of the western nations, whose foreign policies would otherwise have gone their separate ways had not the centripetal force of ideology pushed them together.

The hysteria that greeted the emergence of the People's Republic of China requires some finer brush strokes in the domestic portion of the picture. The fear of communism that blanketed the United States like a dense fog did not spring solely from an abstract Wilsonian sense of global danger. For the American people, still remarkably provincial and insular in their understanding of the external world, the threat from Communism

was mainly *internal*. The kind of romantic celebration of the Soviet experiment that was common during the 1930s and the war years was no longer
tolerated in a postwar scene in which even the New Deal, for many, was
a socialist plot. The sense that the American way of life was on the verge
of being subverted by a communist fifth column generated a wave of
support for administration cold-war policies whose own foreign policy
rationale was literally a world removed from the public's mentality.

All politics is local politics, it is said. Many Americans believed that
the U.S. government was honeycombed with communist traitors. This fear
of domestic subversion was, unfortunately, coupled to a conservative conviction that the country, ever since the swing toward the left in the New
Deal, had been treading the path to socialism. When the demagogue Senator Joseph McCarthy complained of "twenty years of treason" he was
thoroughly fusing and confusing domestic with foreign antiradicalism.
The unnerving discovery that the Soviets had spied on the American nuclear program since its inception, coupled with spectacular accusations of
treachery against Alger Hiss, formerly a highly placed State Department
official, appeared to confirm the existence of communist termites eating
away the support beams of government.

The offspring of this incongruous mating of domestic and international
fears had both good and bad effects for American foreign policy. On the
positive side, the belief that communism was a domestic danger provided
a fervent base of popular support for cold-war policies that otherwise
might have been seduced by neo-isolationism. On the other hand, this
support could become too rabid. In the case of China, the flood of domestic pressures for action threatened to overwhelm the levees of prudence.
In addition, the demands that internal traitors be flushed out of hiding and
punished led to witch hunts within the government that severely demoralized loyal public employees within the State Department and other agencies. Finally, there was a problem that would not come to light for some
years. Like the mule that is the offspring of horse and donkey, this cold
war ideological crossbreed could not reproduce itself.

The domestic side-effects of the fall of China drove home the fact that
cold-war foreign policy was not constructed on a solid foundation of public support. Indeed, that was true of Wilsonianism generally. First Pearl
Harbor in 1941 and now irrational anticommunism a decade later had
papered over an enormous gap between official and popular understanding. For the time being, despite its excesses, popular anticommunism
could be contained and channeled to cold-war uses. However, should the
gap between capital and country reemerge, as it did in the 1960s, Wilsonian internationalism would once again be in deep trouble.

1949 and 1950: The Reemergence of Crisis Internationalism

By itself, the loss of China, even when magnified by doubts about the stability of the American political system, might not have been enough to deflect cold-war foreign policy from its postwar trajectory. But these events, when blended with the news in September 1949 that the Soviets had detonated an atomic bomb, stimulated the Truman administration into some soul-searching that led to far-reaching changes in American cold-war policy. In combination, the fall of China and the Soviet A-bomb had an overpowering effect on American foreign policy because they evoked the two primal fears of Wilsonianism: world war and world conquest.

To this point, the atomic bomb had been America's ace in the hole. Immediately following the war it was widely expected that the nuclear monopoly would last ten to fifteen years. Those early estimates were subsequently recognized as overly optimistic, but the Soviet bomb came as a surprise nonetheless. Knocked for a loop was the widespread assumption that Soviet science, because of ideological distortions and the compulsive secrecy of the Soviet regime, was no match for the Western system of inquiry based on innovation and openness. "This is now a different world," said Senator Arthur Vandenberg.

More than anything else, the bomb had been a security blanket for the United States and its Western allies. However pathetic the state of Western defenses in Europe or elsewhere—and in Europe it was assumed that the Red Army could overrun the Continent in a matter of days—the bomb hovered reassuringly in the background as the ultimate deterrent against Soviet adventurism. Steadily, contingency planning for another war had put more and more of America's military eggs in the nuclear basket. Now, however, in the light of the new strategic situation, policy would have to be rethought. "It changed everything," said Acheson of the bomb.[19]

According to Truman, had it not been for the American nuclear monopoly, "the Russians would probably have taken over Europe a long time ago."[20] (The inability of the U.S. to deliver the bomb on target, thanks to a bumbling Strategic Air Command, was another story.) Inasmuch as the U.S. had not contemplated committing troops to the Continent, America's guarantee of European security in the North Atlantic treaty had little to back it up now that the nuclear guarantee of Europe was no longer credible. Thus, among other things, the Soviet bomb meant that NATO's effectiveness had to be reconsidered. The sense of security essential to economic recovery, according to Dean Acheson, required "a firm belief in the ability of free nations to defend themselves."[21] With confidence apparently on the decline, conventional teeth would have to be put into the

alliance. By the end of 1949, administration insiders were already beginning to think about the unthinkable: rearming the Germans.

Another important by-product of the Soviet atomic explosion was the
decision to develop a thermonuclear weapon, a superbomb based on the
fusion of hydrogen nuclei, whose explosive force was roughly one hundred times greater than that of an atomic bomb. With the physics already
well worked out, Truman decided quickly to make development a national
priority. Although Kennan protested that a thermonuclear bomb had no
military or diplomatic usefulness, the president understood intuitively and
immediately that the hydrogen bomb, because it conferred enormous psychological power upon its possessor, could not be permitted to become
a Soviet monopoly. It would be disastrous if the Soviets possessed such
a device and the United States did not—they "might dominate the world,"
said Paul Nitze, Kennan's hard-line successor at the Policy Planning
Staff.[22] Nitze, says one historian, was "naturally attracted by an instrument
that might serve as a surrogate for the will and resolve of the American
people in the international arena, something in which, as a former isolationist, he had little faith."[23]

The Soviet A-bomb and the fall of China pointed most of all to the
need to reconsider a fundamental assumption of containment to this point:
that the Soviet Union was a reasonable, status-quo power. Prior to the
Soviet nuclear explosion, the ongoing debate about how deeply the Soviet
leaders were committed to communism was moot as long as the United
States had a nuclear monopoly. No matter how radical, socialism's status
as a secular religion meant that the Soviets could not ignore the American
bomb. In the absence of a communist heaven, martyrdom was no service
to the communist cause if it threatened the existence of the Soviet state.

By the end of 1949, Washington was beginning to shift its view on
Soviet ideology away from Kennan's reassuring assertions that the Soviet
leaders were realists. More and more, officials were convinced that the
Soviets were indeed zealous ideologues. "Moscow's faith in the inevitable
disintegration of capitalism is not a passive faith in automatic historical
evolution," argued the CIA. "Instead it is a messianic faith."[24] And indeed,
it appears that the events of 1949 did make Stalin somewhat giddy with
success.

The new strategic situation seemed inherently favorable to ideological
radicalism. Throughout the late 1940s, American intelligence agencies
had discounted the likelihood of a Soviet attack. But now that the Soviets
had the bomb, it was a different story. Though few believed that Moscow
was bent on starting another war, the Kremlin was in a better position to
run dangerous risks on behalf of expanding the communist world, risks

that formerly would have been inconceivable. Again, Kennan dissented, insisting that nothing fundamental had changed since 1945, but his voice no longer carried an authority capable of shaping Washington's view of Moscow's intentions.

Despite frequent comparisons with Hitler's Germany, which, according to Kennan, "drove the experts on Russia to despair,"[25] the Soviet threat was indeed quite different, though in ways that were not reassuring to Americans. Notwithstanding some similarities, Stalin was not like Hitler. Hitler's German nationalism sought to expand through force, whereas Moscow's internationalism sought a victory of communist ideas validated and supported by Soviet power. On the other hand, the communist threat was in some respects more dangerous thanks to communism's undeniable global appeal, whereas the Kaiser, Hitler, and Japan had a comparatively limited ideological allure. Now the atomic bomb had given the Soviets the *perception* of power. With its new military strength, the Soviet Union presented the worst of both worlds: a seductive globalist ideology combined with a superpower state.

The significant differences between Nazi Germany and the Soviet Union were overshadowed by similarities in the ultimate outcomes of their foreign policies. In its structural fundamentals, the threat was in almost all respects the same as the one perceived by Wilson in 1917 and FDR in 1941. By 1950, virtually every element of Wilson's assessment of the Great War was present: the threat of world conquest emanating from an international communist movement; the danger of a world war from a powerful Soviet state that had acquired important satellites and allies; the end of the European balance of power, evident in the continuing inability of the Europeans to restabilize themselves; and the possibility of a small spark somewhere setting off a runaway conflagration. Summing up, Acheson told a group of newspaper editors that the U.S. was "faced with a threat not only to our country but to the civilization in which we live and to the whole physical environment in which that civilization can exist."[26]

This redefined threat called for a dramatic new response that went beyond the many significant steps already taken in the postwar years. In 1947, Congress passed the National Security Act, which brought about an organizational revolution in the conduct of U.S. foreign relations. The oftentimes competitive armed services, formerly represented individually on the cabinet level, were now housed together in the new Department of Defense and coordinated by a secretary of defense. With the intention of preventing another surprise attack like Pearl Harbor, this bill also institutionalized the Central Intelligence Agency, which was only the most prominent of a vast and growing network of intelligence-gathering bodies.

The Defense Department, the joint chiefs, the CIA, and the State Department were all represented on the new National Security Council, an addition to the White House staff that considerably enhanced the president's power to coordinate foreign relations.

The Truman administration had expanded its foreign policy toolshop in other ways, as well. Adopting an innovation it had long been reluctant to accept, in the Smith-Mundt Act of 1948 Congress provided funds for propaganda and cultural relations programs in support of foreign policy. And, in addition to the Marshall Plan, after 1949 the government began giving away large quantities of foreign aid under the Military Assistance Program and technical assistance under Truman's Point Four initiative. More conventionally, peacetime conscription, voted in June 1948, provided the necessary manpower for an enlarged military establishment. Institutionally, then, by 1950 the United States was already well on the way to creating what has been called the "national security state."

But all of this proved to be still not enough, as the Soviet bomb pushed American defense strategy to a whole new level of mobilization altogether. If the bomb was no longer a deterrent, the possibility of a nuclear standoff meant that conventional forces could become the deciding factor in any conflict. In the spring of 1950, the National Security Council completed a far-reaching document, NSC 68, that recommended a quadrupling of America's peacetime military expenditures. While American military spending was high compared to pre–World War II levels, in 1949 Truman had tried ruthlessly to limit military spending to 14 billion dollars, an indication of his belief that the cold war, at that point, could be managed in a relatively frugal way. In a few years, that kind of military budget would seem positively penny-ante.

Kept secret until 1975, NSC 68 was a product of the crisis mentality within Washington in early 1950. It argued that "the integrity and vitality of our system is in greater jeopardy than ever before in our history" because Kremlin policy sought "the complete subversion or forcible destruction of the machinery of government and structure of society of the non-Soviet world." The Soviet bomb, it argued, "puts new power behind its design, and increases the jeopardy to our system." Describing "a descending spiral of too little and too late, of doubt and recrimination" as "the greatest risk of all," the document called for putting the nation on a wartime footing as a way of containing the Soviets, pending "a fundamental change in the nature of the Soviet system." Though he agreed with its recommendations, Truman had little idea at the time of how to gain congressional approval for such a far-reaching program of rearmament.

The fall of China, the Soviet A-bomb, and the reevaluation of commu-

nist ideology led the Truman administration to shift its containment policy away from the monetary and political morale-building measures of
the early postwar years. Once again, though, events outpaced policy. The
adoption of NSC 68 and the decision to proceed with the development
of a hydrogen bomb, while important, turned out to be wholly inadequate
steps in the face of communist military initiatives. None of the challenges
surmounted since 1945 had forced American policymakers to face up to
the core issue of Wilsonian thought: how to deal with military aggression.
That problem was raised by the Korean War.

The Korean War and the Naturalization of Wilsonianism

The fire alarms sounded in earnest on June 25, 1950, when forces from
the communist People's Democratic Republic of Korea, or North Korea,
invaded South Korea. Until that point, Korea had been of little concern
to the United States. Following liberation from Japanese rule in 1945, the
country was divided into Soviet and American zones of occupation and,
as happened with Germany, the advent of the cold war made reunification
impossible. After a futile attempt to promote U.N.-sponsored national
elections, the U.S. withdrew its armed forces from South Korea in 1949,
leaving this rump state to exist on its own under the autocratic governance
of Syngman Rhee, a right-wing strongman who had lived for many years
in the United States. At the State Department's insistence, a pinch of foreign aid was grudgingly granted by Congress to the new country.

With Stalin giving the green light in the expectation that it would be
a low-risk operation, the North Korean dictator, Kim Il-Sung, decided to
reunify the peninsula before South Korea grew too powerful. Numerous
intelligence reports had pointed to the aggressive intentions of Kim's regime, but, as a result of crying wolf too often, the invasion came as a
complete surprise to Washington. With the attack, the *New York Times*
noted that "the world's major concern now is whether the universal conflagration can be avoided."[27] Truman and Acheson acted swiftly and decisively to repel the North Korean assault. A Soviet boycott of the Security
Council, begun in protest of the U.N.'s refusal to seat the People's Republic of China in place of Chiang Kai-shek's Taiwan regime, made it possible for interventionist resolutions to be rammed through without the threat
of a paralyzing veto by Moscow.

As a result, the intervention in Korea proceeded under the cloak of
collective security, as nations contributed troops to the effort. Nevertheless, many did so for reasons that had to do with the pursuit of narrow
local interests wholly unrelated to the Wilsonian rationale that dominated

thinking in Washington. In strictly numerical terms, the U.S. and South Korea were responsible for 90 percent of the troops and material, while the war was run from the Pentagon, not the U.N. headquarters. Over time, significant differences would emerge between the U.S. and its U.N. allies over the military and diplomatic conduct of the war in Korea. Even with the absence of the Soviets in the Security Council (who returned shortly), the halfhearted performance of the organization did not augur well for its future as a peacemaking organization.[28]

The U.N.'s role only underscored the nationalization of internationalism that had taken place. At a meeting of the National Security Council in Washington, the decision to intervene was made with very little discussion of whether it was justified by American security interests. The only question at issue was how to intervene, not whether it ought to be done. As historian Ernest May has explained, the unspoken "axiomatic" assumptions that policy-makers hold in common are more important than the "calculated" policies that form the subject of policy documents. The decision to take military action in Korea, taken with very little deliberation, suggested that the decision to intervene had already been made, in principle.

Afterwards, Truman explained that he was heeding the lessons of history. Recalling the 1930s, when the democracies had failed to stand up to Japan and Germany, he justified intervention as the only way of preventing another slide into world war. The decision was indeed the product of lessons of the past, prompted by memories of the failure in Manchuria and Munich to stop the momentum toward world war. But those crises made sense only from a Wilsonian standpoint, in the context of a Wilsonian narrative of modern world history. From another historical framework, Munich would have taken on a very different retrospective significance. The rapid American response to Korea demonstrated that Wilsonianism, extremely controversial only ten years earlier, had been internalized by the policy elite. If policy owes its existence to the need to make decisions without going over the fundamentals time after time, then the unspoken assumptions behind America's intervention in Korea suggest that Wilsonianism had become policy in its deepest sense. Once a marginal and controversial creed, it had been naturalized.[29] It had come to be so taken for granted that it was now outside the universe of discussion.

Truman's decision to intervene appeared to contradict repeated judgments by the American military that Korea was not essential to American security. "Korea is of little strategic value to the United States," said the joint chiefs just prior to the withdrawal of U.S. forces in June 1949.[30] In January 1950, Acheson let it be known in a speech to the National Press

Club that Korea was outside the U.S. defensive perimeter in Asia. Understandably, Republican critics later attacked the administration for virtually inviting the communists to reunify the country by force. But the paper policy of neglecting Korea had been based on the assumption that it would be a strategic backwater *if* World War III should happen to break out. In contrast, the issue of the moment was *preventing* another world war. "I've worked for peace for five years and six months," Truman wrote later, "and it looks like World War III is here. I hope not."[31]

The war in Korea did not have a traditional strategic justification. The chief clue to its Wilsonian origins was that it was not, strictly speaking, about Korea. By itself, Korea *was* unimportant, not only to the great majority of Americans who would not have known how to locate it on a map, but also to American policy-makers. To be sure, Korea mattered a great deal to Mao, to Japan, and to the Koreans themselves. But for America, it was primarily a token of more important issues.

Korea was a symbolic war, whose meaning was well explained by Truman's successor, Dwight D. Eisenhower. Speaking to his advisers, Eisenhower asserted that "the danger of war does not arise from the intrinsic value to the Communists of the Korean peninsula, but rather derives from the prestige which the Communists would enjoy if they succeeded in destroying a nation . . . set up and maintained by the United States. In short, South Korea had become a symbol throughout the world."[32] The danger of a communist success lay in its demoralizing effect on Western morale or world opinion. A willingness to stand fast, in contrast, would demonstrate the cohesiveness of world opinion. In brief, Korea was a Wilsonian war.

But the Wilsonian lessons of the past went only so far. The question of how exactly to turn the tide could not be answered by consulting history. Here the 1930s, with their record of inaction, provided no blueprint to follow. Consequently, after deciding to intervene, the Truman administration had to improvise a neo-Wilsonian solution to problems that had no exact parallels in the past and for which solutions are still not obvious, even in retrospect. In a process of trial and error, the administration developed an approach to the problem of military aggression that became the core of American containment policy over the next two decades. In other words, Wilsonianism was translated from theory to practice and was itself transformed in the event.

The first steps seemed obvious enough. The communist invasion, having taken the ill-prepared ROK troops by surprise, needed to be stemmed before the peninsula was overrun and conquered. American reinforcements, many of them "desk soldiers" on occupation duty in nearby Japan, were rushed to the Pusan perimeter in Korea's southeast until a counter-attack could be organized. In September, General Douglas MacArthur, the U.S. commander in the Far East, organized a spectacularly successful amphibious assault behind enemy lines at Inchon, on Korea's west coast. With the element of surprise now turned against them, the North Koreans began a pell-mell retreat northward in the direction of the 38th parallel.

At this point, things began to go seriously wrong for the Americans. Responding to the suggestions of those who insisted that the communists needed to be taught a lesson, MacArthur was authorized to pursue the North Koreans across the 38th parallel, all the way to the Chinese border, if necessary. If all went well, Korea would be reunified in the name of collective security and democracy. However, by October, advance elements of U.S. forces began to encounter Chinese troops, the first of more than half a million "volunteers" thrown into service against the Western imperialists. The prospect of a U.S. presence on his Manchurian border offended Mao's revolutionary nationalism. So too did the counterrevolutionary presence of the U.S. Navy's Seventh Fleet in the Taiwan Strait, ordered there at the war's outbreak to block an invasion of Taiwan. The outbreak of the Korean War thus solidified the Truman administration's reluctance to see the Chinese civil war end in a communist victory.

Determined to demonstrate his anti-imperialist bona fides to the world communist movement and to maintain the momentum of the Chinese revolution, Mao intervened in force.[33] Suddenly overwhelmed by sheer numbers, U.N. forces were compelled to retreat southward. The Truman administration was now faced with the enormous implications of its decisions. The intervention in Korea had been undertaken ostensibly to prevent a wider war from breaking out. But with Communist China raising the stakes, the problem of how to deal with aggression had been taken to a higher and far more dangerous level. Taking on the Chinese might lead to a further widening of the war, as Mao had only recently signed a treaty of alliance with Stalin in Moscow.

Though the administration had clearly pushed back too hard, to back off now threatened to repeat the dismal and ineffectual history of the 1930s. In principle, it had to be shown that crime does not pay. But where did one draw the line between a slap on the wrist and a reaction that threatened to slay the criminal and the peace officer alike? Where was the exact point of equilibrium between intervening too little or too much, the golden mean between a foolhardy policy of punishment and a cowardly pursuit of appeasement?

A chastened Truman administration now decided, in an unanticipated twist on the theme of "peace without victory," to pursue a policy of military stalemate aimed at restoring the prewar status quo of two Koreas divided along roughly the 38th parallel. But this new counterpunching strategy left the initiative wholly in the hands of the communists, who appeared to believe that time was now working to their advantage. Its effectiveness depended upon America's willingness to match communist escalation for an indefinite duration. Whether the American public had the patience to take casulties based on a deliberate no-win war of attrition remained to be seen.

The Korean War ended only after two and a half more years of inconclusive fighting that gave rise to much domestic unhappiness before an armistice was signed in July 1953. "Limited war" was quite unpopular to growing numbers of Americans who opposed fighting a war without victory as its ultimate object. The spokesman for this dissenting view became none other than the formidable General MacArthur. At the end of 1950, MacArthur began to go public with his criticism of U.S. strategy and suggested that the war be widened. A blockade of China and aerial bombardment of staging areas in Manchuria, with nuclear weapons if need be, should do the trick, according to the charismatic and politically ambitious general.

Truman and his officials were horrified. After failing to heed repeated warnings to remain silent, MacArthur was fired by Truman for insubordination. Ever after, the episode has been seen as a triumph for the principle of civilian control of the military, which it certainly was, but that was only the immediate issue. Underlying the Truman-MacArthur controversy was the problem of limited war as the new centerpiece of containment policy. Upon returning home to a tumultuous welcome from an adoring public, MacArthur spelled out the traditional view of war in unambiguous terms. "There is no substitute for victory," he said, and many agreed with him.

MacArthur's conviction reflected an outmoded way of strategic thinking. A desire for victory was exactly what the Truman administration could not tolerate. Under modern conditions of world war, meaningful victory no longer existed. To win was to lose. This inability to impose one's will in absolute fashion only underlined another aspect of the Korean war's modern, symbolic character. Limited war was as much an extension of the boundaries of diplomacy and communication as it was a restriction of the traditional definition of war. Besides its effect on world opinion, it was a also a way of signaling between ideological adversaries. It was a continuation of diplomacy whose purpose was to prevent the total breakdown of communication characteristic of all-out war.

Korea as a limited war pointed up another peculiar feature of the cold war: the presidential usurpation of the congressional power, constitutionally given, to declare war. Actually, Truman did consider going to Congress and, had he done so, there is little doubt that he would have received his joint resolution without much trouble. But as time went on, the idea of gaining legislative blessing seemed less and less attractive. Originally, Truman appeared to think that the North Korean invasion could be repelled quickly and with minimum force. As the situation worsened, he could still have gone to Congress and received approval. In that event, however, he probably feared, if war or something like it were formally declared by Congress, that Korea would not remain a limited "police action" because of the political need to pursue a military victory. On the other hand, conducting the war under the auspices of the United Nations provided some independence from Congress within an environment that encouraged diplomatic moderation and military restraint.[34]

Though the presidential usurpation of the congressional war-making power has been much criticized by those critical of presidential recklessness, there is another side to the story. For a nation that prided itself on never having been defeated in a war, public pressure to take any and all measures, including dropping the atomic bomb, would probably have been irresistible. Thus, the emergence of the so-called "imperial presidency" during the cold war was not without its ironies. From one perspective, presidential wars appeared to be the product of executive power run amok, but from a Wilsonian point of view they seemed preferable to the kinds of wars that were likely to be urged by an impulsive and irresponsible legislative branch.

In sum, Wilsonianism in Korea took a far different and unexpected form from the collective security actions contemplated a generation earlier. Despite contributions of troops from sixteen nations, most of them close American allies, the Korean war was preponderantly an American show in which international security proved to be less collective than hoped for. The fact that it was a thinly veiled American war, with the U.S. supplying about 85 percent of the U.N. troops, also suggested that internationalist theory was flawed. If, in practice, American leadership amounted to American unilateralism, the opinion that mattered most was American, not world opinion.

Over the next two years, the decline of Truman's popularity, in large measure due to the public's frustration at interminable bloodletting in Korea, suggested that some grave problems lurked beneath the surface of the cold war consensus. Though overwhelmingly anticommunist, public opinion seemed unable to understand the Wilsonian logic at work in Korea. The public was not alone in its perplexity. Within the Department of

Defense, an increasingly frustrated military establishment began to reconsider its rejection of General MacArthur's proposals. Public disen-
chantment with the policy of limited war was vented by the election of
Eisenhower in 1952, who promised to "go to Korea." After "unleashing"
Chiang Kai-shek by allowing nationalist forces to raid the mainland, the
new administration dropped hints that it would be willing to use the bomb
if the stalemated negotiations, in progress since mid-1951, showed no
forward movement.

Fortunately, by mid-1953 the communists finally agreed to allow the
voluntary repatriation of prisoners of war, thus breaking the deadlock over
an issue that for two years had prevented an end to the fighting. The armistice signed in June roughly confirmed the status quo ante bellum. The
casualties were significant, more than 50,000 dead American troops, and
combined Asian deaths in excess of one million. At a very high cost,
the Korean war had accomplished its minimal objective of turning back
aggression without starting another world war. In that respect, it was a
success. Yet policy in Korea demonstrated that containment created as
many problems as it settled. It left in its wake a chain of foreign policy
headaches that throbbed for decades to come.

CHAPTER SIX

Wilsonianism at Work: Credibility Crises of the 1950s and 1960s

At the heart of America's complex cold-war foreign policy was an abiding obsession with credibility. Descended from Wilson's idea that only a fully committed America could effectively undergird collective security, the cold war pursuit of credibility differed radically from the time-honored conception of prestige as an instrument of power politics. Prestige, as traditionally defined, is the ability to exercise power without having to employ force, to get one's way by speaking softly and carrying a big stick. Credibility, by contrast, required the continual use of force, and not simply the constant assertion of a ready willingness to use it, lest confidence in American leadership unravel and the Soviets become still more emboldened. In the cold war, reputation alone was a short-lived asset.

After Korea, repeated tests of credibility were made more likely by the built-in limitations of containment policy. Carefully controlled interventions, necessary to avoid the spiral to world war, meant that aggressors could be frustrated but not convincingly punished into giving up their expansionist ambitions. Limited war, as one analyst subsequently described it, was a form of warfare "that could neither be deterred nor won by the U.S."[1] Like sandbags when used as instruments of flood control, applications of power could only relieve the pressure from rising communist waters at a particularly critical point. Reinforcement would have to be provided anew, wherever and whenever necessary, until the torrent subsided. Under modern conditions of limited war, then, containment could provide no more than a series of temporary fixes.

Apart from deterrence, credibility was also considered the key to sustaining an effective anticommunist world opinion, which, if left to itself, might well collapse. If America's stock plunged dramatically in the marketplace of world opinion, the resulting panic might lead to a global collapse of liberal institutions worse even than the demoralization that reigned throughout the 1930s. The upside of a robust free world morale was that it could better deter Soviet expansion than an America acting alone, prevent another world war, and organize a global civil society capable of outlasting the Soviet experiment. But these achievements were possible only if world opinion was first shored up and reassured by America's commitment to internationalism. For the time being, the unfortunate truth appeared to be, as NSC 68 complained, that "the rest of the free world lacks a sense of unity, confidence and common purpose."

Ultimately, of course, credibility would pay huge dividends by preventing World War III, but in the meantime it was a form of symbolic capital that could only be banked and not spent.[2] In the cold war context, premiums had to be paid anew each time another credibility crisis arose. Because of the potential impact on world opinion, few places in the world were automatically ruled out as unimportant. In 1953, for example, the National Security Council asserted that the principle of collective security "should be upheld even in areas not of vital strategic importance."[3] Inaction was not even an option because, like appeasement in the 1930s, it seemed likely to lead inexorably to World War III. Only a few years earlier, intervention outside the Western Hemisphere was impossible; now it was unavoidable.

Logically, this kind of universalism was repugnant to the realist mind. To maintain that every place in the world was as critical as any other was to drain the idea of vital interest of meaning. Because of its conceptual promiscuity, global interventionism contradicted a basic precept of realism, advanced by Kennan, influential newspaper columnist Walter Lippmann, and a growing circle of scholars, that interests had to be weighed against capabilities. If a nation persisted in living beyond its military means by chasing every will-o'-the-wisp, it could only result in a dissipation of energy and disastrous overextension. In contrast to Wilsonians who envisioned global disaster resulting from inaction, for realists the diverse and chaotic character of the world guaranteed that there were crises aplenty unrelated to the cold war that could safely be ignored.

American policy-makers were not blind to the force of the realist argument; they were painfully aware that national resources and the patience of the American public were limited. It was politically transparent, for example, that the U.S. could not afford many more successes like Korea. Indeed, one Eisenhower adviser noted with some amazement that "the American people have in fact been extraordinarily docile and cooperative."[4] Yet, despite its obvious liabilities, the Wilsonian argument was never seriously challenged because of the shared understanding that the modern world could no longer be measured by the traditional yardstick of realism. When weighed against the consequences of a failure to intervene, global interventionism seemed absolutely necessary. If sensibly managed, moreover, policy-makers believed that such a policy need not necessarily overburden the U.S.

After Korea, an unhappy experience that seemed to prove that peripheral wars were "uneconomical and weakening," U.S. foreign policy experimented with other ways of maintaining the credibility of containment.[5] One approach was to was to try to spread the burden of defense among like-minded allies. Indeed, credibility was far more important as a force for reassuring allies than for deterring opponents. If it did the former job, the latter would not be necessary. "Our free world system depends on the voluntary alignment of our allies—hence world opinion is quite vital," said President Eisenhower.[6] Another was to rely more openly on the atomic bomb as a deterrent against Korea-like aggressions. Yet another method, favored by the Kennedy administration, was to develop a more complex mixture of conventional and nuclear deterrence capable of meeting all crisis situations. Whatever the form, the intention was to bolster world opinion to the point of creating a "climate of victory" in which a demoralized and delegitimized Soviet system would collapse.

While U.S. leaders understood that world opinion without America would be ineffective, only gradually did it become clear that America would have to be both coxswain and crew. As the failure of collective security in the 1930s and the chaotic postwar situation had amply demonstrated, world opinion was potentially the West's strong point and, at the same time, its major weakness. Because of the factiousness and susceptibility to intimidation of world opinion, the cold war pursuit of collective security turned out to be far more an American project than anyone had expected.

Korea as Catalyst for European Policy

To a shrinking circle of critics, the U.S. was coming to resemble the dreaded "garrison state" whose creation American internationalism was supposed to prevent. But the American cold war situation was fundamentally different. Under the garrison state scenario, as internationalists defined it, the United States would have been alone in a hostile world. The national security state, in contrast, was created to defend and promote a sizeable free world in which democracy and economic liberalism reigned supreme. The existence of formidable allies within a global market system made the two situations fundamentally unlike. Only if that open world and the common values that undergirded it disappeared would the garrison state come into being.

In the 1950s, the center of "world opinion" resided as always, in western Europe. "The defense of Europe is the basis for the defense of the whole free world," Truman told Congress. After the North Korean invasion, it took little imagination to visualize a comparable assault from East Germany.[7] East German leader Walter Ulbricht fanned such fears when he asserted: "If the Americans in their imperialist arrogance believe that the Germans have less national consciousness than the Koreans, then they have fundamentally deceived themselves." But even if the Kremlin did not intend to launch such an invasion, American policy-makers feared that a communist success in Korea might cow the demoralized peoples of Europe into bending their knees to Moscow without the communists having to fire a shot. Indeed, as the Korean war began, morale was already quite shaky among America's allies.

In the post-Korea context, all the steps taken by the United States to stabilize Europe to that point seemed like half measures. With the situation begging for further action, the moment was ripe to extend America's "empire by invitation" on the Continent. In late 1950, Truman sent General Eisenhower to Europe as the Supreme Commander of Allied forces with the mission of making NATO an effective military alliance. With a self-sustaining balance of power in Europe neither possible nor desirable, it was clear that the Continent had to be fortified from the outside, with American soldiers if necessary. Sensing that those troops were only a down payment on a much larger commitment of resources, neo-isolationists in Congress staged a last-gasp "great debate" about the implications of an ongoing American presence in Europe. However, their objections were brushed aside by a coalition of internationalists in a congressional resolution of April 1951 that authorized Truman to rush four combat divisions to western Europe.

Putting the "O" in NATO also meant doing what only a year earlier had seemed unthinkable to many: rearming the Germans. While the Joint Chiefs of Staff insisted that no other option was open, formidable obstacles existed to putting German armies in the field. The French seemed more concerned with a revived Germany than with the Soviet threat. The Soviets themselves were certain to throw major obstacles in the path of a revival of German military strength. The British, divided as always between the global and the European aspects of their heritage, were leery of becoming too deeply involved on the Continent. For their part, the Germans, understandably gun-shy in the wake of Hitler's catastrophic military adventurism, were far from enthusiastic about becoming cannon fodder for the Western cause. With politicians on the left, most notably Social Democratic Party leader Kurt Schumacher, convinced that tethering the Federal Republic to the West would wreck any chances for unification, a policy of neutralism seemed the more appealing course to many Germans.

Hoping to eat his cake and have it too, French defense minister René Pleven came up with an ingenious proposal in the fall of 1950 for a common European army, the European Defense Community or EDC, in which German forces would be folded, like egg whites, in battalion-size units, into a multinational army. Unfortunately, the mixture promised to be as delicate as a soufflé. Since there would be no separate German command structure or general staff, Germany was supposed to be rearmed without creating a separate German army. But—and it was a *big* but—the success of the scheme depended on the creation of effective supranational institutions, nothing less than an embryonic United States of Europe. For the cynically minded, this seemed an impossibly utopian approach to a problem that could only be solved in more sensible ways. Small wonder, then, that many observers doubted the genuineness of the French proposal.

Despite misgivings about the plan's practicality—Acheson thought it "hopeless"—Truman and Acheson felt there was little choice but to take the French at their word and go ahead with the scheme. Acheson knew that the Europeans were likely to bridle at the only other alternative, which was to have the U.S. press for the creation of a German national army. Besides, America *was* deeply interested in furthering western European unity as a way of restoring economic and political stability. A united Europe would have the strength to stabilize a European balance of power minus the old competitive nationalisms and deal independently with the Soviet threat. "If Europe would do what it should do, conceivably it could by itself defeat Russia," said Eisenhower. On the other hand, if Europe remained disunited, it would be like "fighting Communism in handcuffs."[8]

With the West so clearly in need of German manpower, Chancellor Konrad Adenauer of the Federal Republic of Germany had the Allies over a barrel. Ideologically, Adenauer was in full agreement with the proposal. He had long been an enthusiastic advocate of integrating Germany into a federated Europe. But he was also a politician. Pointing to a deeply divided public opinion in his country, he was in an advantageous position to drive a hard bargain. Essentially, Adenauer wanted the Federal Republic to participate as an equal, not as a conquered nation. Plans for EDC therefore had to include an end to the Occupation and a restoration of sovereignty to the Federal Republic. To this end, a complex set of contractual agreements was negotiated and signed in May 1952, at the same time that completed texts of the EDC treaties were completed in Paris. The eagerness of the U.S. to get the Germans on board gave Adenauer an added bonus, a relaxation of the unpopular prosecutions of war criminals.

To steal the thunder from his neutralist opponent, Schumacher, Adenauer promised his countrymen that alliance with the West was more likely to produce reunification than the fantasy of a neutral Germany. This outlook corresponded to a larger "magnet theory" for ending the cold war in Europe that dominated thinking in Washington at the time. Once the West had shown its superiority, this thinking went, the Iron Curtain would rust away. How long this was supposed to take was not spelled out. Indeed, it could not be, for to specify any time limit at all, no matter how long or short, would have been to risk demoralization. In the meantime, Adenauer promised that the West would not flag in its efforts to make the Soviets see reason. To shore up Adenauer—"one of the great men of our time," according to Ike—the U.S. ritually assured the Germans of American support for reunification, even though Western policies were actually making early unity less likely.[9]

With Stalin's death in March 1953, many observers sensed an opportunity for fruitful negotiations with the Kremlin. But the U.S. was not prepared to deal with the dictator's sudden and unexpected demise. "We have no plan. We are not even sure what difference his death makes," said Eisenhower.[10] Though the new Soviet leaders proclaimed what purported to be the reassuring doctrine of "peaceful coexistence," American leaders were unimpressed. If Stalin had been as reasonable as some critics of the cold war have insisted, the situation might well have become more dangerous in the absence of his conservative presence. If nothing else, the continuity of American policy demonstrated that Stalin, unlike Hitler, had not been the chief problem. It was, instead, a well-entrenched Soviet system. In any event, an uprising of disgruntled workers in East Berlin in June 1953, which was suppressed with the help of Soviet tanks, showed no evidence of a more moderate mentality at work in Moscow.

But for many Europeans who were looking for an excuse to avoid creating a powerful Germany, the new situation in Moscow provided a good argument against rearmament. Thus EDC was not to be. In August 1954, four years after it was first proposed by France, the French National Assembly voted decisively against ratification, taking little heed of the threat by John Foster Dulles, Eisenhower's secretary of state, to initiate an "agonizing reappraisal" of American policy should the deputies vote no. Primal fears of Germany, doubts that Germany could be safely contained by the new European institutional structures, and concern for the loss of French national identity in a supranational Europe overpowered cold war concerns. Obviously, by this time, much of the fear that gripped western Europe following the Korean invasion and prompted the EDC idea in the first place had evaporated.

From the American standpoint, the need for German rearmament was greater than ever. Elected president in 1952, Dwight D. Eisenhower was even more concerned with overcoming the "lethargy and inaction in Europe which would allow that Continent to fall into Soviet hands."[11] His administration, which had come to power partly on the strength of its aggressive criticisms of the Truman administration's excessively cautious approach to containment, had an even greater commitment to fighting the cold war. But Eisenhower was also a budgetary conservative. Instead of relying primarily on *American* rearmament, as was true of NSC 68, the fiscally prudent Eisenhower was concerned to rely in the first instance upon America's allies. To his mind, the cold war was a *western* project, an experiment in internationalism, not a unilateral American show.

After noting America's great disappointment with the French decision, the administration took another course: creating a German national army and admitting the Federal Republic into NATO. Eisenhower had earlier resolved that "we simply could not abandon what we had begun in Europe."[12] Though at first sight these moves seemed even more abhorrent to the French, Paris agreed to go along after receiving some additional guarantees. A British agreement to commit troops to service on the Continent reassured the French that they would not be the sole European power called upon to balance the Germans. Also, the Western European Union provided some supranational controls, not on the order of EDC, to be sure, but substantial still. And, last but most important, NATO with a German army would be dominated by the Americans, who would be the ultimate guarantee against a German "breakaway." More than ever, NATO depended on American credibility.

The Federal Republic entered NATO in May 1955 and, at the same time, gained sovereign status. This solution came to be known as "double containment" because it killed two birds with one stone. It was aimed primarily against the Russians, but no less important was its function of keeping West Germany tied closely to the West. As Dulles put it, NATO was a "military magnet to attract and retain the Federal Republic in integration with the free world."[13] There was, from the European standpoint, a third objective, keeping the United States committed to NATO and Europe for the long haul. In Lord Ismay's cheeky phrase, the new NATO was designed was to "keep the Americans in, the Russians out, and the Germans down."

It succeeded in all these purposes, and all too well in keeping the Americans in, as far as Eisenhower was concerned. He hoped originally to keep U.S. troops in Europe as a "temporary expedient" in "a stop-gap operation." As time went on, however, it became clear that a more or less permanent American presence was necessary so long as NATO existed as an institution. Over the years, a fundamental pattern emerged: fearing for alliance solidarity, the United States would take measures to bolster morale. In so doing, more often than not it contributed to dissension within the alliance, which necessitated more tokens of commitment by the United States, and so on. Diplomatic commerce in the coin of credibility was inherently inflationary.

The Symbolic Importance of Asia after Korea

As the fear of war receded on the Continent, it was not long before the European allies began to question the wisdom of America's insistence on seeing the Korean War through. Among those allies, who were initially gratified by U.S. intervention, doubts emerged, as the war dragged on, about an "Asia first" America becoming distracted by a distant quagmire. Would it not be better, they asked, if the United States focused its energies and resources on Europe? This inability on the part of European leaders to understand what seemed an eccentric U.S. preoccupation with Asia would become one of the perennial points of disagreement in the western alliance. The inclination of Great Britain and France, in particular, to follow a softer line in the Far East was an indication that their analysis of the world situation was not synchronized with the global Wilsonian outlook that guided Washington.

To Washington, Asia was precisely the region in which another world war seemed most likely to break out. A degree of order had been restored in Europe, but the situation in the Far East was far more fluid and dangerous. Following the wave of massive decolonization after World War II, the relative stability formerly imposed by the old diplomacy of imperialism was no longer present. In its place was a potent combination of nationalism, communism, and antiimperialism, a volatile mixture oftentimes combined quite effectively in a single political movement.

In stark geopolitical terms, the cause of the instability was traceable to the defeat and demilitarization of Japan, which removed the only natural regional balance to the Soviet Union and China. In Japan, as in Germany, the occupation at first showed little concern for restoring the country as an economic and political factor in the region. That began to change in 1948, when General MacArthur's "reverse course" turned away from a punitive approach, but a settlement of Japan's postwar political status remained beyond the horizon until the Korean War raised concerns about that nation's unsettled future. Following the North Korean invasion, Washington moved to "normalize" relations with Japan. A peace treaty was drafted and signed in 1951. However, with the promulgation of the occupation-inspired constitution of 1947 that prohibited war as an instrument of national policy, Japan was no longer in a position to resume its former role as an East Asian power. Thus a follow-up bilateral treaty between the U.S. and Japan made the United States responsible for the defense of Japan. In this way, Japan's prewar role in the region was taken over by the United States. To make assurance doubly sure on this score, Australia, New Zealand, and the Philippines demanded and received security guarantees from the U.S. in return for their consent to the Japanese peace treaty.

The path followed by American policy toward Japan was markedly different from the postwar course plotted for Germany. Though the U.S. resorted to a mixture of integration and control in both cases, policy toward Japan was tilted far more strongly in the direction of control, at the same time that the emphasis on liberal economic integration was much weaker. As a result, although Japanese economic recovery was quite welcome, the country's subsequent neomercantilist trade policies, with their emphasis on running steady trade surpluses, would cause many problems for the United States and for the world economy down the road.

In other areas of Asia, China and communism appeared to be filling the vacuum left by the departure of the European colonial powers. In the case of Indochina, a communist nationalist movement, the Viet Minh, was struggling impressively to evict their French colonial rulers. France had insisted upon returning to Indochina after WWII, following the surrender of the Japanese occupiers, only to confront a fierce war of national liberation led by the Viet Minh. Barely a year after the Korean armistice, Indochina became the new hot spot in Asia as the French tottered precariously on the brink of military defeat. In May 1954, the surrender of their fortress at Dien Bien Phu to the exhilarated Viet Minh forces broke the back of France's determination to maintain its colonial presence.

For the Eisenhower administration, the fall of Indochina had the makings of a major catastrophe that promised to undo the dearly purchased results of Korea. "The really important spot is Indochina," Dulles told the president, because "if Indochina goes, and if South Asia goes, it is extremely hard to insulate ourselves against the consequences of that."[14] Ultimately, the NSC believed that the fall of Indochina "would endanger the stability and security of Europe."[15] When questioned about the importance of Indochina at a press conference in 1954, Eisenhower introduced what came to be known as the "domino theory," the rationale for American intervention. "You have a row of dominoes set up," he said. "You knock over the first one, and what will happen to the last one is the certainty that it will go over very quickly. So you could have the beginning of a disintegration that would have the most profound consequences."[16]

The domino theory was hardly new. It was only the most recent in a long string of metaphorical expressions of the Wilsonian worldview. In alerting the public to domino-like dangers, Eisenhower was not referring to the threat of direct aggression in southeast Asia. Rather, the concern was with the psychological implications of the fall of Indochina. The impact would be perceptual, on the minds of men. At times, Eisenhower, liked to quote Lenin's view that "the approach to Europe is through the Far East."[17] The reverberations of a defeat would echo throughout Asia but ultimately to Europe, where the EDC crisis was simultaneously coming to a boil. If the United States failed to hold in southeast Asia, collective security would receive a blow from which it would likely fail to recover. In Dulles's words: "There is no place around the orbit of the Soviet world which we can now afford to lose because further losses cannot now be insulated and will inevitably set up a chain reaction."[18]

Despite the perceived gravity of the situation, the use of American ground forces was out of the question. A reluctant president and an American public thoroughly fed up with Korea made sure of that. There was talk for a time of using atomic bombs to rescue the beleaguered French garrison at Dien Bien Phu, but the idea never advanced beyond the trial-balloon stage. Though uncertain about what exactly to do, the administration remained focused on one essential point: any action would have to be taken in concert with the Allies. Unlike Korea, which was a one-man show, Indochina would have to be rescued by what was called "United Action."

Once again, however, the administration found that its internationalist views diverged significantly from the localist perceptions of its allies, who were concerned with events closer to home. The apprehensive British wanted no part of another Asian war, while the demoralized French were bent on cutting their losses. Eisenhower and Dulles were especially disappointed with France, all the more so as the U.S. by 1954 was subsidizing a huge portion of the war in Indochina, partly in the hope of making the French more tractable on German rearmament. But France, as Dulles said later, was "so weak as to make it questionable whether it belongs to the Big 3."[19] Not only were the French wavering in Europe on EDC, they were now hell-bent on exiting from Indochina. Without allied support, Washington could only stand by as a conference held at Geneva ignominiously negotiated the terms of French withdrawal.

Fearful of the consequences of communist victory, yet unable to intervene without willing allies, the administration found itself in a box. Fortunately for Dulles and Eisenhower, the Geneva conference produced a result that was much more favorable than expected. In response to pressure from the Soviets and the Red Chinese, who were eager to liquidate the war, the Viet Minh agreed to a partition of Indochina along the 17th parallel. This was, ostensibly, a provisional measure pending the holding of national elections in 1956, which the communists were expected to win handily. The agreement permitted a regrouping of the forces of the two sides: communists in the north, French forces to the south.

At this point, the French appointed a premier in the south, Ngo Dinh Diem, who proved to be the answer to American prayers. Diem was a Catholic, and thus closely tied to the colonial elite, but he was also a staunch nationalist. After a rocky start, Diem managed to consolidate his authority. Impressed by his energetic leadership, the United States was pleased to find a man who seemed capable of holding the line. Diem was no democrat, but the U.S. gladly settled for an authoritarian solution in the absence of a mature pro-Western democratic public opinion. With no better alternatives in sight, the U.S. decided that "the best and perhaps only chance is to back Diem *unconditionally* on the gamble that he can succeed."[20]

Repeated flirtations of this kind with strongman regimes over the course of the cold war reflected another serious shortcoming in the Wilsonian theory of world opinion, which presupposed the universalization of modern democracy. In Wilson's time, only European opinion counted. But in the early postcolonial era, when the U.S. was competing for the allegiance of the third world, democracy was at best nascent in many newly independent countries; at worst, it was nonexistent. Until it developed, strong leaders would have to suffice. Despite the embarrassment caused by close association with such regimes, they seemed far preferable to communist rule. And since the ultimate concern was, in any case, to reassure the fidelity of the democratic West, an occasional flirtation with autocracy was hardly conclusive proof of having abandoned the marriage to democracy. But even in countries where politics was openly democratic, the United States often preferred to deal with strong personalities. The greater latitude often afforded to leaders in the conduct of foreign affairs, combined with the tendency of local politicians to define the national interest in particularist terms, meant that world opinion in the concrete differed enormously from the ideal type.

With wholehearted American approval, then, Diem ignored the 1956 deadline for national elections, and in the years that followed American influence replaced that of the French. Over the course of the decade,

Washington poured in money, most of it in the form of military aid, in a frenzy of "nation building" in South Vietnam. For a few years, the effort seemed to promise success. In 1957, Dulles reported with satisfaction that "the strength of Vietnam is increasing."[21]

As the Indochina crisis waned after Geneva, the United States sought to stabilize Asia as a whole. Expanding on the theme of united action, Dulles organized an Asian counterpart to NATO, the Southeast Asia Treaty Organization or SEATO. This new grouping—which consisted of Australia, Britain, France, New Zealand, Pakistan, the Philippines, Thailand, and the United States—was much flimsier than its European counterpart. It had no military structures or other regional institutions to bind it together. In contrast to a largely democratic Europe, it consisted of governments whose political systems ran the gamut from democracy to despotism. With its relatively weak dedication to regional security, SEATO's underlying lack of common will would have to be made up by the credibility of the American commitment. Much more so than NATO, SEATO was an American show.

No sooner had the Indochina emergency subsided than another wave of crisis, centering on China and Taiwan, threatened to capsize American policy in the Far East. Among other things, Korea had blown China policy in a new direction. By interposing the Seventh Fleet in the Taiwan straits at the outbreak of the Korean War, the U.S. had intervened directly in the Chinese civil war and snatched near-certain victory from the communists. What began as a temporary measure to prevent a widening of the war turned into a permanent arrangement as a result of the Chinese intervention in Korea. In the Eisenhower administration, the de facto alliance with Chiang Kai-shek's nationalist regime was formalized. A mutual defense treaty was signed in 1954, in which Taiwan was recognized as the legitimate government of all China.

This alliance, which no doubt appeared provocative to Mao's regime in Peking, was functionally conservative in its intent. As the treaty made clear, Chiang was prohibited from attacking the mainland without American approval (though Taiwan remained a significant base for various covert operations). Washington was clearly interested in keeping the lid on the situation and removing the dangers of a larger war that seemed likely to erupt if the noisy calls for the "unleashing" of Chiang Kai-shek were heeded. Without saying so for fear of offending powerful nationalist sentiments in both Taipei and Peking, Washington hoped for a "two-China" mentality to take hold. Unlike in Germany, where reunification was part of the bargain with the Federal Republic, there was no rhetorical commitment to the restoration of Chinese unity. The short-term effect of American policy was to further drive the PRC into the arms of Moscow. The tight embrace, U.S. policy-makers hoped, would in due course lead to a breakup of the two communist giants.

Although the United States would have been content with the status quo in Asia, cold war internationalism failed, here as elsewhere, to keep the lid on the boiling cauldron of nationalist sentiment. Adding to the tension was the Soviet condemnation of American policy in Taiwan for creating "a breeding ground for a new war." Early in 1955, the People's Republic decided to test the resolve of Chiang Kai-shek and his American allies by bombarding some small offshore islands still held by the nationalists. In February, communist troops successfully invaded the Tachen islands. It seemed as if the Chinese, with the backing of the Soviets, were intent on ending the civil war, even if they had to risk all-out war in the process.

The Taiwan Straits crisis created a typical cold war dilemma for the United States. On the one hand, the offshore islands were of little value militarily. American intervention on behalf of Chiang would likely trigger a larger war, far more serious than Korea. Even the brandishing of threats in the hope of avoiding a war had repercussions for western unity. America's nervous allies in Europe, seeing little reason to back Chiang to the hilt on this issue, had no stomach for credibility displays that could well get out of hand.

Yet an American failure to act might have equally dangerous repercussions. Conceding the offshore islands to the communists might have such a devastating impact on nationalist morale that all Formosa might be lost. If that happened, the consequences for SEATO, only recently created, would likely be catastrophic. And, ultimately, the shock waves of demoralization might extend all the way to Europe, where the NATO allies might begin to doubt American steadfastness. The negative implications extended to American policy as well. If the United States failed to act now, could it summon the nerve to do so in the future, when more important issues were on the line? Credibility demanded an ability to take action on the little things, whereas realism suggested that minor issues were not worth the bother.

The crisis lasted until April 1955, when the communists signalled their desire to avoid a major war. To that point, the Eisenhower administration got through the crisis by relying upon a policy of ambiguity. Despite its inner agonizing on the issue, it spoke quite casually in public about the possibility of using nuclear weapons in the region. Nuclear weapons were just like any other munitions, said Eisenhower at one press conference. This position was consistent with the policy of "massive retaliation" announced by Dulles in the 1952 campaign and with his notorious insistence on the necessity of pursuing a policy of "brinkmanship" when dealing with communist challenges. According to this logic, conventional threats would be deterred by "going to the brink" of war, threatening nuclear responses if necessary and not necessarily at the point of attack.

Nuclear Weapons and the Paradoxes of Modern Deterrence

The Quemoy-Matsu crisis of 1955 demonstrated that Eisenhower's administration was far more enamored of the bomb than Truman's. In an era of limited warfare, Korea demonstrated that conventional military deterrence had unpalatable strategic consequences and enjoyed only lukewarm public support. Fiscally, too, the conservative Eisenhower administration worried about budget-busting military spending. Thus, to prevent another situation like Korea from arising, the U.S. threatened the use of nuclear weapons as a first resort against communist aggression. A formidable ring of bases had been built around the world to assure that nuclear weapons could be delivered in devastating quantity against communist nations in the event of war. But, just as limited war and alliance solidarity had significant shortcomings, the same would prove to be true of American nuclear deterrence.

Fearful of turning the relatively open society of the United States into a top-heavy "garrison state" that resembled the totalitarian enemy, Eisenhower was determined to fight the cold war more frugally, hoping to "figure out a preparedness program that will give us a respectable position without bankrupting the nation."[22] Offering the promise of "more bang for the buck," nuclear weapons seemed just the ticket. Eisenhower's "New Look," a modernization of the armed services, emphasized nuclear delivery capability as opposed to conventional combat strength. In Europe, where alliance troop levels never reached goals set in 1952, even after the West German army became part of NATO, nuclear weapons took over the leading role in deterrence. The American stockpile of nuclear warheads mushroomed from 650 in 1951 to more than 18,000 by the end of the decade.

Though American strategy in the 1950s emphasized nuclear weapons as instruments of both war and diplomacy, and U.S. military planners viewed the bomb as a more potent but not qualitatively different weapon, the public face of policy differed considerably from the reservations being expressed in private. To be sure, in the event of major war, Eisenhower left no doubt that the weapons would be used. But at the same time, he was becoming increasingly doubtful about the military utility of nuclear weapons. On one occasion, he "expressed skepticism as to whether any nations as we now know them would continue to exist at the conclusion of this war."[23] The situation only promised to become more troubling over time. According to some NSC projections for the late 1950s, "a total war involving the strategic use by both sides of nuclear weapons would bring about such extensive destruction as to threaten the survival of Western civilization and the Soviet regime."[24]

As George Kennan had warned at the time of the H-bomb decision, these were not weapons that were useful in any conventional sense. Calculated solely in terms of equivalent explosive force, delivering a "small" 15-kiloton Hiroshima-type bomb was the equivalent of dropping a 250-car railroad train loaded with TNT; for a one-megaton hydrogen bomb, the train would be 16,500 boxcars long.[25] The immediate physical destruction from the blast would be multiplied by the lethal effects upon humans caused by the fireball and radioactive by-products of the explosion. While it would take more time to develop a deeper understanding of all the lethal consequences of the bomb, it was rapidly becoming clear that with their near-unimaginable destruction nuclear wars were not likely to be winnable in any meaningful way.

Here, too, as with limited wars and alliances, modernity produced huge differences with past meanings and practices. "If you want peace, prepare for war," went the ancient maxim. This traditional justification of military deterrence supposed that strength would deter an opponent from attacking, an assumption that held true for nuclear deterrence as well. However, in the modern era, the corollary no longer made sense. In the past, if deterrence failed, it was reasonable to go to war. Indeed, deterrence itself stemmed from the certainty in the enemy's mind that you would be quite willing to use your weapons in war. It would have been silly to suppose otherwise. Nuclear weapons, however, made sense *only* as a deterrent. Their usefulness consisted in the prevention of their use, hence the motto of the Strategic Air Command: "Peace Is Our Profession."

An awareness of the paradoxical character of nuclear weapons did not emerge with full force until the late 1950s. So long as the Soviet Union could not deliver its nuclear payloads upon American territory, American willingness to use atomic and hydrogen bombs could have a formidable deterrent effect. The American strategy of preemption, the plan to launch nuclear strikes as soon as general war became certain, was a potent threat. But that traditional kind of thinking began to change following the Soviet launch in 1957 of the first earth-orbiting satellite, "Sputnik." Sputnik had many consequences. It was an enormous psychological coup for the Soviet Union, whose scientific capability had still been considered relatively backward. By raising doubts about the efficacy of the American educational system, it provided the stimulus for a continuing, large-scale federal involvement in education, formerly controlled by local and private hands. Reinforced by reports of impressive Soviet economic gains, Sputnik threw into question the validity of the basic premise underlying containment: that the U.S. system would, in the end, demonstrate its superiority as a way of life. As Sputnik's demoralizing effect at home and abroad sunk in, Vice President Richard Nixon admitted ruefully that the U.S. had "failed to recognize the psychological importance" of space technology.[26]

Sputnik also brought home the military implications of the cold war. The many invasion scenarios discussed prior to the two world wars were more closely related to science fiction than to strategic reality. Indeed, the Wilsonian notion of "world conquest" never envisioned the United States being conquered or physically damaged; the worst-case outcome had always been the "garrison state." Now, however, unstoppable nuclear-tipped missiles had dramatically tipped the scales of the age-old strategic advantage formerly enjoyed by the defense in favor of the offense. The American homeland was lined up in the enemy's cross-hairs and there was no defense against it, as Soviet military strategists delighted in explaining. A Soviet first strike might destroy half the American population. In the words of Eisenhower's biographer, the panicky Gaither Report of 1957 "practically predicted the end of western civilization."[27]

Sputnik also had a major impact on nuclear strategy. A conflict that had been about the survival of the American way of life now became a matter of survival, pure and simple. As codified in "second-strike strategy" of the late 1950s, the effectiveness of a nuclear deterrent depended on its survivability, i.e., the ability of one's nuclear forces to withstand a punishing first strike and return a devastating nuclear blow in return. According to this theory of "Mutually Assured Destruction" or MAD, the certainty of that second strike was supposed to prevent the opponent from launching the first strike. A cottage industry of nuclear strategists, sustained by the toil of intellectuals who now displaced military thinkers, sprouted up to "think about the unthinkable." Strategy became so rarefied, with its own specialized jargon, that relatively few people could understand it.

Quite sensible on its face, MAD provided a fairly stable underpinning for nuclear strategy from the late 1950s onward. Underneath the surface, however, its logic was quite paradoxical. Would it make sense, for example, to launch a full nuclear strike against the enemy if your society was certain to be devastated in a first strike? Politically, one had to answer "yes" to that question in order to deter the enemy. But how much logical or ethical sense did it really make? Nuclear deterrence presupposed a willingness to take action, which, according to the traditional means-ends calculus, was quite irrational. "The more powerful the weapons," wrote Henry Kissinger in a widely read treatise, "the greater becomes the reluctance to use them."[28] Indeed, to a significant degree, that kind of traditional instrumental thinking was wholly beside the point because nuclear deterrence was based less on airtight logic than on political and psychological uncertainty. The more science and rationality were applied to warfare, the less rational warfare actually became. As one source concludes, "it is generally agreed that there is a grey area of uncertainty where credibility is equivalent to dubiety."[29] In nuclear strategy, in other words, anxiety and ambiguity replaced calculated, instrumental precision.

The combination of nuclear warheads and ballistic missiles finally brought about a long-delayed realization of Wilson's intuition that modern all-out war was so radical as to be functionally obsolete; that it made no sense as a useful means of attaining basic national objectives. Wilson's thinking on the nature of modern war had been too avant garde and not universally persuasive, which was one reason why the League project failed. For all their destructiveness, World Wars I and II *had* made sense, to Wilson, FDR, and the American people, in traditional instrumental terms. But to contemplate making nuclear war as a matter of policy was to leave conventional rationality behind altogether. This kind of warfare was almost entirely abstract, with nuclear strategy bearing little relation to social reality.

Thus it made foreign policy sense to possess nuclear weapons but not to use them. But if nuclear weapons were indeed political tools and not battlefield weapons, it was only a matter of time before the imponderables of nuclear deterrence infected diplomacy. In the early and mid-1950s, the Eisenhower administration took advantage of a window of opportunity that opened up briefly until the inevitable day when the Soviet effort to catch up inaugurated the era of nuclear equality. Until that time, the U.S. was free to engage in a form of atomic diplomacy that Dulles called "massive retaliation." Early in the Truman administration, Molotov once accused Secretary of State James Byrnes of carrying the bomb in his pocket. Less sensitive to accusations of "atomic diplomacy," Eisenhower made sure that the bomb was prominently holstered at the hip.

The threat of massive retaliation played a role in a number of crises. In Korea, the Eisenhower administration suggested that it might use the bomb to end the war and intimated a willingness to go nuclear if hostilities resumed. A carrier-based nuclear strike named "Operation Vulture" was briefly discussed as a possible way of extricating the French garrison at

Dien Bien Phu. By the mid-1950s, NATO had gone nuclear. With conventional force levels, even with a German military contribution, insufficient to stem a Soviet attack, NATO adopted a policy of "first use" of nuclear weapons as a way of deterring an invasion. Eisenhower and Dulles also pondered the nuclear option during the Quemoy-Matsu crisis.

Was the administration serious about all this? "But George, what have we got them for?" responded Dulles to an aide who objected to the idea of ever using nuclear weapons against China.[30] At the very least, announcing the intention to use them would have "a very salutary effect" upon the communists.[31] Internally, though, Eisenhower had crippling doubts about the utility of the bomb. "Total war would be an incalculable disaster," said one document,[32] while Eisenhower himself in private understood the policy of "massive retaliation" as only "retaliation against an act that to us means irrevocable war."[33] But it was precisely that kind of crisis that U.S. foreign policy was supposed to avoid. Thus the bomb was useful primarily as a colossal bluff that, one hoped, the other side would never dare to call. As Dulles privately admitted, "one cannot explain everything to our own people, as it also explains things to the enemy."[34]

After Sputnik, though, the one-sided atomic diplomacy of massive retaliation was no longer possible, as Soviet nuclear prowess forced a rethinking of the relationship between American cold war diplomacy and nuclear weapons. As the USSR began to rattle its missiles in a more strident imitation of massive retaliation, an audit of U.S. nuclear strategy was overdue. If deterrence rested on credibility, then it was clear that American willingness to drop the bomb in response to small-scale provocations was less and less believable. In the revolutionary new era of "nuclear plenty," were Quemoy and Matsu worth triggering a devastating Soviet retaliatory strike on the American homeland? Obviously not.

Stalin's successor as Soviet leader, Nikita Khrushchev, was quick to sense the change and take advantage of it in addressing one of his most serious problems, the continuing western presence in Berlin. The western sectors of the city constituted a gaping hole in the Iron Curtain through which dissatisfied East Germans could easily escape. Once through, they were flown into the Federal Republic, where they were welcomed with open arms and showered with generous benefits by the government. The German Democratic Republic, whose successful existence as a socialist state was central to Soviet control of eastern Europe, was not likely to survive such a continued hemorrhage of manpower until the escape route was plugged. In 1958, having been pestered for years by the shrewish Ulbricht (who has been described by scholar Tony Smith as Khrushchev's Lady Macbeth), the Soviet leader decided at last to do something about it. Arguing that the occupation of Germany had long since ended, he described the occupation of Berlin as an outworn relic of the early cold war.

Ending the occupation of Berlin and letting the capital revert to East Germany was the best way for Khrushchev to resolve his problems, but he was willing to entertain other possibilities, perhaps internationalizing West Berlin or making it a free city along the lines of the Vatican, so long as East Germany could restore control of its borders. If the West insisted on the unsatisfactory status quo, he threatened to sign a peace treaty with the GDR, leaving the Soviet puppet state free to assert its sovereignty over West Berlin. If Khrushchev was indeed willing to let the east Germans take over and dictate the course of events, it did not take a Nostradamus to forecast serious trouble in that event.

In a pre–cold war world, as Eisenhower recognized, Khrushchev's reasoning would have been convincing. In military terms, America's position in Berlin was overextended and indefensible. Khrushchev made the point crudely but quite accurately when he described the city as the testicles of the West which he could squeeze any time he desired. But traditional strategic logic no longer governed American policy, which interpreted his proposed solution for Berlin "as direct a threat of aggression as if a bandit kept us out of our own home at gun-point."[35] Again, the U.S. was preoccupied with the logic of credibility, fearing the desertion of world opinion. In this case, the most immediate danger was a massive hemorrhage of German support for the western alliance if the United States were to go along with Soviet demands on Berlin.

By stimulating the creation of the mirror-image Warsaw Pact alliance in eastern Europe and convincing the Soviets of the need to make the communist regime in East Germany more stable, the policy of double containment had made the division of Germany and Europe more rigid still. This was not a bad thing, necessarily, from the standpoint of traditional realpolitik and power balancing, where spheres-of-influence arrangements were conventional ways of creating stability. The absence of any militant western response to the armed suppression of anticommunist revolts in Berlin in June 1953 and Hungary in November 1956 suggested the existence of a shared understanding between the superpowers about their respective spheres of influence in Europe and on the desirability of not disturbing the status quo. Indeed, many in the west had qualms—largely unspoken, for fear of offending opinion in the Federal Republic—about the wisdom of supporting German reunification. One French author humorously expressed the very serious preference of many of his countrymen for continued partition: "I like Germany so much that I am happy that there are two of them."

In this case, however, the de facto partition produced serious instability. The satisfaction with the two-Germany status quo collided with the need to placate German nationalist opinion while simultaneously binding the Federal Republic to the West. American support for unification was not the result of spontaneous enthusiasm or principled commitment to national self-determination. In fact, it was not high on the list of American objectives in Germany, being more a vague long-range desire than a pressing immediate need. But if the Germans were to be kept on board, the U.S. had to do more than give mere lip service to the concept. In Berlin, this rhetorical commitment had especially dangerous consequences, as the United States felt obligated to run the risk of war rather than cause disillusionment within Germany that might sever its ties to the West. Rather incongruously, the cohesiveness of world opinion rested to a staggering degree on the doubtful support of a nationalist German public opinion.

The U.S. presumed that West German participation in NATO and other western institutions had been purchased rather than freely entered into, the price being continued American support for German unification. Within the Federal Republic the NATO bargain had been sold by Adenauer to his people with the slogan "unification through strength," an approach ridiculed by critics who argued quite cogently that a Germanized NATO was likely to prolong German disunity and the cold war. Those who suspected that there was more than a little bad faith behind the American "commitment" to German unity could not help but wonder how long the nationalist impulse of the German people could be suppressed. Among the more prominent discordant voices was a disenchanted George Kennan, no longer in the State Department, who now called publicly for mutual "disengagement" from Germany, with a view to promoting reunification.

But the policy of "double containment" was too deeply entrenched by this time to be reversed. If America retreated from Berlin, the acknowledged capital of a united Germany, it would have been clear to the Germans that unification was no longer an American priority. If that realization sunk in, it was feared that a disillusioned Federal Republic might abandon the West, with ultimate consequences that went far beyond the German problem. The West German foreign minister, well versed in the Wilsonian strategic catechism, threw the domino theory back into the faces of the Americans. "Any concessions to the GDR . . . will start an avalanche which nothing can stop and which will have catastrophic consequences," he said, concluding that "thereby 'The West will have lost the first bloodless blow of World War Three.'"[36]

President Eisenhower fully agreed that Berlin had frightening implications, but he sought to downplay the seriousness of the situation. Afraid that the American public might not understand, he cited the right of Americans to the "pursuit of happiness" as a reason to mute the crisis. "We should not worry the public unnecessarily," said Ike.[37] In the fall of 1959, Khrushchev's sensational visit to the United States resulted in an agreement to defer the issue for a summit conference in Paris the following May. The Paris summit, however, foundered even before it left port when Khrushchev announced the shooting down of an American U-2 spy plane over Soviet territory. Because the pilot had been captured alive, Eisenhower could not issue a plausible denial. Khrushchev saw no alternative but to wreck the conference as a way of appeasing hard-liners within the USSR. But, recognizing that the sands of time were running out for Eisenhower, he again postponed discussion of the Berlin issue, hoping to strike a deal with the incoming Kennedy administration.

Latin America and the Cold War

Until the late 1950s, Latin America remained a diplomatic backwater in the fast-flowing global stream of diplomacy. One measure of the region's relative importance was foreign aid, as transfers to Europe and Asia dwarfed the sums being sent to Latin America. Nevertheless, the cold war did course through the region from time to time. In a departure from the relative openness to social experimentation in Latin America during FDR's New Deal, postwar administrations were quick to clamp down on signs of radical or communist activity in America's back yard. The Rio Pact of 1947 led to the creation the following year of the Organization of American States, which was designed to settle hemispheric problems (under American leadership) without interference by outsiders. The intention, as in the past, was that the region be a placid pool sequestered from the churning waters of world politics.

From time to time, this peaceful idyll was upset by violent events. The Bogotazo uprising of 1948 in Columbia, which interrupted the Pan American conference, attested to the deep discontent of the people on the wrong side of the massive rich–poor divide. In this case, foreign aid funds and democratic leadership within Colombia managed to steer the U.S. through the rapids. Yet another ominous development took form in 1954, when a left-leaning government under Jacobo Arbenz Guzman took over in Guatemala. Arbenz alarmed the United States with his threat to nationalize the massive landholdings of the United Fruit Company and distribute plots to the landless peasants of his country.

Though many liberal observers of Latin America agreed that land reform was a sensible goal to pursue, Washington was convinced that Arbenz's scheme was Communist inspired and therefore intolerable. When an arms shipment from Czechoslovakia reached Guatemala in May, Dulles declared that "a government in which Communist influence is very strong has come into a position to dominate militarily the Central American area." Rather than resort to old-fashioned gunboat diplomacy, the Eisenhower administration relied on the Central Intelligence Agency to orchestrate Arbenz's downfall.

The CIA was an intelligence-gathering organization whose dagger was more influential than its cloak. So powerful was the mystique of CIA success in covert operations that the Eisenhower administration at times viewed the agency as a major tool of foreign policy, particularly useful as an alternative to messy and more expensive conventional military interventions. The agency's most prominent officers tended to be those with "operations" backgrounds who had performed feats of derring-do behind enemy lines in World War II. The CIA had already tested its black arts in Europe in the late 1940s when it acted secretly to prevent communist electoral victories in Italy and France. In 1953, it helped to engineer the return of the Shah to power in Iran in place of Mohammed Mossadegh, a nationalist politician who threatened to nationalize the country's significant western oil properties. The Iranian coup was achieved largely through judicious distribution of money to Mossadegh's enemies.

In Guatemala, the agency created a rebel army in adjoining Nicaragua under the leadership of a Colonel Castillo Armas. This ragtag group hardly constituted a formidable military threat, but it was American-backed. Sensing the hopelessness of resisting the giant to the north, the Arbenz regime buckled and Guatemala returned quickly to its harsh authoritarian ways in which a small landed elite lorded it over an impoverished mass of peasants. This high-handed behavior evoked much criticism from Latin America and from the European allies. Over time, it became clear that the reliance on the CIA in the long-term battle for world opinion resulted, in Henry Steele Commager's words, in the "alienation of much of world opinion."[38] Nevertheless, Eisenhower heaped praise on the CIA for having "averted a Soviet beachhead in our hemisphere."[39]

The persistence of deep undercurrents of dissatisfaction in the region became uncomfortably clear in 1958 when Vice President Richard Nixon took a goodwill trip to Latin America. To his mortification, he was greeted in Caracas by an angry mob that bombarded his motorcade with stones and nearly succeeded in overturning his vehicle. Worse yet, in 1959, another wholly unexpected development threatened to make Latin America a central battleground of the Cold War: the triumph of a communist revolution on the island of Cuba, 100 miles south of Florida.

The swashbuckling romantic rebel Fidel Castro rode into Havana to the cheers of adoring crowds in January 1, 1959, following the abrupt collapse of the corrupt dictatorship of Fulgencio Batista. Initially, the State Department did not take Castro for a communist; nor, for that matter, did the Cuban Communist Party, which played no part in his ascent to power. It was not long, however, before Castro began to bare his anti-American teeth by expropriating American-owned properties in Cuba without adequate compensation. "The revolution may be like a watermelon," said one observer. "The more they slice it, the redder it gets." In February 1960, Castro signed a deal with the USSR that made the Soviet bloc an alternative outlet for his island's sugar crop. In June, the U.S. announced an embargo on Cuban sugar imports. In the same year, Castro announced that he was a communist. Suddenly and without any obvious effort, the Soviets had scored a tremendous psychological coup in the cold war. Communism had been established in the Western Hemisphere, in the belly of the capitalist beast.

Castro took his campaign against the U.S. to the United Nations, but also sought to forge a security connection with the Soviets. Hoping to shelter his precocious new offspring from America's wrath, Nikita Khrushchev declared in July that "the Monroe Doctrine has outlived its time, has outlived itself, has died, so to say, a natural death." Not long after, Soviet officials were announcing the same right to intervene to protect socialist regimes that the U.S. asserted when intervening in Asia and in Europe. In so doing, they created for themselves the same kind of ideologically inspired strategic liability in Cuba that the United States had created for itself in Berlin. In January 1961, Cuba and the United States broke off diplomatic relations, but it was clear that this dramatic story of a communist regime on America's doorstep was only in its beginning stages. For Americans, the inconceivable had incomprehensibly become the intolerable.

The Cold War at High Noon: The Kennedy Administration

The cold war reached a crescendo in the administration of John Kennedy. During the Kennedy years, a string of crises over Berlin and Cuba brought the U.S. and Soviet Union to the brink of direct confrontation. Though the immediate result was a recognition that each side had a fundamental interest in avoiding nuclear war, this new sense of nuclear sobriety failed to resolve the basic problem of how to deter less provocative forms of communist expansionism. The resolution of the crises pointed the United States once again in the direction of limited war as a way of showing western determination and preventing the defection of world opinion to the communist camp.

The glamorous young JFK was a cold warrior through and through who won the presidency in part because of his aggressive critique of the Eisenhower administration's tired cold war strategy. In his well-received inaugural address, the new president pledged "to pay any price, bear any burden, meet any hardship, support any friend, oppose any foe to assure the survival and success of liberty." Kennedy based his foreign policy on a vigorous strategy of "flexible response," which was supposed to be a remedy for a palsied policy of massive retaliation.

The need for a new strategic approach seemed all the more pressing in the aftermath of Khrushchev's January 1960 comments on "sacred wars" that made clear the Soviet Union's obligation to support anti-imperialist "wars of national liberation." Faced with a Soviet equivalent of the Truman Doctrine, the Kennedy administration believed that the West would be soon be confronted by a growing number of local brush-fire wars where the use of nuclear weapons would be wholly out of place. In his May 25, 1961, speech calling for America to be the first nation to put a man on the moon, JFK called the third world "the great battleground for the defense and expansion of freedom today."

All the more reason, then, for a strategy of flexible response that could successfully engage the enemy on his own terms. If sticks and stones were the weapons of choice, the U.S. would use those implements. If the enemy escalated to bows and arrows, the United States would match their move. The point of this mimicry was to be able to meet such raises without putting all U.S. chips in the pot at one time. Since this involved the use of credible force, it would reinforce deterrence and more easily avoid sliding down the "slippery slope" to all-out nuclear war. That was the theory, but the crises actually encountered by the Kennedy administration failed to conform to its conceptual models. Notwithstanding Kennedy's desire to avoid nuclear warfare, his credibility-based policies helped bring the U.S. and the Soviet Union to the brink of nuclear Armageddon.

Kennedy's foreign policy menu was based largely on the Eisenhower administration's leftovers. An early crisis centered on Laos, an obscure landlocked country in southeast Asia, formerly a part of French Indochina, where a communist faction seemed on the verge of besting its center and right opponents. Here was yet another example of cold-war international-ist logic at work, in which upholding America's credibility before an un-easy world opinion (the "key factor" according to the U.S. ambassador in Moscow) demanded that the line be held.[40] The departing Eisenhower told Kennedy that "the loss of Laos would be the loss of the 'cork in the bottle' and the beginning of a loss of most of the Far East."[41]

Fearing the domino consequences of a communist Laos, yet far from eager to intervene in this out-of-the-way jungle land, Kennedy eagerly accepted a patchwork neutralization deal with Khrushchev that eventually produced an uneasy coalition among the three contending factions. However, there was a strong sense among many in Washington that the U.S. had been "frozen in our tracks by the image of the Chinese Communists pouring into Southeast Asia," as Walt Rostow put it.[42] Among America's allies, an intelligence report informed Kennedy that "the common consensus is that the United States must avoid a 'second Laos.' "[43]

The next problem, Cuba, was not so easily finessed. Upon entering the White House, Kennedy inherited a top-secret plan for unseating Castro. The scheme called for a small CIA-financed and trained army of Cuban emigrés to land in Cuba and trigger an island-wide rebellion against Castro. Kennedy, who like many other Washingtonians was blinded by the mystique of CIA success, approved the plan. At the time, its virtues appeared to outweigh its shortcomings. However transparent the American role, a counterrevolution stimulated by an exile army would at least make unnecessary a direct American invasion, for it seemed a foregone conclusion at the time that the U.S. would have to invade Cuba. American public opinion demanded Castro's removal, while policy-makers feared a loss of respect for American leadership if the nation proved powerless to control its own back yard.

The invasion, which went off on April 17, 1961, barely 100 days into JFK's presidency, was a prime illustration of Murphy's Law: everything that could go wrong did go wrong. The invasion plans had become an open secret, well reported in advance by the *New York Times*. A switch in landing sites to the Bay of Pigs marooned the invaders on difficult coral beaches in an area far removed from the sheltering mountains into which they were supposed to melt away. Insufficiently trained for this kind of situation, the invaders were easily isolated and cut to pieces by Castro's forces. The counterrevolution never got under away as the ill-kept invasion secret allowed Castro's secret police to wipe out anti-Castro cells throughout Cuba. Air support from a makeshift air force of B-17s was pitiably insufficient. Interservice rivalry rendered American naval support ineffectual. And, when the chips were down, the American air support which some CIA insiders were counting on was not approved by Kennedy. A report by the CIA's inspector general, long-suppressed, described the agency's operations as "ludicrous or tragic or both."[44]

Kennedy's decision to swallow defeat, however humiliating, was actually quite courageous. Like everything else in the cold war, the balance sheet on specific conflicts had to be judged not by their bottom-line value in the short run, but in terms of their ultimate consequences. The pain of the fiasco certainly paled before the international furor that was certain to arise if the U.S. had gone in with both feet, especially as JFK had already disclaimed any intention of intervening. The western alliance would have been in even greater disarray than was already the case. The Soviets were bound to respond, either by direct support of Castro or by turning up the heat in another area of the world, most likely in Berlin, where the American position was more exposed.

The implications of the defeat for American credibility made it all the more likely that the next confrontation with communism, wherever it might occur, would require a much tougher American response. As Kennedy adviser Walt Rostow noted, "the action in Cuba has temporarily damaged the grand alliance in all its dimensions." The Cuban fiasco, in combination with the Laos deal, suggested that Khrushchev had been fortified in his belief that the U.S. did not know how to deal with his tactics and would "thrash about ineffectively."[45] Later, an intelligence estimate noted matter-of-factly that "Cuba and Laos set back most of the positive expressions of hope expressed earlier in the year."[46]

JFK had barely a moment to catch his breath before the Berlin volcano began once again to rumble and spew smoke. Early in June, at a summit in Vienna, he sought to convince Khrushchev of the virtues of the status quo. But the meeting was a communications disaster. The voluble Soviet leader made it clear that the clock was ticking on Berlin. A somber Kennedy returned to the United States and warned, in a nationally televised address, of the likelihood of a showdown in the near future. Privately, he informed the congressional leadership of "the Soviet sense of a change in the power balance."[47] At the same time, he announced huge military increases and caused a near-panic when he mentioned the desirability of building private fallout shelters.

The Soviets struck suddenly and unexpectedly on August 11, 1961, when their East German puppets began building a wall around the city of West Berlin. Originally a makeshift affair, over time the Wall was refined into an escape-proof structure. Despite its grotesque appearance, the Wall was extraordinarily elegant in its political design. By dividing the city, the Wall effectively closed the escape hatch which had long allowed dissatisfied East Germans to flee the GDR. Meanwhile, because the four-power occupation and the rights of the occupiers remained technically in place, the western powers were in no position to launch legalistic protests.

Publicly, JFK took only a few quite modest symbolic steps in the immediate aftermath of the Wall's construction. He sent an American combat
team down the Autobahn to reinforce the undermanned Berlin garrison.
General Lucius Clay, the hero of the Berlin airlift, was once again pressed
into service as the president's special representative. And Vice President
Johnson headed a team of senior officials who were sent to the scene with
the unwelcome task of restoring the morale of some unhappy Berliners
and West Germans. Despite some tense military moments at "Checkpoint
Charlie" in October, going to war for the sake of reunifying Berlin was
unthinkable. Indeed, within the administration and among the Allies, there
was little enthusiasm for energetically parrying Khrushchev's cynically
brilliant move. The American position in Berlin was too exposed and the
military options too limited for launching a serious counterattack. "A wall
is a hell of a lot better than a war," Kennedy conceded.

Privately, White House officials talked about putting the best face on
the situation for propaganda purposes. They also began to consider more
openly accepting the status quo on Germany that had evolved over the
past fifteen years. However, with West Germany still bent on achieving
national reunification, a frank acknowledgment of the real sentiments in
Washington was impossible. Thus, as all the western capitals wept croco-
dile tears, the decision to strike reunification from the diplomatic agenda
was not much talked about. It risked shocking the West Germans into
slipping their leash to NATO and the West.

Over the next two years, as Berlin receded into the background and the
wall accomplished its mission, Kennedy began to say explicitly what he
felt. In an emotional journey to the Federal Republic in mid-1963, he all
but admitted that reunification was not a realistic prospect and that the
West Germans would have to be reconciled for the foreseeable future to
the fact of a divided country. Even his delirious reception in Berlin, where
he delivered his famous comment, "Ich bin ein Berliner," was unintentionally double-edged. Intended to reassure the cheering throng, it translated
instead as "I am a doughnut" because of the mistaken inclusion of the
article *ein*. Rhetorically, his intention was clear, but the subtext of the
statement said just as clearly that Kennedy was *not* a Berliner.

The Wall brought greater stability to the German issue, but Kennedy
had paid dearly in the coin of credibility, the symbolic currency of the
cold war. All-in-all, he had struck out in his first two at-bats in Cuba and
Berlin. The alliance in Europe seemed shaky, and brush-fire wars of national liberation in the third world threatened to burn out of control if the
Soviets were not brought up short. Kennedy's last at-bat and chance for
redemption came, of all places, in Cuba. In October 1962, photos from

U-2 reconnaissance overflights tipped off CIA analysts to the emplacement of Soviet nuclear-tipped missiles on the island. Ever since the Bay of Pigs humiliation, Kennedy had fended off aggressive right-wing calls to get rid of Castro. Faced with compelling photo evidence of the presence of Soviet nuclear arms in Cuba in defiance of his pointed public warnings against introducing offensive weapons, Kennedy was compelled to act.

The discovery was kept secret for one week while the administration hammered out a response. In that span of time, opinion within "Ex Comm," an ad hoc group of JFK's most trusted foreign policy advisers, shifted from favoring an invasion and air strikes to recommending a "quarantine," a euphemism for a partial naval blockade of the island. A quarantine would buy time for a diplomatic solution, whereas an invasion was likely to breach the dike that held back the waters of escalation. Finally, in a dramatic Sunday evening television address, the president described the ominous situation to an anxious national audience and revealed the administration's plans.

It took a hair-raising week of confrontation before the missile crisis was resolved by diplomatic means. To his everlasting credit, Khrushchev finally agreed to withdraw his missiles from the island in return for a noninvasion pledge *and* the implicit understanding, long obscured after the event, that the U.S. would remove its obsolete Jupiter missiles from Turkey. He had placed missiles in Cuba primarily to defend the Cuban revolution. Assured now of the continuing existence of communism on the island, he turned a deaf ear to Castro's pleas for more aggressive action. "We are not struggling against imperialism to die," he told Castro, "but to . . . [ultimately] achieve the victory of communism."[48] With the exception of Castro, everyone breathed a deep sigh of relief. Thirty years later, the disastrous potential of the missile crisis was made even clearer in retrospect. Battlefield nuclear weapons, it turned out, had also been deployed in Cuba to repel imperialist invaders. Had there been an American invasion, it might well have been the trigger for a thermonuclear war.

The Cuban missile crisis was, from a domestic standpoint, the most successful of Kennedy's foreign policy adventures. As if by instinct, American public opinion instantly sized up Khrushchev's brazen initiative on America's Caribbean turf as a grave threat to the nation's survival. If he did nothing, JFK told his brother, Attorney General Robert Kennedy, he would be impeached. The self-evident character of the crisis preempted discussion of issues other than on the means of rolling back the Soviet move. This manifest, taken-for-granted, do-or-die quality of the crisis illustrated the power of the naturalized Wilsonian assumptions that linked credibility to world public opinion.

However, once one began to verbalize the actual threat posed by Soviet missiles, the issues were not so clear. At an early meeting of the Ex Comm, Secretary of Defense Robert McNamara suggested that, objectively, Soviet missiles in Cuba made no difference to the military balance. This was not simply some quirky opinion on McNamara's part. National Security Adviser McGeorge Bundy recalled that "most of us agreed with McNamara's summary judgment at the outset, that the Cuban missiles did not change the strategic balance—'not at all.' "[49] Reminiscing some thirty years later, presidential intimate Theodore Sorensen said that Kennedy felt obliged to remove the missiles only because he had publicly warned Khrushchev several months earlier about introducing "offensive" weapons into Cuba. That warning had been a piece of rhetorical red meat thrown to the pack of howling anti-Castro wolves. Presumably, had Kennedy been able to see into the future, he would not have given such a warning and, by implication, would not have felt compelled to remove the missiles.

The security threat, then, came not from the missiles themselves but from their political meaning. As Kennedy soon concluded, "They've got enough to blow us up anyway. . . . After all, this is a political struggle as much as military."[50] Although there were those then and now who believed that the presence of ICBMs would have appreciably shifted the military balance, the pros and cons of the precise numbers were a matter of near-theological disputation. In a few years, in any case, Soviet missile-firing submarines would be stationed off the American coast, multiplying many times over the nuclear threat created by Cuba. What *was* crystal clear to Kennedy was that the missiles constituted a political threat. If they were allowed to stand, he believed, America's image in the world would have suffered a serious blow, particularly in Europe, whatever the objective power-equation of the two superpowers. In his address to the nation, Kennedy invoked the ritual language of credibility when he described the missiles as "a deliberately provocative and unjustified change in the status quo which cannot be accepted by this country, if our courage and our commitments are ever to be trusted again by either friend or foe."

Khrushchev's action seemed inexplicable at the time, but it is now clear that he acted out of genuine fear of a U.S. invasion of the island. Even though U.S. policy-makers have since insisted that no invasion was in the works, it is understandable that he would have interpreted the Kennedy administration's anti-Castro obsession as a determination to overthrow the fledgling communist regime. From a symbolic standpoint, the loss of Cuba "would have been a terrible blow to Marxism-Leninism," he recalled. "It would gravely diminish our stature throughout the world." But

Khrushchev had other motives, too. No doubt he saw an opportunity to restore a nuclear balance by compensating for America's huge numerical advantage in ICBMs. By this time, the so-called "missile gap" of the late 1950s, which had allowed Khrushchev to engage in atomic diplomacy, had been discredited by U.S. earth-orbiting spy satellites. Stealing a march on the Americans would also burnish Khrushchev's revolutionary credentials in the face of a growing challenge from Red China for leadership of world communism.

While the outcome of the crisis made clear that the two sides were haunted by much the same kinds of fears, they were not fully symmetrical. Despite being fully alert to Cuba's importance for Soviet credibility, Khrushchev threw credibility to the wind when he had to. Later, in justifying his decision, he explained in typically earthy fashion: "I'm not a czarist officer who has to kill myself if I fart at a masked ball. It's better to back down than to go to war."[51] Perhaps this less weighty view of credibility is what caused him to seriously underestimate Kennedy's fear of losing the allegiance of a wavering world conscience. Although the ongoing war for world opinion would appear to have made the ideological motives of both sides fairly transparent, that fails to take into account the deep mutual ignorance of each other's motives. Unfortunately, the CIA's superb job of exposing the USSR's capabilities was offset by its mediocre record of clarifying its intentions.[52]

The Cuban missile crisis was the cold war's most clear-cut example of the two central fears of Wilsonianism simultaneously in operation. On the one hand, to prevent a collapse of world opinion the U.S. was prepared to run the risk of war for the sake of credibility while, at the same time, it recoiled from war as it became more than a remote possibility. But, at the time, the traditional language of power got in the way of understanding how the stakes were defined. For example, Walter Lippmann described the Cuban missile crisis as "a radical move against the strategic balance of power" that fully warranted the risk of war. JFK himself in the aftermath talked about the Soviet adventure as an attempt to change the balance of power. According to Dean Rusk, "the problem [was] not, as Mr. Khrushchev seems to think, to find a formula to save Western 'face' but for the USSR to refrain from invasions of vital Western interests and commitments."[53] What is important here is how terms like "balance of power" and "vital interests" had been Wilsonianized to the point that they had taken on entirely new meanings in the cold war context.

On the surface, the outcome of the Cuban crisis appeared to be a stunning success for American foreign policy. But beneath the public mask of subdued triumph was the worried face of a president who realized that the United States could not afford more successes of this kind. They were too dangerous. Cuba was a one-of-a-kind affair, not a model for future policy. John Foster Dulles had talked brinkmanship, but Kennedy had been forced to practice it, and the experience was too terrifying to repeat. Khrushchev felt much the same way. In the aftermath of Cuba, then, the chastened superpowers showed a willingness to reopen stalled negotiations on nuclear arms control. If nothing else, the two sides shared an overriding mutual interest in survival, as Kennedy made clear in his American University speech. In the summer of 1963, American envoy Averell Harriman signed a nuclear test ban treaty in Moscow that limited nuclear detonations to underground tests.

These positive developments concealed deeper and dangerous undercurrents beneath the surface of events. Secretary of State Dean Rusk hoped that the crisis had been a "wholesome experience" for the Soviets that had removed any remaining illusions about American determination. That it did, but it also taught the Soviets another lesson: they had been outgunned in Cuba and would see to it that never again would the Soviet military operate from such a disadvantage. Thus, while it led to an arms control success that ought not to be minimized, the Cuban missile crisis also catalyzed yet another phase of an already costly and dangerous arms race.

The Americans had also hoped that Cuba II would finally lay to rest Europe's doubts about American resolve. Here, too, the triumph in Cuba delivered less than it promised, proving once again that credibility in the bank did not assure a solid credit rating. President Charles De Gaulle of France had been the leading critic of American defense policy in Europe. Convinced that the Soviet threat had passed, he argued that NATO had been turned into an instrument of American imperialism. Moreover, he suggested that the American nuclear guarantee was not reliable. Would an American president risk the U.S. homeland to retaliate against an attack against London or Paris? No, he answered. After Cuba, De Gaulle stuck to his guns. Turning a blind eye to the Wilsonian logic of credibility that motivated America's actions in the Cuban affair, he suggested that it proved only that the U.S. would defend an *American* interest by nuclear means.

The success in Cuba also failed to translate into success elsewhere. As JFK was beating down the brush fires in Berlin and Cuba, the leaves of Vietnam smoldered for the three years of his presidency, receiving only occasional attention as the renewed Viet Cong insurgency grew quite serious. Kennedy responded by sending high-level study missions, increasing American aid to Diem, and supplying combat "advisers" who numbered more than 25,000 by mid-1963. By all indications, Vietnam was too important to be allowed to fall to the communists.

In later years, after Kennedy's successor, Lyndon B Johnson, had plunged the United States into what became an extraordinarily unpopular war, Kennedy partisans argued that JFK would *not* have taken the country into Vietnam. The suggestion was that Kennedy the cold warrior had been mellowed and matured by experience. But that argument neglects a number of points that suggest a different conclusion. First, Kennedy had no ideology other than Wilsonianism to rely upon; nor, for that matter, did other policy-makers. Second, American public opinion was, at the time, very solid in its cold war anticommunism. It is difficult to see how a president so sensitive to the polls and attuned to domestic political realities could have struck out on an utterly new and politically risky course.

Third, and most important, Kennedy's experiences in Cuba and Berlin all pointed in the direction of conventional intervention in Vietnam. Each of these crises underscored the desirability of possessing on-the-spot conventional military superiority. Kennedy defended his policy as a "middle way" between appeasement and recklessness. He appeared to mellow only because the all-out pronouncements of his early presidency, those uttered in the Dullesian vein, proved to be impractical. But the limitations of atomic diplomacy only confirmed in practice what had long been understood in principle: that traditional diplomacy, featuring compromise and an occasional retreat, was not yet an acceptable way of conducting cold war foreign policy. By the end of the Kennedy presidency, more so than in the beginning, the logic of graduated response seemed the only way out.

IN THE TEN years following the Korean War, American policy came full circle. The NATO experiment in collective security was equivocal. Policy-makers continued to have serious doubts about allied solidarity and commitment, but at least the situation in developed regions of the world had been stabilized to the point that free-market economies and societies were once again flourishing. The outlook was less promising for other areas of the world, however, where the likelihood of crisis was high and possibilities existed for ruinous defeats in the cold war. After the near-apocalyptic confrontations in Berlin and Cuba and the ill-starred attempt at covert operations in the Bay of Pigs, American policy-makers were left, by default, with limited war as the chief instrument for pursuing a Wilsonian cold war strategy. To avoid an unstoppable blaze down the road, the nation had to be willing to set some controlled burns. Unfortunately, as the forthcoming Vietnam era would show, the necessary base of public and international support for limited symbolic conflicts had become more unstable since Korea.

CHAPTER SEVEN

The Vietnam Era and the Dilemmas
of Wilsonianism

The assassination of John F. Kennedy in November 1963 was followed by a brief period of calm in foreign affairs as Lyndon B. Johnson consolidated his presidency and pursued his vision of "The Great Society," a government-sponsored revolution in social policy. Over the next two years, Johnson launched ambitious initiatives in civil rights, social insurance, education, urban renewal, and a host of other areas. Although the 1964 campaign was, for the first time since 1948, fought out largely on domestic issues, Johnson's political future would be decided overseas. Before long, the unresolved dilemmas of Wilsonian cold war strategy embroiled the United States in one of the most protracted and politically disruptive wars in its history.

The War of 1812 and the Mexican War of 1846–48 showed that unpopular wars were not unusual events in American history. But those conflicts at least ended with a pleasing aroma of victory that the effort in Vietnam, reeking of defeat, could never hope to exude. In the modern era, no other war in American history provoked as much popular controversy, divisiveness, and outright resistance as Vietnam. The war remained at the center of American attention for the better part of a decade; and, like a psychedelic flashback or the pain of an old war wound never fully healed, it resurfaced with remarkably vividness at irregular intervals thereafter.

The tenacity with which American policy-makers stuck to the American position in Vietnam past the point of prudence was testimony to the continued power of the neo-Wilsonian strategy of symbolic deterrence, even as events in Europe, Asia, and the Soviet Union pointed to its growing obsolescence. While Vietnam remained the center of attention through the mid-1970s, other events taking place at the same time proved to be of greater importance in setting the future agenda of American foreign policy. By the end of the period, the ideological volume of the cold war, formerly so piercing as to result in frequent military confrontations, was dialed down and muted.

The Vietnam War

Following the 1954 Geneva conference that divided Indochina into a communist north and a pro-western South Vietnam at the 17th parallel, American policy-makers hoped for a stable situation on the pattern of two Germanies, two Koreas, and the de facto existence of two Chinas. Steady infusions of American aid to Saigon and the energetic leadership of Premier Ngo Dinh Diem promised a successful venture in "nation building" that would force the communists in Hanoi to settle for only half a loaf. American confidence was badly misplaced, however, as South Vietnam plunged into internal and external crises beyond its capacity to surmount.

Shortly after Diem, with America's blessing, refused to hold the 1956 national elections agreed upon at Geneva, a communist insurgency broke out in the south. The Viet Cong rebels fought largely on their own for two years until 1959, when North Vietnam began secretly to provide support. Adroitly mixing antigovernment terror with radical nationalist appeals to the peasantry, the Viet Cong gained control of a large and growing proportion of villages in the countryside. The peasant population had little sympathy for an alien government in Saigon that the Diem family and its cronies controlled on behalf of an oppressive landlord system. With Diem's corrupt and inefficient army hopelessly ill-equipped to deal with the rebels, the insurgency was beginning to spin out of control by the time Kennedy took over as president.

With Cuba and Berlin already occupying his attention, Kennedy was not eager to jump into Vietnam with both feet, as former President Eisenhower was urging him to do. Instead, incrementalism was the order of the day. In response to the dire forecasts of a steady procession of study missions, aid was increased and the number of American military advisers multiplied. Still, despite the obvious reluctance to intervene, Vietnam's importance was never in doubt. "Our security may be lost piece by piece, country by country, without the firing of a single missile or the crossing of a single border," Kennedy told one audience.[1] Like Truman and Eisenhower before him, he and just about everyone else in Washington who had anything to do with foreign policy assumed that the loss of Vietnam would be a devastating defeat in the cold war, leading to the loss of Asia, a collapse of the western defense system, and ultimately, perhaps, to World War III.

Half measures bought time, but, as subsequent events demonstrated, time was not on America's side in dealing with this problem. By the summer of 1963, the contagion of violence in South Vietnam had reached epidemic proportions. Diem's mandarin rule had become increasingly erratic and repressive. Concerned less with military effectiveness than personal survival, Diem appointed army commanders on the basis of personal allegiance. The secret police run by his brother-in-law, Ngo Dinh Nu, freely used terror against opponents. At the same time, Diem's disastrous misapplication of American-devised pacification policies in the countryside gave peasants no reason to identify with his government. Eventually, despite his attempts to keep the lid on, popular discontent boiled over in the summer of 1963 when massive protests rocked the regime. Photos of gasoline-drenched Buddhist monks setting themselves afire shocked American viewers of network television news. Americans were further outraged by comments made by Diem's sister, Madame Nu, who scornfully dismissed the self-immolations as "barbecues."

Diem, once seen as Indochina's counterpart to Adenauer (the "Winston Churchill of southeast Asia," in Vice President Johnson's effusive words), was clearly losing control. Devious, secretive, autocratic, and not a little paranoid, he turned a deaf ear to advice from all but members of his immediate entourage, who tended to reinforce his worst tendencies. Following several failed high-level attempts by Kennedy to talk sense to Diem, it was obvious that he would not change his ways. Indeed, he could not, for many of the reforms being urged upon him would have undermined the foundation of his political support, such as it was. Thus, opinion in Washington hardened: Diem had to go.

Sensitive to changing sentiment within the Kennedy administration, a group of military conspirators in South Vietnam reached the same conclusion. After discreetly sounding out the American ambassador and receiving no signal to stop, the generals launched a brief but violent coup that ended with the murder of Diem and many of his family. Two weeks later, Kennedy was himself assassinated in Dallas. A period of instability followed in Saigon, in which politically ambitious generals succeeded one another in a game of musical chairs. Although the political situation was now less critical than at the peak of the Buddhist crisis, President Johnson and his Kennedy-appointed advisers were growing increasingly concerned at the continued disintegration of Saigon's authority in the countryside.

In the midst of the 1964 election campaign, a confused confrontation between North Vietnamese PT boats and American destroyers in the Gulf of Tonkin gave Johnson the opportunity to respond with retaliatory air strikes on the north, the first in what would become an ongoing series of bombing attacks aimed at punishing Hanoi. LBJ also used the occasion to secure passage of a congressional resolution that had long been in preparation. Approved by overwhelming majorities in both houses, the resolution authorized the president to use whatever force necessary to protect American interests in Vietnam. The resolution, LBJ said, "was like granny's nightshirt. It covered *everything*."

To the extent that foreign policy figured in the 1964 campaign, the Republican candidate, Senator Barry Goldwater of Arizona, was cast in the role of the sinister interventionist. Johnson, by contrast, promised the American people that he would not send American boys to fight and die in Vietnam. Goldwater was buried in an electoral landslide so deep that some commentators were predicting the end of the Republican Party. All this was a change from previous elections, in which the perception of being soft on communism had been the cardinal sin. Though the country was hardly awash in anti-interventionist sentiment at this time, this sequence of events would later cost Johnson heavily in public support, when many critics of the war accused the administration of secretly planning all along to intervene in Vietnam after the election.

That kind of conspiracy thesis was certainly wrong, for LBJ would have been delighted not to have to intervene. Like most everyone else, he had his doubts. In May 1964, for example, he called Vietnam "the biggest damned mess I ever saw," wondered if the U.S. could extricate itself, and added "I don't think it's worth fighting for."[2] But such occasional venting of private misgivings was not in the same conceptual league with a Wilsonian outlook that had reached doctrinal status. At a June 1964 press conference, LBJ described Vietnam as "not just a jungle war, but a struggle for freedom on every front of human activity."[3] Still, no decision to intervene had yet been made. American policy remained incrementalist, doing only what was necessary at the time to stave off collapse.

Intervention began in serious only in the spring of 1965, following a Viet Cong raid on an American base at Pleiku. Heeding the advice of administration insiders who suggested "sustained reprisal" against the communists, Johnson authorized punitive air strikes against the North and, at the same time, announced that a contingent of American marines was being sent to protect the base perimeter. In July, the point of no return was reached. As the military situation continued to deteriorate, additional American troops were rushed over. Bit by bit, but with relentless swiftness, the American presence in South Vietnam swelled to numbers that Defense Secretary McNamara had once called "outrageous." By year's end, there were 200,000 American troops in the South; by July 1968, at high tide, there were 537,000.

For a number of reasons, Johnson felt he could not afford to be candid about American intervention. What later became known as the "credibility gap" had less to do with a cynical desire to deceive the American public than with what, at the time, passed for prudent foreign policy tactics. LBJ wanted to minimize reaction from North Vietnam's allies, the Soviet Union and China, in the hope of avoiding the kind of frustrating stalemate endured a decade earlier in Korea. By slowly turning up the heat, LBJ hoped that the communist frog would fail to realize what was happening until it was thoroughly cooked. Moreover, creating a wartime atmosphere could easily get out of control if "hawks" began, MacArthur-like, to demand all-out victory. Johnson also feared that conservatives might use the war as a convenient cover for allowing the infant Great Society programs to die of neglect.

The increased size of the expeditionary force was matched by the growing ambitions of the American military. No longer content to stand on the sidelines and watch the incompetent South Vietnamese military (ARVN, for short) fumble the ball away, the Pentagon pressed for the first team to take over. The American commander in Saigon, General William Westmoreland, devised a new strategy for fighting the guerrillas. Rather than have his troops sit tight in their bases and leave the initiative to the enemy, Westmoreland proposed to take the war to the communists. Aggressive sweeps of the countryside would be undertaken by U.S. soldiers with the aim of initiating contact.

By forcing the enemy to fight in circumstances of America's choosing, American superiority in firepower and training was supposed to inflict intolerable casualties upon the enemy. Score would be kept by "body count," i.e., running tallies of the number of enemy soldiers killed in combat. If the slaughter was one-sided enough, it stood to reason that at some point the enemy would be forced to cry uncle. This "search and destroy" strategy was a formula for a war of attrition, a struggle of staying power. Its combination of will-cum-firepower was a fitting military corollary to the Wilsonian cold war assumptions that got the nation involved. Designed to avert defeat and demoralization while preventing unstoppable escalation, the strategy was successful in avoiding large-scale Chinese intervention—which was, by the way, more than a purely hypothetical possibility.[4]

Nevertheless, the strategy was deeply flawed because it played directly into the hands of the North Vietnamese foe. Powerfully motivated by an anti-imperialist nationalism which saw the Americans as only a more powerful version of the French colonizers, the North Vietnamese had long been prepared to accept a protracted struggle. Unconsciously repeating the mistakes of the French, the racially and culturally arrogant Americans initially underestimated the resolve and resourcefulness of the North Vietnamese. As one historian has suggested, the lesson of Vietnam was "that it is difficult to fight a limited war against an enemy for whom it is not a limited war."[5] Moreover, it was not clear that the American military was better prepared than the French had been. Despite all the fashionable talk in the early 1960s about preparing for "counterinsurgency warfare," the U.S. army was still being trained for big-unit conventional warfare.

Still, like all Monday-morning quarterbacking, play-calling looks much easier in retrospect than it did at the time. Attrition was virtually the only prudent offensive strategy available. With the exception of wild adventurist types who were willing to run the risk of a major war, few wanted a conflict that invited another Chinese intervention. On the other hand, hunkering down in so-called "strategic enclaves" would have surrendered the countryside to the guerrillas and eliminated any time horizon for ending the war.

The failure of American strategy flowed less from any basic defects in conception or execution than from the public's withdrawal of support. Since the amount of force exerted against the North Vietnamese and the Viet Cong was limited, the material equation was, by definition, balanced. Because attrition is a matter of physical staying power combined with will, the strategy's chief shortcoming was that it assured the multiplication of American casualties over the years to a point that the American public was no longer willing to accept. But the public's disaffection involved more than an unwillingness to accept the frustrations of limited war. Unlike in Korea, there was also much disagreement with the ends for which the intervention was undertaken.

It took a couple of years of creeping interventionism before public discontent finally burgeoned. American policy actually enjoyed a good deal of popular support in 1965. Only later, when the implications of the war became clear—as it became evident that the United States could not win and would not try to win; as foreign criticism increased; and as domestic dissent exploded—did these assumptions come into serious question. In late 1965, only 21 percent of the respondents in a Gallup poll believed the United States should not have become militarily involved in southeast Asia; by May 1967, 37 percent stated that intervention was a mistake. Only by February 1968 did disapproval of the conduct of the war reach 50 percent, although many of these respondents were supporters of an all-out military effort.

By 1966, it was apparent that Vietnam was fast losing its ability to rouse the kind of cold war patriotism so stirringly summoned by John F.

Kennedy in his inaugural address, in which he challenged Americans to ask what they could do for their country. Public criticism came from two sides primarily. With the emergence of a radical "New Left," the thick miasma of anticommunism that had settled on the intellectual landscape throughout the McCarthyite 1950s had lifted, making it possible at last to openly criticize foreign policy on radical grounds. Seizing upon an anti-imperialist critique of American policy, a growing number of college-educated youth rejected the Johnson administration's Wilsonian explanation for intervention. For these young critics, the war was an expression of American imperialism; it was immoral; and, accepting North Vietnam's claims of noninvolvement at face value, the charge of aggression was interpreted as an attempt to cover up what was essentially a civil war.

Many other issues motivated the student radicals, but Vietnam was the catalyst that swelled the ranks of dissent into a mass movement. Peacetime conscription had been a fact of life since 1948, forcing all young men to register for Selective Service and to perform compulsory military service if called, but it received no serious challenge until the Vietnam era when many students worried about being drafted for combat duty in Vietnam. It became a common sight at anti-Vietnam rallies to see draft cards being burned in protest.

Although the fighting and dying was done disproportionately by working-class and minority draftees, college students who received automatic deferments worried nevertheless about being conscripted once their studies were completed. Some dissidents chose to apply for conscientious objector status while a small number of others burned their bridges behind them by fleeing to countries like Canada and Sweden. The unwillingness of Americans to die for internationalism, so evident in the Vietnam years, was the first sign of a coming era of "post-heroic armies" in which technology would have to do the dirty work formerly achieved through patriotic self-sacrifice.

The "generation gap" of the 1960s exposed age-based divisions along a whole spectrum of issues besides Vietnam, most prominently in matters of sexuality, race relations, gender discrimination, and use of recreational drugs. The emergence of such a distinct and iconoclastic generation was a relatively new and shocking demonstration of the difficulties of using tradition to transmit social values in the modern era. This generational divide had much to do with the erosion of public support. Determined to define themselves in opposition to their parents, the young adults of the 1960s saw little relevance in the appeals to memory and the historical analogies that the administration used to justify the intervention in Vietnam.[6]

Increasingly, too, dissident members of the foreign policy elite inside and outside the government began to jump on the critical bandwagon with sophisticated antiwar arguments of their own. Highly respected realists like George Kennan and Hans Morgenthau argued vigorously that the war was not in America's vital interest. In their view, Vietnam mattered far less than Europe and Japan. America could not afford to dissipate its energies fighting in marginal locales when more pressing interests demanded attention. Because Vietnam was so obscure and unimportant, they could not see that it posed any real threat to American security.

Meanwhile, the leftist fringes of the movement openly identified with the Viet Minh as displays of the North Vietnamese flag and chants of "Ho, Ho, Ho Chi Minh" became common sights and sounds at antiwar rallies. Differences over Vietnam divided students, the country, and the intellectual community. Indeed, many scholarly disciplines verged on intellectual civil war over newly revived ideological questions stimulated by the Vietnam intervention. With teach-ins, student protests, and mammoth demonstrations in Washington becoming increasingly common, it was clear that the cold war consensus, if not yet in tatters, had begun to fray around the edges. "We simply hadn't estimated the kinds of new forces that were loose in the land in the middle 1960s," recalled presidential adviser McGeorge Bundy.[7]

America's presence in southeast Asia was the cumulative product of four successive presidential administrations, something that Johnson was always quick to point out when parrying accusations that this was "Lyndon Johnson's War." It was also the product of a generation that, having lived through the 1930s, World War II, and the early cold war, drew direct historical parallels with the events of the past. The Munich analogy and the domino theory argued that just as the appeasement of Japan and Germany in the 1930s had made World War II inevitable, so too the acceptance of communist victory in Vietnam would lead to another, and far more destructive, global conflagration. In making the case for intervention, Johnson tried to use analogies that anyone could understand. "If you let a bully come into your front yard one day . . . the next day he'll be up on your porch and the day after that he'll rape your wife in your own bed," he explained.[8] One wonders how much enlightenment this sort of talk produced.

There was a self-defeating element in this kind of thinking. The domino theory was based in significant part on lessons of the past that were rooted in memories. Obviously, these memories were not part of the internalized experience of the baby-boom generation (the 51 percent of the population that, in the year 1965, was under thirty years of age); they might as well have been ancient history. The argument therefore reached only a shrinking number of the already converted. For those who took historical arguments more seriously, the Munich analogy was easily rebutted by critics like Senator William Fulbright who pointed out—quite correctly—that historical analogies were always flawed: Ho was not Hitler and Vietnam was not Nazi Germany. Memories, moreover, did not automatically inscribe a worldview even in the older generation. Wilsonian policies were popularly accepted and institutionalized after the war thanks largely to the historical accident of Pearl Harbor. But what historical contingency could grant, it could also take away.

Moreover, the deeper Wilsonian rationale was never well understood. The Wilsonian interpretation of modern world history that did away with the idea of *national* interest was the intellectual taproot of American action, but its conceptual depth had always been fathomed by relatively few, with the result that it relied all the more on elite consensus for its efficacy. Thus, while criticism from members of the foreign policy elite tended to take a more conservative line, it was perhaps all the more damaging to an administration that could no longer count on internal unanimity to control the terms of the debate.

Nonconformists like Kennan had long been critical of many aspects of the cold war, so their jumping ship was not unexpected. More hurtful was the desertion of influential politicians like Senator William Fulbright of Arkansas, who had been the major sponsor of the Gulf of Tonkin Resolution. Fulbright complained of an "arrogance of power" and a slavish adherence to outworn myths as the causes of the nation's disastrous embroilment in southeast Asia. As head of the Senate Committee on Foreign Relations, Fulbright chaired televised hearings that provided a national forum for early dissenters. Within the administration, the number of doubters swelled over time. George Ball, the undersecretary of state, was the earliest high-ranking dissenter, but his influence was negligible by virtue of his unofficial status as "devil's advocate," which meant that he was always politely heard and routinely ignored. But in time Ball was joined by others, most prominently Secretary of Defense McNamara, so that by early 1968 the administration was itself a house divided.

The way in which Johnson dealt with these criticisms illuminated some of the contradictions of a Wilsonian internationalism that depended in the first instance on support from the American public. While fuming privately and giving vent to the suspicion that critics of the war were communist-inspired, Johnson could not play the card of anticommunist patriotism. Any attempt to rouse patriotic sentiment against sedition, he believed, would ruin American policy because it was likely to be *too* successful. Unlike World War I, when Wilson was able to demand the application of force without limit, once the beast of patriotism was awakened, it was likely to devour American foreign policy as well as the protestors. Warlike passions would demand victory, which could be achieved only by a full-scale effort that would in turn raise the threat of escalation. And it was precisely the danger of escalation to World War III that American policy sought to prevent. Thus, LBJ's complaints about the decline of patriotism were irrelevant, since the administration was doctrinally prohibited from conjuring it up.

Far more damaging to Johnson's war effort was the fact that the internationalist outlook, which was even more urgently needed than patriotism, was in short supply. It was one thing to fight for the defense of one's country in the face of an immediate threat; it was quite another to fight without seeking victory in obscure locales whose relevance to American security might become clear only after a long chain of hypothetical events had come to pass. Internationalism's subjective cognitive status as an interpretation of the world, its high level of abstraction, and its peripatetic character—as a doctrine that was embodied first in the League, then migrated to the UN, and lastly took up residence in U.S. policy—made it a creed that was very difficult to translate into dogma. In direct contrast to the nationalist emotion and hatred of the enemy that would have been conjured up by patriotic appeals, the internationalist logic of America's commitment in Vietnam required a dispassionate, complex, nuanced, and controlled perspective. Even for the committed, internationalism was a demanding faith.

In an attempt to demonstrate his reasonableness to the doves and to the growing throng of critics in friendly nations, Johnson from time to time halted the massive bombing raids on the North. These were, as the administration knew and its critics on the left suspected, mere public-relations exercises. But the more frequently they were tried, the more they enraged the hawkish right-wing opinion that Johnson was at pains to keep under control. At the same time, the bombing halts made absolutely no progress toward negotiations that might appease LBJ's left-wing critics. Indeed, the pattern soon became numbingly familiar: the failure of the bombing halts to produce negotiations led to increased escalation and still more denunciations from both hawks and doves.

Likewise, the administration's search for approval and support abroad produced only frustration. The European allies were at best unenthusiastic supporters while the French were downright opposed. The massive bombing campaign against North Vietnam had an extraordinarily negative impact on world opinion as the noisiness of protests abroad nearly matched, at times, the unrest on American streets. In 1967, mock war-crimes trials in Stockholm, presided over by world-famous philosopher and social activist Bertrand Russell, condemned American barbarism. In Asia, where America's regional partners presumably had major stakes in the war's outcome, support was similarly difficult to come by. Though the legal justification for America's military presence in South Vietnam came from the SEATO treaty, only a few nations contributed token contingents of troops, but without enthusiasm and usually only after they been bribed or pressured by the U.S. into so doing. Unlike Korea, where UN resolutions had provided some cover of internationalist legitimacy to what was essentially an American war, the U.S. was exposed and alone in Vietnam, an internationalist community of one. If the war was indeed a credibility struggle, Hanoi was clearly winning the battle for the hearts and minds of the West.

The loss of public support at home and abroad led U.S. policy-makers to fear a widespread return to isolationism. Administration officials routinely attributed the timidity of the allies to self-absorbed national outlooks that failed to take into account the big global picture. They often wondered why America's friends failed to understand that the United States, bearing the burden of leadership, was acting in *their* best interests. Still, support from allies, though highly desirable, was not indispensable as long as the United States was prepared to act. But a failure of will seemed altogether possible if the American people reverted to an underlying isolationism that, policy-makers suspected, had never been killed off. If American internationalism weakened, world opinion and the American alliance system would collapse in a heap, making cold war defeat all but inevitable. Or so it was widely believed in Washington.

The inability to generate national and international support was indicative of the insecure intellectual foundation upon which cold war Wilsonianism had been built. Abroad, American globalism was welcomed when it accorded with the self-interest of allies, but it seemed eccentric and utopian when they derived no immediate benefit from it. At home, meanwhile, elite policy-makers had become habituated to the Wilsonian worldview to the point that it was second nature. But basing policy on unspoken normative assumptions, while it had its advantages, also had its downside. These assumptions were so embedded in analogies and so confused by talk of "realism," that it is not clear that *anyone* fully understood, in a self-conscious and articulate manner, what American internationalism was about. Precisely because they defied precise articulation, those assumptions were difficult to get across. Because these assumptions were embodied, the product of lived experience, they were all the more difficult to understand for younger people who defined themselves, in large measure, by their differences with their parents. Thus the government found it increasingly difficult to sell its policies, both to an American public that had never fully assimilated the Wilsonian worldview in the first place and to a younger generation for whom the book of historical memory opened with the Eisenhower years.

Yet the future of Wilsonianism was far from bleak. For all the opprobrium heaped upon LBJ and his administration, no alternative to the worldview that called for American intervention in Vietnam came close to being generally accepted. Like the isolationists of the 1930s, the opponents of the war were members of a discordant coalition: leftist radicals, pacifists and moralists, a large number of young people who feared conscription, some Europe-first types, and a small sect of realists. This antiwar grouping was very good at mobilizing dissent, but poor at proposing a politically viable alternative to cold war internationalism. Unlike the 1930s, a decade in which worldviews were up for grabs, in the 1960s a fully institutionalized ideology, for which the Vietnam war was only one element in the larger scheme of things, was already in place.

Indeed, as respected opponents of the war like Fulbright and George Ball (both of whom carried solid internationalist credentials) demonstrated, one did not have to be anti-Wilsonian to be anti-Vietnam. It was possible to take issue with the Vietnam War while remaining within the intellectual framework of the cold war. In arguing that more attention needed to be paid to European opinion, critics like Ball were suggesting that an overgrown Wilsonianism needed to be pruned back to its more modest original dimensions. Moreover, they made clear that by ignoring European desires and acting unilaterally, the U.S. was violating its internationalist precepts.

By early 1968, Vietnam as an issue in American domestic politics came to a critical pass. Politically, South Vietnam had been stabilized with the accession to power of General Nguyen Van Thieu, but militarily the situation continued to decline as the North matched every American escalation with increased infiltrations of NVA troops. On January 30, a wholly unexpected Viet Cong offensive on the lunar new year holiday, Tet, saw the guerrillas capture many South Vietnamese cities. A few even penetrated the U.S. embassy compound in Saigon before being repulsed. The Viet Cong were eventually beaten back, suffering heavy losses in the process, but not before they had inflicted an enormous psychological defeat on the U.S. and succeeded in what was lamely described as their "desperate attempt to take the world's headlines."[9] For all the optimistic talk about "light at the end of the tunnel," Tet proved that there was no end in sight to the war and that the enemy was, if anything, more determined and dangerous than ever.

Tet was no less a shock to the administration. After General Westmoreland demanded 200,000 more ground troops, which would have gone far toward transforming Vietnam into a full-scale war, many of Johnson's advisers decided that it was time to throw in America's hand. A meeting of the "Wise Men," leading members of the cold war elite who had formerly supported the war, advised LBJ that it was hopeless. With more than enough manpower available in the North to make up for American-inflicted casualties, the war was unwinnable under the self-imposed restrictions dictated by Wilsonian strategy. Moreover, the systematic bombing of North Vietnam, besides causing only limited damage to a largely agricultural society, was counterproductive because it cemented North Vietnamese morale. It was also exacting a high toll in captured American pilots, who were sure to become pawns in any peace negotiation. Above all, the American people could not be counted on to stay much longer on the military treadmill.

An astounded president could scarcely believe his ears, thinking at first that the wise men had been given faulty information in their briefing. After reluctantly absorbing the unwelcome advice, he took limited action. Westmoreland's whopping request for more troops was denied. Johnson shocked Americans by announcing that he would not be a candidate for the presidency and promised more actively to seek negotiations, ordering yet another bombing halt as a show of earnest money. But all this produced little change in the war itself. LBJ showed little flexibility, telling his advisers that "I am not hell-bent on agreement."[10] Preliminary talks in Paris made no progress whatsoever as the North Vietnamese negotiators continued to insist on an unconditional American withdrawal.

Domestically, events spiraled out of control. Johnson had become virtually a prisoner in the White House, reluctant to hazard public appearances for fear of being harassed by demonstrators chanting "Hey, hey, LBJ, how many kids have you killed today?" JFK's younger brother and hated rival, Robert Kennedy, having recently adopted an antiwar position, appeared to have a good chance at winning the nomination until he was shot to death at a campaign rally in Los Angeles. The Democratic national convention in Chicago in August turned into a chaotic scene as out-of-control local police confronted a horde of antiwar protesters on the city's streets. The pandemonium outside was nearly matched by the tumult within the convention hall, where Vice President Hubert Humphrey was finally nominated, but without promising any change in the conduct of the war.

It fell to the Republican victor in 1968, Richard Nixon, to end the war.

Although by 1969 he was willing to acknowledge privately that "we had been wrong"[11] to get into Vietnam, Nixon insisted, for the sake of America's credibility, on securing a "peace with honor." His influential national security adviser, Henry Kissinger, who openly admitted that the U.S. "may have exaggerated the significance of Vietnam in the early stages of its involvement," dismissed early errors as irrelevant to the current situation. "What is involved now is confidence in American promises," he insisted.[12] The substantial involvement and its heavy costs "had settled the issue of whether the outcome was important for us," he recalled.[13]

In for a penny, in for a pound. Like the banker who has invested so much in a delinquent borrower that there seems no other choice but to keep lending more money to stave off disaster, the United States was less concerned with ultimate success than with staving off collapse. Nixon and Kissinger believed that the U.S. had *created* a vital interest in Vietnam. In view of their much-trumpeted "realism," it is worth pointing out that this idea that vital interests are created rather than preexistent was an argument very much in the modern, Wilsonian mold. By contrast, the realist approach to bad investments is to cut one's losses by getting out while the getting is good.

Long an exemplary cold warrior, Nixon took a leaf from Eisenhower's 1952 campaign book by promising vaguely "to end the war and win the peace" in Vietnam. He hoped at first that his reputation as a fierce anticommunist would frighten North Vietnam into meaningful negotiations, but it soon became evident that Ho Chi Minh could not be bluffed. Taking another tack, Nixon, like Lyndon Johnson before him, urged Moscow to exert a moderating influence on North Vietnam. But the Soviets, with one eye on their Chinese rival, felt obliged to continue aiding Hanoi even though the North Vietnamese ungratefully declined to accept Soviet advice. Fully aware that the reserve of public tolerance was running on empty, Nixon had somehow to square the circle by securing American withdrawal while at the same time preserving American credibility.

He finally settled on a multitrack policy. On the one hand, he announced phased withdrawals of American forces, accompanied by an accelerated program of "Vietnamization" that was supposed to prepare the South Vietnamese military, only recently the object of American mockery, with new equipment and training, to take over the war. At the same time, Nixon realized that a unilateral American withdrawal was not likely to persuade the North to sit down at the negotiating table. So he chose also to escalate the war in various ways.

In 1970, bombing attacks on the North were resumed and intensified. The ground war was expanded to Cambodia as American forces attempted to wipe out North Vietnamese base camps that had formerly served as sanctuaries. A secret bombing campaign against Cambodia was also authorized in an attempt to increase the pressure. In the spring of 1972, Nixon took the risky step of mining the approaches to Haiphong harbor, North Vietnam's chief port, a step that had been avoided in the past for fear that the sinking of a Soviet vessel might lead to Moscow's direct involvement in the war.

At first, Nixon's attempts to regain credibility with North Vietnam caused further damage to the ultimate source of credibility, the American public, as his daring moves provoked antiwar critics to new levels of frenzy. A few of the demonstrations ended tragically when student protesters were shot by national guardsmen at Kent State and Jackson State Universities. Undeterred, some 500,000 protestors besieged Washington in the spring of 1971, leading to wholesale arrests of demonstrators and a bizarre early-morning chat on the Mall between a disoriented Nixon and some surprised young people. Eventually, though, Nixon's strategy began to work. By July 1972, American troop strength in Vietnam had shrunk to 45,000 and average monthly combat deaths were down to 36, compared with a monthly toll of 1,200 in January 1968. Antiwar demonstrations subsided accordingly.

There was also progress on the long-stalemated negotiating front in Paris, as Kissinger managed by the autumn of 1972 to patch together an agreement for ending the war. "Peace is at hand," he announced shortly before the presidential elections, thereby squelching the already meager chances of the Democratic peace candidate, Senator George McGovern. McGovern's landslide loss to Nixon showed that Vietnamization had taken the wind out of the sails of the antiwar movement. A snag in the negotiations, caused by cold feet on the part of both the North and South Vietnamese, led Nixon to launch a ferocious new wave of "Christmas bombings." But finally, in February 1973, an accord was reached. It called for an as-is cease fire in the South, a complete withdrawal of American forces, the return of all American POW's held by the North, and the formation of a "National Council of Reconciliation and Concord."

It was still possible at this juncture to put the best face on the matter by declaring a victory of sorts. To be sure, the American public had become fatigued, while in Vietnam the various civic action programs designed to promote democracy and win the "hearts and minds" of the people had apparently failed, even though the situation in the Vietnamese countryside was, in fact, better than it had been for years. Elsewhere in the region, however, things looked much brighter. In 1973, the editor of the *Far Eastern Economic Review* argued that the US effort in Vietnam had "won time for southeast Asia, allowing neighboring countries to build up their economies and their sense of identity to a degree of stability which has equipped them to counter subversion."[14] From this regional strategic perspective, the war had been successful as a holding action, and the fate of Vietnam itself, never a matter of major concern, was unimportant.

The war had not yet run its full course, however. Following two years of uneasy truce, during which Nixon resigned the presidency as a result of his implication in the Watergate scandal, the North Vietnamese launched a limited offensive in March 1975. Encountering little or no effective ARVN resistance, they quickly expanded their campaign into a war-winning effort that ended with the fall of Saigon in April. Once again, American television viewers witnessed a humiliating scene, as military helicopters at the American embassy managed to evacuate only a few of the many South Vietnamese clamoring desperately to escape the new regime. Nixon's successor, President Gerald Ford, requested emergency aid for the South, but there was no chance at all by this time that Congress would authorize another leap into the quicksand.

The political aftermath of Vietnam failed to substantiate the dire predictions of the domino theory, though at first it seemed as if it would hold true for at least southeast Asia. Cambodia fell to communist Khmer Rouge rebels in 1975 and Laos became a vassal state of Vietnam. But then some strange things happened that the domino theory had failed to predict. Responding to simmering border tensions with the nationalist Khmer Rouge, the Vietnamese army invaded and conquered Cambodia and set up a puppet regime. In return, in February 1979, communist China, upset by Vietnam's tilt toward the USSR, launched a limited invasion of Vietnam's northern border to punish the Vietnamese for their Cambodian adventure and to rein in their ambitions.

A classical balance of power had emerged in southeast Asia! According to Wilsonian thinking and the domino theory, this was not supposed to happen. To some who generalized on the basis of European experience, the balance of power was a historical curiosity, an outmoded relic of past political practices. However, this surprising development did not signal a return to traditional power politics, in the region or elsewhere. The surprising turn of events in southeast Asia was related to broader ideological changes that channeled the cold war into a less destructive course. This transformation, which occurred at the same time that the war in Vietnam was still raging, set the stage for the end of the cold war and the end of the Wilsonian century.

As the first war lost by the United States, Vietnam tends to be seen as a deep national trauma, a psychologically debilitating sign of America's fall from grace. But the relatively moderate casualties suffered in comparison to losses incurred in other conflicts, the affluent and tolerant social climate of the home front, and the absence of catastrophic consequences for American foreign policy suggest that its importance has been overstated. Only a disastrous failure or complete victory in the cold war could have challenged deep-seated Wilsonian assumptions, and Vietnam was neither. When viewed as part of the larger narrative of U.S. foreign relations in the twentieth century, the conflict declines in significance. Seen in perspective, Vietnam, the abiding preoccupation of a generation, can be seen for what it was: a painful defeat in a victorious century-long struggle for world order. The Vietnam War vindicated Senator Fulbright's critique of America's "arrogance of power" by reminding policy-makers that there were some serious external and internal constraints on the lengths to which cold war Wilsonianism could be carried. But the war was a defeat only for the way policy had been applied in this instance, not a repudiation of the underlying principles for which it had been fought.

The Institutionalization of the Cold War

The Vietnam War and its discontents were logical fruits of a neo-Wilsonian containment policy that touted world opinion as the only force capable of preventing another global crisis. To this point in the cold war, the two superpowers had careened from crisis to crisis, trying to take advantage of any openings while looking all the while to avoid World War III. But with each step that the United States took, it also undermined some basis of public support indispensable to the long-term credibility of containment. How long it would have been possible to continue along the same lines is impossible to tell, but Vietnam suggested that it would not be much longer. By the mid-1960s, the ideological surge of the cold war had overloaded America's political and cultural circuitry.

Fortunately, in this case, the impact of modern complexity was so thoroughgoing that even ideology was demoted from the status of an absolute creed. Even as the war raged on, the Vietnam era was simultaneously inaugurating a new phase in the cold war in which some of the outstanding causes of tension were successfully institutionalized; that is, they were made subject to mutually agreed upon procedures. While neither superpower had thus far succumbed to outright fanaticism, the cold war's normalization was a product of the recognition that the resistance to ideological voltage spikes needed to be increased sharply if disaster was to be avoided. After Vietnam, then, the cold war continued to be fought, but in a far less dangerous way.

The nuclear arms race provided the best example of how competition and cooperation could work hand in hand. In the late 1950s and early 1960s, atomic diplomacy was still the order of the day. As the diplomatic credibility of massive retaliation began to fade, American strategists looked for some other way of making nuclear weapons useful. But every alternative explored over the course of the next few years—the resort to small-scale tactical nuclear warfare, civil defense, a "war-fighting strategy" of targeting only the enemy's nuclear missiles, and development of an antiballistic missile defense network—had a fatal drawback. Each of these options risked destabilizing the balance of nuclear terror, thereby increasing the chances that a full-blown nuclear would take place.

With usefulness in the traditional military sense ruled out, nuclear weapons more than ever became defined as instruments of credibility in the struggle for world opinion: the more formidable the arsenal, the more impressive the national image. Having been stared down during the Cuban missile crisis thanks in large measure to American military superiority, the Soviets pressed ahead with their nuclear weapons development program. By the time Nixon assumed the presidency, the American lead had vanished. Indeed, in some quarters the Soviets were ahead, especially in the prestigious category of "throw weight," or payload delivery capacity. Soviet missiles had to be larger and capable of delivering bigger bombs because they were less accurate, but, somehow, in the double-entry bookkeeping of nuclear status a debit was accompanied by a larger credit.

By the end of the decade, the number of land-based ICBM's on each side was roughly 1,600 for the Soviets and 1,054 for the United States. But numbers failed to tell the entire story, for the arms race was also surging forward on the technological front. By mid-decade the U.S. had perfected MIRVed (multiple independently targeted reentry vehicles) missiles, hydra-headed weapons that could hit widely separated targets with the multiple warheads housed in a single nose cone. MIRVing multiplied the destructive power of the American nuclear arsenal many times over. By decade's end, both sides were also on the verge of completing rudimentary, but workable, antimissile systems that threatened to upset the delicate balance of terror. Should one side achieve near-invulnerability to enemy attack, the prospect could well tempt the other to launch a preemptive first strike before the system was installed; otherwise, in the face of an effective ABM system, the nuclear arsenal would be useless.

The steady progress of weapons development threatened further destabilization still. The U.S. had been the first to deploy missile-firing submarines. These were, at first, ideal weapons for a second-strike strategy of deterrence because their mobility made them difficult to locate in the vast reaches of the ocean, thereby assuring survivability in the event of a Soviet first strike. But soon enough the inexorable development of new missiles with greater accuracy and range, which allowed for more precise targeting and greatly expanded operating areas that made them even more difficult to find, transformed these submarines into first-strike weapons. Naturally, these developments evoked counterdevelopments, as vast sums were poured into developing hunter-killer subs capable of tracking and destroying the "boomers" before they could release their missiles.

In the nuclear era, being ahead was, in its own way, nearly as dangerous as being behind. The inherent instability and precariousness of the nuclear arms race prompted statesmen to think seriously about ways of restricting the competition. In large measure because of the recognition of mutual danger, the 1960s brought convincing evidence of one of containment's key predictions: the "mellowing" of the Soviet system. In 1964, Khrushchev was deposed by the Politburo in part because he was considered a dangerous plunger in foreign relations. The other Soviet leaders, including the new number one, Leonid Brezhnev, wanted more stability and predictability in the relationship with the United States.

Following the signing of the Nuclear Test Ban Treaty in 1963, the Soviets agreed to continue negotiations on nuclear issues. At a minimum, there was a mutual Soviet-American interest in limiting the membership list of the nuclear club: the fewer the better. Thus, even as the Vietnam War heated up following Kennedy's death, the U.S. and Moscow worked toward a nonproliferation treaty. After brushing off numerous complaints from America's allies that such a pact would compromise their own national interests, by 1968 the treaty was ready for signing. In return for their pledges to become nuclear teetotalers, nonnuclear nations received promises from the superpowers that they would reduce their nuclear arsenals and permit the peaceful expansion of atomic energy. In 1969 and 1971, two additional treaties banned nuclear weapons from outer space and the seabed.

This drift in the direction of nuclear cooperation received a helpful nudge when Nixon announced in 1969 that "sufficiency" would replace "superiority" as the guiding principle of American nuclear armament. In other words, beyond a certain point, enough was enough. Skillfully using the threat of further development of an ABM system as a "bargaining chip," Nixon negotiated the first strategic arms limitation treaty with the Soviets. So powerful was the Soviet desire for this arms control pact that Nixon risked mining Haiphong's harbor prior to his scheduled May 1972 trip to Moscow for the signing ceremony. The gamble worked. In distinct contrast to the U-2 affair a decade earlier, Brezhnev passed on the chance to use a provocation to cancel a summit. From this point on, despite many ups and downs in the relationship, SALT talks would become an ongoing feature of the cold war.

The American change of heart about continuing as nuclear top gun was motivated to a considerable extent by Kissinger's historical pessimism about America's ability to maintain its level of energy. In his career as a scholar, Kissinger was an admirer of the classical balance-of-power techniques employed by his hero, Prince Klemens von Metternich of Austria, at the Congress of Vienna. Convinced by his reading of American history that the United States had alternated historically between fits of idealistic enthusiasm and petulant bouts of withdrawal, Kissinger saw the ugly public mood over Vietnam as a sure sign that another cycle of change was in the offing.

The United States could not afford such mood swings in the face of an ongoing threat, Kissinger believed. He warned that "today, for the first time in our history, we face the stark reality that the [communist] challenge is *unending*. . . . We must learn to conduct foreign policy as other nations have had to conduct it for so many centuries—without escape and without respite. . . . *This condition will not go away*."[15] An alternative to cold war was necessary, Kissinger believed, because "it was a serious issue whether the American people could sustain a long-drawn-out contest on grounds other than a moral crusade."[16] Whereas a retreat to isolationism could spell disaster, a shift to a conservative balance-of-power approach had the virtue of transforming what otherwise seemed an almost certain rout into a tactical retreat. Thus emerged the policy of détente, or relaxation of tensions, that became the signature theme of the Nixon administration.

Kissinger enjoyed celebrity status in the news media, but few Americans bought into his version of realism. Realpolitik as a statesman's creed had never been congenial to a country in which values, in one form or another, had always played a central role in foreign policy and in which the amoral pursuit of power as the core necessity of national existence tended to be viewed as an un-American activity. As with George Kennan's influence some twenty years earlier, the readiness of Americans to accept Kissinger's advice was more easily accounted for in the Wilsonian terms of cold war logic. Indeed, one wonders how much credence Kissinger himself gave to his realism; or, for that matter, Nixon, who hung a portrait of Woodrow Wilson in the Cabinet Room. After Vietnam, Kissinger voiced concerns about the decline of American credibility that yielded to no cold warrior in their stridency. In 1975, for example, he argued that "peace is indivisible. The United States cannot pursue a policy of selective reliability. We cannot abandon friends in one part of the world without jeopardizing the security of friends elsewhere." But, for the moment at least, his outlook and the Wilsonian strategic culture happened to intersect.

If Wilsonian thought was undergoing an ideological crisis, so too, fortunately, was international communism. Equally important as a force for restraint was the historic shift toward ideological moderation then taking place in Moscow and Beijing. In the Soviet Union, communist ideology was beginning to experience a hardening of the arteries. The enthusiasm that had made the USSR so dynamic under Lenin and Stalin and so dangerously unpredictable under Khrushchev was transformed, under Brezhnev, into a bureaucratic concern with protecting vested interests. Members of the "new class," the party elite or *nomenklatura,* were more interested in enjoying the present than in sacrificing for the future. In destroying an old society, Stalin had created a new aristocracy that lost its zest for pressing recklessly toward a global utopia. The Soviet Union of the 1960s was finally becoming the kind of ideologically fatigued regime that Kennan and other realists believed already existed under Stalin's rule in the 1940s.

By the end of the decade, ideology was also reaching its zenith in the radical communist China of Mao Zedong. Since the 1950s, the Chinese strain of communism had been more virulent than the Soviet variety. At first, the Russians and the Chinese placed the need for unity against Western imperialism ahead of their considerable differences. But by 1960 the Sino-Soviet split was well advanced, as Mao accused the Soviets of appeasement in foreign affairs and conservatism in their domestic policies. Pooh-poohing the dangers of nuclear warfare, the Chinese argued for greater pressure against the American-led West. China's explosion of a nuclear device in 1964 heightened fears in Moscow as well as in Washington of Red Chinese recklessness. Indeed, when justifying the American presence in Vietnam, more often than not American policy-makers cited China as the primary danger.

At first, the long-awaited Sino-Soviet split failed to live up to expectations. It had long been supposed that the end of monolithic communism would enable the United States to successfully play off one side against the other and "to exploit the areas of common interest between the Soviet Union and the West."[17] Initially, though, things worked the other way around, as Beijing and Moscow each sought to burnish their radical credentials as leaders of world communism. However much they may have wished to turn down the ideological volume in the cold war, the Soviets could not afford to be perceived as collaborators with the imperialists. Consequently, despite numerous attempts by the U.S. to convince Moscow of the mutual benefits to be derived from reining in the impetuous Chinese and the North Vietnamese, the Soviets felt compelled to stay abreast of their more strident ideological mates while hoping that the U.S. would wind down its Vietnam adventure.

But the long-fraying strands of ideology could not hold the communist giants together forever. In the spring of 1969, barely repressed Sino-Soviet hostility broke out into open warfare when a long-standing border dispute in Manchuria flared into a brief but nasty shooting war. So unnerved were the Soviets by the possibility of a Chinese invasion that they even took soundings of the U.S. position in the event that hostilities should go nuclear. The Nixon administration made sure to signal the Soviets that a Soviet attack on China would not be welcome, a response that would later be used to U.S. advantage in dealing with the Chinese. "A Soviet attack on China could not be ignored by us," recalled Kissinger in Wilsonian language. "It would upset the global balance of power; it would create around the world an impression of approaching global dominance."[18]

Within China, too, momentous changes were in the offing. Beginning in 1965, the country became absorbed in an upheaval known as the Great Proletarian Cultural Revolution, an extraordinary attempt on Mao's part to revitalize a revolutionary regime and save it from the bureaucratic dry rot afflicting the USSR. For nearly five years, China was unsettled by the crusading zeal of the Red Guards, young students unleashed by Mao to stand in revolutionary judgment on the failings of their elders and to administer ad hoc punishment. Probably millions died in this orgy of ideological enthusiasm run amok. But, by the decade's end, Mao realized he had gone too far. The turmoil had been enormously harmful to essential institutions and had done serious damage to China's economic base.

The conditions were now in place for the U.S. to capitalize on the Sino-Soviet split by playing a new game of "triangular diplomacy." To their credit, Nixon and Kissinger recognized that the time was finally ripe for a move that had been anticipated since 1950, now that the crumbling façade of ideological solidarity could no longer be patched. Early in 1972, Nixon shocked the world by making a trip to China, secretly arranged by Kissinger, for a summit with Mao. Each leader, for his own reasons, hoped to put pressure on Moscow. For Nixon, playing the "China card" would make the Soviets more pliable on arms control and other important issues. Realizing that the Chinese needed something in return, Nixon held out the hope of diplomatic recognition of the People's Republic of China, thereby abandoning support for Taiwan's claim that it was the "real" China. Meanwhile, the U.S. no longer stood in the way of the PRC's admission to the U.N. Security Council. The Shanghai communiqué of February 1972 codified the new understanding.

Nixon followed up this stunning success by visiting Moscow in June for the signing of the first SALT treaty. This summit featured a blizzard of other accords, including a new statement of principles that committed both sides to a policy of moderation in which neither would attempt to seize an advantage. It ended in a frenzy of agreement-signing, including such innocuous symbolic measures as joint scientific cooperation in cancer research and a joint space mission.

Still another momentous change occurred within the Atlantic alliance, which, since the early 1960s, had been in a state of chronic crisis. The most serious internal threat came from French President Charles de Gaulle, who, in the belief that the Soviet threat to Europe had passed, was determined to undermine America's imperial role in NATO. In 1965, he announced the end of French participation in the military half of the alliance and set a two-year deadline for the removal of all American troops from his country. The U.S. had little choice but to comply. "When a man asks you to leave his house, you don't argue. You get your hat and go," said President Johnson.[19]

For a time, De Gaulle's nationalism caused great concern in Washington, which feared that the old adage, "when Paris sneezes, the rest of Europe catches cold," still held true. No one was seriously worried about De Gaulle or France running amok; rather, the concern was that French-style nationalism, with its proud insistence on fielding its own nuclear deterrent, might catch on in West Germany and lead to "the end of NATO and the neutralization of Germany."[20] Should the contagion of French nationalism spread to the Federal Republic, it might conceivably withdraw from the alliance and perhaps even seek its own nuclear deterrent, the better to dictate its own national destiny. For a brief but frightening moment, the signing of the Franco-German Treaty of Friendship in January 1963 suggested that the Germans had decided to follow the Pied Piper of Paris.

Subsequent German protestations of fidelity did little to calm imaginations that were running wild with worst-case scenarios. "The Germans have gone off the reservation twice in our lifetimes, and we've got to make sure . . . that they don't go berserk," said Lyndon Johnson.[21] To assure that the Federal Republic did not succumb to the nuclear temptation, the U.S. proposed a multilateral force or MLF, which would have created a NATO nuclear force, which the West Germans and the other allies would control equally. But with so many fingers on the nuclear trigger and with the U.S. still possessing the veto power, the MLF was too unwieldy to succeed. The plan was dropped in 1965 and replaced by more frequent and systematic consultation on nuclear matters within the alliance.

The concern with Germany was due, in significant measure, to the realization that American policy, since the 1950s, had been based on a contradiction. On the one hand, maintaining popular support in the Federal Republic required appeasing German nationalist sentiment by claiming that the surest and most direct route to unification lay through affiliation with the western alliance. But it was hardly a secret that unification was impossible as long as the cold war was still in force. The Berlin crisis had only underlined the Soviet determination to maintain the two-Germany status quo. Nevertheless, so long as reunification was thought to be the key to winning the allegiance of the West German public, the Americans saw little choice but to halfheartedly pursue an inherently dishonest policy that inhibited the negotiation of a more stable relationship with the Russians in Europe.

Fortunately, these nagging concerns about German nationalism faded as the result of a sea change in West German political sentiment. The Berlin crisis made clear to politically astute Germans that talk of reunification was merely the diplomatic equivalent of window shopping. As long as Konrad Adenauer remained at the helm as chancellor, the official German view of "reunification through strength" did not change. But with his retirement in 1963, the situation became more fluid. The movement was most noticeable in the Social Democratic Party, which to this point had been advocating the wholly unworkable idea of cold war neutrality as the best route to German unity. Henceforth, it was the Christian Democrats who would have great difficulty in tearing themselves away from an ideological security blanket that they should have outgrown.

Under the leadership of Willy Brandt, the mayor of West Berlin at the time the Wall was constructed, the Social Democrats slowly hammered out a new approach based on the two-Germany status quo. A policy of "change through contact" accepted the existence of the other Germany; but it also sought to promote contacts of all sorts to maintain a sense of common German identity lest the two Germanys grow too far apart. Brandt was able to implement his ideas in 1969, when he became the first Social Democratic chancellor of the postwar era. He quickly inaugurated his *Ostpolitik* or "eastern policy," which meshed nicely with the détente being pursued by the Nixon administration. In short order, he signed a treaty with Poland, which guaranteed the still controversial post–World War II borders and concluded a treaty of friendship with Moscow.

In parallel with these initiatives, the Nixon administration pursued new four-power accords on Berlin that were finally hammered out in 1971. Berlin's status as an occupied city did not change as a result of these accords, nor did the Wall come down, but the agreements finally ended Berlin's brief but spectacular career as a cold-war flash point. Henceforth, there would be no new Berlin crises. American eagerness to see a new Berlin regime was made clear when the White House, using secret "back channels" to communicate its desires to the Soviets, circumvented State Department negotiators who were suspected of being foot-dragging prisoners of the old cold war mentality.

Ostpolitik was capped off in 1973, when Brandt concluded a "Basic Treaty" with East Germany in which the two states recognized each other's existence and agreed to promote the economic and human contacts that were the linchpin of Brandt's approach. The ideal of unity was not thrown away; it was to be placed in storage and lubricated periodically until the end of the cold war. Although Kissinger worried often and loudly that *Ostpolitik* was *too* eastern in orientation and might end in the de facto neutralization of the Federal Republic's policy, Washington went along with Brandt. Indeed, it had been explicitly urging the Germans to some such reconciliation with the GDR in the east ever since the Johnson administration. By putting unification on the back burner, it was clear that the U.S. had conquered its fears of German nationalism. On the whole, this transformation signaled a quiet but enormous success for American policy: the effective Europeanization and westernization of German civic and cultural consciousness.

The process of domesticating the cold war in Europe came to a logical conclusion in 1975 at the Helsinki Conference. Helsinki was the product of an often-stated Soviet desire to normalize and legitimize the post–World War II status quo in Europe. Obligingly, the diplomats at Helsinki signed a document attesting to the sanctity of existing European borders. The Soviets, in turn, agreed to a western demand that human rights be respected, and they consented to follow-up meetings to assess compliance with this "cultural basket."

These developments did not mean that ideology was being superseded by realism. Rather, they suggested that the two ideologies were undergoing mid-course corrections, attempting to steer between the Scylla of total war and the Charybdis of complete accommodation. Neither Wilsonianism nor communism was a particularly warlike ideology. True, they were both universal creeds, but their foreign policies were each rooted in a wariness of the contradictions inherent in the *other* system that led to expansionism. Détente allowed each system to concentrate on what was believed to be its strong suit—economic development.

The Return of Economics

Although the cold war could be lost militarily, victory was attainable only on the economic playing field. Containment could never have succeeded without a successful economic strategy. Prosperity was essential to western solidarity and as an attractive ideological model for the allegiance of the nonaligned world. World opinion could not be coerced by a military superpower commanding deference. It could be won over only through seduction, by the voluntary decisions of bystanders and the members of the Soviet bloc to join a world organized by performatively superior market mechanisms that were inspired by a liberal ideology. In other words, the success of Wilsonianism was dependent upon the underlying appeal of normal internationalism.

Throughout the 1950s, the United States enjoyed something approaching economic supremacy. Despite the success of the Marshall Plan in Europe, the relative weakness of the other western economies prevented the Bretton Woods system of freely convertible currencies from coming into effect until 1958. Throughout this initial period, when the dollar was as good as gold, the U.S. could afford to spend its dollars with abandon for the purpose of shoring up one ally or another.

While militarily the United States had no choice but to play the role of Atlas holding up the world, economically it could not afford to play the hegemonic role forever, notwithstanding the enormous postwar vitality of the American economy. The continuing export of dollars, the emergence of balance-of-payments difficulties, and domestic inflation caused by spending on Vietnam necessarily shifted attention to economic fundamentals. If the U.S. expected to continue playing the dominant role in the free-world coalition, it would have to come up with a remedy for the problem of "imperial overstretch."

The balance of payments had already shifted into deficit by 1963, suggesting that America's allies had regained their economic health. The German economic miracle, which started in the late 1940s, went into overdrive in the 1960s. So prosperous was Germany that a shortage of labor led the government to welcome *Gastarbeiter,* "guest workers" from southern and southeastern Europe, to fill the gap. Countries like France similarly resorted to immigration to address the labor shortage. Other European nations also benefited from the surge of prosperity. In Asia, the Japanese were creating an economic miracle of their own that would shortly make the German effort look humdrum by comparison. As in Germany, the surge in growth of the export-oriented Japanese economy was made possible by the existence of open markets abroad. The most significant importer of all was the United States, which, in contrast to the 1920s, kept its allies happy by purchasing their goods.

These economic success stories were neither accidental nor unwelcome. The global mind-set of American policy-makers since World War II emphasized the health of the entire economic system. As many observers noted at the time, it would have been impossible for the United States to maintain the unnatural position of economic hegemony that it enjoyed at the end of World War II, when the American economy was responsible for one half of the world's production. The U.S. could not expect to maintain its huge economic lead because the logic of a free market system favored an equalization of wealth over time as a result of the tendency of capital to flow into areas with lower costs of production. Thus, in creating the conditions for the spectacular growth of Europe and Japan, the U.S. was actually creating the conditions for its own hegemonic decline. In consciously promoting global economic integration, the United States was forced to adjust to the same market forces that it had successfully unleashed. Changing the world required changing itself, though at times Washington had difficulty in gracefully accepting the inevitability of its diminished political influence.

As always, interdependence was a two-sided process: on its advantageous side, it enhanced security; gone awry, it generated vulnerability. The new American reliance on Middle Eastern oil was a prime example of how new economic necessities could become mixed up with political and ideological imperatives. From the 1950s onward, the United States became steadily more dependent upon oil imports for the functioning of its economy. Once wholly self-sufficient in oil (it had been the world's largest producer in the 1930s), by 1973 the nation purchased about one-half of its oil abroad. As the world's high-revving economic engine became thirstier, the control of oil moved to center stage.

No region was as important as the Middle East, which, after Vietnam, became the flash point of world politics. Although the U.S. imported most of its oil from more convenient nearby sources in Latin America, the European allies and Japan were far more dependent upon assured supplies from sources clustered in the Persian Gulf area. A reliable flow of crude, essential to the functioning of modern industrial economies, was continually threatened by virtue of the fact that the lion's share of the world's proved reserves lay beneath the shifting sands of a politically unstable region.

U.S. support for Israel made the U.S. position more contradictory than it would have been if only economic interests had been at stake. President Truman's hurried recognition of the Israeli state in 1948 was not at first mixed up with the cold war because the Soviets were also quick to recognize the new political entity. But that coincidence of viewpoints was only temporary. In the 1950s, the Soviets began shopping for client states in the region. Their prize purchase was Gamal Abdal Nasser's Egypt, which became a recipient of Soviet economic and military largess in 1954.

In the Suez crisis of 1956—the result of a British, French, and Israeli invasion of Egypt which erupted following Nasser's nationalization of the Suez Canal—the U.S. was still able to side against its allies out of a desire to placate Arab nationalism. However, Arab sentiment, long anti-Western, coalesced in a fierce opposition to the Israeli state's presence in the region. Henceforth, America's desire to maintain good will in the Middle East had to be balanced against a wish to guarantee Israel's survival, all the while blocking Soviet inroads in the region. As Arab opposition to Israel mounted, egged on increasingly by the Soviets, America was pulled ever more deeply into the region's increasingly violent conflicts. Though American policy-makers claimed to be even-handed, the pro-Israeli tilt of American policy was evident to all.

The Six Day War of 1967 dangerously escalated the stakes in the Middle East. Israel's swift and one-sided victory was much admired in the United States, but its conquest and occupation of the Sinai Peninsula, the Golan Heights, and the West Bank of the Jordan River made the Arab-Israeli dispute well-nigh intractable. U.N. Security Council resolution 262 proposed a formula of "peace for land," but this presumed the willingness of each side to give up what was most precious to it. The Arabs were interested only in a peace in which Israel had disappeared, and the Israelis were definitely not interested in giving up land. The formation of the rejectionist Palestine Liberation Organization in 1964 under the leadership of Yasir Arafat further rigidified the situation. Within a decade, the PLO was officially recognized by most Arab states as the representative of the Palestinian people. The PLO was a state without territory to govern, but it did control an apparatus of terrorism that helped keep Arab-Israeli tensions at a boil.

The situation nearly got out of hand in 1973 in the Yom Kippur War, when a successful Egyptian surprise attack across the Suez Canal boomeranged in the face of an Israeli counterattack that soon endangered Cairo. At that point, the Soviets threatened to introduce paratroop forces to save the collapsing Egyptian army. Brezhnev was dissuaded only by a coun-terthreat by Nixon, who placed American forces on alert and by an Israeli agreement to a cease-fire and withdrawal to the other side of the canal. Israeli armored columns were also called back from their deep penetration into Syria.

The war climaxed in a shocking manner with the announcement of an Arab oil embargo against the West by the Organization of Petroleum Exporting Countries. In existence since 1960, this would-be cartel had, to this point, enjoyed no success in its desire to control the world's petroleum markets. Things began to look up for OPEC in the late 1960s, when the oil companies began to cede control of petroleum properties to the govern-ments in the region. With upstream sources of supply increasingly in Mid-dle Eastern hands, the international oil companies who had formerly called the shots were now transformed into dependent downstream distrib-utors. In effect, one cartel was in process of being replaced by another.

By 1973, OPEC was in position to call an embargo and make it stick. The resulting oil shortage sent shock waves through the international economy. The most visible and worrisome sign was the emergence of long lines at gasoline stations in the United States as American driv-ers sought anxiously to top off their tanks. The supply situation in the U.S. was aggravated by America's decision to share oil with the Euro-pean allies. Ultimately, the embargo was lifted in return for American-sponsored negotiations for Israeli withdrawal from the Sinai, but OPEC made sure that oil prices did not return to their former levels. In short order, the price of oil on international markets doubled, and then doubled again. When the Iranian revolution caused another interruption of supply in 1979, the price reached 36 dollars per barrel. By comparison, six years earlier a barrel had fetched only two dollars.

Because oil was crucial to the manufacture of plastics, chemicals, fertil-izers, pharmaceuticals, artificial fibers, and every imaginable kind of prod-uct, the inconvenience was not limited to drivers and the automotive in-dustry. The inflationary shock reverberated through the international economy, and the price echoes would not subside for a full decade. Even-tually, as conservation measures, more fuel-efficient technology, and eco-nomic recession reduced demand, the cartel was unable to maintain price and production discipline among its members and oil prices drifted sig-nificantly downward in the 1980s. New sources of oil in the North Sea and Alaska also helped break the cartel's brief but powerful grip.

The price increases led to one of the largest short-term transfers of wealth in world history, creating serious imbalances in the world mone-tary system that were ominously reminiscent of the 1920s. Understandably, policy-makers worried about what the nouveaux riches oil states would do with their immense disposable income. Part of it went toward support of the PLO and part into enormous arms purchases that could create an even more serious threat to Israel's existence should there be another round of war. But in general, the oil states behaved responsibly. The industrialized nations were able to straighten out their balance of payments with the OPEC countries thanks to their enormous imports from the West. Meanwhile, the huge amounts of capital transferred to the oil-rich states were deposited in western banks.

These petrodollars were recycled as loans to underdeveloped third world countries strapped to pay for their suddenly high-priced energy imports. Eventually, this recycling led to a debt crisis which, according to one analyst, "provided the international financial system with its greatest test in fifty years."[22] By the early 1980s, the ability of the less-developed countries (LDC's) to repay their enormous loans was becoming doubtful. The oil shocks, aggravated by the growing cost of borrowing and a collapse of world commodities markets, made it impossible for many of the LDC's to meet their obligations. Fortunately, a combination of emergency loans to significant debtors like Mexico and Brazil, debt restructuring and rescheduling, and liberal write-offs of bad loans got the international financial system over the hump by the late 1980s.

As for the political aftermath, Henry Kissinger worked hard to produce a limited withdrawal of forces in the Sinai, but his success came at the cost of promising lavish economic support to both Egypt and Israel. Indeed, these two nations shortly became the primary recipients of American financial aid. Israel, a small nation of two million, was soon receiving the astounding sum of 1,500 dollars annually for each man, woman, and child. But neither recipient believed that accepting these payments created a political obligation to follow American wishes in the Middle East. By the mid-1970s, it was clear that the Middle Eastern situation was a problem that could not be resolved; at best, like the cold war as a whole, unremitting hostility would have to be managed so as to prevent total calamity.

The oil shock coincided with yet another economic jolt. In 1971, Nixon concluded that the Bretton Woods guarantee in which the U.S. dollar was redeemable in gold could no longer be honored. Because the amount of precious metal in America's vaults no longer sufficed to meet all the dollar claims from abroad, Nixon announced the closing of the "gold window" as a temporary solution, but it soon became clear that the gold standard was beyond revival. Unlike in the 1920s, when the fetish for maintaining the gold standard made trade and payments more difficult, Bretton Woods was interred by western finance ministers in the Smithsonian Agreement of 1971 and replaced by a new system of floating exchange rates that, after a period of experimentation, went fully into effect in 1978.

Under the new regime, gold was no longer the international unit of account; international payments were no longer settled by shipments of gold. Instead, balance was imposed by a new and wholly untried system of flexible exchange rates governed by international currency markets. The value of a nation's currency would henceforth be judged by all kinds of factors, depending on which were uppermost in the calculations of the market at any moment: political stability, inflation, interest rates, overall economic health, investment opportunities, and so on. Overall, the system would work well over the next two decades, as market discipline forced most nations (with the notable exception of the United States) to toe the line fiscally and make the necessary adjustments signaled by international currency flows.

It was clear from this development that the United States had lost its formerly commanding influence over the international financial system. Now that international monetary flows were too vast to be controlled by a single nation, they were managed increasingly by cooperation among central bankers and regulators. The same was true of international macroeconomic policy. Beginning with the Rambouillet meeting of 1975, the heads of government of the leading western economies (beginning as the Group of Five, then Seven) met annually to discuss global economic issues and to coordinate policy whenever possible. The United States was still the world's leading economic actor, but the stage was getting crowded with other stars who were eager to share the limelight.

BY THE mid-1970s, the Vietnam War, the crisis in the Middle East, and the decline of American economic dominance had produced deep scars in the national psyche. Even the brilliant successes of détente that took advantage of the divisions in the communist world were accompanied by a sense of pessimism about American staying power. And yet, despite the gloominess of those who lamented the nation's exhaustion, it was not long before the U.S. found its second wind in the cold war marathon. Indeed, in retrospect the Vietnam era marked a successful transition. It finally allowed the cold war to be fought out as originally intended, as a struggle of social systems whose success was measured by the staying power of the beliefs about economic development that undergirded them.

CHAPTER EIGHT

Ideological Renewal and Exhaustion:
Stumbling to the Finish Line of the Cold War

Unlike most instances of major change in international systems, which have often been punctuated by violence, the cold war lived up to its metaphoric name by ending in a way common to all ice ages. From the 1970s onward, the glaciers and ice sheets of cold war politics retreated slowly, creating space for a new environment hospitable to new species of behavior. As energy, trade, Islamic fundamentalism, terrorism, and the Middle East took up a growing share of policy-makers' time and public attention, cold war arguments lost the compelling urgency of previous decades. By the time the cold war ended in 1991 most of the issues that would dominate the international agenda of the post-cold-war era were already well in place.

The End of Detente

As the closing act of the tragedy in Vietnam unfolded, the nation turned inward. Saturation coverage by the media of the Watergate scandal absorbed the public's attention for a full two years prior to Nixon's resignation in August 1974. Even the sharp Soviet-American disagreement during the Yom Kippur War was suspiciously interpreted by many as a shameless attempt by Nixon to divert attention from his Watergate miseries. The War Powers Resolution of November 1973, which limited the president's authority to commit troops to combat for more than sixty days, symbolically dethroned the "imperial presidency." (Cynics pointed out, however, that once troops were engaged by the president, Congress would not be in a position to force their withdrawal.) The administration's decision to end the draft also put a huge dent in the nation's globalist capabilities, though some argued that a professional military was more readily usable for interventionist purposes.

Under Nixon's successor, Gerald Ford (who had been chosen by Congress to succeed Spiro Agnew as vice president following Agnew's resignation in the wake of revelations of corrupt practices while governor of Maryland), foreign policy was turned over to the trusted hands of Henry Kissinger. Now the secretary of state as well as national security adviser, Kissinger was expected to manage with dexterity the policy of détente, which well-suited America's introspective post-Vietnam, post-Watergate mood.

However, for a number of reasons détente soured quickly and it became clear that the cold war was far from over. Détente was temporary because it was dependent in the first place on significant ideological transformations that were taking plasce in the USSR, China, the Federal Republic of Germany, and the United States. But in the Soviet Union and the U.S. events soon showed that ideology was alive and well. Moreover, even when taken on its own terms, détente as a geopolitical strategy was not a radically new outlook but merely a variation on the cold war view that it sought to replace. The geopolitical "structures" and "global balance of power" of which Nixon and Kissinger were so fond were themselves products of the kinds of imaginative historical fears that formed the taproot of Wilsonian thinking.

Nixon had envisioned détente as a comprehensive bargain with the Soviets, not realizing that each side would have very different interpretations of its meaning. Disagreements over intervention in the third world, the nuclear arms race, and human rights emerged in the mid-1970s and remained as irritants to U.S.-Soviet relations through the 1980s. The quarrels over these issues were heated enough to fuel talk of a second cold war. While it is true that the relationship became more frigid, this time around unpredictable confrontation was replaced by managed competition which featured a complex blend of conflict and cooperation between the superpowers.

Whatever its impact on Asia, Vietnam failed to solve the problem of revolution in the third world. Beginning in 1975, the Soviets interfered in various conflicts in Africa, the most important being a civil war in the West African country of Angola, only recently freed from Portuguese rule. In support of a Marxist faction, the Soviets airlifted more than 150,000 Cuban troops, supplied willingly by Fidel Castro in the spirit of socialist fraternity, into the country. Kissinger, who worried about the reaction in Africa, Europe, and China "when they see the Soviets pull it off and we don't do anything," demanded money to support the non-Marxist forces but was overruled by a Congress understandably sensitive to the possibility of entering another Vietnam-like quagmire. For once, Congress got it right. Contrary to Kissinger's fears, it is likely that Angola and other Soviet interventions in Africa were prompted less by a coherent strategy than by an inability to refrain from taking advantage of ideologically favorable events occurring spontaneously on the periphery.

The questionable realism of détente was thrown into relief by the Ford administration's by now familiar assessment of the implications of the loss of Angola. Indeed, Kissinger's concerns were identical to the earlier cold war preoccupation with credibility. In testimony before Congress, Kissinger asked rhetorically: "If the U.S. is seen to emasculate itself in the face of massive, unprecedented Soviet and Cuban intervention, what will be the perception of leaders around the world as they make decisions regarding their future security."[1] But a gun-shy Congress disagreed, and forbade the administration to provide men or money to the anti-Marxist rebels.

Kissinger also fretted about the prospect of communism coming peacefully to power in western Europe, where "Eurocommunism" was making electoral headway under the banner of reformed communist movements that distanced themselves from Moscow. Increasingly anxious to quiet criticism coming from the right that equated détente with appeasement, President Ford declared that the word "détente" would be dropped from his diplomatic vocabulary. The growing concerns of Kissinger, right-wing critics, and significant numbers of cold war liberals were an indication that the cold war preoccupation with credibility and world opinion was beginning to reassert itself.

At first, this mood of revived militancy was at odds with the thinking of the new president, Jimmy Carter, who came to office in 1977 convinced that the cold war was just about over. Carter recalled that "too many of our international concerns were being defined almost exclusively by the chronic United States–Soviet confrontation mentality, which seemed to me both shortsighted and counterproductive."[2] In the post-Vietnam climate, he could not imagine another intervention. "We have learned that we cannot and should not try to intervene militarily in the internal affairs of other countries unless our own nation is endangered," he said. Instead of zeroing in on the usual east-west coordinates, he was by temperament more attracted to the social and economic problems of north-south relations. Forecasting the imminent emergence of a post-cold- war world, he insisted that the United States "was now free of . . . inordinate fear of communism." At the same time, he spoke of the need to "reestablish a spirit of common purpose among democratic nations." In a 1977 western economic summit, he used the phrase "dollar diplomacy," suggesting that Wilsonian fears could, at long last, be set aside. The following year, echoing Taft's normal internationalism, he confirmed his preference for "dollars over bombs."[3]

One of Carter's more innovative departures from the cold war was his rediscovery of fundamental liberal principles that all too often had been ignored or even ridiculed by cold war foreign policy professionals. During his presidential campaign, Carter hit upon the theme of human rights, which satisfied the public's post-Watergate craving for a return to morality. He spoke of principles "which have made us great and, unless our foreign policy reflects them, we make a mockery of all those values." In a speech at the University of Notre Dame, Carter talked optimistically about "dramatic worldwide advances in the protection of the individual from the arbitrary power of the state." "Our commitment to human rights must be absolute," he proclaimed. "We can no longer separate the traditional issues of war and peace from the new global questions of justice, equity, and human rights."

Carter also tried to pay greater attention to Africa, long an area where benign neglect had been the rule and where former European colonial powers, particularly France, continued to exercise far more direct influence than the United States. As a southern liberal on civil rights, Carter was quite distressed by the denial of liberties to black African majorities in South Africa, Namibia, Rhodesia, and areas still under European colonial control. The appointment of African-American Andrew Young to the post of U.N. ambassador symbolized Carter's willingness to attack the international color line. The international politics of race was morally driven, but Carter also believed that he was siding with the future in a continent brimming with important natural resources.

Carter may have been seeking to deemphasize U.S.-Soviet issues, but human rights, because they epitomized the enormous contrast between the ways of life created by the two ideologies, was also useful as a symbolic way of fighting the cold war. Carter's national security adviser, Zbigniew Brzezinski, criticized the Nixon administration for having "elevated amorality to the level of principle" and thereby forfeiting a major asset in the ideological struggle. His assistant saw human rights as "a 'brilliant policy'. . . a very pragmatic tactic to really beat up morally on the Soviets."[4] The issue had roiled U.S.-Soviet relations as early as 1973, when Congress passed the Jackson-Vanik amendment, which refused most-favored-nation status to the Soviets unless they relaxed their restrictions on Jewish emigration. It had also been raised by America's allies at Helsinki, where the Soviets reluctantly agreed to a human rights package as part of the overall deal on boundaries.

As post-Helsinki dissident communities formed within the eastern bloc, Carter felt obliged to provide at least moral support and sympathy when they suffered periodic persecution at the hands of communist leaders who undoubtedly assumed that the West would obligingly look the other way. A 1977 post-Helsinki review conference raised Soviet hackles when the U.S. insisted on releasing a report critical of the Soviet bloc record on human rights. Predictably, Brezhnev did not take kindly to what he characterized as interference in the Soviet Union's internal affairs. But the utility of human rights as a cold war weapon was seriously compromised when Carter was forced to criticize nations in the so-called "free world" for human rights abuses, leaving the U.S. open to mud-slinging arguments about which side was entitled to play holier than thou.

The inability to escape the embrace of the cold war was nowhere more evident than in the increasingly acrimonious arms control negotiations, which made a mockery of Carter's ambitious hopes for negotiating sweeping reductions in nuclear weaponry. Indeed, by this time the nuclear arms race had replaced limited wars as the supreme symbolic issue of the cold war. In arms policy, as with the interventions in Korea and Vietnam, it proved impossible to strike a perfect balance between appeasement and foolhardy escalation.

SALT I was in part the product of the Nixon-Kissinger belief that the United States, traumatized by Vietnam, did not have the stamina to finish the cold war marathon while running at full speed. Indeed, under Nixon, defense spending as a percentage of GNP declined dramatically as the Vietnam War wound down. In the Vladivostok meeting between Ford and Brezhnev, the two sides agreed to limit their nuclear launchers to a maximum of 2,400 each on the basis of a principle of "equal aggregates," which was not unlike establishing a basis of comparison between apples and oranges. Despite the emergence of new weapons systems like cruise missiles (relatively inexpensive terrain-hugging pilotless jet drones capable of carrying nuclear warheads) and the Soviet Backfire bomber, it appeared that arms control was well on its way to being institutionalized by the time Carter took office in 1977.

However, that moderate climate of opinion began to change by mid-decade. Carter set sail for SALT II in the face of a stiff headwind emanating from the defense establishment. In 1976, Ford backed away from pursuing SALT II in part because a new team of CIA analysts, "Team B," concluded that Soviet strength had been grossly underestimated. By 1977, a formidable new defense lobby, the Committee on the Present Danger, headed by long-time cold warrior and NSC 68 author Paul Nitze, warned that the United States was being overtaken dramatically in the arms race by the Soviet Union.

Arms control had a rocky career from this point on. The committee and sympathetic defense intellectuals were particularly critical of the advantages conceded to the Soviets in numbers of launchers and throw weight in the SALT negotiations. Advocates of arms control like Arms Control and Disarmament Agency director Paul Warnke and Secretary of State Cyrus Vance believed that the complexity and dissimilarity of weapons systems made precise equality impossible to achieve; nor was equality particularly meaningful in an era of "overkill" in which each side had the capacity to destroy the other many times over. From their perspective, because "superiority" had no strategic significance, the numbers had to take a back seat to the overriding need to reach an agreement.

These kinds of views were ridiculed as "asinine" by Paul Nitze.[5] For the conservatives, numbers mattered. They were convinced that the Soviets did not believe in overkill and made much of the fact that the Soviet strategic planners were prepared to fight and win a nuclear war, if it came to that. The United States could afford to do no less, they reasoned. Moreover, in a crisis situation, they feared that the United States might find itself forced to back down in the face of intimidating Soviet nuclear forces. The willingness to accommodate the Soviet demand for numerical superiority was therefore interpreted as appeasement, the gravest neo-Wilsonian sin of all.

In 1977, Carter managed the improbable feat of riling both his conservative domestic critics and the Soviets by proposing reductions in the number of nuclear launchers from 2,400 to 1,800. Recoiling from this suggestion, the Soviets charged the Americans with trying to renegotiate to their advantage what had already been decided at Vladivostok. Despite this spat, the mutual interest in arms control was strong enough to produce a SALT II treaty. In marathon talks that lasted long beyond the October 1977 expiration of SALT, negotiators finally hammered out a new treaty based roughly on the Vladivostok limits. Full of obscure details understood by few but fought over with a passion, the document was ready for signing at a Carter-Brezhnev meeting in Vienna in June 1979. After four days, as a fitting conclusion to a successful summit, the two leaders embraced.

The treaty immediately ran into a political buzz saw back home from those who considered it a sellout, appeasement, and worse. Arguing that SALT II would benefit the United States, the administration pointed out that Carter had decided to proceed with the development of the new MX missile, a "silo buster" first-strike missile capable of delivering ten nuclear warheads precisely on target. Unfortunately, his cancellation of two other projects, the B-1 bomber and the enhanced radiation weapon or, neutron bomb, left him vulnerable to accusations that he was pursuing a weak-kneed approach to arms policy. The negotiation of the Panama Canal treaty in September 1977, in which the U.S. agreed to surrender control of the canal to Panama by the end of the century, had already stigmatized Carter in the eyes of conservatives.

With the Soviet invasion of Afghanistan in December 1979, support for SALT II dried up entirely. SALT II enjoyed little public confidence as measured by opinion polls, while even conservative backers like Kissinger and Ford conditioned their support of SALT on significant increases in defense spending. Carter's successor as president, Ronald Reagan, had no interest in seeing the treaty ratified at all. In a 1981 speech at West Point, he asserted the new hard line: "The argument, if there is any, will be over which weapons [to build], not whether we would forsake weaponry for treaties and agreements."

A crisis over Afghanistan further accelerated the downward spiral of U.S.-Soviet relations. On December 25, 1979, the Soviets sent in their troops following a coup that ousted a Marxist leader in Kabul and installed a puppet regime headed by Babrak Karmal. To his diary, Carter confided that "this is the most serious international development that has occurred since I have been President."[6] Calling the invasion "a qualitative new step involving direct invasion of a country outside the Warsaw Pact," Brzezinski suggested that the era of Soviet military conservatism was now over. Carter called Brezhnev a liar for claiming that Soviet troops had been invited into the country. All but confessing that he had been naive about the cold war, Carter revealed that Afghanistan had caused a "dramatic change in my opinion of what the Soviets' ultimate goals are." Shortly thereafter, he asked the Senate to defer consideration of SALT II. In January 1980, he announced the "Carter Doctrine," in which he designated the Persian Gulf as a vital interest of the United States.

Carter also looked for appropriate ways to punish the Soviets for their brazen aggression. Since it was unthinkable to rain nuclear missiles on Moscow or even to intervene with conventional forces in Afghanistan, the President had to settle for largely symbolic sanctions. Grain exports under a 1975 agreement were embargoed and Soviet fishing rights in American waters were revoked. Sales to the USSR of high technology devices like computers were prohibited. Most important, as a "powerful signal of world outrage," the president announced that the United States would not compete in the 1980 Moscow Olympic games. The Wilsonian justification for these measures was by now trite. "History holds its breath," Vice President Walter Mondale told the U.S. Olympic Committee. "For what is at stake is no less than the future security of the civilized world. If one nation can be subjugated by Soviet aggression, is any sovereign nation truly safe from that fate?"

The sanctions were highly unpopular. American farmers grumbled at the loss of revenues, arguing correctly that the Soviets would fill the gap by purchasing grain from other western nations. Far from hurting the Soviets, the embargo was only causing pain in America's farm belt. More acrimonious yet was the response of the U.S. Olympic Committee and many American athletes who had their hearts set on competing for gold medals. With Carter worrying that "the outcome was always in doubt,"[7] the Olympic Committee, against its inclination to view the Olympics as being above politics, was pressured into boycotting the games. Altogether, sixty nations agreed to follow Carter's lead, a sizeable number. The Soviets, who were counting on the Olympics to showcase the achievements of socialism, were stung once again at being labeled pariahs. Nevertheless, the western measures failed to force them to reconsider their war in Afghanistan.

By the time Carter left the presidency, cold war II was firmly under way. Military expenditures were nearly double the level of spending when he took office. At the same time, the Afghanistan crisis demonstrated that, despite heightened official concern, post-Vietnam America no longer possessed any obviously effective means of dealing with aggressions in out-of-the-way locales. Despite the modest nature of Carter's countermeasures, the American public was hardly enthusiastic about taking actions that caused as much pain to America as to the USSR. The Olympic boycott showed that the only way to demonstrate political will was to intrude upon an area long viewed—with too much idealism, perhaps, given the nationalism that fueled the success of the modern Olympic games—as unpolitical.

But even if the administration had succeeded in restoring a sense of urgency about Soviet behavior, the rapidly improving relationship with China made impossible any full-throated revival of the first cold war's global sense of threat. Carter was determined to pursue the "normalization" envisaged in the Shanghai communiqué, which had been placed on hold for five years. His task was made easier by the liquidation of Mao's failed Great Proletarian Cultural Revolution and by Mao's death in 1976.

After a transitional period in which the neo-Maoist "Gang of Four" was purged from the party hierarchy, the Chinese communist leadership set out on a venturesome and ideologically perplexing course that introduced market mechanisms in the economy at the same time that the party continued to play a dictatorial role in politics, never mind that all this was impossible to justify in Marxist terms. Under Deng Xiao Ping, the pragmatic new "paramount leader," China set its sights on pursuing the "Four Modernizations" of science, the military, industry, and agriculture. Economic modernization, long delayed by revolution, war, and internal ideological turmoil, was thus finally set on the rails.

Carter recognized the PRC in December 1978, simultaneously de-recognizing Taiwan in deference to Beijing's claim that there was only one China. In a bit of bureaucratic hocus-pocus, the American embassy in Taipei became the American Institute in Taiwan, and all the former State Department personnel were instantaneously transformed into "private" individuals charged with carrying on commercial and cultural relations with Taiwan. In return for derecognition, the PRC agreed to allow "unofficial" relations between Washington and Taipei, while insisting for the record that reunification was entirely an internal Chinese matter. Meanwhile, the United States continued to provide arms to the Taiwanese for their self-defense. In the Taiwan Relations Act, Congress later declared that the use of force against Taiwan would be of "grave concern" to the United States. Following the completion of the deal, Deng Xiao Ping visited the United States in January 1979, where the aged Chinese leader sought to impress upon Carter the common danger presented by Soviet "hegemony."[8]

The two leaders also talked about China's eligibility for "most-favored-nation" status, which would have given China an open door to the U.S. market. Trying to bargain, Carter raised the issue of emigration, to which Deng replied: "If you want me to release ten million Chinese to come to the United States, I'd be glad to do so." End of discussion. The two also agreed on cultural exchanges, which allowed westerners into China in numbers not seen since the revolution and made it possible for tens of thousands of Chinese students to enrol in American universities. Somehow, the improbable cultural relationship between the two countries originally nurtured early in the century was reestablished. The irony was that these relations between two civilizations so culturally distant were in practical terms so relatively close, whereas the U.S.-Soviet relationship, starting from a much greater degree of family resemblance, was virtually nonexistent.

The denatured quality of the second cold war was also evident from the contentiousness besetting the Atlantic alliance. Hoping to restore NATO to its traditional place at the center of the American scheme of things, Kissinger had planned a "year of Europe" in 1973, only to have it overtaken by events. The alliance system persisted throughout these years, albeit with diminished sense of urgency and purpose. With the danger of a Soviet invasion reduced to near zero after the Helsinki accords, NATO drifted and became prone to crippling disagreements.

A newly confident Federal Republic of Germany, under the leadership of the imperious Helmut Schmidt, had discovered in *Ostpolitik* a foreign policy of its own. As Kissinger had feared, maintaining close relations with its communist sister state, the GDR, appeared on occasion to take precedence over the country's commitment to NATO goals. Increasingly, the Federal Republic began to criticize the U.S. on matters such as Carter's decision not to develop the neutron bomb. More contentious was a dispute over the modernization of NATO's intermediate-range nuclear forces in Europe as a response to Moscow's ongoing deployment of SS-20 missiles in the European portion of the Soviet Union. As always when it came to deploying nuclear missiles on the Continent, the Americans were suspected of being willing to fight a nuclear war to the last European.

Despite attempts to read portentous consequences into these disagreements, they were more in the nature of family squabbles. As if to underscore the absence of a substrate of compelling issues, much of the discussion on alliance matters had to do with surface personality differences, especially the tiffs between the ingenuous Carter and the abrasive Schmidt. In any case, the alliance could well afford its occasional spats. The disarray in the west was fully matched by a loosening Soviet grip on eastern Europe. In Poland, the revolutionary trade union movement Solidarity was making enormous strides in popularity; while within Hungary, a more relaxed brand of communism had already emerged.

The Middle East and the Iranian Crisis

As the cold war declined in intensity, issues like the interminable Arab-Israeli confrontation and the Iranian crisis sprouted like weeds that threatened to crowd out the long-established cold war vegetation. The oil crisis of 1973, with its price increases and long lines at gas stations, had already announced the coming of a new era in north-south relations. The Iranian crisis that broke out in 1978 marked the beginning of a still deeper American involvement in the Middle East that went beyond the Arab-Israeli problem and outlasted the cold war. Indeed, by upstaging the Afghanistan invasion, the Iranian affair, with its huge claim on the public's attention, demonstrated that non-cold-war issues could no longer be considered peripheral annoyances.

Progress in resolving the Arab-Israeli standoff had been modest since the October 1973 war. In a virtuoso display of "shuttle diplomacy," Kissinger managed to negotiate a disengagement of Egyptian and Israeli forces in the Sinai peninsula. Financial inducements, it turned out, were a crucial factor in getting the two sides to budge as the U.S. began throwing huge amounts of foreign aid money at the two chief enemies in the region. But money was the least of it. The chief cost of Kissinger's modest achievement was to involve the United States even further in the region's tangled affairs.

Ambitiously, Carter decided to break the deadlock. Taking advantage of the goodwill generated by Egyptian president Anwar Sadat's path-breaking visit to Israel, he invited Sadat and Israeli Prime Minister Menachem Begin to the United States for negotiations in September 1978 at the presidential retreat at Camp David. At the end of two grueling weeks of discussion in which Carter played the role of mediator and paid little attention to anything else, the Camp David accords were reached. The two sides agreed to end their state of war in return for a complete Israeli withdrawal from the Sinai peninsula. The accord also provided for further discussions on Palestinian autonomy in the occupied west bank of the Jordan River.

Camp David was a remarkable triumph for Carter's brand of personal diplomacy, but the enormity of his failures in the region more than matched his successes. The crisis that capsized his presidency began with a 1978 revolution against the shah of Iran. Led by Shi'ite Muslim clerics who were outraged at the repression, insider corruption, and unrestrained westernization of the Shah's regime, crowds of fervent protesters in Tehran and other cities demanded the shah's ouster and the creation of an Islamic republic.

Unfortunately, the United States had tied itself very closely to the autocratic ruler's fortunes. To many Iranians he was reviled as "the American Shah" at the same time that he was lionized by Americans. In the 1970s, the Nixon and Ford administrations designated Iran as a regional policeman. Enormous sales of the most up-to-date American weaponry benefited the defense industry, eased the U.S. balance of payments problem, and fed the shah's overweening ego. In a state visit to Tehran early in 1978 notable for its ill-timed comments, Carter praised Iran as "an island of stability in one of the more troubled areas of the world." As for the shah, a gushing president revealed that "there is no leader with whom I have a deeper sense of personal gratitude and personal friendship."[9]

As the love affair with the shah bloomed, no one saw trouble coming. But by the end of 1978, the shah's regime was in tatters as his troops grew increasingly reluctant to fire into the growing crowds of hostile demonstrators. The Ayatollah Ruhollah Khomeini, a religious leader living in exile in Paris, became the galvanizing figure of a movement powered by millenarian faith, whereas the self-confidence of the shah's regime appeared to drop daily. The shah himself dithered, unable to choose between a convincing program of reform or an effective plan of repression.

With reluctance, Carter and National Security Adviser Brzezinski soon joined the many high-ranking policy advisers who had already concluded that the shah was a goner and that the United States would have to accommodate itself to his successors. The shah finally got the message. In January 1979, after a brief stay in California, the "king of kings" departed for Egypt, leaving to the newly appointed prime minister, Shahpour Bakhtiar, the impossible task of rolling back the tide of revolution. By mid-February, Khomeini was back in Tehran, greeted with shouts of "Imam," a messianic title for Shi'ites, and the future of Iran rested firmly in his anti-Western hands.

For a time, the regime's anti-Americanism seemed to abate. It seemed as if the two republics could unite at least on a program of opposing the Soviet intervention in neighboring Afghanistan, where Russian troops were attempting to exterminate Muslim *mujahedin* freedom fighters. But the relationship took an irretrievable turn for the worse in October when Carter allowed the shah to enter the United States to receive treatment for advanced cancer. Though fear of stirring up trouble had caused Carter to retract an earlier invitation to allow the shah to reside in the U.S., humanitarian reasons prevented him from saying no to a medical visit. On November 4, a swarm of students seized the American embassy compound in Tehran, capturing and holding hostage seventy-six Americans. With Khomeini applauding the seizure, the government in Tehran was powerless to do anything about a situation that had as much to do with an internal struggle for power within Iran as it did with hatred for the "American Satan." The hostages were now pawns in a campaign for further radicalization of the revolution.

For the United States and for Carter, the 444-day hostage crisis became an ordeal in which American will and power were more seriously challenged than at any time since the Cuban missile crisis. The Iranian hostage crisis soon became every bit the abiding national obsession that Watergate had been for domestic affairs a half decade earlier. As in Watergate, the crisis was kept alive and even inflamed by the news media, whose provocative images—Iranian militants parading blindfolded American hostages and burning American flags—affronted a nation that had still to recover its balance from Vietnam.

Carter never recovered. He tried to exert pressure through an embargo on imports of Iranian oil and a freeze of Iranian assets, all the while attempting to secure release of the hostages through diplomacy, but the Iranian militants had no intention of giving up the revolution's ace in the hole. They demanded the return of the shah, repatriation of his enormous personal fortune, and an American apology for past misbehavior—conditions which they surely knew were impossible for Carter to fulfil.

Out of desperation, Carter approved a risky rescue attempt. In April, a helicopter team was flown into the Iranian desert, only to abort the mission because of equipment failures caused by heavy sandstorms. Making matters worse, a number of men were lost when a chopper collided with an airplane. The bungled operation struck hard at America's sense of technological pride. Completing the picture of incompetence and disarray, Secretary of State Cyrus Vance submitted his resignation to the president shortly after the failed mission was made public. As a known opponent of a rescue attempt, he had been cut out of the planning for the operation. The crisis abated somewhat when the Iranians moderated their terms for the release of the hostages and agreed to negotiations through Algerian intermediaries. The shah's death in Cairo in July 1980 helped things along. The United States agreed not to interfere in Iran's internal affairs and a complex solution was worked out for the return of Iranian assets. But despite the progress of the negotiations, Carter's hopes were dashed by the Iranian decision to delay releasing the hostages until his successor, Ronald Reagan, was sworn into office. As a final slap in the face to Carter, they were let go on the very same day as the inauguration.

It has since been suggested that the delay was prompted by a secret deal between insiders on Reagan's campaign team and the Islamic regime in Tehran. Given the bizarre connection that later emerged between Tehran and Washington, the speculation was that a delay in the release of the hostages, calculated to increase Reagan's chances of election, was bought by promising a relaxation of the embargo on arms sales to Iran. Whatever the real story, it is clear that the Reaganauts viewed Iran as a sideshow to the cold war main event. The USSR "underlies all this unrest that is going on," said Reagan. "If they weren't engaged in this game of dominoes, there wouldn't be any hot spots in the world." He came into office determined to restore foreign policy fully to its Wilsonian fundamentals.

Ronald Reagan and Cold War II

The revival of the cold war, already well under way as Carter's presidency drew to a close, peaked under Ronald Reagan, a professional movie actor turned politician. Long a major force in the Republican Party's right wing, Reagan's dislike of big government was matched only by his detestation of the Soviet Union. Reagan criticized Carter for being weak on Panama and craven in Iran, but most of all for blindness in his dealings with the USSR. Agreeing with the Committee on the Present Danger that a "window of vulnerability" faced the United States, Reagan was determined to restore America's military supremacy. Otherwise, his first secretary of state, Alexander Haig, warned that "unchecked, the growth of Soviet military power must eventually paralyze Western policy altogether."[10]

Public anti-Soviet condemnations of a kind not heard since the 1950s once again abounded, as Reagan's rhetoric stirred the dying embers of the cold war to a robust blaze. Speaking of the Soviets in an early press conference, the new president said that "the only morality they recognize is what will further their cause, meaning that they reserve unto themselves the right to commit any crime, to lie, to cheat. . . . I think when you do business with them, even at a détente, you keep that in mind."[11] In March 1983, Reagan called the Soviet empire "the focus of evil" in the world. The next year, while the sound level was being tested prior to his weekly radio broadcast, an open microphone captured Reagan announcing, in mock seriousness: "My fellow Americans, I'm pleased to tell you today that I've signed legislation that will outlaw the Soviet Union forever. We begin bombing in five minutes."

Underlying the Reagan administration's policies was a new note of self-confidence. "Civilizations thrive when they believe in themselves. They decline when they lose this faith," said Haig's successor, George Shultz. "History is on freedom's side."[12] The administration's anticommunism was unapologetic and openly contemptuous of what it considered faint-hearted and self-defeating liberal pieties that shrank from making hard choices. For example, his U.N. ambassador, Jeanne Kirkpatrick, made her reputation by bluntly defending the long-standing but much criticized practice of supporting anticommunist dictators. There was nothing to be ashamed about in this practice, she argued. Authoritarian rulers deserved the benefit of the doubt since they were certainly better than their totalitarian alternatives and, like tyrants in classical Greece, were oftentimes stepping-stones to democracy.

Catching up to and surpassing the Soviet Union militarily was only the means to grander political ends in the Reagan administration's strategic design. According to Reagan, Soviet communism was a "sad, bizarre chapter in history whose last pages are now being written." Rearmament was necessary if the U.S. were to take advantage of a historic opportunity to end the cold war. The idea, as one adviser put it, was to launch "a full-

court press against the Soviet Union."[13] Containment had always been a
defensive approach, but Reagan believed that the passive zone-defense
then being played had to be energized. If successful, the economic and
ideological pressure exerted by U.S. rearmament would force the Soviets
to focus their attention inward. William Clark, Reagan's national security
adviser, argued that "we must force our principal adversary, the Soviet
Union, to bear the brunt of its economic shortcomings."

This policy of forcing the Soviet system to spend itself into bankruptcy
marked a significant change in the logic of the cold war. It came at a
time when CIA analyses indicated that Soviet defense spending had been
stagnant since the mid-1970s. The possession of huge inventories of nuclear weapons and delivery systems had always played a large symbolic
role in the struggle, but the intention now was to stress the economic
infrastructure that produced such weapons. Consequently, in place of external confrontation, the cold war came to resemble a modern potlatch
ceremony, the kind of lavish display ritually practiced by west coast
Kwakiutl Indians whereby those intent on showing themselves to be a
"big man" literally consumed all their resources in the process.

In contrast to Eisenhower's conservative suspicion of *all* government
expenditures, including the defense budget, Reagan had no inhibitions
about military spending. Thus, while he actively sought dramatic cuts in
domestic outlays, he asserted that "defense is not a budget item. You
spend what you need." His activist secretary of defense, Caspar Weinberger, proposed 10 percent annual increases over the last Carter budget,
which was itself significantly increased from mid-70s spending levels.
With Weinberger refusing to engage in budgetary give-and-take with
Congress on his appropriations requests, by 1985 defense spending bal-
looned to 300 billion dollars per year, a 34 percent jump in real terms from
1981 spending. In combination with the tax cuts that Congress passed at
Reagan's insistence, the result was massive budget deficits that probably
left Eisenhower, fiscally a much more traditional conservative, rolling in
his grave.

The list of military hardware purchased by this spending spree was
extensive. Reagan went ahead with the development of the MX missile,
even though he caved in to political pressures from residents of western
states who, fired by the "not in my back yard" syndrome, refused to consider new basing schemes. Instead, Reagan chose to deploy the missiles
in existing Minuteman silos, even if this meant increasing their vulnerability. The administration also went ahead with the B-1 bomber; the B-2
"stealth" bomber and stealth fighter, designed to be invisible to enemy
radars; a 600-ship navy; the Trident missile for the nuclear submarine

fleet; and new Pershing II intermediate-range missiles for Europe. Other agencies besides the Pentagon also benefited from this spending binge. The propaganda programs of the U.S. Information Agency, long viewed with suspicion by Congress, were infused with new funds to spread the idea of freedom.

There was also tough talk about a new war-fighting strategy for making use of these weapons. Since the late 1950s, nuclear war had been considered a strategically irrational course of action. The Reaganauts, however, decided to resume thinking about the unthinkable. Instead of viewing a nuclear war as Armageddon in which victory was denied to both sides, the United States would now fight to "prevail." The Civil Defense director caused a stir by discussing the enormously positive impact that a few shovels would have in assuring individual survival into the post-nuclear-holocaust world.

Most worrisome to the Soviets was Reagan's March 1983 announcement of a research program into a new space-based antimissile system that would make use of futuristic technologies like lasers and particle beams. This Strategic Defense Initiative, or SDI, rapidly dubbed "Star Wars" by the press after the hugely successful science fiction movie, threatened to launch the arms race into orbit. In response to arguments that SDI would violate the ABM treaty and inaugurate a new arms race, Reagan declared: "Why don't we just go ahead on the assumption that this is what we're doing and it's right. . . . Don't ask the Soviets. Tell them."[14] Although Reagan argued that the new technology would "free the world from the threat of nuclear war," and even suggested that it would be given to the Soviets after development, its real-world significance was far different from that sketched by the president.

The Soviets saw Star Wars as an American bid to achieve a first-strike capability, an attempt to "disarm the Soviet Union" in the words of Yuri Andropov, thereby upsetting the balance of terror, based on mutually assured destruction, that had been in effect since the 1960s and institutionalized in SALT. To be sure, the system would not be perfect. Even if 95 percent effective, this space shield or high-tech Astrodome could still be overwhelmed by the relatively simple expedient of the other side deploying more missiles. That, however, would require a Soviet economy already groaning under the weight of militarization to further tighten its belt. That was the benign interpretation of SDI's intent. Since it was conceded that it could not provide a perfect defense and could be readily overwhelmed, the more sinister view was that it was an offensive first-strike technology, designed to "mop up" any Soviet missiles remaining after a first strike.

Not surprisingly, then, Reagan's first few years featured some shrill confrontations with the Soviets. Washington condemned as act of babarism the September 1983 downing of a Korean Airlines flight that strayed over Soviet air space in the Pacific en route to Seoul with 269 people. The Soviets responded bitterly with a cascade of anti-Western vitriol. Reagan's decision in October 1983 to invade the Lilliputian Caribbean isle of Grenada following the installation of a Marxist government generated yet more name-calling. The intervention demonstrated his determination to avoid another Cuba in the Western Hemisphere and suggested symbolically the administration's willingness to intervene with force if need be. However, it also raised a storm of international criticism about the high-handed behavior of the Americans in the Caribbean.

Nevertheless, there were also many moderating factors at work that prevented the situation from getting out of hand. In a number of cases, Reagan was not willing to allow cold war rhetoric to damage his domestic political base. The basing of the MX missile demonstrated that domestic politics took priority over ideology. Reagan's decision to cancel Carter's grain embargo, which was justified by the lame argument that the Soviets, by purchasing American grain, would be forced to expend funds otherwise destined for defense, showed a similar sensitivity to local interests.

The military's desire to avoid another Vietnam provided another example of the administration's failure to live up to its rhetoric. In 1984, Defense Secretary Weinberger publicly insisted that a number of conditions had to be fulfilled before committing American troops abroad. In this updated military definition of just-war doctrine, any commitment had to be in the nation's vital interest; it must be made only as a last resort "with the clear intention of winning"; and it must have clearly defined military and political objectives, with reasonable assurance of support from Congress and the American people. Haig's successor as secretary of state, George Shultz, could not imagine this doctrine striking terror into the hearts of would-be wrongdoers. He complained that "In the face of terrorism, or any other of the wide variety of complex, unclear, gray-area dangers facing us in the contemporary world," Weinberger's doctrine "was a counsel of inaction bordering on paralysis."[15]

Reagan's striking personal popularity also did not translate into automatic public endorsement of his positions. By 1983 a nuclear freeze movement calling for an end to the arms race had emerged in America. An ABC television movie depicted the horrors of the post-nuclear environment, while Jonathan Schell's widely read book, *The Fate of the Earth*, predicted a "republic of insects and grass" in the aftermath of a nuclear shootout. With the revived fixation on the horrors of nuclear war, it was questionable whether public opinion provided the consensual base of support for some of the administration's more extreme views on the role of nuclear weapons. Meanwhile, scientists continued to discover new and more disturbing consequences of nuclear war, the most horrifying being the prospect of a "nuclear winter" descending upon the earth and destroying food-producing vegetation in the process.

Compounding its internal problems, Reagan's anticommunist vision ran into further contradictions in the attempt to impose it on the rest of the world. The Reaganauts discovered soon enough the limitations imposed by their tunnel vision. Haig's desire to forge "a consensus of strategic concerns" in the Middle East was a crude attempt to pound the square pegs of regional issues into the round hole of anticommunism. Not surprisingly, it was widely ignored by the Arab states in the region, who refused to take communism as a serious threat, while the Israelis, as always, followed their own counsel. In Europe, meanwhile, America's NATO allies refused to go along with economic sanctions imposed by Reagan following the imposition of martial law in Poland in December 1981. Although the U.S. government prohibited American firms from supplying the technology to the Soviets for building a massive natural gas pipeline stretching from Siberia to western Europe, the west Europeans refused to follow suit. Eventually, Washington gave up on the attempt to coerce its allies.

Even in the arms arena, the Reagan administration's actions were less ferocious than its rhetoric. Despite all the invective heaped upon it, Reagan agreed to abide by the terms of SALT II for fear that the Soviets would otherwise surge forward in the arms race. Reagan also saw the wisdom of entering into arms negotiations with the Soviets on a whole series of issues, if only to take the sting out of antinuclear sentiment in America and in Europe. In November 1981, he offered to cancel the deployment of Pershing II missiles in Europe if the Soviets withdrew their SS-20 launchers. This so-called "zero option," in which the US offered to trade a nonexistent horse for one already on the track, was dismissed by the Soviets as a nonserious propaganda ploy. Moscow responded with a heavy-handed attempt to sway opinion on the Continent against the Euromissiles.

After a decent interval, the administration expressed interest in going from SALT to START—seeking, in Eugene Rostow's words, "a dramatic and equitable cut in each side's arsenal—to achieve a real breakthrough in the mad spiral of arms accumulation." In May 1982, Reagan suggested sweeping cuts in the number of launchers allowed each side. Later in the year, Soviet leader Yuri Andropov made a counteroffer, proposing a 25 percent reduction in strategic missiles and an even greater reduction

in the number of warheads. For the time being, further progress was interrupted by Reagan's announcement of the Star Wars program, but in time
even Star Wars would play a significant role in accelerating the momentum of arms talks.

Economics, Terrorism, and the Middle East

Reagan, who was never accused of having a steel-trap mind, was notorious for confusing history with his former movie roles. Similarly, his administration's retelling of the how it allegedly won the cold war bore little
resemblance to what actually happened. Despite the Reagan administration's original intentions, as the cold war became less intense and more
contradictory, post-cold-war blooms continued to sprout up uninvited in
the garden of cold war issues. Out of necessity, Reagan's extremely narrow foreign policy agenda expanded considerably as time went on.

One major issue was trade, specifically the huge balance of payments
deficits that the United States began to run in the 1980s. The trade deficit
was related to the budget deficit that resulted from Reagan's relentless
promotion of tax cuts without making corresponding cuts in spending.
The Treasury, needing to borrow massive amounts to cover the deficits,
raised the interest rates on its bonds above world levels, thereby attracting
foreign investors. In a reversal of the financial flows of the 1920s, nations
like Japan were now lending the U.S. the foreign currency to purchase
their own products. Once the world's banker, the United States became
the world's biggest debtor nation. The problem was compounded by a
weakening of the country's manufacturing sector. As companies disappeared across the midwestern "Rustbelt," American consumers were purchasing growing quantities of foreign manufactured goods, which were
cheaper and often of better quality than comparable U.S.-made products.

It had been anticipated that the revival of exporting nations like Japan
and West Germany would be beneficial to the free world economy. However, in the case of Japan and a growing number of countries eager to
emulate her export-led success, it seemed as if the rules were being rigged
in their favor. Governed by a bureaucratic elite with a neomercantilist
mentality that valued trade surpluses as a positive good, the Japanese
made it very difficult for foreigners to sell in their country. It was claimed
that different Japanese snow made it difficult to import American skis;
dissimilar Japanese intestines did not allow for healthful digestion of
cheaper American beef products, and so on. From the Japanese perspective it was the Americans who were guilty—of shoddy manufacturing,

insufficient attention to the minutiae of marketing in foreign societies, and a lack of domestic discipline that rang up huge budget and trade deficits.

In an endless series of negotiations, the Reagan administration prodded the Japanese into slowly opening up their economy. But, in a major move that went counter to free trade ideology, agreement was reached on import quotas for automobiles. By this time, Japanese manufacturers had captured nearly 30 percent of the American automotive market. Although consumers certainly suffered from this protectionist deal, the import quotas allowed Detroit's big three manufacturers to raise prices on their cars and to generate the profits needed to build new generations of automobiles capable of holding their own in the new global economy. But the quotas had little effect on the trade deficit, as the Japanese went upscale with their auto offerings by creating new luxury lines like Lexus, Acura, and Infiniti that offered greater profit per unit sale. Fearing further restrictions on imports, the Japanese built new auto manufacturing plants in the U.S., thereby combining superior Japanese manufacturing methods with lower costs of production.

These trade tensions were, however, always subordinated to the strategic relationship in which the United States continued to be responsible for Japanese security. The situation was nothing if not strange, for Japan was economically a superpower and militarily a protectorate. But for Washington, still governed by Wilsonian concerns, the good of the whole was more important than narrow self-interest. As is often the case with patron-client relationships, the Japanese held the high cards, for no one wished to see them pushed to the point of once again deciding to go it alone. From the Japanese perspective, this process of negotiation and concession in which they would never have to pay too high a price could go on indefinitely.

By this time, the place of Asia in America's mental picture of the world had changed radically. Once primarily of symbolic importance for its relation to Europe and the global system, Asia was now the scene of the world's most dynamic economies as other "dragons" like South Korea, Singapore, Taiwan, and Hong Kong repeated Japan's export-based success. Soon China would be joining the caravan. These striking changes, coupled with America's traditional connection with Asia, led some European statesmen to worry aloud that the United States was becoming an Asia-first power. This stunning regional transformation, however, was in large measure the realization of an old vision of development that saw global civilization enveloping the East. What was once a fantasy was rapidly becoming reality.

Events in the Middle East also eclipsed cold war concerns. In 1980, war erupted between Iran and Iraq. The Iraqi dictator, Saddam Hussein, took advantage of Iran's revolutionary chaos and pariah status to seize a piece of strategic real estate at the mouth of the Persian Gulf. This conflict, one of the more brutal and bloody wars since the end of World War II, caused some three million deaths and lasted eight years before it ended with modest Iraqi gains that in no way made up for the loss of life and waste of resources.

From 1981 to 1986, the U.S. professed neutrality, its chief concern being to keep open the international shipping lanes for oil tankers. By 1985, as the tide of battle began to shift in favor of Iran, Washington tilted toward Baghdad, which began shopping around for a diplomatic resolution of the conflict. Fearing expansion of the Iranian revolution, the U.S. provided intelligence information to the Iraqi regime. The pro-Baghdad bias of U.S. policy became evident when Iraqi airplanes attacked and severely damaged an American destroyer in the Persian Gulf in May 1987, causing significant loss of lives, only to be absolved by the U.S. of any blame.

The endless Arab-Israeli dispute was another non-cold-war quagmire in which the United States had sunk to the waist. Hopes for a comprehensive Middle East peace faded rapidly in the wake of Camp David when negotiations on Palestinian autonomy and remaining territorial issues stalled. Meanwhile, the PLO continued its guerrilla assaults on Israel from base camps in Lebanon, a country racked by civil war in which the PLO had become a state-within-a-state. Determined to punish the Palestinians at the source, in 1982 the Israelis launched an invasion of Lebanon that carried quickly to the capital city of Beirut.

Because the operation only displaced the terrorists without defeating them, Israel was forced to withdraw. Much to Reagan's shock, 239 American marines on peacekeeping duty in Beirut were killed by a massive car bomb. Threats of punishing the PLO with military retaliation proved empty. How, after all, could the U.S. succeed where the Israelis, who never hesitated to order eye-for-an-eye reprisals, had failed? Following a decent interval, the United States ignominiously pulled out its troops. This unhappy episode would have much to do with the formulation of the Weinberger doctrine.

As cold war issues faded after the mid-1980s, the administration conjured up a new global specter in what George Ball called an "obsession with terrorism."[16] Though the odds of becoming a victim of terrorism were incredibly low, the issue was nevertheless highly charged from a psychological viewpoint. Moreover, it was easy for the administration to suggest a close connection between terrorism and Soviet policy. Reagan insisted that regional conflicts, far from being peripheral, were "a fundamental part of the overall U.S.-Soviet relationship."[17] Despite a CIA estimate that openly belittled this view, the administration did little to discourage the public perception that Soviet machinations were behind it all.

The symbol of the new terrorist enemy was Colonel Muammar al-Kadaffi, the military strongman in Libya, an oil-rich Arab nation of some two million. Kadaffi was an ideologically ambitious Arab revolutionary who combined flamboyant anti-American rhetoric with support for anti-Western terrorist activities. The list of terrorist outrages in the 1980s was lengthy, including an attempt on the life of Pope John Paul II. Following a string of spectacular hijackings, bombings, hostage-taking of American nationals in Lebanon, and assassination attempts, all of which made for sensational television news, the administration finally gave vent to its anger.

In March 1986, in response to Libyan complicity in the bombing of a U.S. servicemen's club in Berlin, the United States gave Kadaffi a whiff of grapeshot. Following a confrontation between U.S. carrier-based planes and Libyan jets in the Gulf of Sidra, in April Reagan authorized direct strikes against in-country targets, including one of Kadaffi's residences. In the aftermath of this demonstration of American wrath, Kadaffi's pugnacious visage disappeared almost entirely from network newscasts, but terrorism itself was far from vanquished.

Terrorism, anticommunism, and regional conflict became hopelessly entangled in the Iran-Contra affair, a scandal that for a time threatened to explode into Reagan's Watergate. That they should come together as a *domestic* crisis suggests that these regional connections existed primarily in the minds of American policy-makers rather than in the play of external events.

The Iran-Contra affair originated in the Sandinista revolution of 1978 in Nicaragua, which overthrew the long-time despotic ruling family, the Somozas. The Sandinista leadership was incontestably leftist and Marxist in persuasion, but Reagan ignored the indigenous roots of their radical revolution and preferred to see them as "surrogates" of the Soviet Union. In neighboring El Salvador, where another bloody civil war raged between radical rebels and a right-wing military, the administration perceived the war as "a global issue because it represented the interjection of the war of national liberation into the Western hemisphere."[18] If communism succeeded in establishing a beachhead in Nicaragua, the U.S. would be facing another Cuba, and Reagan predicted that another row of dominoes would be set in motion.

Determined to reverse the Carter administration's policy of accommodation, Reagan sought to mimic Eisenhower's 1954 success in Guatemala by backing a group of so-called rebel "Contras." In addition to funneling money and equipment to these "freedom fighters," the CIA played a more direct role in the conflict by planting mines in Nicaraguan harbors, contrary to international law, causing damage to a Soviet freighter in the process. "We are like mushrooms," said one member of a CIA oversight committee. "They keep us in the dark and feed us a lot of manure."[19] In contrast to its see-no-evil approach to such goings-on in the past, an appalled Congress in 1984 passed the Boland Amendment, which forbade further arming of the Contras. In March 1986, all aid to the Contras was cut off.

Convinced that a group of wrong-headed legislators was endangering national security, the administration began to raise funds for the Contras from private sources. Better yet, an imaginative White House aide, U.S. Marine Corps Colonel Oliver North, hit upon an ingenious scheme for killing two birds with one stone. The plan worked something like this. Using Israel as an intermediary, the CIA sold missiles and spare parts for U.S. military equipment to the Iranians, who were sorely pressed in their war against Iraq. In return, the Iranians used their influence with Islamic radicals in Lebanon to secure the release of the hostages. The proceeds of the sales (not actually "profits," since the weapons were given to the CIA at fire-sale rates) were then used in Central America to support the Contras.

These secret and quite illegal dealings came to light in the fall of 1986, following the shooting down of a plane by the Sandinistas, whose captured pilot admitted to being part of a CIA operation. Shortly thereafter, a Lebanese newspaper revealed the arms-for-hostages side of the scandal. From that point on, the Reagan administration struggled to limit the political damage. The implausible White House story portrayed the administration as reaching out to "moderates" within Iran and seeking to buttress their position. In February 1987, a commission headed by former Texas senator John Tower absolved the president of responsibility, but subsequent investigations by Congress and a special prosecutor suggested high-level White House complicity. However plausible these intimations, the quicksand of official forgetfulness swallowed up any evidence that might disprove White House denials.

Besides demonstrating an extraordinary confusion of issues, Iran-Contra also showed the degree to which exhaustion with the cold war had taken over. The affair suggested an unwillingness on the part of Congress and the American people to turn a blind eye to cold war illegalities in the name of anticommunism. Even Reagan's Teflon-like ability to prevent damaging criticisms from sticking to his presidential image was marred. Far from reinforcing American credibility in the struggle against communism and terrorism, Iran-Contra became a millstone around the neck of the Reagan administration. With the single exception of massive increases in defense spending, approved by a Congress more interested in pork barrels than rifle barrels, Reagan's attempt to revive the cold war failed to generate much in the way of successful policy initiatives. So unpopular was the administration's anticommunist fetishism that it was reduced to carrying out a secret foreign policy.

Later, Reagan would claim that his policies had created the conditions for victory in the cold war. However, his unimpressive record suggests otherwise. The cold war was an ideological marathon in which the biggest question was which of the two contestants would survive to cross the finish line. As it happened, it was less the strength of American cold war ideology than the relative weakness of Soviet communism that proved to be the deciding factor. In a bizarre turn of events, the loser would receive most of the world's cheers. Only the disastrous attempt to revive socialism in the USSR made the tepid revival of cold war Wilsonianism look vigorous by comparison. Here the U.S. had one huge advantage: despite the increasingly apparent lack of enthusiasm for pursuing the cold war, the American national security state and its global alliance system had been successfully institutionalized. The same could not be said for the Soviets.

From Evil Empire to Feeble Empire

Simultaneous developments in the Soviet Union demonstrated that Reagan's brand of anticommunism was out-of-date as well as ineffective. Though militarily a superpower, economically the USSR lagged far behind the West and continued to lose ground. The command economy system, once believed to be capable of overtaking capitalism, reached its limits in the 1970s, only a meager 14 percent or so as large as the American economy. Following the quick deaths in office of two post-Brezhnev leaders, Yuri Andropov and Konstantin Chernenko, in March 1985 the Soviets selected a dynamic young Mikhail Gorbachev to head the party. By the fall of 1986, it was clear that Gorbachev was a reform communist. Shortly thereafter, he became much more than that. Early in 1987 he characterized his agenda as one of promoting "essentially revolutionary changes."

Gorbachev's battle cries were *perestroika,* or restructuring, and *glasnost,* a policy of critical openness to new thinking. The two went hand in hand, since economic reform could not begin without open criticism of the country's ossified state-controlled economy. But criticism, including an honest look at the officially distorted Soviet past, had immense political implications, since it challenged the monopoly of infallibility, maintained since Lenin's time, that was the basis for the Communist Party's legitimacy. Gorbachev quickly realized that his program made necessary a democratization of society. However, like a homeowner who begins a renovation only to discover that the entire structure needs to be rebuilt, Gorbachev, with his reforms, exacted a cost that the party was ultimately unable to pay. By 1989, in a move unheard of in communist societies, elections to party positions were actually contested.

Gorbachev's domestic program had enormous implications for the cold war, since the success of *perestroika* depended on the USSR's ability to reduce the enormous burden of military expenditures, which, by some estimates, amounted to as much as 25 percent of the gross domestic product. Economizing on the military could only be achieved by cutting down on Soviet commitments, by negotiating reductions of armaments and forces with the United States, or, unthinkably, by unilaterally disarming. Either way, the Soviet Union could no longer afford to trade technological punches with the United States at existing levels of spending. However, this hardly proves the Reaganite argument that American military spending drove the Soviets into fiscal and ideological bankruptcy. Sooner or later, even without an escalation of the arms race, the poorly functioning command economy of the USSR would have led its leaders to conclude that their system could never match the productivity of the capitalist world.

Gorbachev was able to produce movement by seizing the Wilsonian high ground of world public opinion and in the process transformed himself from a Soviet politician to a world leader. Hitherto resistant to blatant Soviet propaganda, the West began to melt upon hearing his inspiring words. Noting that "Europeans are sick and tired of nerve-racking confrontation,"[20] Gorbachev began to articulate what he called "new thinking" in foreign relations. He was determined to lead by "force of example" rather than by "force of arms." An influential *Pravda* article in 1987 declared that "Interstate relations cannot be the sphere in which the outcome of the confrontation between world socialism and world capitalism is settled."[21] The "Gorbymania" that broke out in western Europe in response to these ideas was reminiscent of the kind of adulation that greeted Woodrow Wilson after World War I. It would not be long before the United States was bowled over by Gorbymania, too.

Early in 1986, Gorbachev told the 27th Party Congress that "peaceful

coexistence" needed to be replaced with more radical measures of concili-
ation. Referring to the overarching themes of a "European common home"
and the needs of a single global civilization, he spoke of going beyond
the balance of power, ending the cold war and the division of Europe,
and allowing the satellite states of eastern Europe more freedom to run
their domestic affairs as they saw fit. The 1968 Brezhnev Doctrine was
explicitly repudiated. Gorbachev reconfirmed his commitment to "freedom of choice" and universal human values in a December 1988 speech
to the United Nations, while looking forward to a future free of ideological
conflict and the use of force. Above all, he emphasized the need for new
efforts in arms control in order to prevent the disaster of nuclear war.

All this, Gorbachev insisted, reflected a "more realistic approach"
which took account of the "broad evolution of concrete facts, rather than
viewing everything only from the point of view of one's own interests."[22]
By 1990, he was arguing against traditional alliances and their principles
of mutual opposition, proposing a new tenet of alliance-building based
on "unity to create the conditions for a life worthy of a human being."[23]
These were very much internationalist statements, all the more appealing
to western liberals because they were not particularly Marxist in inspiration.[24] The greater attractiveness of Gorbachev's international vision was
the result of his ability to look beyond the cold war to a future in which
Wilsonian fears had been left behind. It was an odd and unexpected development, in which Gorbachev's internationalism, based on "new thinking,"
was juxtaposed with Reagan's somewhat dated Wilsonianism. The scales
had fallen from his eyes, he admitted, and he had left his ideology behind.
Could the U.S. do the same?

At first, Gorbachev's statements were met with suspicion from the
West's leaders. In Berlin in June 1987, Reagan suggested that Soviet
moves might be only "token gestures, intended to raise false hopes in
the West or to strengthen the Soviet system without changing it."[25] He
challenged Gorbachev to tear down the Berlin Wall and to withdraw from
other areas, a challenge which, if accepted, would have been tantamount
to conceding defeat in the cold war. Within a few years, Gorbachev would
do all that and more, demonstrating to Reagan that the Soviet leader's
"New Thinking" was more than rhetoric. Because Gorbachev made a
habit of meeting western proposals more than halfway, the Reagan administration could not refuse to negotiate with him, despite the intense suspicions of hard-wired cold warriors.

Whether western leaders understood that Gorbachev's foreign successes were undermining the legitimacy of the communist empire is unclear. But, to Reagan's credit, he was willing, from an early date, to curb

his anticommunist impulses and gamble on the possibility that fundamental change was taking place. At Chernenko's funeral, Vice President George Bush delivered Reagan's personal invitation to Gorbachev to meet with him in Washington. In July 1985, the hard-line Andrei Gromyko was removed as foreign minister and replaced by the more flexible Eduard Shevardnadze. The way was being paved for a renewal of summitry, in which leadership would replace the institutional inflexibility of the cold war.

A November 1985 summit in Geneva produced little more than an opportunity for the two leaders to get acquainted. Reagan was charmed by Gorbachev, itself a notable development in a relationship in which the dense fog of ideology rarely permitted the rays of personal friendship to penetrate. Soon afterward, Gorbachev made a stunning proposal for the phased abolition of all nuclear arms by the year 2000, accompanied by deep cuts in conventional weapons. Though it was transparently obvious to all that this offer was cannily intended to put Star Wars out to pasture, it was equally apparent that dramatic offers of this kind were winning battles for the Soviets in world opinion, and on America's home field yet.

Though many American hawks were far from enthusiastic about scuttling what they considered to be their nuclear advantage, Gorbachev kept up the pressure. For the skeptics who believed that political summits, like mountain peaks, were barren, another get-together in Reykjavik, Iceland, in October 1986, demonstrated why many policy-makers did not look forward to high-level personal meetings. Gorbachev unveiled an astonishing proposal for a 50 percent cut in nuclear missiles, only to be topped by an American counteroffer of a total ban after ten years. The Americans fully anticipated that Gorbachev would reject this bid, since it left the United States superior in bombers and cruise missiles. But Gorbachev just threw more chips into the pot and raised again, suggesting that all nuclear weapons be abolished by 1996. Ultimately, though the two sides came tantalizingly close, the deal foundered on the rock of Gorbachev's insistence that SDI remain confined to laboratory research for the duration. "SDI proved an insurmountable stumbling-block," Gorbachev recalled.[26]

The two sides parted without agreement, trailing clouds of recrimination as they left. Nuclear theologians were appalled at the president's cavalier willingness to destroy in two days doctrines that had been framed with great difficulty over the course of a generation. West Europeans were upset at the president's readiness to get rid of NATO's nuclear deterrent without first consulting them. Still, the pressures to reach agreement were very real. The revival of antinuclear sentiment in the early 1980s, with its advocacy of a nuclear freeze, implied that go-for-broke nuclear spending did not enjoy solid public support. An unprecedented string of monstrous budget deficits, in part attributable to the defense buildup, could not be sustained forever. In Moscow, mounting domestic difficulties and a rapidly souring war in Afghanistan promised disaster. For both men, foreign policy successes promised relief from domestic distresses.

Gorbachev was still willing to propose, while Reagan, more than ever, was willing to listen. In February 1987, Gorbachev gave up for the time being on strategic missiles and offered instead a "zero option" deal on Euromissiles in which the U.S. and USSR would remove their intermediate-range missiles (INF, for short) from Europe without taking into consideration the sizeable French and British missile inventory. In so doing, he accepted an American proposal so one-sided that it had been floated as a propaganda ploy in the belief that it had no chance of being accepted. In September 1987, the two sides agreed to destroy all missiles with a range of 300 to 3,400 miles. On-site inspection, something long resisted by the Soviets, would allay any suspicions of cheating.

The signing ceremony of the INF treaty took place in Washington in December, where Gorbymania swept the capital. "He's one of us—a political animal," said one star-struck Congressman. Yet, however stunning the treaty was, the Reagan administration was well aware that the INF accord was only a modest step forward within the cold war context. "There is nothing in the 'new political thinking' to date which suggests that the end of the adversarial struggle is at hand," said a cautious George Shultz.

Then, as if to underline his seriousness, Gorbachev announced in February 1988 the beginning of Soviet withdrawal from Afghanistan. A few months later, Reagan paid a ceremonial visit to Moscow. Though nothing much was accomplished, the trip was full of symbolism as the cold war president became a guest in the citadel of the evil empire. In the uphill climb to the clear air of nuclear sanity, Gorbachev had clearly dragged along his more reluctant partner, Reagan. Now both paused for a moment to enjoy the view. The evil empire, Reagan now admitted, belonged to "another time, another era."[27]

The End of the Cold War

Following the Republican victory in the 1988 elections, the baton was passed to George Bush who, rather unusually, had risen to power on the strength of his administrative experience in foreign policy positions as ambassador to the United Nations, U.S. envoy in Beijing, and director of the Central Intelligence Agency. As his secretary of state, Bush appointed the crafty James Baker, formerly White House chief of staff and treasury secretary in the Reagan administration. The two made a good team. Building on the Reagan-Gorbachev legacy, they saw the cold war through to its conclusion and opened the door, tentatively, to a new era in world politics and history.

Bush was more cautious than the sometimes impetuous Reagan, less inclined to take Gorbachev at his word, and more comfortable with the established cold war outlook. In an attempt to make good his self-admitted shortcomings on what he called "the vision thing," in May 1989 Bush spoke of moving "beyond containment" while looking forward to a "Europe whole and free." But Gorbachev would not be upstaged. As one political-control rod after another was inserted in 1989, the ideological reactor that fueled the cold war began to shut down.

Thus Gorbachev announced unilateral conventional-force reductions and his Warsaw Pact allies followed suit. The Soviet withdrawal from Afghanistan was completed on schedule. In Poland, after seven years, the Solidarity movement was once again legalized; and, with Gorbachev advising against repression, by August a Solidarity-led government had been elected to power. In Hungary, long a stronghold of unorthodox socialism, the country's name was changed simply to "Republic of Hungary" and the barbed-wire border separating Hungary from Austria was torn down. The Baltic republics of Lithuania, Latvia, and Estonia, under Soviet rule since 1939, declared their sovereignty in May and June. By July 1989, Gorbachev declared that "the cold war is passing into history."

Without a pause, the pace of change accelerated throughout the eastern bloc. In November, hard-line party leaders were removed in Czechoslovakia and Bulgaria. By year's end, a "velvet revolution" installed the dissident intellectual Vaclav Havel as president of Czechoslovakia. In Rumania, the capricious despot Nicolae Ceausescu was murdered by a firing squad in December. These epochal events were explained by the Soviets in a humorous fashion that only a few years earlier would have been inconceivable. Citing a new "Sinatra doctrine" based on his song "My Way," a Soviet spokesman explained that the eastern European states "were doing it their way."

The events taking place on the socialist side were an illustration of something American policy-makers had long feared: how nations could collapse like tumbling dominoes following a collapse of credibility. For a time, it even appeared that the chain reaction would spread to China. In June 1989 pro-democracy protesters in Beijing's Tiananmen Square erected a goddess of liberty that bore a strong resemblance to the Statue of Liberty, only to be dispersed in brutal fashion by tanks sent in to quell a potential revolution against the regime. Gorbachev, meanwhile, despite pressure from horrified conservatives in Moscow, refused to follow the example of Chinese repression in dealing with a revolutionary situation in the keystone of the Soviet empire, East Germany.

Long blocked by the Berlin Wall, East Germans intent on fleeing the workers' paradise now found a new escape route in Hungary, which allowed them transit to Austria. Once the East German government plugged this hole, other leaks quickly sprung up. Pressure on the regime also emerged from within, as a protest movement whose demonstrators chanted "we are the people" spread through major cities in October. Whatever thoughts the East German regime may have had about pursuing a tough line were scotched by Gorbachev, who visited the GDR in October to celebrate the fortieth anniversary of its creation. Met with acclaim in his public appearances, Gorbachev counseled his East German hosts to follow the path of reform. "Life punishes those who come late," he told them. Obviously, there would be no support from the Big Brother in the Kremlin for a policy of brutality.

With that, the dam of repression burst and the long-contained waters of political freedom thundered forth. A decision by the East German leader Egon Krenz to allow unrestricted travel back and forth between east and west turned into a disaster for the regime. Once the Berlin Wall was opened, hundreds of thousands of Germans surged through and began to dismantle the structure amidst joyous tumult. Long a symbol of the GDR's viability, the Wall's opening-up marked the point of no return for East Germany's collapse. Seizing the moment, the normally phlegmatic West German Chancellor Helmut Kohl surprised everyone by presenting a ten-point proposal to the Bundestag looking forward to German unification.

At this point, alarm bells went off in east and west. German unification had been a pious catch-phrase for forty years, but it was doubtful whether anyone but the Germans believed in it. The cold war division of Germany was not entirely a bad thing. A divided Germany was at least controllable. Though increasingly influential, the Federal Republic could not overawe or bully its other European partners. A reunited Germany, however, was another matter. Prime Minister Margaret Thatcher in London, President François Mitterand in Paris, and various east European leaders all expressed reservations about reunification and the creation of what Thatcher called a "German juggernaut." Raw memories of belligerent German nationalism were still very much alive. Similarly, the Soviets finally came to grips with the full implications of the Sinatra Doctrine when Shevard-

nadze announced in December that unification was "not on the agenda."
In promoting change in the eastern bloc nations, Gorbachev had hoped
to create reform regimes that could bolster his own efforts within the
USSR. The outright collapse of socialism was another matter altogether.

Realizing that the United States could not afford to alienate the Germans by saying no, Bush laid down some conditions for reunification:
consultation with allies and neighbors, continued membership in the European Community, respect for Soviet security needs, and membership of
a united Germany in NATO. This last item might well have proved too
repulsive for even the accommodating Gorbachev to swallow. Even so,
these proposals were not thrown out for effect only, for Bush was not a
die-hard opponent of German unification. "The Germans aren't any kind
of threat at all," he was quoted as saying at a state dinner. "They are a
totally different country from what they used to be."[28] A united Germany
would be dangerous only if the demon of German nationalism was
aroused. Bush, backed by American opinion polls, was betting that the
evil spirit had long since been exorcised and that the German people had
been successfully democratized and westernized. If he was right, opposition to unification would only be self-defeating. And if he was not, it
would have been impolitic to oppose it openly.

Over the course of the next year, the U.S. and the Soviets strived alter-
nately, and without much success, to pull hard on the reins of the runaway
stagecoach of reunification. There was talk of a "new architecture" for
Europe which suggested the desirability of a leisurely pace. But as the
German Democratic Republic unravelled far more quickly than anyone
anticipated, the diplomatic masonry work was, of necessity, a slapdash
affair. In a whirligig of meetings, Baker assured Gorbachev that a united
Germany within NATO was far preferable to a Germany outside it. The
east European countries agreed. To sweeten the pill, Kohl assured Gorbachev that NATO troops would not move farther east within Germany in
the event of unification. By February 1990, agreement was reached on a
process for regulating reunification. This approach left the domestic details of unification to the two Germanys, while the international aspects
were regulated by the four occupying powers.

In February 1990, Kohl proposed monetary union and followed up with
a seductive monetary proposal that allowed East Germans to exchange
worthless *Ostmarks* at a one-to-one ratio for gilt-edged West German
Deutsche Marks. In March, East German elections produced a startling
victory for parties who advocated the GDR's absorption into the West
under the Basic Law, thereby disappointing those who believed that reunification should be negotiated between the two Germanys for the purpose

of creating a unique hybrid of capitalism and socialism. With the election of a friendly government in the East, Kohl was able to step on the accelerator of the unification process. Financial unification went into effect in July. In late August, the East German Parliament voted to unify with West Germany on October 3, and a unification treaty was signed on the 31st.

Meanwhile, the Soviets were having second thoughts about Germany in NATO, which was, after all, an opposing alliance. At a summit in Washington in May, where Gorbymania was running riot, Gorbachev suggested to an amazed Bush that Germany be made a member of both NATO and the Warsaw Pact. Sensitive to Gorbachev's difficulties with domestic hard-liners, who actually booed Shevardnadze when he attempted to explain German policy, Bush and Baker decided that a few digestives were in order to make the meal easier to swallow. In July, a NATO summit in London promised a "kinder and friendlier NATO" by accepting various self-denying doctrines. The final details were worked out during a Kohl-Gorbachev summit in the Caucasus in July. Security assurances were coupled with economic incentives, as the Germans promised to pay the cost of Soviet troop withdrawals. All-German elections took place on December 2, 1990, with the Christian Democrats again winning a plurality. The division of Germany was at an end.

In its diplomatic aspects, the cold war was all but over. The denouement came with the collapse of the Soviet Union in 1991. This was an ironic outcome for Gorbachev, who remained to the end a communist dedicated to reinvigorating rather than destroying the Soviet system. Falsely believing that he was ideologically in control, he failed to realize the power of the winds of revolution blowing from the west. Once he let loose the spirit of democratic nationalism abroad, Gorbachev quite unwittingly conjured up the spirit of nationalism in the Soviet republics that to this point had been kept in tight check by Moscow. Gorbachev's revivalism, it turned out, like the Ghost Dance of the late nineteenth century that sought to restore American Indian societies, was an enormous delusion.

Although the Soviets tried to clamp down on Lithuania with military force, independence movements in other republics—Ukraine, Armenia, Azerbaijan, and Moldavia among the first—could not be halted, and by year's end all had issued declarations of sovereignty. Anti-Soviet nationalism was most pronounced in Russia, where Boris Yeltsin, formerly a Gorbachev ally, was elected president of the Russian republic in May 1990. Yeltsin quickly proclaimed Russian sovereignty, thus inserting a dagger into the heart of the Soviet system.

Gorbachev sought to remain in control by tacking to the right. Domestically, he leaned toward antireform groups. He allowed Soviet troops to impose control in Lithuania and Latvia. Ironically, the American invasion of Panama in 1990 to oust the corrupt dictator Manuel Noriega provided Gorbachev with the precedent to justify intervention in his own sphere. Amidst these tremors of change, the conclusion of Soviet-American agreements took on even more urgency. President Bush, hoping to avoid the chaos that would result from opening the cages of the Soviet empire, traveled to Moscow at the end of July to sign a historic START treaty in which the two sides agreed to reduce their nuclear weapons by about one-fifth each.

Shortly after Bush's departure, Soviet hard-liners attempted to remove Gorbachev in a coup d'état. Thanks largely to Yeltsin's heroic stance, popular opinion in the streets prompted significant defections from among the armed forces. Without military support, the plotters lost their nerve and the coup attempt collapsed. Released from house arrest, Gorbachev rushed back to Moscow only to discover that Yeltsin was the man of the hour. Ironically, the coup plotters had subverted the one man capable of saving the Soviet system. The movement toward sovereignty in the other republics accelerated, slowed little if at all by the creation of an amorphous new political entity called the Confederation of Independent States. By Christmas, Gorbachev had resigned, while the hammer and sickle flag disappeared, replaced by the blue, white, and red Russian banner over the Kremlin. The cold war was definitely over.

Over the long term, the faith in containment had been well placed, as the Soviet tactics aimed at exploiting contradictions in the western bloc were frustrated by the ability of the United States to create a voluntarily more cohesive world than the fragile, forcefully maintained Soviet sphere of influence. But this solidarity did not occur spontaneously, despite the fact that the American empire was one of invitation. It was doubtful the West would have maintained its cohesion had not the United States counteracted—and disregarded—the particularist views of its allies and clients, no matter how reasonable they seemed at the time.

The dramatic end of the cold war came as a huge surprise to all those who made a business of punditry in foreign affairs. The way in which the Soviet system collapsed confirmed the predictions of John Foster Dulles in the 1950s, who noted that "despotisms always look formidable and impregnable from the outside," but "they are usually rotten on the inside."[29] "Once a crack appears in a despotic system such as the Russians had under Stalin, it can go fast," said Dulles.[30] Well aware that such periods of rapid change could be extremely dangerous, the Bush administration moved cautiously throughout, taking care not "to rub the Soviets'

noses in their defeat and possibly undermine Gorbachev and his policies."[31] Fortunately, the cold war's conclusion was successfully managed
by the statesmen in a way that avoided a crash landing.

The rather abrupt end of the cold war was also unmistakably anticlimactic. Its closing phases resembled a prizefight in which two heavyweights
had punched themselves out, with the later rounds degenerating into
clumsy pushing and shoving. At its conclusion, the spectators seemed less
thrilled about a victory than relieved to see the contest finally come to an
end. What in normal circumstances would have been a story of victory
had become simply the long overdue victory of the Wilsonian story.

The Return of Normal Internationalism and the End of the Wilsonian Century

Even though the struggle for control of the world's ideological tiller ended in the best way imaginable with a peaceful victory, the conclusion of the cold war was far from euphoric. This lack of exhilaration owed something to the fact that the cold war had already been winding down for more than a decade while, over the same period, many of the contentious issues that would dominate the post-cold-war period had been emerging. Inevitably, the world's messy complexities were bound to produce a letdown. But this anticlimactic mood had little to do with the discovery among some naive souls that the world was an imperfect place. It was, rather, the result of a natural process of accommodation to the kind of normal, nonutopian world that Wilsonianism had been intended to preserve.

There was some triumphalism, to be sure. In a widely discussed essay, Francis Fukuyama announced that the end of the cold war marked "the end of history"— that is, if one conceived of history as the logical working out of the principles of freedom embodied in all human beings. Because it was no longer possible to *imagine* a world founded on principles superior to triumphant liberal ideas, the only task remaining was to universalize liberal democracy throughout the globe. The completion of this process would take some time, the author conceded, but ultimate victory was no longer in doubt. The last challengers to liberalism—fascism and bolshevism—had been eliminated. Given the tumultuous excitement of the past hundred years, Fukuyama predicted, the future by comparison would be boring.

However, to most onlookers, the post-cold-war world was nothing like a foreign policy paradise. The end of superpower conflict had made some things better, but it also made others worse, thus making the world seem, paradoxically, more secure and more violent at the same time. On the positive side, the arms race was shifted into reverse. In 1993, a Start II treaty further reduced the number of nuclear warheads. The 1969 nonproliferation treaty was renewed; and, in 1996, 158 countries agreed to ban all nuclear explosions. In the Middle East, the end of the cold war contributed to an easing of the Arab-Israeli dispute, as both sides realized that they would now receive less support from their former patrons. The 1993 Oslo accords, sealed by a symbolic handshake between Yitzhak Rabin and the PLO's Yasir Arafat at the White House, committed both parties to an ongoing process of mutual accommodation in which Israeli-occupied territories in Gaza and the West Bank would gradually be turned over to a Palestinian authority.

But the story was far from uniformly pleasing. Relations between the West and Boris Yeltsin's Russia, the great-power successor state to the USSR, were often testy. Driven by the century-old fear of a dysfunctional European balance, the United States moved to expand NATO eastward at the insistent urging of eastern European countries who continued to worry about their giant Russian neighbor and about their own propensities toward violence. Russia also had serious internal problems. Afflicted by inflation, gangsterism, corruption, authoritarianism, erratic privatization, and huge disparities of income, its transition to democracy and a market economy promised to be a rocky voyage. With the reemergence within Russia of the old debate between slavophiles and westernizers, the only certainty was that the jury would be out a long time on Russia's future.

In the other Soviet successor states, the adoption of democracy seemed more unlikely still, while a number of nasty boundary wars reaffirmed the continuing capacity of nationalism for violence and disruption. In Russia, meanwhile, Chechnya declared its independence, inducing Moscow to launch an inept but brutal war to prevent a breakaway that might prove an irresistible precedent for other discontented peoples within the Russian federation. Nuclear weapons proliferation among the Soviet successor states was worrisome. "Rogue states" like North Korea, Iran, and Iraq posed significant regional dangers. In other conflict-ridden areas of the world, Afghanistan for example, anticommunist rebel groups continued to fight endlessly among themselves following the Soviet troop withdrawal.

China, increasingly nationalist because communism no longer provided ideological legitimation for the regime, continued to commit human rights violations, habitually transgressed international commercial norms, engaged in arms sales to customers of dubious reputation, and threateningly voiced its displeasure at Taiwan's refusal to move toward reunion with the mainland. Its prearranged 1997 takeover of the British crown colony of Hong Kong raised concerns that heavy-handed bureaucrats in Beijing would stifle one of the world's most successful free enterprise economies.

The China situation was nothing if not ironic. After more than a century of western fantasizing and anticipation, the country was finally set firmly on the road to modernization. But the path was a crooked one. For one thing, trade with China was not quite what had been expected. It was, to be sure, booming, but the mirage of the China market continued to remain beyond reach as China exported far more to the U.S. than she imported. In addition, China, formerly the symbol of progressive great-power cooperation, was for many onlookers emerging as the primary danger to world order. Perhaps, though, the new "yellow peril" was overblown. Just as China was once the exaggerated symbol of modernity's benign possibilities, it was quite possible that the Chinese danger was now the product of overheated alarmist imaginations.

Even within the Western world, the story line was by no means upbeat. Structural unemployment in Europe remained alarmingly high, leading to a growing sentiment for closing Europe's borders to further immigration. Continued economic integration and the adoption of a common European currency, or Euro, were in doubt, thanks in part to huge budget deficits incurred by Germany in the attempt to modernize the economy of the former German Democratic Republic and the inability of other countries to get budget deficits below predetermined limits. The Clinton administration's decision to expand NATO into eastern Europe as a way of keeping the alliance alive suggested that, among high policy-makers at least, the century-long failure to provide a substitute for the old balance of power made necessary a continuing American presence on the continent.

The situation in Asia also had its gloomy and threatening aspects. Japan's economy was stagnating, as the bursting of the stock market and real estate bubbles, combined with structural rigidities in the economy, took the air out of the inflated image of "Japan as Number One." No longer was it possible to joke that "the cold war is over, and Japan won." Late in 1997, Asian stock markets collapsed in a wave of panic selling, leading to fears that the rest of the world's' financial markets and manufacturing sectors would soon catch the contagion.

Economic globalization, long considered a good thing, began to encounter serious resistance from those who refused to worship every decision made by international markets. For the critics of the globalization of production, the growing attractiveness of low-wage countries as production platforms placed downward pressure on wages, eroded job security, damaged the environment, and threatened the American standard of living. Even successful regional integration posed potential problems. The United States concluded a North American Free Trade Agreement with Canada and Mexico in 1992 with the aim of forming a huge free-trade bloc, but it also kicked up a good deal of economically nationalist protec-

tionist sentiment within the country in the course of the debate over ratification. Simultaneous with the 1995 launch of a new World Trade Organization to succeed the various GATT agreements, there was persistent talk
of a coming trade war among the world's three regional trading blocs. In
a move that set off alarm bells among economic internationalists, Congress in 1997 refused to grant the Clinton administration the "fast track"
authority to negotiate trade deals without having the details reviewed and
reopened by Congress.

The United Nations fared even worse, though at first its future seemed
quite promising. With the end of the cold war, at long last the time seemed
ripe to make the UNO the kind of institution whose development had
been arrested in 1945: an effective institution of great-power cooperation
against lesser threats. The organization faced an early test in the summer
of 1990 when Iraqi dictator Saddam Hussein invaded and annexed the
oil-rich sheikdom of Kuwait to the south. Saddam's brazen action, if left
unchallenged, would have given the capricious dictator direct control of
a significant share of the world's oil supply; indirectly, his leverage would
have been much greater, allowing Iraq to exert extraordinary influence
on other important petroleum-rich states in the Middle East. His success
would also, in all likelihood, have destabilized the Arab-Israeli standoff.
Not least, it would have been a monument to UN impotence.

Although unsure at first how to respond, President Bush declared that
Iraq's aggression would "not stand." The UN Security Council voted resolutions threatening Iraq with punishment if she failed to withdraw. In short
order, Bush orchestrated an economic embargo of Iraq and began transfer-
ring American forces to the Saudi Desert where by year's end U.S. troop
strength totaled more than 500,000. Displaying an enthusiasm that had
been lacking in many cold war crises, America's allies contributed significant numbers of soldiers and sizeable cash contributions. In justifying
the buildup, Bush resorted to classical domino rhetoric about the consequences of aggression. The difference between this episode and previous
credibility crises, however, was that this time the United States was intervening on behalf of a specific economic interest. As James Baker
spelled it out, that interest reduced to a four-letter word: "jobs."

After softening up Saddam's forces with a sustained series of punishing
air strikes, the UN forces quickly finished up the stunningly successful
Operation Desert Storm. Within a few days, and with remarkably few
casualties, Kuwait was liberated and the Iraqi army completely routed.
On March 6, 1991, the president delivered a victory speech to Congress
in which he drew optimistic conclusions about the war's meaning. "Now
we can see a new world order coming into view," he said, "a world where

the United Nations—freed from the cold war stalemate—is poised to ful-
fill the historic vision of its founders." But the euphoria generated by the
Persian Gulf War dissipated quickly thanks to the unsavory taste of its
aftermath. The decision to allow Saddam to remain in power for fear that
Iraq would fall apart and destabilize the entire Middle East struck many
as a last-minute triumph of expediency over principle. In the following
years, the weakened but unrepentant dictator continued to jangle nerves
by thumbing his nose at the Security Council, despite the continuation of
UN sanctions and controls.

Subsequent interventions on behalf of the UN proved even less satisfying. In the east African nation of Somalia, a land in which disruptions
to agricultural production and distribution caused by an interminable civil
war had produced a disastrous famine, televised images of mass starvation
produced a clamor for action. The UN responded by landing troops to
support the distribution of humanitarian food aid. Thanks to a sizeable
American military presence, the back of the famine was broken. However,
the American public grew impatient when "mission creep" added a new
objective for the intervention: forcibly ending the civil war. As U.S. casualties multiplied in a fruitless attempt to capture an elusive warlord, popular support dried up and the troops were brought home.

The American people showed similar reluctance to sanction intervention in Yugoslavia when that country began to disintegrate. Following
Tito's death in 1980, the collective communist leadership struggled to
keep together the various republics, all of which had strong ethnic and
religious identities. When nationalism, fanned by shortsighted local political leaders, took hold at the end of the cold war, Yugoslavia quickly frag-
mented. In June 1991, first Slovenia seceded, then Croatia, then finally
the multiethnic republic of Bosnia-Herzegovina. In the latter, a three-way
civil war broke out among its Serbian, Muslim, and Croatian populations,
with the Serbs determined to join their republic to a "Greater Serbia."
"We ain't got no dog in this fight," explained Secretary of State Baker
following a failed last-ditch diplomatic attempt to prevent the fragmenta-
tion of the country.

The war attracted the world's attention when news reports exposed the
Bosnian Serb practice of "ethnic cleansing." With the connivance and
support of Slobodan Milosevic, the nationalist leader of Serbia and the
rump state of Yugoslavia, the Bosnian Serbs were determined to purify
their area by deporting or massacring the Muslim populations. In the face
of continuing reports of systematic rapes of women and other atrocities,
and with the disturbing images being broadcast daily over television from
the siege of Sarajevo, a city that as the site of the 1984 winter Olympic

games had only recently symbolized the ideal of global brotherhood, the international community was finally embarrassed into taking action, however unenthusiastically.

After some failed negotiations headed by former Secretary of State Cyrus Vance and British David Owen, America's NATO allies reluctantly stepped into the breach. The French and the British inserted troops into Bosnia under UN auspices, but handcuffed their commanders by denying them the authority to impose a settlement on the feuding factions. In response to American criticisms about continued toleration of genocide under their very noses, the Europeans lashed back at the United States for its unwillingness to contribute to a solution.

Finally, faced with a deteriorating situation and sickening new evidence of massacres of Muslims committed by the Bosnian Serbs, President Bill Clinton agreed in 1995 to introduce American troops, with the mandate to use overpowering force if necessary. By that time, the tide of battle had begun to run against the Serbs and the new military lines suggested the possibility of agreement on ethnically realistic and stable boundaries. A cease-fire and a peace accord worked out in Dayton, Ohio, envisioned elections for a federal republic of Muslims, Orthodox Serbs, and Catholic Croats in Bosnia. However, American troops were kept on a short leash by Congress and the public. Their removal was promised to come shortly following the 1996 presidential election, though it soon became apparent that they would have to stay on indefinitely because withdrawal was likely to bring a renewal of violence.

Whatever the on-the-ground successes of these UN operations, it was clear that the organization was severely overburdened and incapable of living up to the high expectations that sprouted like crocuses following the end of the cold war. In the United States, anti-UN opinion was on the rise. Congress refused to authorize payment of U.S. membership fees long in arrears; liberals and others complained about the UN's unwieldy and inefficient bureaucracy; conservatives carped about the organization's anti-American bias and made it appear as if the American military were in danger of being swallowed up by the UN chain of command. Meanwhile, extreme right-wing groups propagated the mindless myth that the U.S. itself was in danger of being taken over by the United Nations Organization. President Clinton's promise in his inaugural address to take action "when the will and conscience of the world is defied" seemed in danger of being undercut by a lack of American will.[1]

But it should have come as no surprise that the UN received mediocre or failing grades in its first post-cold-war tests. That body's difficulties simply underscored the inability, repeatedly demonstrated, of international organizations to handle major political disputes. In the 1930s, the League's noble dream of eliminating great power wars was shown to be an illusion. Now in the 1990s, the possibility of attaining the much more modest UN goal of quelling lesser disturbances was also cast into doubt as the growing American reluctance to lead was more than matched by a reluctance of its partners to follow. It was not long before the Security Council settled into a familiar pattern in which, even without the ideological schism of the cold war, great-power cooperation was by no means assured.

The UN's troubles only confirmed what historical developments had already suggested: that the real story of internationalism's survival in the twentieth century had little to do with supranational organizations. Wilsonianism had triumphed as a creed only because, having been blown off course into strange waters, it was adopted by the United States as a national program for preventing the kinds of global calamities first prophesied by Wilson. Even then, the Americanization of Wilsonianism had been quite limited. Because the American public never fully understood the complex, counterintuitive logic of internationalism, it never became a creed for the masses.

America's Wilsonian outlook met with similar puzzlement abroad, where other nations continued to operate on the basis of a traditional logic of realism that made it difficult for them to think beyond their immediate interests. The Americanization of internationalism was essential to the creation of a global society, but at the same time it reflected the absence of a global culture—or world opinion—that was capable of organizing internationalism outside the traditional boundaries of nationalism and nation states. Because America's internationalist reasoning tended to make others nervous, support for American "leadership" had often been difficult to come by. In practice, world opinion was all too often an illusion, a will-o'-the-wisp. Even among highly developed core countries, the superficial similarities of material culture appeared to mask thought-worlds that were completely alien to one another.

With world opinion so problematic and unreliable, the success of Wilsonianism was the result of its adoption and internalization by American elites, whose cohesiveness made possible American leadership. As the 1920s and 1930s demonstrated, Wilsonian ideas did not easily find a home but, once installed, they endured. To be sure, the elites argued on occasion about means, as in Vietnam, but they remained united on the all-important issue of ends. In addition, Wilsonianism managed to prosper because it was successfully institutionalized in a host of government agencies that endured throughout the cold war and after, even though their original raison d'etre had disappeared. Not least, Wilsonianism endured because the alternatives always seemed worse and because, despite its shortcomings, it worked.

While the understanding of the past was hazy, the sense of the present was clear: disappointment with the UN and the unruliness of the world created a feeling of emptiness in American internationalism. With all the turmoil in the world, it was understandable why some people viewed the passing of the cold war with nostalgia. Along with a sense of high purpose, it had also brought a measure of stability and predictability to the conduct of foreign affairs, combined with a certain seductive excitement. In contrast, the future, for which little had been done by way of preparation, was unpredictable. Though still committed in principle to world leadership, it seemed as if America's heart was no longer in it.

Was this not a dangerous situation? In the past, changes from one system to another had often been accompanied by instability and war. This time, the pessimists suggested, was no different. The cold war would be succeeded by inflamed nationalisms; perhaps by a conflict of civilizations, in which the West would be pitted against "the rest," most likely Islam or rising Asian powers. Some feared an American reversion to isolationism, which would once again allow the world to slide into chaos. As conceptual drift appeared to take over, politicians and intellectuals were chastised for failing to produce a new foreign policy vision to replace containment.

But such calls were misplaced because they operated from a poor understanding of the purpose of Wilsonianism and cold war internationalism. Wilsonianism's rise to prominence in the 1930s and the cold war was an emergency response to a century-long global crisis of belief in a modern world order. Fascism was a rejection of liberalism and cosmopolitanism, as, in effect, was communism. In the face of these challenges, Wilsonianism as it emerged in practice was not an idealistic creed. As implemented by the U.S., it provided a way of muddling through the century-long crisis until the kind of world envisioned at the beginning of the century once again came into view.

Far from being the centerpiece of American utopianism, then, Wilsonianism was a self-liquidating creed because, as Warren Harding had long ago recognized, it was not an ideology suited to "normalcy." It owed its existence in the first place to the emergence of the extraordinary threat that was embedded within modernity. Once the threat vanished, so too did Wilsonianism. This was evident from the amazing swiftness with which the cold war became historically distant and foreign, a relic of a strange past that now required an effort of anthropological imagination to understand. The ideology, which only recently had been second nature to policy-makers, had been so quickly and thoroughly denaturalized that its potency and influence were difficult to credit except on the assumption that cold warriors had collectively succumbed to some weird mental disorder. Thus the post-cold-war world was not a third chance to institutionalize Wilsonian policies; rather, it provided the occasion for dispensing with them altogether.

With the UN and Wilsonianism hors de combat, the world was back to where it had been in 1900. From the perspective of this book, the cold war and the Wilsonian century were a lengthy interlude in a story whose next chapter had long been anticipated. The end of the cold war marked a resumption of the kind of historical evolution that Taft and the Republican statesmen of the 1920s believed had already come to fruition, the kind of world that FDR in World War II had hoped for with fingers crossed, the kind of world anticipated prematurely by Jimmy Carter. After a century of turbulence, the world could look forward to a smoother stretch of great-power relationships and focus its energies on the tasks of development.

The United States in the 1990s had returned to normal internationalism, to the kind of benign but hazy global vision that was in vogue at the turn of the century. American foreign policy through the twentieth century was remarkably consistent in its aspirations for a world of liberal capitalism, democracy, and great-power cooperation, undergirded by commercial and cultural cooperation. Because this was a conception to which the nation returned again and again in untroubled times, the post-cold-war world was in no way strange. It was in fact nothing more than the kind of liberal world that the United States had long been anticipating. And, thanks to Wilsonianism, it was "a world of its own making."[2]

Of course, much had changed since 1900. The concept of global society was being broadened and deepened to encompass nations, races, cultures, and genders that formerly would never have been accepted as equals. It was now widely understood that this was a world whose structural faults, unless closely monitored, threatened its self-destruction. The faith in progress was now partially clouded over with an ironic self-awareness of the perils of modernity. But, in its main outlines, it was the kind of world that Americans imagined a hundred years ago. Though that world was bathed in optimism, it was hardly a utopian place. It was plagued by uneven development and populated by great powers who were themselves at different stages of historical evolution. It was a world of forced contact in which cultural intrusions were passionately but fruitlessly resisted. It was a world of minor conflicts. But above all, it was a world of progressive possibilities.

Much had changed in American policy, too. With full public support, in principle at least, America was self-conscious about the need to act as world leader. Militarily, the U.S. continued to be the ultimate guarantor of security in Europe, East Asia, and the Middle East, as demonstrated by the deployment of forces to Bosnia, the Taiwan straits, and the Persian Gulf. Indeed, its defense spending, while down considerably from the 1980s, continued at levels that critics charged, to little noticeable effect, was grossly disproportionate to any threats the nation might face. Economically, the chronic trade deficit allowed the American economy to absorb large quantities of imports without, however, jeopardizing the country's image as the model of free enterprise dynamism and efficiency. Culturally, despite complaints about cultural imperialism, American media, mass culture, and consumer values flooded the globe.

Thus the problems of the UN and the emergence of petty nationalisms concealed the degree to which internationalism had triumphed. Most obviously, the challenges of a series of contending ideologies, incarnated in great powers like Germany, Japan, and the USSR, had been surmounted. At a deeper level, while nationalism, authoritarianism, and cultural differences appeared to be so deeply ingrained as to make impossible any global culture, it was also true that cosmopolitanism had never before been as broadly and deeply rooted as at the end of the twentieth century. Though far from solidary, a world opinion, the mirage brought to life by Wilson and his successors, was at work. Wilsonianism made it possible for this complex, untidy, and uneven world of liberalism to continue its problematic development.

As our story began, normal internationalism was more a fanciful possibility than an established fact of international life. When it first came to dominate American thinking on foreign affairs, normal internationalism was not "normal" at all. It was quite exceptional, actually existing primarily as an image in the minds of some members of the American foreign policy elite and a modest number of like-minded internationalists abroad. While it correctly identified some of the world's positive features, it failed utterly to anticipate its soon-to-be-revealed threatening aspects. The world of great-power relations then in being, which was based on age-old practices of realpolitik and war, would not begin to be displaced until the middle of the century. As one scholar reminds us, "only since World War II has it been possible to write about 'global liberalism' or 'liberal world order' and expect a reasonable, if not automatic, understanding of what is meant by these terms."[3]

Just how and why this image of internationalism managed to become a reality is not clear. Indeed, it is remarkable that it happened at all. Because images were involved in constituting this world, it is clear that imagination played a significant role in the process. Nations, one historian has argued, are "imagined communities," while still another scholar speaks about "the imaginary institution of society."[4] Given the outcome of the Wilsonian century, I would suggest that the scope for the creative exercise of human imagination is just as great in international affairs, if not more so, than it is in domestic life. How else can one explain the tenacity, which otherwise would seem absurd, with which Americans pursued the realization of the historical "grand narrative" that they carried inside their heads?

But creative policy in the service of imagination is only part of the story, and a small part at that. It is important to realize that foreign policies rooted in the Wilsonian imagination did not, of themselves, create the post-cold-war world. To be sure, these policies, which perceived problems in global Wilsonian terms and addressed them with a variety of Wilsonian solutions, were themselves quite extraordinary. In pursuing its Wilsonian agenda, the United States abandoned traditional definitions of national interest—not simply American conceptions, but interest- and power-based ideas that had dominated thinking about international relations for thousands of years. Nevertheless, these policies, though their achievements were considerable, did not shape history directly. They merely provided the political space in which the kind of world imagined by normal internationalism could take root and grow to maturity. Wilsonianism was based on a faith in allowing history to proceed "normally."

Somehow, it did. To explain why things turned out this way is not the purpose of this book. The philosopher Ludwig Wittgenstein used to argue that the purpose of philosophy was to rid oneself of the need to do philosophy. In a somewhat different way, the purpose of doing diplomatic history is to rid oneself of the need to do traditional diplomatic history, to suggest how politics points beyond politics. In this case, the challenge is to understand how hard power and economic power made for integrative power.[5] It is that improbable, impossible-sounding process of world integration— more clouded over than explained by terms like "globalization" and "modernization"—that awaits historical excavation by diplomatic historians of the future. Just as Wilsonianism pointed to a more fundamental vision of internationalism, a study of the Wilsonian century points beyond Wilsonianism to a concern for understanding a process in which a world full of strangers has become a global society.

History is not necessarily progressive in its outcomes. The coming of the millennium brought with it all kinds of predictions of epochal change caused by overpopulation, resource depletion, environmental degradation, epidemic disease, mass migration, nuclear catastrophe, and cultural dislocation. Forecasts of highly skewed development raised the possibility of a permanent, swollen international underclass. If it came to pass, this situation would undoubtedly cause a crisis of liberalism, whose legitimacy rests on the idea of universal progress. But it is unlikely that anything can be done to adequately address such issues in advance. If and when a crisis does emerge, perhaps another Wilson—not necessarily an American—will come along. But given the unhappy circumstances that evoked Wilson's vision and plagued America through the Wilsonian century, one may be pardoned for hoping that another Wilson will not be necessary.

Unfortunately, there is no way to demonstrate, even after the fact, whether the fears of Wilson and his ideological heirs were or were not objectively grounded. Was autocracy the threat that Wilson said it was? Would Hitler and the Japanese eventually have burned themselves out? Were Stalin and the USSR bent on global domination? Historians, with much more information at their disposal than policy-makers ever had available, continue to argue these issues with passion, as inconclusively as ever and with little likelihood of reaching a unanimous verdict.

Far from being scandalous, this inability to zero in on necessary causes in the past is but another confirmation of the role of indeterminacy and freedom in human affairs. Over the course of the twentieth century American policy-makers created, sustained, and made a historical reality of the kind of interdependent world that they imagined in their minds' eyes. Despite its contradictions, it was a world more united in structure and sentiment than ever before in the history of humankind.

To drive home the extraordinary character of this achievement, it helps to ask oneself: What kind of contemporary world would a power-based realism have produced? There is no conclusive answer to that question, of course, but I, for one, find it difficult to suppose that the outcome would have been more benign. Despite all its adversities, it is easy to imagine how critical passages in this century's turbulent voyage might have come to complete disaster.

"History is bunk," said Henry Ford. Maybe so, but the story of American foreign policy in the twentieth century is a testament to the power of historical understanding and imagination to shape human destiny. The Wilsonian imagination fathered the post-Wilsonian world. If nothing else, the Wilsonian century demonstrated the power of historical imagination to illuminate and create its own reality.

NOTES

Introduction

1. David Campbell, *Writing Security: United States Foreign Policy and the Politics of Identity* (Minneapolis: University of Minnesota Press, 1992), p. 4.

2. Henry Kissinger, *Diplomacy* (New York: Touchstone Books, 1994), p. 46. For the bible of neorealism, see Kenneth Waltz, *Theory of International Politics* (Reading, Mass.: Addison-Wesley, 1979).

3. Extract from Hans J. Morgenthau and Kenneth W. Thompson, *Politics Among Nations: The Struggle for Power and Peace* (New York: Knopf, 1985), in Herbert M. Levine, ed., *World Politics Debated,* 4th ed. (New York: McGraw-Hill, 1992), p. 117. Actually, these kinds of speculations lead in an interesting direction. One could argue that *all* nations are similarly subject to illusions, in which case misunderstanding and the resort to settling issues by power are unavoidable. Although this would appear to describe a pluralist, realist kind of world, this kind of scheme is inherently unpalatable to objectivists because an international system that is subjectively and irrationally driven leaves little room for objectively rational people to understand and manage the system.

4. Alfred North Whitehead, *Symbolism* (New York: Capricorn Books, 1959), p. 61. For the argument that realists are much better at arguing that certain interests are not vital than they are at establishing an objective and universally accepted foundation of national interest, see John Ruggie, *Winning the Peace: America and World Order in the New Era* (New York: Columbia University Press, 1994), p. 3.

5. Frank Ninkovich, "Interests and Discourse in Diplomatic History," *Diplomatic History* 13 (Spring 1989): 135–61.

6. Harold Garfinkel, *Studies in Ethnomethodology* (Englewood Cliffs, N.J.: Prentice-Hall, 1967), pp. 66–70. For an extended discussion of this point, see John C. Heritage, "Ethnomethodology," in Anthony Giddens and Jonathan H. Turner, eds., *Social Theory Today* (Stanford: Stanford University Press, 1987), p. 229.

7. Thomas Kuhn, *The Structure of Scientific Revolutions,* second edition, enlarged (Chicago: University of Chicago Press, 1970), pp. 110–11.

8. John B. Thompson, *Ideology and Modern Culture: Critical Social Theory in the Era of Mass Communication* (Stanford: Stanford University Press, 1990), p. 225.

9. For a condensed summary of realism's assumptions, but with other apt descriptions scattered throughout the essay, see James Der Derian, "A Reinterpretation of Realism: Genealogy, Semiology, Dromology," in James Der Derian, ed., *International Theory: Critical Investigations* (New York: New York University Press, 1995), pp. 373–74.

10. Herbert Blumer, *Symbolic Interactionism: Method and Perspective* (Englewood Cliffs, N.J.: Prentice-Hall, 1969), p. 22.

11. Pierre Bourdieu, *The Logic of Practice,* trans Richard Nice (Stanford: Stanford University Press, 1990), pp. 135–41.

12. Martin Heidegger, "The Age of the World Picture," in Heidegger, *The Question of Technology and Other Essays,* trans. William Lovitt (New York: Garland, 1977), p. 120.

13. Blumer goes so far as to suggest that structures are reifications. "The conception of human society as structure or organization is ingrained in the very marrow of contemporary sociology," he says, whereas a symbolic aproach "sees human society not as an established structure but as people meeting their conditions of life." Blumer, *Symbolic Interactionism,* p. 74. See also Bourdieu, *The Logic of Practice,* pp. 10–11, for his realization that the structures he was "mapping" existed in his mind rather than in the reality he was observing. Both of these people are, mind you, sociologists.

14. David Harvey, *The Condition of Postmodernity* (Oxford: Blackwell, 1990), p. 306.

15. See, e.g., Judith Goldstein, *Ideas, Interests, and American Trade Policy* (Ithaca: Cornell University Press, 1993), pp. 253–54.

16. On this point, see Roger E. Kanet and Edward Koldziej, *The Cold War as Cooperation* (Baltimore: Johns Hopkins University Press, 1991), p. 30.

17. John F. Kennedy, *The Strategy of Peace* (New York: Popular Library, 1960), p. 264.

18. See especially the many works of Akira Iriye, most recently *Cultural Internationalism and World Order* (Baltimore: Johns Hopkins University Press, 1997), and, for an extended argument on the importance of ideology, Michael Hunt's pioneering *Ideology and U.S. Foreign Policy* (New Haven: Yale University Press, 1987).

19. Niklas Luhmann, *The Differentiation of Society,* trans. Stephen Holmes and Charles Larmore (New York: Columbia University Press, 1982), p. 354.

Chapter One

1. Remarks by Professor Edmund J. James, *Proceedings of the American Academy of Political Science: The Foreign Policy of the United States* (Philadelphia, 1899), p. 215.

2. Archibald Cary Coolidge, *The United States as a World Power* (New York: Macmillan, 1908), p. 148.

3. Norman Graebner, *Ideas and Diplomacy: Readings in the Intellectual Tradition of American Foreign Policy* (New York: Oxford University Press, 1964), p. 340.

4. For the generational difference in attitudes toward imperialism, see Robert Beisner, *Twelve against Empire: The Anti-Imperialists, 1898–1900* (New York: McGraw-Hill, 1968). In a classic work, Ernest May, *American Imperialism: A Speculative Essay* (New York: Atheneum, 1968), argues convincingly that American elites

followed the lead of European opinion leaders, who served as their "reference group" on the issue of imperialism.

5. Richard H. Collin, *Theodore Roosevelt, Culture, Diplomacy, and Expansion* (Baton Rouge: Louisiana State University Press, 1985), p. 108.

6. David Healy, *U.S. Expansionism: The Imperialist Urge in the 1890s* (Madison: University of Wisconsin Press, 1970), p. 247.

7. William C. Widenor, *Henry Cabot Lodge and the Search for an American Foreign Policy* (Berkeley: University of California Press, 1980), p. 76.

8. Coolidge, *The United States as a World Power,* p. 7.

9. David S. Patterson, *Toward a Warless World: The Travail of the American Peace Movement, 1887–1914* (Bloomington: Indiana University Press, 1976), p. 126.

10. Theodore Salisbury Woolsey, *America's Foreign Policy* (New York: The Century Co., 1898), p. viii.

11. Albert B. Hart, *The Foundations of American Foreign Policy* (New York: Macmillan, 1901), p. 52.

12. Herbert Croly, *The Promise of American Life* (Indianapolis, 1965), p. 297.

13. William Justin Mann, *America in Its Relation to the Great Epochs of History* (Boston: Little, Brown, 1902), p. 224.

14. Quoted in William Appleman Williams, *Empire as a Way of Life* (New York: Oxford University Press, 1990), p. 99.

15. Quoted in Richard Heindel, *The American Impact on Great Britain, 1898–1914* (New York: Octagon, 1968), p. 138.

16. Ibid., p. 2.

17. *Omaha Bee,* 13 October 1898, quoted in Robert Rydell, *All The World's a Fair* (Chicago: University of Chicago Press, 1984), p. 122.

18. Draft of Columbia University address, 12 May 1954, White House memoranda series, John Foster Dulles Papers, Princeton University, Seeley Mudd Library, Princeton University, box 1.

19. George S. Morison, *The New Epoch as Developed by the Manufacture of Power* (Boston: Houghton Mifflin, 1903), p. 57.

20. Donald M. Lowe, *History of Bourgeois Perception* (Chicago: University of Chicago Press, 1982), p. 39.

21. Quoted in Julius W. Pratt, *Expansionists of 1898* (Chicago: Quadrangle Books, 1964), 19.

22. Theodore Roosevelt, "History as Literature," *The Works of Theodore Roosevelt,* national edition, ed. Hermann Hagedorn (New York: Scribner's, 1926), 12: 7.

23. Quoted in May, *American Imperialism,* p. 185.

24. Extracts from McKinley speech of 5 September 1901, in Arthur S. Link and William L. Leary, Jr., eds., *The Diplomacy of World Power: The United States, 1889–1920* (New York: St. Martin's Press, 1970), pp. 39–41.

25. Croly, *The Promise of American Life,* p. 297.

26. Tyler Dennett, *John Hay* (New York: Dodd, Mead 1933), p. 181.

27. Quoted in David Healy, *U.S. Expansionism,* p. 33.

28. Dennett, *John Hay,* p. 189.

29. Quoted in Bradford Perkins, *The Great Rapprochement: England and the United States, 1895–1914* (New York: Atheneum, 1968), p. 154.

30. Quoted in David Dimbleby and David Reynolds, *An Ocean Apart: The Relation-*

ship between Britain and America in the Twentieth Century (New York: Vintage Books, 1989), p. 34.

31. Hart, *Foundations of American Foreign Policy,* p. 238.

32. Quoted in Ragnhild Fiebig-von Hase, "The United States and Germany in the World Arena, 1900–1917," in Hans-Jürgen Schröder, ed., *Cooperation and Confrontation: Germany and the United States in the Era of World War I, 1900–1924* (Providence, R.I.: Berg, 1993), p. 45.

33. Quoted in Holge W. Herwig, *Politics of Frustration: The United States in German Naval Planning, 1889–1941* (Boston: Little, Brown, 1976), p. 104.

34. *The Education of Henry Adams: An Autobiography* (New York: Time, 1964), 2: 145.

35. Croly, *The Promise of American Life,* p. 296.

36. Warren I. Cohen, *America's Response to China,* 2d. ed. (New York: John Wiley and Sons, 1980), p. 43.

37. Ibid., p. 311.

38. Quoted in Eugene Anschel, ed., *The American Image of Russia, 1775–1917* (New York: Frederick Ungar, 1974), p. 179.

39. Ibid., p. 202.

40. Ibid., p. 195.

41. Ibid., p. 188.

42. Ibid., p. 200.

43. Theodore Roosevelt to Cecil Arthur Spring Rice, 13 June 1904, *The Letters of Theodore Roosevelt,* ed. Elting W. Morison (Cambridge: Harvard University Press, 1950), 4: 830.

44. TR to George von Lengerke Meyer, 12/26/1904, ibid., 1079–80.

45. Norman E. Saul, *Concord and Conflict: The United States and Russia, 1867–1914* (Lawrence: University of Kansas Press, 1996), p. 420. This shows clearly that Taft did not expect the Russians to knuckle under.

46. Quoted in Rydell, *All the World's a Fair,* p. 50.

47. Quoted in Akira Iriye, *Pacific Estrangement: Japanese and American Expansion, 1897–1911* (Chicago: Imprint Publications, 1994), p. 167.

48. Rockefeller Foundation, *Annual Report,* 1939, p. 70.

49. Quoted in Jerry Israel, *Progressivism and the Open Door* (University of Pittsburgh Press, 1971), p. 94.

50. Warren I. Cohen, *The Chinese Connection: Roger S. Greene, Thomas W. Lamont, George E. Sokolsky and American-East Asian Relations* (New York: Columbia University Press, 1978), p. 68.

51. Coolidge, *The United States as a World Power,* p. 119.

52. Brooks Adams, *America's Economic Supremacy* (New York and London: Harper, 1947), pp. 70–71.

53. Dennett, *John Hay,* p. 328–29.

54. Hart, *The Foundations of American Foreign Policy,* p. 240.

55. "Germany and American Public Opinion," *The Living Age,* 246 (August 12, 1905), 436–37, quoted in Graebner, *Ideas and Diplomacy,* p. 397.

56. Andrew D. White, as quoted in H. Wayne Morgan, *William McKinley and His America* (Syracuse: Syracuse University Press, 1963), p. 459.

57. Paul Reinsch, *Public International Unions* (Boston: Ginn and Company, 1911) p. 3.

58. Quoted in H. Wayne Morgan, *McKinley,* p. 450.

59. See Paul Wolman, *Most Favored Nation: The Republican Revisionists and U.S. Tariff Policy, 1897–1912* (Chapel Hill: University of North Carolina Press, 1992).

Chapter Two

1. Woodrow Wilson to Ellen Axson Wilson, 30 October 1883, in John M. Mulder, *Woodrow Wilson: The Years of Preparation* (Princeton University Press, 1978), p. 74.

2. News report of an address in Youngstown, Ohio (15 March 1906), in Arthur Link, ed., *The Papers of Woodrow Wilson* (Princeton: Princeton University Press, 1966–), 16: 333 (hereafter cited as *PWW*).

3. After-dinner remarks in NYC to the Friendly Sons of St. Patrick (17 March 1909), *PWW,* 19: 107.

4. Quoted in Thomas J. Knock, *To End All Wars: Woodrow Wilson and the Quest for a New World Order* (New York: Oxford University Press, 1992), p. 18.

5. Press conference, 28 April 1913, *PWW,* 27: 300.

6. Press conference, 24 November 1914, *PWW,* 50: 636.

7. Knock, *To End All Wars,* p. 44.

8. Frederick S. Calhoun, *Uses of Force and Wilsonian Foreign Policy* (Kent: Kent State University Press, 1993), p. 32.

9. An appeal to the American people, 18 August 1914, *PWW,* 30: 394.

10. From the diary of Colonel Edward House, 30 August 1914, *PWW,* 30: 462.

11. Memo of an interview with Wilson by Herbert Bruce Brougham, 14 December 1914, *PWW,* 31: 459.

12. Wilson to House, 12 July 1915, *PWW,* 33: 492.

13. Quoted in Arthur Walworth, *America's Moment, 1918: American Diplomacy at the End of World War I* (New York, 1977), p. 344.

14. Fourth of July address, 4 July 1914, *PWW,* 30: 251.

15. Remarks to the Associated Press in New York City, 20 April 1915, *PWW,* 33: 40.

16. Speech accepting a second nomination for the presidency, 2 September 1916, in Ray Stannard Baker, ed., *The Public Papers of Woodrow Wilson* (New York: Kraus Reprints, 1970), 4: 282 (hereafter cited as *PPWW*).

17. Quoted in Thomas Bailey, *A Diplomatic History of the American People* (Englewood Cliffs: Prentice-Hall, 1980), p. 565.

18. Press conference, 2 March 1915, *PWW,* 50: 705.

19. An address to the Senate, 22 January 1917, *PWW,* 40: 535–37.

20. From the diary of Colonel House, 4 January 1917, *PWW,* 40: 409.

21. Second Inaugural Address, 5 March 1917, *PWW,* 41: 333.

22. Speech of September 11, 1919, *PWW,* 63: 182.

23. Jules Jusserand to Foreign Ministry, 14 April 1917, *PWW,* 42: 70.

24. Tasker Bliss to Newton Baker, 25 May 1917, *PWW,* 42: 409.

25. Memo by John Howard Whitehouse of conversation with Wilson, *PWW,* 42: 66.

26. Wilson to House, 21 August 1915, *PWW,* 34: 271.

27. A Flag Day Address, 14 June 1917, *PWW,* 42: 501–2.

28. Address in Buffalo to the American Federation of Labor, 12 November 1917, *PWW,* 45: 14.

29. Address to the officers of the Atlantic Fleet, 11 August 1917, *PWW,* 43: 429.

30. Robert Lansing, *War Memoirs of Robert Lansing, Secretary of State* (Indianapolis: Bobbs-Merrill, 1935), p. 21.

31. House to Wilson, 3 February 1916, *PWW,* 36: 123.

32. Memo by Sidney Edward Mezes, David Hunter Miller, and Walter Lippmann [December 1917], *PWW,* 45: 460–61.

33. Walter Hines Page to Wilson, 23 July 1915, *PWW,* 34: 19.

34. Quoted in Perkins, *The Great Rapprochement,* p. 242.

35. Remarks to representatives of livestock growers, 13 March 1918, *PWW,* 47: 3.

36. Address in Denver, Colorado, September 25, 1919, in Ray Stannard Baker and William E. Dodd, eds., *The Public Papers of Woodrow Wilson* (New York: Kraus Reprint, 1970), 6: 388. My emphasis.

37. Fourteen Points address, 8 January 1918, *PWW,* 45: 536.

38. Excerpts from Lincoln Colcord, "Danger of Junkerism Drawing U.S. Into War," *Philadelphia Public Ledger,* 10 February 1917, in *PWW,* 41: 192.

39. Address in Buffalo to the A.F. of L., 12 November 1917, *PWW,* 45: 12.

40. Flag Day Address, 14 June 1917, *PWW,* 42: 500.

41. Stephen Kern, *The Culture of Time and Space, 1880–1918* (Cambridge: Harvard University Press, 1983), p. 240.

42. Second Inaugural Address, 5 March 1917, *PWW,* 41: 336.

43. Remarks to the Associated Press in New York City, 20 April 1915, *PWW,* 33: 37.

44. Remarks to the New York Press Club, 30 June 1916, *PWW,* 37: 335.

45. Address at the Metropolitan Opera House, 27 September 1918, *PWW,* 51: 131–32.

46. An address in Atlantic City to the New Jersey State Teachers' Association, "The State and the Citizen's Relation to It" (28 December 1909), *PWW* 19: 638.

47. Quoted in David W. Levy, *Herbert Croly of the New Republic* (Princeton: Princeton University Press, 1985) p. 221.

48. An Address, "The Course of American History," (16 May 1895), *PWW,* 9: 267.

49. An Address in Washington to the League to Enforce Peace, 27 May 1916, *PWW,* 37: 114.

50. Memo of conversation by Thomas Lamont, 4 October 1918, *PWW,* 51: 22.

51. See Wilson's interview of 31 December 1918, in *PWW,* 53: 573–75.

52. From the diary of Dr. Grayson, 5 April 1919, *PWW,* 58: 112.

53. Wilson to Robert Lansing, 24 May 1919, *PWW,* 59: 470–71.

54. Roland Stromberg, "The Idea of Collective Security," quoted in Sondra Herman, *Eleven against War* (Stanford: Stanford University Press, 1969), p. 72.

55. Wilson letter to Democratic senators, 18 November 1919. quoted in Bailey, *Diplomatic History of the American People,* p. 621.

56. Hamilton Foley, *Woodrow Wilson's Case for the League of Nations* (New York: Kraus Reprints, 1969), p. 201.

57. The treaty with reservations was defeated 55–39 on November 19, 1919; the vote on the treaty without reservations was 53–38; the last treaty vote on the Lodge resolutions went down 49–35 on March 19, 1920.

58. From the diary of Dr. Grayson, 6 May 1919, *PWW,* 58: 462.

Chapter Three

1. Ray Stannard Baker, *Woodrow Wilson and World Settlement* (Gloucester, Mass.: Peter Smith, 1960), 1: 82–83.

2. Hoover, "Problems of Our Economic Evolution," address to Stanford University seniors, 22 June 1925, "The Bible," No. 00, in Herbert Hoover Presidential Library, West Branch, Iowa.

3. As Michael Hogan has put it, "the theory of cooperative capitalism required important concessions by the great powers to a broader community of interests along with enlightened action by private leaders in managing the international economy." Michael Hogan, *Informal Entente: The Private Structure of Anglo-American Economic Diplomacy* (Columbia: University of Missouri Press, 1977), p. 212.

4. Akira Iriye, *The Cambridge History of American Foreign Relations,* vol. 3, *The Globalizing of America, 1913–1945* (New York: Cambridge University Press, 1993), p. 97.

5. Quoted in Robert D. Shulzinger, *The Making of the Diplomatic Mind* (Middletown: Wesleyan University Press, 1977), p. 77.

6. Quoted in Charles Beard, *The Idea of National Interest* (New York: Macmillan, 1934), p. 425n.

7. Dwight Morrow, quoted in Robert Freeman Smith, *The United States and Revolutionary Nationalism in Mexico, 1916–1932* (Chicago: University of Chicago Press, 1972), p. 222.

8. Ibid., p. 246.

9. Gaddis Smith, *The Last Years of the Monroe Doctrine* (New York: Hill and Wang, 1994), p. 32.

10. Quoted in Robert James Maddox, *William E. Borah and American Foreign Policy* (Baton Rouge: Louisiana State University Press, 1969), p. 95.

11. Quoted in Graebner, *Ideas and Diplomacy,* p. 510.

12. Hogan, *Informal Entente,* p. 95.

13. Quoted in Betty Glad, *Charles Evans Hughes and the Illusions of Innocence* (Urbana: University of Illinois Press, 1966), p. 158.

14. Denna Frank Fleming, *The United States and World Organization, 1920–1933* (New York: Columbia University Press, 1938), 93–98.

15. Quoted in Charles Cheney Hyde, "Charles Evans Hughes," in Samuel Flagg Bemis, ed., *The American Secretaries of State and Their Diplomacy* (New York: Cooper Square, 1963) 10: 248.

16. Quoted in Bailey, *A Diplomatic History of the American People,* p. 629.

17. Quoted in Melvyn P. Leffler, *The Elusive Quest: America's Pursuit of European Stability and French Security, 1919–1933* (Chapel Hill: University of North Carolina Press, 1979), p. 41.

18. Frank Costigliola, *Awkward Dominion: American Political, Economic, and Cul-*

tural relations With Europe, 1919–1933 (Ithaca: Cornell University Press, 1984), p. 264.

19. John Maynard Keynes, *The Economic Consequences of the Peace* (New York: Harper Torchbooks, 1971), p. 146.

20. Quoted in Joan Hoff Wilson, *Herbert Hoover: Forgotten Progressive* (Boston: Little, Brown, 1975), p. 186

21. Quoted in Frank Ninkovich, *Germany and the United States The Transformation of the German Question since 1945,* updated edition (New York: Twayne Publishers, 1995), p. 10.

22. Joan Hoff Wilson, *American Business and Foreign Policy, 1920–1933* (Lexington: University of Kentucky Press, 1971), p. 128.

23. Betty Glad, *Charles Evans Hughes and the Illusions of Innocence,* p. 232; Kenneth Paul Jones, *U.S. Diplomats in Europe, 1919–1941* (Santa Barbara: ABC-Clio, 1981), p. 31.

24. Quoted in Jean-Baptiste Duroselle, *France and the United States: From the Beginnings to the Present Day* (Chicago: University of Chicago Press, 1978), p. 125.

25. Quoted in Gordon A. Craig and Felix Gilbert, *The Diplomats, 1919–1939* (New York: Atheneum, 1974), 1: 295.

26. James T. Shotwell, *War as an Instrument of National Policy and Its Renunciation in the Pact of Paris* (New York: Harcourt, Brace, 1929), p. vii.

27. Robert Ferrell and Howard Quint, eds., *The Talkative President: The Off-the-record Press Conferences of Calvin Coolidge* (Amherst: University of Massachusetts Press, 1964), p. 219.

28. Baker, *PPWW,* 6: 431.

29. Alfred Eckes, Jr., *Opening America's Market: U.S. Foreign Trade Policy since 1776* (Chapel Hill: University of North Carolina Press, 1995), pp. 106–9.

30. Joan Hoff Wilson, *American Business and Foreign Policy, 1920–1933,* p. 122.

31. Henry L. Stimson, *The Far Eastern Crisis: Recollections and Observations* (New York: Harper & Brothers, 1936), p. 241.

32. Stimson letter to William E. Borah, 23 February 1932, in *Foreign Relations of the United States, Japan 1931–1941* (Washington, D.C.: GPO, 1943), I: 86–87.

33. Shotwell, *War as an Instrument of National Policy,* p. 30.

Chapter Four

1. Quoted in Robert Dallek, *Franklin D. Roosevelt and American Foreign Policy, 1932–1945* (New York: Oxford University Press, 1979), p. 29.

2. FDR to Arthur Murray, 14 April 1933, in Edgar Nixon, ed., *Franklin D. Roosevelt and Foreign Affairs* (Cambridge: The Belknap Press, 1969), 1: 54.

3. FDR speech, 28 December 1933, in ibid., pp. 560–62.

4. Machiavelli, *The Prince* (Northbrook, Ill.: AHM Publishing, 1947), p. 44.

5. Quoted in Dallek, *Roosevelt and American Foreign Policy,* p. 68.

6. *Congressional Record,* 74th Congress, first session, pp. 1221–22.

7. Dallek, *Roosevelt and American Foreign Policy,* p. 128.

8. Ibid., p. 133.

9. Ibid., p. 137.

10. *Roosevelt's Foreign Policy, 1933–1941: Franklin D. Roosevelt's Unedited Speeches and Messages* (New York: Wilfred Funk, 1942), p. 105.

11. In Graebner, *Ideas and Diplomacy* (New York: Oxford University Press, 1964), pp. 574–75.

12. Ibid., p. 574.

13. FDR to James Roosevelt, 20 January 1938, *FDR: His Personal Letters, 1928–1945,* ed. Elliott Roosevelt (New York: Duell, Sloan and Pearce, 1950), 2: 751.

14. Quoted in Robert Divine, *The Illusion of Neutrality* (Chicago: University of Chicago Press, 1962), p. 49.

15. Douglas Little, *Malevolent Neutrality: The United States, Great Britain, and the Origins of the Spanish Civil War* (Ithaca: Cornell University Press, 1985).

16. Charles Beard, *The Devil Theory of War* (New York: Greenwood Press, 1969), 110. Emphasis in the original.

17. Charles Beard, *The Open Door at Home: A Trial Philosophy of National Interest* (New York: Macmillan, 1934), p. 267.

18. Beard, *The Devil Theory of War,* p. 124.

19. Divine, *The Illusion of Neutrality,* p. 120.

20. I shall continue to call it Wilsonianism on the assumption that it is understood that important elements of the ideology were dropped or modified and new elements added as the situation demanded. Still, the basic resemblance warrants referring to the ideology as Wilsonian.

21. For the classical argument along these lines, see Bruce M. Russett, *No Clear and Present Danger: A Skeptical View of the U.S. Entry into World War II* (New York: Harper Torchbooks, 1972).

22. 1936 Chautauqua address, in *Roosevelt's Foreign Policy,* p. 104.

23. Ibid., p. 101.

24. Ibid., p. 102.

25. Ibid., p. 103.

26. Quoted in Dallek, *Roosevelt and American Foreign Policy,* p. 91.

27. Proclamation of National Emergency, May 27, 1941, in Russell D. Buhite and David W. Levey, eds., *FDR's Fireside Chats* (New York: Penguin Books, 1993), p. 178.

28. Fireside Chat of December 29, 1940, ibid., p. 166.

29. Claude G. Bowers to FDR, 20 February 1938, in Donald B. Schewe, ed., *Franklin D. Roosevelt and Foreign Affairs* (New York: Garland Books, 1979), No. 853.

30. Quoted in Melvyn P. Leffler, *A Preponderance of Power: National Security, the Truman Administration, and the Cold War* (Stanford: Stanford University Press, 1992), p. 22.

31. Cordell Hull, *Memoirs* (New York: Macmillan, 1948), 1: 577.

32. William C. Bullitt to FDR, 7 December 1937, in Schewe, *Roosevelt and Foreign Affairs,* No. 654.

33. G. R. Sloan, *Geopolitics in U.S. Strategic Policy, 1890–1987* (Brighton, Sussex: Wheatsheaf Books, 1988), p. 110.

34. Quoted in Eric Nordlinger, *Isolationism Reconfigured: American Foreign Policy for a New Century* (Princeton: Princeton University Press, 1995), p. 57.

35. Diary entry, 26 May 1939, in *Navigating the Rapids, 1918–1971: From the*

Papers of Adolf A. Berle, ed. Beatrice Bishop Berle and Travis Beal Jacobs (New York: Harcourt Brace Jovanovich, 1973), p. 224.

36. Doc. 1685a, draft of a radio broadcast for FDR by Welles, March 29, 1939, in Schewe, *Roosevelt and Foreign Affairs.*

37. See, e.g., the Gallup polls of September 7 and November 14, 1941, in George H. Gallup, *The Gallup Poll, 1935–1971* (New York: Random House, 1972), 1: 296, 306.

38. Quoted in John L. Harper, *American Visions of Europe* (New York: Cambridge University Press, 1996), p. 121.

39. Abba Eban, "The U.N. Idea Revisited," *Foreign Affairs* 74 (September/October 1995): 43.

Chapter Five

1. Had the U.S. and the Soviets been motivated by realism, that would be reason to agree with the cold war critics who assert that there was no need for a cold war. But they were not motivated by traditional realpolitik, and to suggest that they ought to have been is to miss the point about what the cold war, not to mention American foreign policy in the twentieth century, was about. As this book argues, U.S. policy cannot be understood in terms of so-called "objective" factors. This is so, in part, because American political philosophy was hostile to power politics. But quite apart from the particulars of a hostility to power politics, America's unrealistic behavior was rooted in a built-in conceptual tension, even incompatibility, between globalism and realism.

The same argument holds for Stalin and the Soviet side. As with the United States, one must weigh the specifics of communist ideology in relation to realism. Thus, while many historians have suggested that Stalin was a "realist" with whom it was possible to make sensible bargains on a live-and-let-live basis, that view fails to grapple with the fact that realism's views of human nature and nations are quite incompatible with certain fundamental principles of Marxism. Stalin could not have been *doctrinally* a realist while hewing to Marxism. For those who insist on pointing to his allegedly prudent behavior, his alleged realism is more consistently explained by reference to the fact that ideologies are flexible operational codes that enable believers to develop pragmatic ways of surviving in the world. Wilsonianism was one such code; Soviet Marxism was another. But pragmatism is one thing, and realism is quite another. As subsequently demonstrated by a series of Soviet misadventures that in some ways paralleled America's cold war Wilsonianism, in the Soviet case globalism was equally antithetical to the kind of prudent and limited—realistic—foreign policy based on local knowledge.

2. Handwritten memo, 24 July 1946, in Papers of George M. Elsey, Harry S. Truman Presidential Library, Independence, Missouri, box 63.

3. The first intelligence estimate, ORE-1 of July 23, 1946, was the product of a single individual in the Central Intelligence Group who wrote the paper much in the frantic way a college undergraduate might complete a senior thesis. See Arthur B. Darling, *The Central Intelligence Agency: An Instrument of Government to 1950* (University Park, Pa.: Pennsylvania State University Press, 1996), pp. 130–31.

4. Vladislav Zubok and Constantine Pleshakov, *Inside the Kremlin's Cold War: From Stalin to Khrushchev* (Cambridge: Harvard University Press, 1996), p. 3.

5. Walter Millis, ed., *The Forrestal Diaries,* 15 August 1946, 192.

6. On the Wilsonianism of the Baruch Plan, see Gregg Herken, *The Winning Weapon: The Atomic Bomb in the Cold War* (New York: Knopf, 1980), pp. 152, 165.

7. Morrell Heald and Lawrence S. Kaplan, *Culture and Diplomacy: The American Experience* (Westport, Conn., Greenwood Press, 1977), pp. 215–24.

8. Quoted in Richard M. Freeland, *The Truman Doctrine and the Origins of McCarthyism* (New York: Schocken, 1971), p. 94.

9. Memo, Marshall to Truman, 27 February 1947, *Foreign Relations of the United States, 1947*, 5: 61 (hereafter *FRUS*).

10. Minutes of meeting, 26 February 1947, *FRUS, 1947*, 5: 57.

11. Draft memo of Acheson's presentation at the White House on 27 February 1947, Joseph Jones Papers, Truman Library, box 2.

12. Quoted in Donald White, *The American Century* (New Haven: Yale University Press, 1996), p. 178.

13. Stimson quoted in Paul Y. Hammond "Policy Directives for the Occupation of Germany," in Harold Stein, ed., *American Civil-Military Decisions* (Birmingham: University of Alabama Press, 1963), p. 367.

14. Quoted in Carolyn Eisenberg, *Drawing the Line: The American Decision to Divide Germany, 1944–1949* (New York: Cambridge University Press, 1996), p. 44.

15. Quoted in ibid. p. 427.

16. Martin H. Folly, "Breaking the Vicious Circle; Britain, the United States, and the Genesis of the North Atlantic Treaty," *Diplomatic History* 12 (Winter 1988): 67.

17. Anders Stephanson, *Kennan and the Art of Foriegn Policy* (Cambridge: Harvard University Press, 1989), p. 141.

18. NSC-68, in Thomas H. Etzold and John Lewis Gaddis, *Containment: Documents on American Policy and Strategy, 1945–1950* (New York: Columbia University Press, 1978), p. 429.

19. Quoted in Frank Ninkovich, *Modernity and Power* (Chicago: University of Chicago Press, 1995), p. 183.

20. Quoted in Robert Donovan, *Tumultuous Years: The Presidency of Harry S. Truman, 1949–1953* (New York: Norton, 1982), p. 100.

21. Walter LaFeber, "NATO and the Korean War: A Context," in Lawrence S. Kaplan, ed., *American Historians and the Atlantic Alliance* (Kent: Kent State University Press, 1991), p. 35.

22. Quoted in Melvyn Leffler, *A Preponderance of Power* (Stanford: Stanford University Press, 1992), p. 327.

23. John L. Harper, *American Visions of Europe*, p. 224.

24. CIA memo, "Recent Soviet Moves," 8 February 1950, President's Secretary's Files, Truman Library, box 187.

25. Ernst Reuter lecture, 12 October 1955, George Kennan Papers, Seeley Mudd Library, Princeton University, box 19.

26. Acheson statement in address before ASNE, 22 April 1950. A CIA report to the president of 7 April 1950, PSF: Foreign Affairs File, Truman Library. One document was "momentous, involving the fulfillment or destruction not only of this Republic but of civilization itself."

27. *New York Times*, 26 June 1950.

28. For details, see William Stueck's splendid *The Korean War: An Internationnal History* (Princeton: Princeton University Press, 1995).

29. The unspoken character of Wilsonianism raises some puzzling questions: How is it possible to call American policy-makers Wilsonians if they didn't recognize themselves as such? Isn't it more sensible to suppose, given the numerous deprecating references to Wilson's outmoded idealism that were made throughout the cold war, that Wilsonianism was not operative? No, it does not. For one thing, the strategic assumptions on which American policy-makers were acting, and one finds these scattered everywhere throughout the documentation, are recognizably Wilsonian. So too is the emphasis on world opinion which, in cold war dress, takes the form of credibility.

But still, one might ask, if that is the case, why didn't people recognize it and talk about it? Why didn't policy-makers refer to Wilson the way the Soviets referred to Lenin? The reason appears to be, as Ernest May has suggested, that policy-makers internalized certain ideas through experience to the point that they became "axiomatic." No one needed to talk about them because everybody was agreed on their meaning and their validity. But this explanation, in turn, raises questions of its own. What, exactly, does it mean for ideas to be internalized, buried, or "sedimented" in this way?

Pierre Bourdieu, the French sociologist, has articulated a concept of *habitus* that may provide a helpful approach to thinking about this problem. *Habitus* is defined as an embodied, i.e. visceral, predisposition to understand and behave in certain ways, a culturally learned disposition that *cannot* be fully articulated by those who practice it. Perhaps this idea is made a bit clearer by its resemblance to the argument by philosopher of language Ludwig Wittgenstein about the rules for speaking a language. In his view, we don't *obey* rules; rather, the rules are retrospectively inferred from practice. The point is that rather complex cultural constructions like Wilsonianism can be learned to the point of becoming second nature. If formal rules cannot be understood even as they are being applied, this helps to explain why Wilsonianism was misrecognized by Wilsonians during the cold war.

30. *FRUS, 1949,* 7: 1056–57.

31. Quoted in Bruce Cumings, *Korea's Place in the Sun: A Modern History* (New York: Norton, 1997), p. 288.

32. Meeting of 31 January 1957, Papers of Dwight D. Eisenhower, AWF: NSC series, Eisenhower Library, box 82.

33. Chen Jian, *China's Road to the Korean War: The Making of the Sino-American Confrontation* (New York: Columbia University Press, 1993); Shu Guang Zhang, *Mao's Military Romanticism: China and the Korean War, 1950–1953* (Lawrence: University Press of Kansas, 1995).

34. Stueck, *The Korean War,* p. 46.

Chapter Six

1. Robert E. Osgood, *Limited War Revisited* (Boulder: Westview Press, 1979), p. 6.

2. NSC 162, 30 September 1953, *FRUS, 1952–1954,* 2: 496.

3. Pierre Bourdieu's notion of "symbolic capital" would thus appear to have limited applicabiliity to our understanding of the cold war. Bourdieu's notions of situated interest are more readily used to explain traditional notions of prestige than the free-floating idea of credibility that motivated cold warriors. For a definition of symbolic capital, see Bourdieu, *The Logic of Practice,* pp. 112–21.

4. C. D. Jackson as quoted in Nancy E. Bernhard, "Clearer than Truth: Public Af-

fairs Television and the State Department's Domestic Information Campaigns 1947–1952," *Diplomatic History* 21 (Fall 1997): 548.

5. *Foreign Relations of the United States, 1952–1954,* vol. 2, *National Security Affairs* (Washington, D.C.: GPO, 1984), p. 439.

6. Notes on a Bipartisan Conference, 12 July 1955, *FRUS, 1955–1957,* 5: 307.

7. Quoted in John Lewis Gaddis, *We Now Know: Rethinking Cold War History* (New York: Oxford University Press, 1997), p. 124.

8. Solarium discussion by NSC, 30 July 1953, *FRUS 1952–1954,* 2: 437; Eisenhower conversation with Senator Walter George, 7 January, AWF: Diary Series, Dwight D. Eisenhower, Presidential Papers, Eisenhower Library.

9. Eisenhower-Dulles phone conversation, 4 October 1954, AWF: DDE Diary Series, Eisenhower Library, box 7.

10. Quoted in Robert Divine, *Eisenhower and the Cold War* (Oxford University Press, 1881), p. 106.

11. Minutes of NSC meeting, 31 March 1953, *FRUS 1952–1954,* 2: 271–72.

12. NSC meeting, 7 October 1953, *FRUS 1952–1954,* 2: 528.

13. Memo of NSC meeting, 21 November 1955, *FRUS, 1955–1957,* 5: 805.

14. *Executive Sessions of the Senate Foreign Relations Committee (Historical Series),* 6: 168.

15. NSC 124/2, "U.S. Objectives and Courses of Action with Respect to Southeast Asia," 25 June 1952, NSC Series: Policy Papers Subseries, Eisenhower Library.

16. Presidential press conference, 7 April 1954, quoted in George C. Herring, ed., *The Secret Diplomacy of the Vietnam War: The Negotiating Volumes of the Pentagon Papers* (Austin: University of Texas Press, 1983), 1: 596.

17. Eisenhower meeting with Charles Bohlen, 2 December 1954, AWF: Diary Series, Eisenhower Library, box 3.

18. Notes on remarks at NSC meeting March 31, 1953 dictated by Dulles, 1 April 1953, Dulles Papers, White House Memoranda Series, Princeton University, box 7.

19. "Think Piece" Drafts, 1956, Dulles Papers, Subject Series, box 7.

20. Unsigned Memo, 11 May 1955, Dulles Papers, Subject Series, box 9.

21. Minutes of Cabinet meeting, 29 March 1957, AWF: Cabinet Series, Eisenhower Library, box 8.

22. Minutes of NSC meeting, 11 February 1953, *FRUS 1952–1954,* 2: 236.

23. NSC meeting, 25 March 1954, ibid., p. 642.

24. Study prepared by the NSC planning board, 14 June 1954, ibid., p. 655.

25. Calculated at a 60-ton load per boxcar.

26. Quoted in Robert A. Divine, *The Sputnik Challenge* (New York: Oxford University Press, 1993), p. 72.

27. Stephen E. Ambrose, *Eisenhower: The President* (New York: Simon and Schuster, 1984), p. 434.

28. Quoted in Johnathan Schell, *Time of Illusion,* p. 354.

29. Graham Evans and Jeffrey Newnham, *The Dictionary of World Politics* (New York: Simon and Schuster, 1990), p. 71.

30. George V. Allen oral history, Dulles Papers, Princeton University, 2: 32.

31. Undated, unsigned Department of State memo on nuclear weapons policy submitted to National Security Council, Dulles Papers, White House Memoranda Series, box 7.

32. *FRUS 1952–1954,* 2: 774.

33. Eisenhower-Dulles conversation, 20 July 1954, AWF: Diary Series, Eisenhower Library, box 2.

34. Conversation with Richard Nixon, 19 April 1954, Dulles Papers, telephone conversations memoranda, box 2.

35. Talking Paper for Khrushchev visit, 8 September 1959, President's Official File, Papers of John F. Kennedy, John F. Kennedy Presidential Library, box 125.

36. Briefing on Berlin, 25 November 1958, White House Office, Office of the Staff Secretary, International Series, Eisenhower Library, box 6.

37. Memo of conference on Berlin, 8 March 1959, White House Office, Office of the Staff Secretary, International Series, Eisenhower Library, box 6.

38. Quoted in Rhodri Jeffreys-Jones, *The CIA and American Democracy* (New Haven: Yale University Press, 1989), p. 82.

39. Quoted in Stephen G. Rabe, *Eisenhower and Latin America: The Foreign Policy of Anticommunism* (Chapel Hill: University of North Carolina Press, 1988), p. 61.

40. G. Llewlyn Thompson to State, 23 January 1961, POF, Kennedy Library, box 125A.

41. Ambrose, *Eisenhower,* p. 614.

42. W. W. Rostow to Kennedy, 12 May 1961, POF, Kennedy Library, box 114.

43. ONI research note, 18 August 1961, NSF, Kennedy Library, box 82.

44. *New York Times,* 22 February 1998, p. 6.

45. Rostow to McGeorge Bundy, 6 May 1961, POF, Kennedy Library, box 126.

46. ONI research note, 18 August 1961, NSF, Kennedy Library, box 82.

47. JFK meeting with congressional leadership, 7 June 1961, NSF, Kennedy Library, boxes 70–71.

48. Quoted in Raymond L. Garthoff, "Some Observations on Using the Soviet Archives," *Diplomatic History* 21 (Spring 1997): 255.

49. McGeorge Bundy, *Danger and Survival* (New York: Random House, 1988), p. 452.

50. Quoted in Alexander Fursenko and Timothy Naftali, "One Hell of a Gamble," *The Secret History of the Cuban Missile Crisis* (New York: Norton, 1997), p. 226.

51. Quoted in Richard Ned Lebow and Janice Gross Stein, *We All Lost the Cold War* (Princeton: Princeton University Press, 1994), p. 110.

52. One ought not be too critical of the CIA on this point inasmuch as historians are *still* arguing about how best to reconstruct the thought-world of the Soviet leadership.

53. Memo, Dean Rusk to JFK, 20 September 1961, POF, Kennedy Library, box 125A.

Chapter Seven

1. JFK address to the American Society of Newspaper Editors, 20 April 1961, in *The Pentagon Papers: The Senator Gravel Edition* (Beacon Press: Boston, 1971), 2: 799.

2. Tape recordings of 27 May 1964 phone conversation with McGeorge Bundy, quoted in *New York Times,* 15 February 1997, p. A:12.

3. LBJ press conference statement, 22 June 1964, *Pentagon Papers,* 3: 718.

4. On this point see the forthcoming work on Chinese–North Vietnamese relations by Qiang Zhai.

5. David C. Hallin, *The "Uncensored" War: The Media and Vietnam* (Berkeley: University of California Press, 1989), p. 214.

6. For a discussion of public opinion that minimizes the role of generational change ("cohort succession") in the 1960s, see William G. Mayer, *The Changing American Mind: How and Why American Public Opinion Changed between 1960 and 1980* (Ann Arbor: University of Michigan Press, 1992), pp. 166–73. Mayer places more emphasis on *intracohort* changes.

7. Quoted in William Conrad Gibbons, *The U.S. Government and the Vietnam War* (Princeton: Princeton University Press, 1989), 3: 148.

8. Quoted in Doris Kearns, *Lyndon Johnson and the American Dream* (New York: Harper and Row, 1976), p. 258.

9. Lloyd Gardner, "Lyndon Johnson and Vietnam: The Final Months," in Robert Divine, ed., *The Johnson Years,* vol. 3, *LBJ at Home and Abroad* (Lawrence: University Press of Kansas, 1994), p. 200.

10. Ibid., p. 222.

11. Memo of conversation, Acheson, Nixon, and Kissinger, 19 March 1969, Acheson Papers, series 4, Sterling Library, Yale University, box 58.

12. Quoted in George Herring, *America's Longest War* (New York: John Wiley), 1979, p. 219.

13. Henry Kissinger, *White House Years* (Boston: Little, Brown, 1979), p. 235.

14. Quoted in Noam Chomsky, *Rethinking Camelot: JFK, the Vietnam War, and U.S. Political Culture* (Boston: South End Press, 1993), p. 11.

15. Quoted in Francis Fukuyama, *The End of History and the Last Man* (New York: Avon Books, 1992), p. 8.

16. Henry Kissinger, *Years of Upheaval* (Boston: Little, Brown, 1982), p. 1031.

17. Memo, Rostow to JFK, 15 May 1961, NSF, Kennedy Library, boxes 70–71.

18. Henry Kissinger, *White House Years* (Boston: Little, Brown, 1979), pp. 185–86.

19. Quoted in H. W. Brands, *The Devil We Knew: Americans and the Cold War* (New York: Oxford University Press, 1993), p. 129.

20. George Ball, *The Past Has Another Pattern* (New York: Norton, 1982), p. 271.

21. Quoted in Thomas Alan Schwartz, "The United States and Western Europe," in Diane B. Kunz, ed., *The Diplomacy of the Crucial Decade* (New York: Columbia University Press, 1994), p. 134.

22. Ethan Kapstein, *Governing the Global Economy* (Cambridge: Harvard University Press, 1994), p. 101.

Chapter Eight

1. Walter Isaacson, *Kissinger: A Biography* (New York: Simon & Schuster, 1992), p. 684.

2. Jimmy Carter, *Keeping Faith* (New York: Bantam Books, 1982), p. 188.

3. Quoted from Timothy P. Maga, *Hands across the Sea? U.S.-Japan Relations, 1961–1981* (Athens: Ohio University Press, 1997), p. 116.

4. Quoted in David A. Mayers, *The Ambassadors and America's Soviet Policy* (New York: Oxford University Press, 1995), p. 230.

5. Gaddis Smith, *Morality, Reason and Power: American Diplomacy in the Carter Years* (New York: Hill and Wang, 1986), p. 75.

6. Carter, *Keeping Faith,* p. 473.

7. Ibid., p. 526.

8. For details, see Nancy Bernkopf Tucker, *Taiwan, Hong Kong, and the United States, 1945–1992* (New York: Twayne Publishers, 1994), p. 131–35.

9. Quoted in Smith, *Morality, Reason, and Power,* p. 186.

10. Seyom Brown, *The Faces of Power: Constancy and Change in United States Foreign Policy from Truman to Reagan* (New York: Columbia University Press, 1983), p. 572.

11. Ibid., p. 571.

12. Quoted in Tony Smith, *America's Mission: The United States and the World-wide Struggle for Democracy in the Twentieth Century* (Princeton: Princeton University Press, 1994), p. 270.

13. Quoted in Brown, *The Faces of Power,* p. 607.

14. Raymond Garthoff, *The Great Transition: American-Soviet Relations and the End of the Cold War* (Washington: Brookings Institution, 1994), p. 309.

15. George Shultz, *Turmoil and Triumph: My Years as Secretary of State* (New York: Charles Scribner's Sons, 1993), p. 650.

16. Ibid., p. 651.

17. Garthoff, *The Great Transition,* p. 271.

18. Alexander Haig, *Caveat: Realism, Reagan, and Foreign Policy* (New York: Macmillan, 1984), p. 118.

19. Quoted in Rhodri Jeffreys-Jones, *The CIA and American Democracy,* p. 236

20. Garthoff, *The Great Transition,* p. 584.

21. Quoted in Allen Lynch, *The Cold War is Over—Again* (Boulder: Westview, 1992), p. 25.

22. Ibid., 263.

23. Quoted in John Ruggie, *Winning the Peace: America and World Order in the New Era* (New York: Columbia University Press, 1996), p. 27.

24. Tony Smith, in *America's Mission,* p. 108, argues that Gorbachev's new thinking "echoed Wilson's appeals of seventy years earlier," although it seems likely that the differences between Gorbachev and Wilson are just as striking, if not more so, than the similarities.

25. Garthoff, *The Great Transition,* p. 315.

26. Mikhail Gorbachev, *Memoirs* (New York: Doubleday, 1996), p. 418.

27. Quoted in Smith, *America's Mission,* p. 272.

28. Michael Beschloss and Strobe Talbott, *At the Highest Levels: The Inside Story of the End of the Cold War* (Boston: Little, Brown, 1993), p. 136.

29. John Foster Dulles to Clare Booth Luce, 1 September 1954, General Correspondence and Memoranda Series, Dulles Papers, box 2.

30. Richard Harkness memoranda on visits with Dulles, Additional Papers, Dulles Papers, box 1.

31. Stephen Szabo, *The Diplomacy of German Reunification* (New York: St. Martin's Press, 1992), p. 42.

Conclusion

1. Jonathan Clarke, "Rhetoric before Reality," *Foreign Affairs* 74 (September–October 1995), p. 4.

2. John Ikenberry, "The Myth of Post-Cold-War Chaos," *Foreign Affairs* 75 (May–June 1996), pp. 79–91.

3. Robert Latham, *The Liberal Moment: Modernity, Security, and the Making of the International Postwar Order* (New York: Columbia University Press, 1997), p. 3.

4. Benedict Anderson, *Imagined Communities: Reflections on the Origin and Spread of Nationalism,* revised edition (New York: Verso, 1995), p. 3; Cornelius Castoriadis, *The Imaginary Institution of Society,* translated by Kathleen Blamey (Cambridge: MIT Press, 1987).

5. On integrative power, see Kenneth Boulding, *Three Faces of Power* (Boulder: Sage Publications, 1989).

INDEX